INTO THE MOUNTAIN

INTO THE MOUNTAIN

A LIFE OF NAN SHEPHERD

CHARLOTTE PEACOCK

GALILEO PUBLISHERS
CAMBRIDGE

First published by Galileo Publishers © 2017
First paperback edition 2018
16 Woodlands Road, Great Shelford, Cambridge,
UK, CB22 5LW

www.galileopublishing.co.uk
Galileo Publishers is an imprint of Galileo Multimedia Ltd.

Text © 2017 Charlotte Peacock,
The moral right of the author has been asserted.

ISBN:
978-1-903385-78-4

Cover design by NamdesignUK
Editor: George Allan
Cover photograph by permission Erlend Clouston

Printed in the UK
by TJ International

2 4 6 8 10 9 7 5 3 1

For my daughters

ISBN 0 900015 40 3

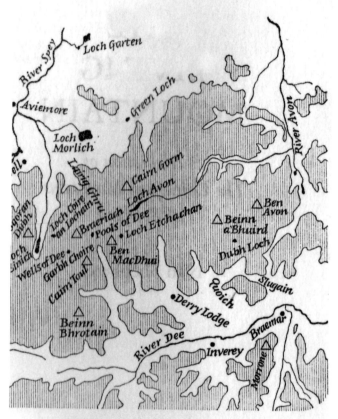

The plateau and a few place names

The original copyright page from the Aberdeen University Press
first edition of *The Living Mountain*, drawn by Ian Munro.

I believe I that I now understand in some small measure why the Buddhist goes on pilgrimage to a mountain. The journey is itself part of the technique by which the god is sought. It is a journey into Being; for as I penetrate more deeply into the mountain's life, I penetrate also into my own. For an hour I am beyond desire. It is not ecstasy, that leap out of the self that makes man like a god. I am not out of myself, but in myself. I am.[1]

Nan Shepherd, *The Living Mountain.*

CONTENTS

PREFACE

During the last weeks of her life, in a letter to her friend, the artist Barbara Balmer, Nan Shepherd said: 'As for writing about my experiences, if I did that recognisably, I'd be for it'.[2] She left no journals and much of her correspondence was pitched out.[3] What little is extant in the archives has been heavily censored. Lines are scored through, pages snipped into and in some places completely excised, presumably by Nan herself. Even in her two commonplace books there is rarely any personal comment made alongside the extracts she has carefully copied in. Renowned for her reticence, in death it seems Nan Shepherd wished to remain as enigmatic as she was in life.

Examined for insight into a writer's life and works, diaries and journals are often considered an authentic resource, revealing 'truths' unavailable elsewhere. However, as biographers and life-writing theorists know very well, such a supposedly authentic resource is often a careful construct, a conscious act of self-presentation written with an audience of some kind in mind—even if it is the diarist themselves, reading in the future. So if Nan Shepherd *had* left behind endless journals, diaries and correspondence, they could not be relied upon. But as the late Jenny Diski points out, there are infinite ways of telling the 'truth', including fiction.[4]

A fictional work is, of course, assumed to be an invention, a narrative describing imaginary events and people. Yet because of this assumption, fictions often enable more of 'truth' about a life to be written than a supposedly factual account.[5] A contemporary of Nan Shepherd's, Scottish writer Catherine Carswell knew this. 'The literature of imagination has always been rich in autobiography, confessed and unconfessed', she wrote in *Proust's Women* in 1923. 'It is in essence, perhaps one should say in its impulse, largely an affair of passionate reminiscence'.[6]

From the correspondence which survives, it seems the only person to whom Nan might have 'confessed' was her close friend, the author and historian, Agnes Mure Mackenzie (known as 'Mure') and their correspondence, too, has been carefully edited. But what Nan does not divulge in her letter to Barbara Balmer is that she had already written about her life *unrecognisably* (or so she hoped) in her novels—particularly her first, *The Quarry Wood*.

Mure Mackenzie saw immediately that the book was heavily autobiographical and reported how much she had enjoyed unpicking the 'transmutation, ordering, supplementing, modifying and blending' in Nan's creative process. 'Naturally', she went on, 'I can't do this as a rule with other people's work. With yours as you know I can to a large effect (including tracing some bits of my own in it!).'[7] In fact, there was so much that was autobiographical in *The Quarry Wood* that Mure felt it would take a second book to see what Nan could really do creatively. 'I'm not quite satisfied yet that you can get your stuff away from yourself',[8] she wrote in 1927. *The Weatherhouse,* and *A Pass in the Grampians* which followed, *did* show what Nan could do, but even these are, to some extent, drawn from her own experiences.

It is because of this, that rather than devoting discrete chapters to her novels, commentary and reference to them is woven into my version of Nan Shepherd's life. Wherever possible, I have drawn on those primary sources available to me, including unpublished material written by her friends as well as the testimonies of those who knew her. But while all these add flesh to the biographical bones of a subject, the biographer's job is to try to portray not just what is known about the person, or how they came to be in the context in which they lived, it is to try to reveal their essence.

Here, Nan Shepherd helped, because what she *did* leave behind was *The Living Mountain* and in this slim volume is all her spirit—spirit of the untameable mountain. To grasp Nan Shepherd's essence is to grasp what prompted her to take that journey into the mountain and what she apprehended from it. Because *The Living Mountain,* of course, is a metaphor; 'It is to know its essential nature that I am seeking here',[9] she writes in her opening paragraph. By the end she knows, 'with the knowledge that is a process of living' that the deeper she penetrates into the mountain's life, the deeper she penetrates into her own.

Her 'journey into Being' is therefore integral to this first, literary biography of Nan Shepherd in which I have attempted, too, to examine the role of friendships in her life, her place within the Scottish 'Renaissance' movement and her work, as well as her writing. It is only one of an infinite number of perspectives. It will take further works and other perspectives before Nan Shepherd begins to be understood in the round for, as she said herself, 'knowing another is endless…The thing to be known grows with the knowing'.[10]

Charlotte Peacock. June 2017.

ACKNOWLEDGEMENTS

This book began in Autumn 2014 when I was living in Suffolk, a flat land with huge skies, where mountains were not on my horizon any more than they were on my mind. Then I read Robert Macfarlane's *The Old Ways* and it is to him I am indebted, for it was in his book I first came across Nan Shepherd and *The Living Mountain*. Intrigued by the woman who turned herself upside down to see the earth as it must see itself, arching its back and bristling, I set off in pursuit of her.

It has been a fascinating and, at times, frustrating journey. When I began my search for the elusive Nan Shepherd, biographical information about her was scant. But so many people have been enormously helpful, patient and generous with their time and hospitality during the making of this book and have encouraged me along the way—I am deeply grateful to them all.

In particular, I would like to thank: Erlend Clouston, Nan Shepherd's literary executor, for appointing me to write this first authorised biography, for his unflagging optimism and humour and for allowing me access to Nan's effects and books; Robert Hyde, of Galileo Publishers for commissioning the work and for his support and editorial insight; and the Society of Authors, Author's Foundation, for awarding me a grant, without which research for this book would not have been possible.

Huge thanks are due, too, to Deirdre Burton, Neil Roger, Hélène Clouston, Malcolm and Ruth Sutherland, Helen Bain, Grainne and Dan Cullen, Cameron Donaldson, Jack Kelly, Frances Watts, Calum and Jackie Innes, John Duff, Adam Watson, Jenny Aitchison, Fiona and George Herraghty, George Mackie, Mary Gall, Grace Law, Jon Morrice, Bill Malcolm, Jack Costello, Ian Burnett, Lizzie MacGregor, June Ellner, Michelle Gait, Scott Docking, George Allan and Amelie Prevost.

For permission to quote from manuscript sources I am extremely grateful to Jocelyn Campbell, Avril Kesson, Dairmid Gunn, the National Library of Scotland, Aberdeen University and the University of Edinburgh. I am also indebted to Gill Lowe who first encouraged me on this path, to Dr Helen Smith who first suggested I write a literary biography and to Professor Kathryn Hughes for her invaluable advice when this project was still in its infancy.

Many thanks are due, too, to Jamie Byng and Canongate for allowing me to quote extensively from Nan Shepherd's novels and *The Living Mountain*. Finally, I am grateful to family and friends for their continuous support and belief in me and for tolerating my unavailability and preoccupation during the past couple of years and especially to Flora and Cassia Peacock, Bridget and Tom Pettigrew and Judith Steventon Baker.

For putting me up during my research trips to Scotland, thank you to Sam and Stephanie Laird and Sam Sinclair; for his foot-stepping companionship, thank you, Mark Devereux-Renny; and for his patience and ever-listening ear, thank you, Steve Gibb.

Chapter One

1941

It was only two years into World War Two, but already the number of bombing raids on Aberdeen had earned it the epithet 'Siren City'. Glasgow may have been the worst bombed of the Scottish cities, but Aberdeen endured most attacks. Returning to Germany and Norway after sorties over Britain, enemy aircraft regularly rid themselves of any leftover bombs on to Scotland's North East, wiping out houses and farmland as well as the fishing fleet. 'Don't lose your head', the government warned. But it was hard to keep smiling through the fear and uncertainty that came from not knowing when the next attack might come.

By then in her late forties, Nan Shepherd had already lived through one world war. She was sickened by this second one, arriving so soon after the first. 'How, in this disrupted world are we to reach any sort of unity?'[11] she despaired in a letter to her friend, the novelist Neil Gunn, in May 1940. The following Spring, she had spent an Easter made meagre by wartime rationing with her mother Jeannie and their housekeeper Mary Lawson at her Lower Deeside home, 'Dunvegan', in Cults.

Four miles west of Aberdeen, Cults was then still a village. To its residents, the war at times felt frighteningly close, the bombardments by faceless enemies shooing them to shelter on palliasses strewn on the Old School floor in Cults. At others it seemed distant, surreal almost, taking away their men and killing them apparently randomly. During daylight hours they watched the road anxiously for the yellow telegrams which seemed just as arbitrary, handing death to people who felt little connection with the origins of the conflict. When darkness fell it was unrelieved: a wartime night of blackout. Along the Deeside Railway Line, where Dunvegan and most of the other houses of Cults were clustered, dull blurs of light were visible. In front, all was dark. Behind them, the Quarry Wood, quieter since the quarrymen had downed tools and gone to war, rose up to Blacktop Hill and beyond it, far to the west, soared the ice-cold peaks of the Cairngorm Mountains.

From her thirties, the Cairngorms had been Nan Shepherd's refuge.

An escape from the domesticity of Dunvegan, they were her secret place of ease, somewhere she could just *be*. During those disturbed and uncertain years of the war her need for escape grew more insistent. And the hills were different during the 1940s. So many were away, fighting or doing their bit for the war effort, there was nobody there. That suited Nan, who would rather walk alone than with the wrong sort of companion.

> The presence of another person does not detract from, but enhances the silence, if the other is the right sort of hill companion. The perfect hill companion is the one whose identity is for the time being merged in that of the mountains, as you feel your own to be. Then such speech as arises is part of a common life and cannot be alien. To 'make conversation', however, is ruinous, to speak may be superfluous...I have walked with brilliant young people whose talk, entertaining, witty and incessant, yet left me weary and dispirited, because the hill did not speak....[12]

Already made weary and dispirited by the war, Nan needed to hear the hill speak. With a precious few days' holiday left before term began again at the teacher-training college in Aberdeen where she was Lecturer in English, she was heading for the hills that Easter Monday of 1941, the day she met Jessie Kesson on a train. Although the two women might not have met at all—Jessie nearly missed the train that day.

Jessie had been getting ready to make one of her twice-yearly visits to her syphilitic mother, dying slowly at Craigmoray Institution in Elgin, when she heard the news broadcast on the radio that Charles Murray, one of Scotland's best-loved poets, had died aged seventy-seven at his home in Banchory. 'Hamewith', she remembered as she set off to cycle the eight miles from her cottar home near Old Meldrum to Inverurie station, 'Hamewith'.... 'The road that's never dreary'[13] was how Charles Murray's poems had been introduced to her as a school-girl and as 'Hamewith'—never Charles Murray—he had remained to Jessie ever since. Meaning 'homewards' in Doric,[14] the dialect of North East Scotland, 'Hamewith' was the title of one of Charles Murray's short works as well as a collection of his poetry, which was so rich in the vernacular it earned him the title 'the King of Doric'.

Arriving at Inverurie station just as the guard was about to raise his green flag, Jessie scrambled into a carriage, falling over the long, slim, brogue-shod feet of its only other occupant. Gathering herself together, as she dusted herself down, she surveyed the woman sitting opposite. Pale skinned, with clear, hazel eyes, her auburn hair wound into 'earphones' either side of her head in a style harking back to the 1920s, the woman was dressed in clothes matching her tawny colouring: browns, russets and muted greens. Below a flowing, calf-length skirt, her slender legs were uncrossed, neatly pressed together ankle to ankle. This, Jessie decided, was 'A Lady'.

Until then, the only 'Lady' Jessie had ever come across was the President of the Rural society at their once a month social-cum-craftsmanship meetings and theirs was no more than a smiling acquaintance. But Jessie was a talker. Dark-haired, bright-eyed and bubbly, she was a nervous person who disguised it with non-stop chatter and Charles Murray's death was still very much on her mind.

'Hamewith's dead', she blurted out as she sat down. From the look on the other woman's face she could see this was news to her. 'This morning,' Jessie assured her. 'I heard it on the wireless'.[15]

As Jessie said later, 'little did I know then of her long friendship with, or deep appreciation of Charles Murray's work. Nor did she inform me'.[16] But Nan Shepherd had a talent for silence. For her, to listen was better than to speak and when she did, it was quietly. In an accent which, to an English ear, bore a trace of soft, Scottish burr, the only information Nan volunteered about herself during their entire conversation that Spring morning was that she was off to walk in the hills. Jessie was a little more forthcoming. 'My name is Jessie', she informed her, in her rather 'seductive husky voice,'[17] as Nan was later to describe it. 'My husband is a cattleman at a dairy farm not far from Old Meldrum'.

As the train steamed out of Inverurie station, from their carriage window, the rocky-topped snout of Bennachie, the blue hill that tugged most at Charles Murray's heart, reared in the distance. 'Bennachie…An' wast ower Keig, Wi' a' the warl' to me, atween'.[18] In 1964, Nan would quote Murray's lines from memory during the Centenary Celebrations held at Murray Park, land donated to the people of Alford by the poet. And for the rest of their journey, the two women 'tired the sun with talking'[19]—Murray's poems and Doric words flowing between them.

Before she left the train, Nan rummaged in her knapsack and pulled out a strawberry-pink, silk headscarf. 'A small memento of a lovely journey,' she said, handing it to Jessie. But if Jessie thought that was the last she would see or hear of the 'Lady in the Train', she was mistaken.

A few months later, she was surprised to find the postman on her doorstep. A visit from the postman was a rare event for Jessie. 'I never got letters. I had no one to write to…Thus a visit from the postman was unusual indeed. The letter he delivered that day was also unusual. The wonder is that it found me at all. Addressed as it was—

Miss Jessie—Now Mrs—
At a Dairy Farm
Near Old Meldrum'.

'Do you remember a lovely train journey in April?' the letter began and went on to tell Jessie about a Short Story Competition—*Sangschaw for Makars* run by the Aberdeen Scottish Literature and Song Association. Suggesting she should enter the competition and offering to help her with the 7/6 entry fee, the letter was signed 'Nan Shepherd'.[20] For the first time, Jessie learned the identity of 'the Lady in the Train'.

Jessie entered the competition and, to her amazement, won first prize for her short story 'Sleepin' Tinker'. An invitation followed to write for BBC Scotland. She accepted and her writing career took off. Over the next forty-odd years, Jessie Kesson published three novels, contributed poetry and short stories to *The Scots Magazine, The People's Friend* and the *North East Review* and wrote over ninety plays for television and radio. It was Nan Shepherd Jessie Kesson always credited with starting her writing. A great one for telling stories, the one about her momentous meeting with 'the Lady in the Train' Jessie told over and over, until it reached almost mythical proportions. The trouble was, she was not the most reliable of narrators and her stories changed often in the telling.

In one account of their meeting, published in 1990 in *The Aberdeen University Review*, Jessie is certain she first met Nan Shepherd on 4th April 1941 because it was the day Charles Murray's death was announced on the radio. As Murray died on 12th April 1941, this could not have been the case. In that same account Jessie also says Nan left the train at Rothiemurchus. As the train from Inverurie to Elgin did not stop there, this is impossible. It is most likely to have been at Keith that Nan changed trains for Aviemore. More importantly, Jessie's claim that Nan Shepherd was responsible for her starting to write is not strictly accurate. When the two women met in 1941, Jessie was already a published writer, albeit in a small way: several of her poems had been printed the year before in the *North East Review.*

It was certainly from Jessie, though, that Nan Shepherd first learned of Charles Murray's death. She confirmed this by letter in December 1979, adding, 'and I remember that train ride well. It was a lucky meeting.'[21] But Nan always felt that the role played by 'the Lady in the Train' was somewhat exaggerated. 'What the lady in the train relished so much about that journey', she said, 'was just the sense of life gushing out in all sorts of ways—it was a life-enhancing journey.'[22] Out of Jessie's mouth that day, spilled stories and experiences and inevitably a joke, leaving her laughing herself speechlessly to tears. Her vivacity was infectious. Quick to spot and nurture talent in others, Nan was sure that if Jessie's 'bubbling immediacy could be caught between the pages of a book',[23] she had the makings of a writer. She was correct.

Whether or not Nan can be given complete credit for kick-starting Jessie's writing career, she certainly encouraged her. From then on it was Nan's critical opinion of her work that really mattered to Jessie:

> More, in all the years, whatever the critics wrote about my work, in praise or blame, it was Nan Shepherd's verdict that I awaited. *Her* opinion I accepted. It was always constructive. She rarely generalized[sic], but pointed a sure and firm finger on the strengths or in the flaws, so that I never felt confused. Disliking my constant use of exclamation marks she pounced on them but with imaginative kindness. "You are a much better writer than you allow yourself to believe. There is no need for !!!!!! ...."[24]

Few letters between the two women survive. Those that do suggest they corresponded fairly frequently. Jessie's upbringing was markedly different to Nan Shepherd's modest, middle-class one and in correspondence, their class differences were retained, at least formally—Nan's letters are addressed to 'Jessie' while Jessie's begin 'Dear Miss Shepherd'. But both women had a talent for friendship and despite differences in class, education, occupation and distance (the Kessons moved to London in 1951) during the thirty or so years of their friendship, until Nan's death in February 1981, the bond between them deepened. How often they actually met is uncertain. But if Jessie was bothered by their class differences, Nan was not.

Some months after their first meeting, she turned up out of the blue at the farm near Old Meldrum. Jessie was working in the byre with her husband, milking the cows of the last dregs, when her neighbour hurried in. 'A Lady' was looking for her, she said. To Jessie, that could only mean Nan Shepherd. She began to panic. How on earth was she to entertain 'Miss Shepherd' to tea in the manner to which she was surely accustomed? None of her crockery matched and she did not even own a proper butter dish.

But Jessie need not have worried. Truth was, whether Nan was sitting in ingles, drinking black tea stewed for half an hour on the hob, or went formally to high tea in front parlours with crochet eight inches deep on the tea-cloth, the best china and butter in silver dishes, she did not mind which she had. She was the same to everyone.[25]

In October 1945, Jessie's poem 'To Nan Shepherd' was published in the *North East Review.* Revealing the depth of their friendship, it speaks, too, of their shared love of landscape. Jessie Kesson was 'the right sort of hill companion':

> Two hoors did haud oor years o'kennin each the t'ither's sel'
> While words poored forth, swift burns in spate,
> syne tint themsel's in the myrrh's thick smell.
> We twa grew quate tae listen till oor thocts
> gang loupin' through the wuds, and owre the distant hills.
> Jist aince we cried them back, and changed the wi' each
> other like tokens,
> Sayin', 'Keep mind o' that still river faur trees glower lang an'
> deep at their reflections.'
> Nor could the jostlin' fowk and noisy street touch for a
> meenit oor communion.
> Tho' I held oot a hand in pairtin'
> I wisna aince my lane on the homeward track,
> For, through myrrh's smell, past wud's tremendous green,
> My frien' jist followed me, the hale way back. [26]

Forty years of 'kennin each the t'ither's sel' they may have had, but as Jessie said after Nan's death in February 1981, 'Although we corresponded for many years, I know as little of Nan Shepherd's life as I did on the day we first met. She was elusive. Reticent about herself'.[27] Like Martha, the heroine of her first novel, *The Quarry Wood*, Nan Shepherd had a 'habit of self-control and silence'[28] that she maintained to the last and was rarely more forthcoming than she had been that first day on the train.

It was three years into their friendship before Jessie discovered that Nan was a published author. Even then she found out, not from Nan herself, but from one of her ex-students. Reluctantly, Nan was persuaded to lend Jessie a copy of one of her novels. On its return, Nan put the book to one side and immediately began to talk of other things.[29] Yet by the mid-1940s Nan had published not just one, but three novels, as well as a collection of poetry and was writing the work now considered her masterpiece, *The Living Mountain*.

Published in quick succession between 1928 and 1933 while she was still in her thirties, *The Quarry Wood, The Weatherhouse* and *A Pass in the Grampians* achieved immediate critical acclaim on both sides of the Atlantic. Described as 'a novelist to put alongside Virginia Woolf',[30] her first fictional work, *The Quarry Wood,* was lauded by Hugh Walpole as 'a real addition to English literature'[31] for its lyrical descriptions of nature. While not formally as radical as Woolf's *Mrs Dalloway* with its 'stream of consciousness'-style narrative voice or collage-like structure, *The Quarry Wood* reveals Shepherd as a pioneer of narrative technique, who was experimenting with the use of Scots language and idiom several years before Lewis Grassic Gibbon's much-celebrated *Sunset Song* burst on to the Scottish literary scene. Her poetry collection, *In the Cairngorms,* published in 1934 then sealed Shepherd's reputation as one of the North East's most highly respected literati and a key contributor, along with the likes of Hugh MacDiarmid, Neil Gunn, Lewis Grassic Gibbon, Catherine Carswell and Edwin and Willa Muir, to the Scottish literary revival of the early twentieth century.

Yet time and again, interviewers remarked on how taciturn Nan Shepherd was on the subject of her writing. 'A literary enigma', she would talk happily about 'her garden' or 'her hills' said 'Cynthia' in an article on Scottish women authors for *The Scotsman* in 1931, but would say little about her work.[32] 'She never mentioned her novels', said Helen Bain, a friend in the 1950s who, until recently, was unaware Nan was also a poet.[33] The Scottish belief that 'self-praise is nae recommendation' might perhaps account for some of her modesty, but it was not just on the subject of her writing that Nan was reticent.

A great story-teller, inimitable with a tale that was a little earthy, a robust, wry, Scottish sense of humour and a gift for its terse expression, Nan Shepherd was also an intensely private person. She had a talent for 'untroubling silences'[34]—an interesting description suggesting her reticence amused rather than irked, possibly because it was accompanied, more often than not, by a twinkle in her eye and a shrug or a smile.

Enigmatic and elusive are the adjectives most used about Nan Shepherd. To one ex-student at Aberdeen's Training Centre where she was a lecturer for over forty years, Nan 'always seemed far away, somewhere else',[35] an observation backed up by her friend and fellow hill-walker, Jean Roger. Nan Shepherd's mind 'was a little detached from the average Aberdonian's…you were just aware that she lived almost on another plane'[36] she said. This far-away, elusive quality of hers is perhaps best explained in *The Quarry Wood*. Martha, the novel's heroine, coming home each day from university where the 'widening world of ideas grew more and more the true abode of her consciousness', realises that 'the cottage did not reabsorb her afternoon by afternoon: it received her back. She was in its life but not of it'.[37]

In the 1970s, Jean Low, a neighbour of Nan's, introduced her to Barbara Balmer who was then a visiting lecturer at Gray's School of Art in Aberdeen. It was a brief, but intense, friendship, during which Barbara painted 'Nan Shepherd's Sun Porch'. Hanging now at the top of the stairs leading up from the entrance hall in the Deveron Arts Gallery in Huntly, the oil-on-panel painting in pale, pastel hues shows the conservatory, viewed through the open door leading from the dark, oak-panelled hallway at Dunvegan. Through thinly curtained glass, light pours into the room on to shelves lined with potted plants. The garden beyond, which falls steeply down to the old Deeside Railway Line, is a mere suggestion: a single spike of conifer in a watery sky uninterrupted by cloud.

The conservatory was Nan's favourite room in the house. In photographs taken of her over the years she is often shown seated there in her wicker chair among the pots of clashing scarlet and pink geraniums. In Barbara's picture, however, the chair is empty, turned instead towards the door to the garden, which stands invitingly open. It feels as though at any moment, with her quiet walk, Nan might suddenly appear over the threshold—or, that she has just left. The painting is all about Nan Shepherd—her chair, her home, her garden— and yet, like Martha in *The Quarry Wood,* she is in it, but not of it; she is somewhere else.

'It's a grand thing to get leave to live'. These words, engraved on the paving stone dedicated to Nan Shepherd outside the Makar's Museum in Edinburgh, now also appear on the Royal Bank of Scotland's new, polymer, five pound note, along with a portrait of her, Brunnhilde-like in headband and plaits, gazing into the distance. It would amuse Nan that this image of her as a teenager has been selected to represent her. Coming across it in a pile of family photographs in the early 1960s, she held it up chuckling, 'I was just fooling around at the photographers and picked up a piece of film which I put round my head and stuck a brooch on the front'.[38] The quotation, however, would please her.

It comes from a scene towards the end of her first novel, *The Quarry Wood* published in 1928:

> Geordie stood with an admirer's eye upon the fat breast of the fowl, holding her out from him until her spass of involuntary twitching were over. Martha watched, breathing the clean sweet air of a July morning. When she raised her head she saw the wet fields and the soft gleam of the river. "How fresh it is," she said.
> "Ay, Ay," answered her father. "It's a grand thing to get leave to live".[39]

Born a late Victorian in 1893, Nan Shepherd lived through a period of dramatic change during the twentieth century. Opportunities for women were expanding. The right to vote, access to higher education and into the professions, allowed women to penetrate the public sphere in ways that were unthinkable to her mother's generation. It was finally becoming possible, it seemed, for women to see themselves as something other than wives, mothers and homemakers. But it was a slow process. The Aberdonian society in which Nan grew up remained a heavily patriarchal one and its expectations of women were not just down to Scottish male attitudes. As Nan's novels reveal, it was often, paradoxically, conservative women like the Leggatt aunts in *The Quarry Wood*, satirised as the epitome of middle-class, staid respectability, who upheld these patriarchal prejudices.

To belong to a tight-knit community, where everybody knows everybody else, from their pedigree to their pets, where these traditional, patriarchal values are upheld and to actually *get* leave to live is a recurring theme in Nan's fiction. Her female protagonists are educated young women living in the early decades of the twentieth century, each of whom, realising there must be more for them in life than the roles allocated to them by society, tries to find space in it for the self.[40]

Nor is it just her heroines Nan Shepherd uses to explore this conflict. Her fiction is strewn with female characters, old and young, grappling with their social situation, trying to strike a balance between challenge and acquiescence. Among them are the quietly anarchic Josephine Leggatt in *The Quarry Wood,* who 'made haste for no man, no, nor woman neither'; the 'earthy smelling' Bawbie Paterson 'with her goat's beard, her rough hairy tweed like the pelt of an animal' in *The Weatherhouse;* and the strident, brassy Bella Cassie 'with her cheap cardboard case finished to look like leather, and her impudent copper hair puffed out in front', carrying 'her curves like a Queen' in *A Pass in the Grampians.*

To define Nan Shepherd's novels solely as a discourse on class and gender conflict, however, would be an injustice. Threaded through them all is a more universal, metaphysical and very human concern: what it means *to be.* All three of her fictions, too, are to some extent autobiographical. Their backdrop, her native North East Scotland, is wrought from her own experience and reveals her unsentimental affinity for its people, its culture and its landscape. Her acute sensitivity to what life was like for women living in Scotland and the stringent, social limitations imposed on them during the early decades of the twentieth century was because she lived it. It mirrored her own.

In her first, most heavily autobiographical novel, *The Quarry*

Wood, Martha Ironside's working-class family background could not be further from Nan Shepherd's modest, middle class upbringing. A *Bildungsroman,* the book charts Martha's growth from girl to a young woman of intellectual and emotional maturity. Quietly determined and ravenous for knowledge, she fights her way to university and a teaching career, discovering along the way 'that man does not learn from books alone'. Knowledge alters; wisdom is stable, learned through living, Martha finally understands. And it is her aunt who embodies this: 'Aunt Josephine at every turn chose instinctively the way of life. The flame of life burned visibly in her with an even glow'.[41] By the end of *The Quarry Wood,* Martha has decided to remain at home, apparently fulfilled by life as a teacher and mother to her adopted child, Robin. 'Acquiescent to her destiny, having delivered herself from the insecurity of the adventurer' Martha chooses to *'Sail not beyond the Pillars of Hercules'*.[42]

Flanking the entrance to the Straits of Gibraltar, gateway to the Mediterranean and the world beyond, these symbolic pillars reappear as a mountain pass and are given the title role in Shepherd's third novel, *A Pass in the Grampians.* Unlike Martha, Jenny decides to leave, to cross that pass. Her life at 'Boggiewalls', in Kincardineshire she loves 'as the only life worth having, but she must know the other. She must find a thousand answers to a thousand questions. She must get beyond the Pass'.[43]

It is no coincidence these symbolic gateways haunt Nan Shepherd's work, nor that she explores their implications through her female characters. Well-educated, with her middle-class background affording her the luxury of university, her profession as Lecturer in English at Aberdeen's Teacher Training Centre brought financial independence. She was relatively well-travelled too, holidaying in South Africa and Europe as well as exploring remote corners of her homeland. Yet, despite the opportunities opening up to women of her generation, Nan never did get 'beyond the pass'. At least not physically. Instead, like Martha in *The Quarry Wood,* she remained at home. She never married. Her entire life was lived in that cold shoulder of Scotland lying between the North Esk and Spey rivers known to the Scots (somewhat confusingly for the English) as 'the North East'—most of it in the same house.

'Nan was always understood to be a rather tragic 'left-over' from World War One, one of so many single women who were left spinsters through the terrible cull of young men during that war',[44] said Jocelyn Campbell, who knew Nan from the 1960s. Spinster: a woman whose occupation is to spin. It's such a pejorative term nowadays. There was a spinning wheel at Dunvegan. Several visitors remember seeing it in the house and it was found, somewhat dilapidated, still in the garage by Dunvegan's current owners. But it was certainly never used by Nan who would no doubt have shrugged off the perception of her as a tragic 'left-over' which saw no deeper than the surface. [45]

Twenty-first century readers have criticised Martha in *The Quarry Wood* for being 'irritatingly passive' compared to another female character, 'ardent feminist' Lucy Warrender. Nan herself was far from passive on the subject of feminism; she just didn't shout about it. Like the indomitable Aunt Josephine, Nan led an outwardly conventional, but quietly anarchic, life. A 'doer' rather than a 'sayer', through her own actions she rebelled against the power structures, laws and social conventions that conspired to keep women servile, subordinate and second best, while on the surface, at least, she appeared to conform.

'Oh aye, she was a feminist', said Cameron Donaldson, a close friend and neighbour of Nan's:

> 'Not in a militant way. It was all to do with the worth of woman…She thought they were seriously undervalued… Even then it was quite a modern attitude. It's only become mainstream recently. But Nan was way ahead of her time in many respects. She did what she did, going on her own to the hills, for example, partly to prove this was what women could do. It was a statement. And then of course there was her job. If you married, you had to give up your job and she loved teaching. She loved her students. She was so committed.'[46]

Once asked by Jessie Kesson if she believed in an afterlife, Nan responded: 'I would like it to be true for those who have had a lean life. For myself…',[47] and making a wide, embracing gesture with her hands, enigmatic as ever, she said no more. Jessie's impression was that Nan meant she had lived a happy and fulfilling life—and she was right. Because Nan Shepherd had a secret life. It was not something she talked about to many people, because few understood, but it was fundamental to the writing of *The Living Mountain*.

First published in 1977, this slim volume is now considered a 'masterpiece of mountain literature', 'one of the finest books on nature and landscape in Britain ever written'.[48] Always disparaging about her novels, *The Living Mountain* was the work of which Nan Shepherd was most proud. 'She was radiant about that book', said Jessie Kesson 'and rightly so'.[49] It is telling, then, that after the book was politely rejected in 1946, she put the manuscript in a drawer where it remained for the next thirty years. And in all that time, she never mentioned it again.

It was on a cloudless July day in 1934 at Loch Avon, when Nan was forty-one years old, that she first found a way in to this secret life. A long, shining sheet of water stretching a mile and a half, bordered in places by bright, white sands, Loch Avon is one of the more inaccessible places in the Cairngorms. It lies at an altitude of over seven hundred metres in a deep, crag-ringed gash in the rock between the soaring sides of Cairn Gorm and Ben MacDhui. Once you're in, higher up the loch, the only way out again is either to scramble up one of the burns tumbling from the heights, or through the gap above the Shelter Stone between the hills, to Loch Etchachan. From the lower end, there is an easier but much longer exit route along Glen Avon to Inchrory, a ten-mile walk Nan describes 'as lonely and unvisited as anything in the Cairngorms'.[50]

For Nan, the inaccessibility of this remote, freshwater loch was its initial draw. Later, she was to understand this was part of its power. In 1934, she had been walking in the Cairngorms for twelve years. She had come across Loch Avon before, but only to look down on it from the surrounding cliff-tops. The sight of it, such a startling blue in its deep-set, granite girdle, inspired her poem 'Above Loch Avon', but three years passed before she actually clambered down into the cleft containing it.

Of all the seasons, Nan liked summer least and the summer of 1934 was the third in a succession of heat waves that had begun in 1932. Most years in the Cairngorms, winter hangs on stubbornly through the summer months, when patches of old snow can still be seen standing like wraiths high in the corries. But by August of 1934 only a small patch in the innermost recess of the Garbh Choire of Braeriach had stayed the course. July's first few days were particularly hot. Temperatures hit eighty degrees in some parts of the country and stayed there.[51] Aberdeen was stifling. Nan's body functioned at its best in the rarer mountain air; too long at sea-level and she started to suffocate and as the Training Centre was on its summer break, she took herself off to the Spey side of the hills, to Aviemore. On this occasion, Nan was accompanied by a female friend and although it is not known who, she was clearly 'the right sort of hill companion'.[52] Setting out at dawn that morning, they crossed Cairn Gorm around nine o'clock, and headed for the Saddle—an approach which gives the best view along the water and upwards to the Shelter Stone. Making their way to the lower end of the loch the two women lazed around at the water's edge for a while.

On that sweltering day, after several sweaty hours of walking and a scramble down to the loch's side, the water was tantalising in its transparency. No sediment is carried by the burns flowing over the granite ramparts into the loch. The water is limpid. But its clearness is deceptive. There are stories of men walking into the Avon and drowning, supposing it shallow because they thought they could see its depth.

At noon, when the sun penetrated directly into the water, they stripped and waded in. Over ten years later, Nan reconstructed what happened next in *The Living Mountain*:

> The clear water was at our knees, then at our thighs. How clear it was only this walking into it could reveal. To look through it was to discover its own properties. What we saw under water had a sharper clarity than what we saw through air. We waded on into the brightness, and the width of the water increased, as it always does when one is on or in it, so that the loch no longer seemed narrow, but the far side was a long way off. Then I looked down; and at my feet there opened a gulf of brightness so profound that the mind stopped. We were standing on the edge of a shelf that ran some yards into the loch before plunging down to the pit that is the true bottom. And through that inordinate clearness we saw to the depth of the pit. So limpid was it that every stone was clear. I motioned to my companion, who was a step behind, and she came, and glanced as I had down the submerged precipice. Then we looked into each other's eyes, and again into the pit. I waded slowly back into shallower water. There was nothing that seemed worth saying. My spirit was as naked as my body. It was one of the most defenceless moments of my life.[53]

It was not any sense of danger that had so unnerved her, although as she admitted 'I might, of course have overbalanced and been drowned' (an interesting comment that suggests she could not swim[54]). As her gaze penetrated the depths of the loch, Nan felt not fear, but the exhilarating shock of sudden illumination, a flash of intuitive insight known in Zen Buddhism as 'satori'.[55] As she says in *The Living Mountain*, 'the mind stopped'. Not '*her* mind', '*the* mind'. The use of the definite article is deliberate. 'That first glance down', she wrote afterwards, 'shocked me to a heightened power of myself' experiencing a perceptual shift, when for the first time she saw the world undistorted by the lens of self. Everything, she now saw, was interrelated.

Henry Thoreau, who in many ways anticipated Zen practice and thought, describes the lake (in his opinion the most beautiful and expressive feature of the landscape) as 'the earth's eye, looking into which the beholder measures the depth of his own nature'.[56] Suzuki explains that the discipline of Zen consists in opening the mental eye in order to look into the very reason of existence.[57] What happened to Nan, then, was symmetrical. The mind-stopped, the mental eye opened and, looking deep into the lake, the earth's eye, she saw into the depths of her own nature. It was an exchange. An interaction Nan sums up in the final paragraph of *The Living Mountain:* 'as I penetrate more deeply into the mountain's life, I penetrate also into my own'—a 'movement of being'[58] she first described it but which she was eventually to call 'traffic'.[59]

It had taken going *into* the mountain, clambering down into that gash in the rock and seeing into the deep-most pit of the loch to achieve this clarity. But what Nan Shepherd also knew was that she had only just begun to see; that this first encounter was merely the beginning of what she called 'her journey into Being', a journey that was itself part of the technique.[60]

That experience at Loch Avon haunted Nan. Reconstructed in *The Living Mountain* it also inspired a poem written shortly afterwards. Dated July 1934, it is not in her manuscript book of poetry but tucked into it on a separate sheet:

> Loch A'an, Loch A'an, hoo deep ye lie!
> Tell nane yer depth and nane shall I.
> Bricht though yer deepmaist pit may be,
> Ye'll haunt me till the day I dee.
> Bricht, an' bricht, an' bricht as air,
> Ye'll haunt me noo for evermair.[61]

'Loch A'an' is one of only three poems in her poetry collection *In the Cairngorms* which is written in dialect. Nan only used Doric when a word suggested itself to her and felt right.[62] It is entirely appropriate here. In English, the poem has none of the same rhyming resonance. To read it only once or twice is to be able to commit it to memory. It leaves its own haunting.

When Nan was writing this poem, to her knowledge, Loch Avon had yet to be sounded. It has now. At its deepest, the latest edition of the OS Landranger map makes it 30 metres. In *the Living Mountain,* she claims, rather ambiguously, 'I know its depth, but not in feet'. So she pinpoints a truth about Zen. It is an infinite riddle, a labyrinth, a knot that never quite unravels. Just as you think you might arrive at your destination, it leads you onwards. As she explains in *The Living*

Mountain, 'Knowing another is endless: the thing to be known, grows with the knowing'.[63] As a result, 'one never quite knows the mountain, nor oneself in relation to it'.[64] It is an astonishingly profound insight in an era when Eastern Philosophy was only just beginning to infiltrate Western thinking.

Buddhist works had been circulating in the West since the mid-nineteenth century, the by-product of a surge of scholarly interest in Oriental studies. But these texts were an esoteric taste for the learned few and even by the early twentieth century Buddhism was still something only under investigation by academics—it didn't occur to any of them to actually practise it. By 1924, Travers Christmas Humphreys had founded the first Buddhist Society in London (it still exists) but while many of its original members thought of themselves as Buddhist, most were armchair philosophers, only there to discuss ideas. In the intellectual and artistic circles of the West, interest increased dramatically after the Second World War, related, no doubt, to the fad for Japanese culture. It would take until the 1950s and early 60s when Buddhist teachers like the Tibetan lamas fleeing the Chinese occupation, actually emigrated to the West during a period which coincided with the rise of the 'Beat Generation'—Ram Dass, Jack Kerouac and Allen Ginsberg—for Buddhism to begin to be seen as more than just an interesting concept.

In Zen, all the philosophy of the East is crystallised, and although there is an intellectual element to it, Zen is not philosophy as we understand the term: rooted in logic and analysis. If anything it is the polar opposite. Zen is not something that can be grasped by the rational mind, any more than it can be explained; nor can it be learnt from books:

> Zen is the whole mind, and in it we find a great many things; but the mind is not a composite thing that is to be divided into so many faculties, leaving nothing behind when a dissection is over. Zen has nothing to teach us in the way of intellectual analysis; nor has it any set doctrines which are imposed on its followers for acceptance. In this respect Zen is quite chaotic... Zen followers may have sets of doctrines, but they have them on their own account, and for their own benefit; they do not owe the fact to Zen. Therefore, there are in Zen no sacred books or dogmatic tenets, nor are there any symbolic formulae through which an access might be gained into the signification of Zen. If I am asked, then, what Zen teaches, I would answer, Zen teaches nothing. Whatever teachings there are in Zen, they come out of one's own mind. We teach ourselves; Zen merely points the way.[65]

So said Professor Suzuki. In 1957, Alan Watts put it another way: Zen 'is an experience, nonverbal in character, which is simply inaccessible to the purely literary and scholarly approach. To know what Zen is… there is no alternative but to practise it'.[66]

As far as we know, Nan was not familiar with Suzuki's essays. First published in Japan in *New East* magazine in 1914 (making it most unlikely she would have read them then) they later formed the basis of his *Introduction to Zen Buddhism* published in America in 1934. Nor can we be certain she read Watts's works. We do know, however, that she was interested in Eastern writing from an early age. Among the collection of books she left to her literary executor, Erlend Clouston, is a beautifully-bound copy of the *Rubaiyat of Omar Khayyam* purchased in 1909 when she was just fifteen. But it was around 1917 that her interest in Eastern philosophies really began to take hold. This is obvious from her commonplace books.

From May 1907, Nan kept commonplace books. Into *Gleanings,* as she named the first one which she began in May 1907 and her later *Medley Book* (started in 1911) she carefully copied quotations which inspired her. To leaf through these is to see a young woman of precocious intellect. Page after page is filled with extracts gathered from widely disparate sources. English, Scottish and European prose and poetry mingle with Ancient Greek works and quotations from religious and philosophical texts. Among these is a long passage from 'Nirvana' in Lafcadio Hearn's *Gleanings in Buddha Fields* published in 1897.

Greek by birth, Hearn lived and worked as a journalist and writer in America until 1890 when he moved to Japan.[67] Well-known in America for his somewhat florid, Stevensonian-style prose, the works he produced while living in Japan until his death in 1904 are his finest, their language simpler and as a late nineteenth century guide to those completely uninformed on the subject of Japanese Buddhism Hearn's work is hard to beat. Less specialised than Zen, Hearn's brand of Buddhism was the popular form practised by the ordinary Japanese people rather than the 'higher', profoundly metaphysical and more complex Buddhism of the monks. This, combined with his simple diction, made his works much more accessible.

Into *Gleanings* Nan carefully copied extracts from Chapter IX of Hearn's work, taking up four pages of her book. It is worth repeating here, what she would have read before she reached the passage she transcribed—Hearn's explanation that Buddhist philosophy is antithetical to Descartes's 'Cogito ergo sum'—'I think, therefore I am':

Self is false, ego is merely a temporary 'aggregate of sensations, impulses, ideas, created by the physical and mental experiences of the race—all related to the perishable body, and all doomed to dissolve with it'. What to Western reasoning seems the most indubitable of realities, Buddhist reasoning pronounces the greatest of all illusions. The mind, the thoughts and all the sense are subject to the law of life and death. With knowledge of Self and the laws of birth and death, there is no grasping, and no sense-perception. Knowing one's self and knowing how the senses act, there is no room for the idea of 'I', or the ground for framing it. The thought of 'Self' gives rise to all sorrows— binding the world as with fetters; but having found there is no 'I' that can be bound, then all these bonds are severed.[68]

The extract Nan copied into *Gleanings,* recounts 'The Sutra of the Great Decease's account of the Eight Stages of Nirvana.'[69] Listing them she ends, 'the eighth stage all sensations and ideas cease to exist. And after this comes Nirvana' and in her version, Nan underlines the word 'after', before continuing:

The same Sutra, in recounting the death of the Buddha, represents him as rapidly passing through the first four stages of meditation to enter into "that state of mind to which the Infinity of Space alone is present"—and thence into "that state of mind to which the Infinity of Thought alone is present"— and thence into "that state of mind to which nothing at all is specifically present"—and thence into "that state of mind between conscious and unconsciousness"—and thence into "that state of mind in which the consciousness both of sensations and of ideas has wholly passed away.

Leaving a line, she then adds a further paragraph:

In this Oriental philosophy, acts and thoughts are forces integrating themselves into material and mental phenomena— into what we call objective & subjective appearances. The very earth we tread upon—the mountains and forests, the rivers and seas, the world and its moon, the visible universe in short—is the integration of acts and thoughts, is Karma, or at least Being conditioned by Karma. When every phase of our mind shall be in accord with the mind of Buddha, … then there will not be even one particle of dust that does not enter into Buddhahood.[70]

Hearn was influenced by the philosopher Herbert Spencer. He includes a quotation of Spencer's which Nan also copied out:

> Every feeling and thought being but transitory;—an entire life made up of such feelings and thoughts being also but transitory;—nay, the objects amid which life is passed, though less transitory, being severally in the course of losing their individualities whether quickly or slowly—we learn that the one thing permanent is the Unknowable Reality hidden under all these changing shapes.[71]

This 'unknowableness' is what Nan apprehended for the first time at Loch Avon some seventeen years later.

Zen, according to Suzuki, 'perceives and feels, and does not abstract and meditate. Zen penetrates and is finally lost in the immersion. Meditation, on the other hand, is outspokenly dualistic and consequently, inevitably superficial'.[72] Nan tried meditation but it did not work for her: 'at one time I used to try to induce the right sensitivity, by deep relaxation, by stringent discipline; but it is rather like the way religious writers tell how for all their self-abrogation, the vision refused to come and the dark night of the soul descended on them'.[73] Instead, from July 1934 onwards, these flashes of illumination came when she stopped trying to force them, 'unpredictably, yet governed, it would seem, by a law whose working is dimly understood', she wrote in *The Living Mountain*. 'Moments, of sheer shock and joy' which felt, she said, 'like a renewal of life itself',[74] and which lasted well into old age.

They came most often when she was waking from outdoor sleep, or gazing 'tranced' at running water, listening to its song. Most of all, they came: 'after hours of steady walking, with the long rhythm of motion sustained until motion is felt, not merely known by the brain, as the still centre of being...Walking thus hour after hour, the senses keyed, one walks the flesh transparent. But no metaphor, *transparent*, or *light as air*, is adequate. The body is not made negligible, but paramount.'[75]

In the final paragraph of *The Living Mountain* Nan expresses something hard to articulate and what Hearn identified, that this way of thinking is the antithesis of the dualism of Descartes' theory which had long been a mode of thought in the West. The Western assumption is that because 'I' am doing this, then 'I' must be separate from the world, doing something 'to' it. Eastern philosophy on the other hand, understands that without the 'I', man and universe are not separate, but inseparable. With the 'self' removed from the equation, Nan explains that she still feels very much herself but more so; more alive than ever before: 'It is not ecstasy, that leap out of the self that makes man like a god. I am not out of myself, but in myself. I am'.[76]

Hard to describe because it has to be experienced to be appre-hended, even Suzuki explains it through another's words:

> When Bodhidharma[77] was asked who he was, he said "I do not know". This was not because he could not explain himself, nor was it because he wanted to avoid any verbal controversy, but just because he did not know what or who he was, save that he was what he was and could not be anything else.[78]

'I am as I am and I can't be any ammer', wrote a young Nan Shepherd on the frontispiece of *Gleanings.* No explanation or attribution accompanies this statement. The only other words on the page are in a slanted, slight and careful hand: 'Nan Shepherd, Dunvegan, Cults' and the date: '7th May, 1907'. Judging by the handwriting, which grows progressively bolder, more rounded and upright later in the book, this epigraph was added some years afterwards, in about 1917, around the same time she copied Hearn's 'Nirvana' into the book.

Nan's statement suggests that long before she actually apprehended it in 1934, she could grasp that 'that leap out of self', ironically, is the most intense state of being. It would take another decade before she began to articulate it in *The Living Mountain.* In the meantime, she remained, like Martha Ironside, in her life, but not of it: her real life, she lived somewhere else. And during all this time, she strove to be able to translate this *felt* experience into the written word. She was in awe of anyone who could.

Barbara Balmer, although impervious to mountains, responded to Nan immediately,[79] grasping this other life of hers, there, but hidden below the surface. The two women, however, met in the 1970s, by which time Eastern philosophies had really begun to permeate Western ideas. Theirs was an intense, but short-lived friendship. Barbara and her husband George Mackie, also an artist and lecturer at Gray's in Aberdeen, moved south in 1980 and although they corresponded for a couple of years, their bond was broken by Nan's death in 1981.

During her lifetime, there was only one other person who really understood and with whom Nan could share her 'secret life', because for him, too, it was a living reality, and that was the Scottish novelist Neil Gunn. Not only could he comprehend it, however, he was also able to express it in words.

It was not until the 1950s, towards the end of Gunn's writing career, when a friend introduced him to Herrigel's *Zen in the Art of Archery,* that he began to recognise the parallels between Eastern thinking and his own, fundamental philosophies—philosophies which permeate his work. From then on he read widely on the subject, including texts by Suzuki and Watts. Neil Gunn valued Nan's comments on his writing because, from the outset, she understood the inner awareness in his works that the critics had missed.[80]

In a letter she wrote to him on 14 May 1940 about his latest two novels, *Wild Geese Overhead* and *Second Sight,* published consecutively in 1939 and 1940, she is reverent in her praise for his ability to explain the unexplainable:

> Laddie you frighten me whiles. Not because of the theme, or any consideration of its implications: but because of the uncanny way you enter my breathing and living and seeing and apprehending. To apprehend things—walking on a hill, seeing the light change, the mist, the dark, being aware, using the whole of one's body to instruct the spirit—yes, that is a secret life one has and knows that others have. But to be able to share it, in and through words—that's what frightens me. The word shouldn't have such power. It dissolves one's being. I am no longer myself but part of a life beyond myself when I read pages that are so much the expression of myself. You can take processes of being—no that's too formal a word—<u>states</u> is too static, this is something that moves—<u>movements</u> I suppose is best—you can take movements of being and translate them out of themselves into words. That seems to me a gift of a very high and sane order.[81]

The Living Mountain, of course, illustrates that she, too, had this gift and although that slim volume is the best of her writing, it is developed in her novels, too. In her third novel, *A Pass in the Grampians* published in 1933 a year before she actually began to know it intuitively at Loch Avon, you can see she is already trying to describe the concept that man and universe are inseparable, interrelated. She contemplates this idea through sheep farmer Andrew Kilgour:

> He had made his covenant with the moor: it had bogged him and drenched him, deceived, scorched, numbed him with cold, tested his endurance, memory and skill; until a large part of his nature was so interpenetrated with its nature that apart

from it he would have lost reality.[82]

Using free indirect speech here, which she does often and to great effect, she reveals her empathy for her subject, an empathy which was deep-rooted.

Chapter Two

1893-1901

Nan Shepherd was no stranger to hills. As a child, the Deeside hills near her home and the Monadhliaths flanking the Spey on the other side of the Cairngorms were her idea of the perfect playground. It was from a shoulder of the Monadhliaths she first glimpsed the 'stormy violet of a gully on the back of Sgoran Dubh' that haunted her dreams and '*thirled*' her for life to the mountain, as she recounted in *The Living Mountain*.[83] But her affinity for her native landscape, she felt, went back further than this. It was innate. 'My forebears were sheep farmers—shepherds—the whole process of life is somewhere in my blood',[84] she explained in a letter to Neil Gunn in April 1947. And Nan's surname, which derives from the Middle English 'schepherde' meaning 'herdsman' or 'guardian' of sheep, suggests this was probably the case. .

From the middle to late nineteenth century, census figures reveal that the highest concentration of Scottish 'Shepherds' was in the North East, in Aberdeenshire, Angus and Kincardine and nearly half of them were farmers. It is not surprising, then, that both Nan's parents were Aberdeenshire people and both were descended from farming stock.

The 'son of a petty crofter in a Deeside Glen'[85] as Nan describes her father, thinly disguised as John Grey in *The Weatherhouse,* John Shepherd was born on the 15th December 1852 in Wester Cullerlie in the parish of Echt, twelve miles west of Aberdeen. Named after his father, grandfather and great-grandfather, with not a middle name to distinguish them, he was the fourth of five children born to Ann and John Shepherd, and the second son.

His grandfather, the son of an agricultural labourer, was Master Blacksmith at the Smithy in Wester Cullerlie, a cluster of dwellings surrounded by open farmland lying about three miles south-east of Echt—not far, somewhat aptly, from the famous horseshoe-shaped circle. At the heart of every village, despite its grimy, working-class image, the smithy was often one of the wealthiest enterprises in the community. Regardless of the industrial revolution, the nineteenth century was still the age of the horse, both on farms and in the towns. Blacksmiths, skilled crafters of tools and ironmongery, were more in demand than ever.

On his father's retirement, John Shepherd Junior, as was expected of the oldest son, took over the smithy (which in 1851 was prosperous enough to employ two men and an apprentice).[86] But the blacksmith's life was not for John-Junior, 'petty crofter' of Nan's description, who as well as running the smithy, was already farming six acres of land locally. He was married by then, too, to Ann Barron, a farmer's daughter from nearby Echt.[87]

Ann was marrying relatively late. Aged thirty-two on their marriage in 1849, she was three years older than her husband and some seven months pregnant with their first child, a son, Robert, who arrived on April Fool's day the same year. Whether or not the pregnancy was a calculated move and the couple married under pressure from their families, we do not know. But four more children followed in the space of seven years: a daughter Ann, then John, Andrew and Mary.

Sometime after Mary's birth in 1856, John-Junior left the Smithy and moved his family to Strachan[88] in Kincardineshire taking on the tenancy of the Haugh,[89] a substantial, traditional, U-shaped, stone steading, sitting between the Waters of Dye and Feugh, tributaries of the River Dee, with 115 acres of farmland.

How much Ann had to do with the move can only be conjectured. She might well have had a competitive nature. George Barron's fourth daughter, she was the fifth of nine children and very much, then, the middle child. What we do know, however, is that over the next ten years, John-Junior increased his acreage. After all, as well as the four labourers he employed, he had three sons to help on the farm. But while Robert, the oldest of the Shepherd brood, seemed happy to follow his father into farming, his younger brothers had other ideas.

Before the 1872 Education Act made schooling compulsory, children went to school only if their parents could spare them and could afford the fees. If Nan's fictionalised account of her father's upbringing is anything to go by, this was almost certainly the case for the Shepherd boys. All three will have laboured on the farm taking their schooling as and when they could, mostly in the winters. But the Dominie of Strachan's Free Church school did well by the three youngest and brightest Shepherds. Andrew became a pupil teacher there before going on, in true Scottish style, to be educated for the Church. He headed for Glasgow to study theology and by 1891 was a Senior Minister of

Chryston West Church, in Cadder, comfortably settled in its Manse.

John, the smithy's iron still smouldering in his veins, set his sights on mechanical engineering and by the age of eighteen had left the farming life behind and begun an apprenticeship at James Abernethy & Co of the Ferryhill Foundy in Aberdeen. By 1871, along with his thirteen year old sister Mary (who had outstripped the village school and been dispatched to the town to continue her education) he was living with his unmarried and elderly aunt, Margaret Barron, at 7, Black's Buildings.

A towering tenement on Mutton Brae, Black's Buildings stood in front of Woolmanhill overlooking the old bleaching greens on the banks of the fast-flowing Denburn. Tenement life was tough. Despite the town's growing prosperity, before the slum clearance of the 1920s many Aberdonians lived in squalor. The best of the working-class housing available in Aberdeen, tenements were far from comfortable. There was no piped water, families were often crowded into one room and the privies at the 'backie' were shared.

Disease was rife. Cholera, despite disappearing in 1854, was still much feared. Typhus, scarlet fever, measles, typhoid and tuberculosis were widespread. The 1870s were years of continuous smallpox outbreaks in Aberdeen and in 1872, so many were afflicted, the hospitals overflowed. Poor Mary Shepherd. She escaped the 1872 epidemic only to die of bronchitis in June that year, aged just fifteen.

John Shepherd had a stronger constitution than his sister, and was determined. He worked hard and put himself through night school, too. So that by the time he was twenty eight, he'd been promoted from apprentice turner to Mechanical Draughtsman at Abernethy's. And had survived another ten years of tenement living.

From the 1820s until the 1930s Aberdeen was the largest granite-producing area in the world, its industry employing some 25,000 of its men. Established in 1806, James Abernethy & Co was the world's largest maker of granite-working machinery producing a vast range of castings and equipment. 'Ironfounders, Boilermakers & Bridge Builders, Makers of Tea Machinery, Sugar Mills, Fish Guano & Manure machinery Etc' reads a 1905 advertisement.[90] It shows the foundry buildings were impressive, numerous and sprawling and at either end, stood tall, smoke-spewing chimneys. In older parts of the city the company's drain covers and 'branders' (gratings) can still be seen, but by the 1960s Abernethy's had ceased operating.

Back in 1881, though, business was booming and there were around four hundred employees some thirty five years later when John Shepherd retired as Works Manager. Among his work is the Pollhollick

Suspension Bridge and the much more elegant, white suspension bridge at Cambus O'May—all latticework and fret-worked towers. Opened over the Dee in 1905, the footbridge survived countless torrential floods but the battering of December 2015 has closed it for now.

'His voice was soft and persuasive. His men revered him and trusted his judgement', Nan says of John Grey in *The Weatherhouse* and by all accounts John Shepherd was a quiet, unassuming man. Like his daughter, however, there was more to him than met the eye. As fond of botany and books as he was of engineering, he, too, was a hill lover. He 'went out early on Sunday mornings, taking long walks in the country, teaching himself botany and learning by heart the works of the English poets, studying Carlyle and Ruskin, John Locke and Adam Smith', according to *The Weatherhouse*. But if it is true that John Shepherd bought himself 'an eighteenth century *Paradise Lost,* leather bound with steel engravings of our First Parents in a state of innocence' to which he added 'for Eve, a skirt, for Adam short pants, of Indian ink'[91] he shared his daughter's wry sense of humour.[92]

How he met Nan's mother, Jeannie Kelly, is not known. But while John was living and working in Aberdeen, his parents moved again, to Tersets, an even bigger farm of 140 acres in Drumoak. Jeannie Kelly was born and raised in Aberdeen, but she often visited her grandparents, James and Jean Tough, who lived only a couple of miles east of Tersets at the Mains of Drum. Now Drumoak has never had a large population. Its 811 inhabitants in 1846, by 1972 had reduced to a mere 650. So, in a small farming community, where everybody knew everybody else, it was highly likely to have been here, rather than in Aberdeen, that John and Jeannie first met. And by 1881, when John Junior finally retired and installed himself and his wife, Ann in Drumoak's Park Cottage, John had moved in too.

'Dalmaik' to its inhabitants, Drumoak is eleven miles south-west of Aberdeen. Bounded by the Dee, it is closed on the south by the Grampians, while to the west lie the snow-clad peaks of the Cairngorms. Its farmers had much to contend with. One of the driest Deeside parishes, its land, was like the 'small land; poor; ill to harvest, its fields ringed about with dykes of stone laboriously gathered from the soil of *The Weatherhouse*. Except where it had been cultivated the longest, the soil was inferior.

Originally a sheep-farming community, by the mid-nineteenth century numbers of sheep dramatically dwindled as large tracts of their pasture were converted to arable farming. Sheep no longer filled the fields, but years of their grazing the good grass had ruined the land. It took time and labour to restore the balance.

Like his father before him, Jeannie Kelly's maternal grandfather, James Tough, was a farmer. A genial fellow, whose kind heart and obliging nature were proverbial in the parish of Drumoak[94], his early working life was in the service of the Irvines. The name, from the Scots 'Veine', means resolute and worthy and perhaps the Laird saw this in James Tough, who as his own surname suggests, was resilient and apparently indefatigable. At the age of seventy seven he was far from well, yet still out and about on the farm overseeing the finishing of a well-filled corn yard.

A photograph shows him in middle age, bearded and bewhiskered, his hair in stiff tufts over his ears, like horns. In his long coat and high-buttoned waistcoat with its gleaming curve of watch-chain, top hat in one hand, the other holding a chair-back, his weight on one leg, the other crossed in front, he had something of Nan Shepherd's direct gaze about him. Unusually for Victorian portraits, he looks at ease, too, and comfortable, exuding prosperity.

By 1857, his hard work and flair for farming meant he was in a position to take over the lease of the Mains of Drum. The nearest to the 'big house', the Mains was often the largest tenancy with the best facilities and richest pasturage.

A less ornate, smaller but still imposing version of Drum Castle, the grey-turreted Mains is now an award-winning garden centre and restaurant set in immaculate landscaped grounds. In the late 1850s, it was a farm of ninety acres and home to eleven people. Along with James's wife, Jean, lived five of their eight children, his elderly father, a ploughman and field labourer as well as a lodger whose occupation was a clerk but who probably also tutored his four younger daughters, then still living at home.[95]

Busy though he was with the farm, James still found time to indulge his passion for literature: 'It was a pleasure and profit to hear him discuss the newest biography with a fine appreciation of its merits', reads his obituary, which describes the cause of his death as a serious attack of 'congestion'[96] from which he never rallied. It killed him just two days after the birth of his great-grandson Frank Shepherd, on 7th October 1890. He was survived by Jean, his wife of fifty-three years, and five of their children.

Descended from James Smith, who is recorded in the parish Register of Edzell in Angus as a 'rabbler' in the Jacobite Rebellion of 1714, Jean was the oldest daughter of David and Elisabeth Smith's brood of nine. Until her father's death in 1834, Jean lived at the family's farm, Dalfouper, a farm which still sits on a bend of the North Esk river and just south of the Kincardine border. Twenty-four when her father died and still unmarried, she moved three miles away to Westerton in Strathcathro to live with a childless aunt, along with a cousin of hers, a Miss Gray, who married a George Falconer—both surnames Nan used in *The Weatherhouse*.

Between 1841 and 1931 around two million Scots emigrated. Among them were several of Nan's relations. While two of Jean's siblings died young (her brother David drowned in childhood and her younger sister Kate, forced to flee her doctor husband in Aboyne, walked the thirty miles home overnight only to die on the doorstep) others went 'beyond the Pass'. Jamie went to New Zealand; Margaret to a Sydney-suburb in Australia and another sister, Mary, also went abroad.

Cousins of Jean's also left Scotland. Charles Smith found work in Cape Colony, before returning home to Aberdeenshire in the 1880s to marry an 'old romance'—sounding suspiciously like Roy Foubister who came back for Aunt Josephine in *The Quarry Wood*. Nan often used her relations' lives for inspiration—sometimes borrowing more than their names. She would have known these cousins and may well have used the story, although she changed its ending. Other relatives, too, ended up as missionaries in South Africa, connections that would prove useful to the Shepherds in the early 1900s.

By October 1836, aged twenty seven, Jean Smith was married to James Tough and proceeded to produce eight children in the space of sixteen years (the last in her early forties). Trim, still, in her late twenties, a formal portrait shows her, exuberantly curly hair fastened with flowers, seated, a book in her hand, opened towards its end. She might well have shared James's love of literature, but it's possible this was the photographer's prop, given to her so she had something to do with her hands. Less relaxed than her husband, she looks anxiously away from the lens. In this portrait, she seems plain, rather than the 'good-looking woman' Nan's mother, Jeannie, describes as having highly arched brows, dark hair and eyes and a high complexion'.[97] Those brows give her a look of constant, faint surprise.

Jane Tough bore a striking resemblance to her mother, brows and all. The oldest of the eight Tough offspring, she was born on 15 January 1837, three months exactly after her parents' marriage. But while we cannot be sure if her parents married for love or out of necessity, we can be certain that their oldest daughter's marriage to Francis Bonnyman Kelly was a love match.

Francis Kelly was courting 'Jeannie' (as Jane Tough, like her mother and daughter, was rather confusingly known) for over two years before their marriage on 6th March 1861 when she was twenty-four. A token of affection he gave her is embroidered with the date: 29th December

1858,[98] but as the Kellys also lived in Drumoak, at Wardmill, only a mile north of the Mains of Drum, they had probably known each other all their lives.

Both Francis and his older brother were tailors, like their father William. Francis began his working life as a journeyman tailor for Cook & Davidson in Market Street Aberdeen and shortly after wedding Jeannie, left on horseback to drum up business door-to-door in villages lying north of Aberdeen from Udny to New Deer. Jeannie stayed at home with 'Grannie'.

The roads were dreadful, the ground frost-hardened and often snow-covered. Some days Francis was riding through driving sleet and snow. Riding was not his forte. In letters addressed to his 'darling Jeannie', he reassured her he was managing the horse so well, 'you should really think I had served my apprenticeship to be a jockey'. He was taking orders and had 'a good many promised', he said, but there were days when he would call at eight houses in a village without leaving his saddle before riding another twenty miles to the next. [99]

In *The Weatherhouse* Nan gives us a portrait of a 'Journeyman':

[Weelum] was a taciturn man: he wasted no words; and when his master's clients gave orders about the detail of the work he undertook he would listen with an intent, intelligent expression, and reply with a grave and considering nod. Afterwards he did exactly what he pleased. Folk complained…in the end his master dismissed him; reluctantly for he had clever hands.[100]

Francis was not dismissed. Instead he proved a good enough salesman to leave Cook & Davidson and establish his own business at 10 St Nicholas Street, Aberdeen (now demolished). In a photograph of Francis and Jeannie Kelly with their two oldest sons, James sits on his lap. Standing in front of his mother—already tall for his age—is their oldest son, William. They look affluent, and as you would expect, well-turned out.

By 1881, Francis was indeed prospering and had joined the ranks of Aberdeen's moneyed, middle-class. Elected to the City Parish, his staff at the St Nicholas street shop now numbered eleven plus several apprentices and he had moved his wife and seven children and their servant into 11 Albert Street in Aberdeen. He was wealthy enough to pay for secondary education for all his children and for two of his sons to go to university.

His oldest, William Kelly, was by 1881 already a practising architect. Responsible, amongst other works, for improvements to King's

College Chapel made towards the end of the nineteenth century, he is most famous now for the leopards on Union Bridge, installed when it was widened in 1908—although there is some dispute over whether he actually designed them.[101] Years later, an amused Nan related her uncle's outrage, when, during rag week, the undergraduates tied ribbons round the leopards' necks. The future of 'Kelly's Cats' is currently uncertain,[102] but for now they remain, on suicide watch alongside Samaritans' posters urging would-be jumpers to think again. Of the other Kelly boys, James, became a tailor and Francis, a doctor. In 1881, the Kelly girls, of whom Jeannie, at sixteen, was the eldest, were still being educated. The Census records no governess or tutor living in, so they were probably at St Margaret's, the oldest private girls' school in Aberdeen founded in 1846.

Then in 1885, the Kellys moved again. Albert Street had been a pretty smart address. Granite terraces line the road, without much in the way of a front garden, but separated from the pavement by iron railings still intact today. Less than a mile away, the Kelly family's new address was even smarter. Gladstone Place is a wide, tree-lined avenue of substantial, bay-fronted, terraced houses, all with large front gardens set behind low walls, ironwork and hedging. Still much sought-after, it was a prime location in Aberdeen's West End in the mid-1880s. The Kellys were now daily rubbing shoulders with the professional classes. Among their neighbours were solicitors, a university professor, a builder, a bookseller, and a dentist. It was from Gladstone Place that a twenty-one year old Jeannie Kelly married John Shepherd, eleven years her senior, on 23rd September 1885.

It was not unusual for Victorian women to marry young. In fact, rather than risk the humiliation of spinsterhood, there was pressure on young women to marry if a suitable opportunity presented itself. Most families, especially those like the Kellys with a large number of children, were only too happy if their daughters married around the age of twenty and since women were supposed to age faster than men, husbands were often expected to be older, ideally by three to seven years. Scottish society, even by the early twentieth century, was still heavily patriarchal and the age difference helped reinforce women's 'naturally subservient' position. Of course, this was also for financial reasons. A potential bride-groom was required to prove he had the means to support his wife and children before he was granted permission by the girl's father.

The first of the Kelly girls to marry, Jeannie was a beauty and certainly the most striking, physically, of the three. They were a tall family. William was described as 'endowed with commanding height, a fine leonic head and a rich resonant voice…His tall figure and rapid walk made him noticeable among Aberdonians at the time. Men with shorter legs found it trying to come down Albyn Place with him in the morning'.[103] Jeannie, too, was very tall, with the straight high shoulders and long, swinging legs which Nan inherited. Pale-skinned, with delicate, white hands that look as though they never held anything except a pair of gloves or an embroidery needle, in early photographs, Jeannie's round, dark eyes brim with intelligence. She has her mother's high forehead, but not her eyebrows—in fact, perhaps rather fortunately, none of the Kelly girls inherited those. Educated and accomplished, from a respectable, professional, middle-class Aberdonian family, she was an extremely desirable match.

Talented, ambitious and hard-working, John Shepherd was already making his mark at the Ferryhill Foundry when he and Jeannie married. But Nan's fictionalised portrait of her father in *The Weatherhouse* is supported by photographs of him. In sharp contrast to his wife's elegant, lithe, legginess, his was 'a squat, plebeian figure, redeemed by its alert activity and by the large and noble head. The brow was wide and lofty, the nose aquiline, shaggy eyebrows emphasised the depths of the eye sockets, in which there shone a pair of dark, piercing and kindly eyes.'[104] His hair, those 'shaggy eyebrows' and a bushy beard which he never shaved off and which dominated his face, emphasising his receding hairline, were intensely black in youth. Like Nan, in photographs, John Shepherd's eyes often twinkle, as if at some private joke.

'The well-bred love with discrimination', [105] says the narrator of *The Weatherhouse* and in *The Quarry Wood* Nan Shepherd illustrates the still strictly-stratified, late-Victorian, Aberdonian society and the repercussions of marrying out of your own class. As far as the Leggatts were concerned Emmeline had thrown herself away on Geordie Ironside and aside from Aunt Josephine, they had turned their backs on her:

> 'If she hadna the wit to pit a plooman by the door, nor the grace to mind on fat was due to her fowk and their position, she can just bid the consequences…ye've gotten fat ye hae gotten by mairryin' aneath ye'.[106]

But there is no evidence that the Kellys considered Jeannie had married beneath her. After all, Francis Kelly was much younger and still a journeyman in the early days of his marriage and John Shepherd's career was very much in the ascendant by the time he wed Francis's daughter. In any case, both John and Jeannie were descended from tenant farmers, the middle-class of the agricultural sector.

Access to higher education and a profession was not a possibility for middle-class women of Jeannie Shepherd's era. Women were supposed to want marriage because it allowed them to become mothers. Even Nan's generation was subject to society's still very much patriarchal attitudes and its views on marriage and motherhood. Into *Gleanings* in around 1908 she has dutifully copied poems like 'The Virtuous House-wife', 'Madonnas' from *Songs of Motherhood* and Charles O'Donnell's 'The Blessed Barren'—and this was while she was a pupil at Aberdeen's most progressive secondary schools for girls.

Before marriage, Victorian women were expected to remain chaste (although as we know, neither Jeannie's grandmother nor John's mother fulfilled this particular expectation). And, as women of her class and generation weren't even permitted to speak to a man unless they were chaperoned, aside from her father and brothers Jeannie would have had little contact with the opposite sex. When she did, she had to be careful not to seem too forward as this might indicate a sexual appetite—most unseemly in a Victorian woman. The 'angel in the house' who relished sex risked being dubbed 'hysterical' and locked-up, either in an asylum or, like Bertha in *Jane Eyre,* up in the attic.

Faced with all these emotional frustrations, 'getting leave to live' was as important an issue for Jeannie Shepherd's generation as it was for her daughter (even if Nan lived through a period when societal attitudes to women had begun to change). But in the early years of her marriage to John Shepherd, Jeannie looks content. In a picture of them both taken in 1888, three years into their marriage, they are unsmiling, but Jeannie looks relaxed, without the stiff Victorian formality of earlier photographs we have of her. It is taken in a doorway opened onto a garden, thin drapes billowing behind them. Both seated, John positioned slightly higher than his wife, they are so close as to be touching. There looks to be an easy intimacy between them.

* * *

'I've had the same bedroom all my life!' an elderly Nan Shepherd exclaimed to an interviewer in the 1970s[107] leading the way up the staircase, throwing open the first door on the left. Her little room under the eaves with its coom[108] ceiling and wide, Deeside valley view had changed little over the years and contained only the furniture that could be squeezed in: a large chest of drawers scattered with innumer-able hairpins, a well-stacked bookcase under the window, a single bed, covered in an assortment of rugs, pushed against the wall and next to it, her bedside table. There was no chair. To read, which she often did until the wee hours, she would squat on a cushion on the floor. With no room for a closet either, the rest of Nan's clothes were kept packed carefully into trunks in the old maid's room.

Certainly Nan's bedroom at Dunvegan was the only one she would have remembered and she was not to know then that her final months would be spent at a nursing home in Torphins. Her life began elsewhere too: less than a mile away, in Westerton Cottage, Cults at 9 o'clock precisely, on the morning of Saturday 11th February 1893.

Children were slow in coming to John and Jeannie Shepherd. It was five years into their marriage before their first, a son, was born on 5th October 1890. Named Francis after Jeannie's father, Frank, as he was always known, was followed three years later by a daughter they named Anna, after John Shepherd's mother. 'Annie' to her parents, she was 'Nan' to the rest of the family and close friends; to everyone else, she was 'Miss Shepherd'.

Victoria's reign was drawing to a close. The year of Nan's birth a bronze statue of the stout old Queen replaced a white marble version in Aberdeen, too delicate to cope with its hard frosts. Moved in 1964, it now stands at the Queen's Cross roundabout looking west towards her beloved Balmoral, the castle Prince Albert built for her in 1856, knocking down the original house which was deemed too small to accommodate the Royal Family.

Victorian marriage had been all about large families. Since the infant mortality rate remained high and the average wife could expect to bury at least one baby as well as lose children to chronic diseases, large numbers of children were the norm. John Shepherd was one of five, Jeannie one of seven, his mother one of nine and Jeannie's grandfather, one of eleven. The bigger the family though, the more child death-beds a woman would likely have to remember. Grief and years of continuous child bearing took their toll, turning bright young women into sickly, miserable matrons like Emmeline In *The Quarry Wood,* who 'after twelve pinched and muddled years, with her trim beauty slack, two dead bairns...increased in flabbiness of temper as of body'.[109] As living standards and health care provision improved, from the 1880s Scotland's birth rate dropped. A wife's 'breeding years' were no longer earmarked for motherhood, her energy sapped by endless pregnancies and there were fewer dead babies to mourn.[110]

Westerton Cottage, where John and Jeannie Shepherd set up home after their marriage in 1885, was one of a few dwellings then dotted around Inchgarth Farm, a dairy farm of seventy acres spread over fields on the low-lying land within a meander of the River Dee. It was certainly large enough to house one child and live-in domestic help in the shape of fourteen year old Maggie MacGregor. With the arrival of a second child, its five rooms were apparently becoming cramped.

Shortly after his daughter's birth, John Shepherd borrowed £300 from Aberdeen & Northern Friendly Society and bought 'Dunvegan Cottage' a large, granite, semi-detached villa in West Cults.

Now one of the most affluent areas of Scotland, lying on the western fringes of Aberdeen, these days Cults is a city suburb. North Deeside suburbia stretches over several miles of continuous riverside communities: Cults, Bieldside, Murtle, Milltimber and Peterculter, all served by the North Deeside Road. Despite the existence of so many more houses in the village since Nan's day, in the summer months, from across the river Dee, these are barely distinguishable among the green canopy of trees from which the village takes its name: 'Coiltean', a Scots derivative of 'Quelytis' meaning 'wooded place'.

'Bountiful as she is in greens, Deeside is not a green land', Nan wrote of the countryside surrounding her home.

> It is predominantly a blue landscape…I think this is partly because of the trick distances have (even green distances) of turning blue; and partly because long views almost invariably end in heather: because, too, the width of the land gives one such a sweep of sky. So blue and brown are the colours I should choose as of the very nature of this country…The colour itself seems to have body; to be substance. It lies like the bloom on a plum, or the pile of plush. Sometimes in a hill hollow it would seem to have its own existence, apart from both earth and sky. The result is to give the landscape depth and at least the illusion of significance.[111]

Passion for her 'blue valley' is palpable in this article of Nan's published in *The Deeside Field* magazine in 1938. Deeside is renowned for its beauty and its 'significance' is not lost on others.

The Dee, which rises high in the Cairngorms, flows swiftly east through some of Scotland's most picturesque scenery till it reaches its brim at Aberdeen. Midway on the river's run, lying in the shadow of Lochnagar, is Balmoral, holiday home for five successive monarchs since Queen Victoria and Prince Albert first made Deeside 'Royal', building their huge granite castle there. When the Queen first clapped eyes on Deeside in 1848, it was love at first sight: 'All seemed to breathe freedom and peace, to make one forget the world and its sad turmoils. The scenery is wild, and yet not desolate', she wrote in her journal.[112]

Lying on the North side of the Dee valley, until the mid-nineteenth century, Cults was a sleepy, agricultural area, its population sparsely spread. Its settlement sprang from the Den of Cults, whose waters drove the timber-cutting and grain-grinding mills dotted around the old Deeside Road, running west from the old Brig of Dee. When newly-weds John and Jeannie Shepherd moved there, Cults was just a hamlet in the parish of Banchory-Devenick with a post office, a couple of smiddys, a coaching inn and a church.[113]

Railway fever was slow to reach the North East, but the *Aberdeen Herald's* prophesy in 1845 that the existence of a cheap, speedy railway would 'cause the whole of Deeside to be studded with villas and cottages as thickly as the banks of the Clyde', proved accurate. With stations at East and West Cults originally, the opening of the Deeside Railway Line in September 1853 provided a faster link with Aberdeen than horse-drawn coaches. In 1866 it expanded in the other direction to Ballater, through some of the 'finest scenery in the world'. A railway advertisement of that year sang Deeside's praises:

> The scenery's grand, the air, oh! It's charming,
> Deeside being famed for its excellent farming;
> The mountains stupendous, and sweet heathery plains—
> Travelling's pleasant, there's well-arranged trains.[114]

In the early 1890s, the 'subbies' were introduced. These commuter trains, which ran ten times a day to and from Aberdeen, made Cults an even more desirable place to live and sparked a building boom which, by the end of the nineteenth century, had dramatically picked up its pace.

'The Square', in Cults, as it is still known today and which is little more than a single street, remains its shopping nucleus. The coaching inn still sits on the road's curve, renamed Cults Hotel. As the numbers of incomers to Cults grew, a grocer's shop appeared with a beautiful new post-office adjoining it, as well as a chemist and fishmonger—both of which were more usually found in a town.

As for recreation, there were already bowling, tennis and cricket clubs before Allan Park was opened to commemorate the Queen's Diamond Jubilee in 1897. There, when the weather turned icy, in the hollow between the steep bank and the wooded ridge, villagers could go skating and curling; curling being the only activity aside from hill-walking that Nan Shepherd ever admitted enjoying. There was even a school, run by the Church and headed by Dominie Donald—as famous for his school-house garden as his teaching. By the end of the nineteenth century, Cults was an ideal place to raise a family and despite its growth, until the 1930s half its acreage was still open fields. When Nan was small, it was still rural enough to spy deer wandering down the village street.

In April 1873, a local builder, Alexander Hendry, constructed several houses along the Deeside line. Dunvegan Cottage, into which John Shepherd moved his family in March 1893, was one of these handsome new houses built of locally-quarried granite, with their backs to the road and their faces turned Dee-wards, squarely to the track. Beyond the railway line lay the wide, shallow valley and running through it, the silver streak of fast-flowing river that so often broke its banks in rebellion during Nan's lifetime (and continues to do so). Over the river, Blairs College could be glimpsed to the right and a scattering of farmhouses here and there among fields and trees lifting the eye to the horizon, where the Kincardineshire hills meet the sky. This, then, was the view of Nan's 'blue valley' from her little bedroom—a view soon enlarged when its original skylight was replaced by a dormer, bay window. Her little bedroom sounds eerily reminiscent of the one in the quaint irregular hexagon of *The Weatherhouse* in Nan's second novel, a room 'that was all corners and windows—an elfin inconsequential room'.[115]

Undoubtedly, for John Shepherd, much of Dunvegan's appeal lay in its proximity to West Cults station which was just a short walk from the bottom of its front garden making his twice daily commute to work at the Ferryhill Foundry a mere twelve minutes on the subbie. But like many of the Cults incomers, the Shepherds were members of the professional middle-class and these Victorian well-to-do, had homes large enough for several family bedrooms as well as servants' accommodation. Dunvegan was certainly spacious compared to Westerton Cottage, but John Shepherd saw there was scope for further enlargement, which he now needed.

In 1892, John's father died of pneumonia, just a few months before Nan was born on her grandparents' wedding anniversary. Perhaps this was significant for Ann Shepherd, as although she had two other children living not far away who would have plenty of room to accommodate her, it was to Dunvegan she came. As its four existing bedrooms were already occupied by John, Jeannie, their two children and their maid, Isabella Morrison, John set about extending the house. First, building sideways over the passage running from the front to the back of the house he added a further two bedrooms and an upstairs bathroom. Then to the front, looking Dee-wards, he built on a conservatory and later, at the same time Nan's skylight was replaced, he attached a turret-topped bay, enlarging Jeannie Shepherd's bedroom as well as the parlour below.

Today Dunvegan is little changed. White, weather-proof windows have been swapped for the old, painted, wooden-framed ones. The side extension, its original concrete crumbling, has had to be rebuilt and the conservatory has been replaced with a larger one. From the garden gate opening on to the old Deeside line, a neat, gravel path still leads up to the house, grassed to the left, terraced towards the house and separated from the steeply sloping lawn by iron railings. Some of the trees, though, are gone.

But if John Shepherd imagined Dunvegan would soon be filled with more children, he was mistaken. Over the years, photographs of Jeannie reveal her deterioration, from svelte, striking beauty to a gaunt, sallow, shadow of her former self. This, however, was not the result of years of endless childbearing and mourning dead infants. Miscarriages or still-births there might have been, but the 1911 Census records the number of children born alive to the Shepherds during their, by then, twenty five year marriage, as two. After the birth of her daughter, Jeannie Shepherd took to her bed and rarely left it again for the rest of her long life—except, apparently, when no-one was looking.[116]

Visitors to Dunvegan arriving unannounced would sometimes spy Jeannie through the windows, but by the time they had been ushered inside, there would be no sign of her. For some, the only sign she existed was the ornate wicker wheelchair, standing empty in the conservatory or parked under the covered walkway at the side of the house. No-one recalls ever seeing her out and about in Cults in the wheelchair.

If the Shepherds themselves knew what ailed her, it was not discussed outside the family. Opinions vary as to what was actually wrong with Jeannie Shepherd, but the general consensus in the village seems to be... not very much. Described as one of the 'worrit well' by her friend and sparring partner, Euphemia Cruden, the story in the village was that Jeannie had a weak heart.[117] There is a case for this: the cause of her death in the early hours of the morning of 18th March 1950 was given as Arterio Sclerosis, a thickening of the arteries gradually restricting blood flow to the organs which led to a cerebral thrombosis—bleeding on the brain caused by a stroke. But she *was* eighty-eight.

It is perfectly possible that Jeannie Shepherd's 'illness' was either psychosomatic, or a case of malingering. It might also have been her way of rebelling against the restrictions imposed by Victorian marriage—a way of finding space for self—getting leave to live. Elizabeth Barrett Browning, who was supposed to have used illness as a way to escape to her room to write poetry, suffered symptoms that sound remarkably similar to Jeannie Shepherd's: incapacitating weakness; heart palpitations; exhaustion in bouts that lasted from days to months or even years.

In an article written in 1986, five years after Nan's death, Vivienne Forrest suggested her mother had 'one of those mysterious Victorian wasting diseases with no diagnosed name but which included mental depression'.[118] Depression, perhaps even post-natal depression, it might have been. But if this is what Jeannie Shepherd was suffering from, she was lucky to remain at home in her own bed. An inordinate number of women with post-natal depression during the late nineteenth and well into the twentieth century were carted off to asylums.

May Anderson, a friend of Nan's at university, was diagnosed with neurasthenia and committed to Craig House Hospital in Edinburgh's Morningside where, in 1944, she underwent a frontal lobotomy. Unrecognisable to her friends after the operation, May, who had good reason to be depressed after the deaths, in quick succession, of her brother and both her parents, was eventually released from the hospital, only to endure cancer and a mastectomy before dying in 1961.

Those 'mysterious' Victorian illnesses were usually diagnosed as 'Neurasthenia' a term used first in 1869 by the American psychiatrist George Beard[119] for an illness that bore many similarities to what we now call M.E.[120] and for which there is still no cure. Thought to be a disease of the nervous system, its onset often triggered by an infection, it was young women who seemed to be most susceptible to it. A condition of 'nervous exhaustion', while its symptoms included headaches, dizziness and nausea, insomnia, as well as muscle and joint pain, the primary characteristic of Neurasthenia was chronic mental and physical fatigue after the slightest exertion. Given what we know of Jeannie Shepherd from the years after Nan's birth until her death in 1950, M.E. is the most likely explanation for her withdrawal from life.

In the early years of marriage, Jeannie participated in village life. The Kelly girls were brought up to be an accomplished lot and as well as being highly skilled with an embroidery needle (which, of course, with a tailor for a father, you would expect). Jeannie, like her older brother William, played the piano and loved to sing. Although by the mid-1850s they were becoming less popular, in the late 1880s Cults still had a Glee Society which Jeannie and John joined, taking it in turns with the other members to host the meetings.

This was how the Shepherds first met Charles Murray. The same age as Jeannie, Charles Murray was a good-looking man. Tall and athletic with a thick head of curly hair, aquiline nose and full lips hidden beneath an exuberant moustache, his piercing eyes below bushy brows gave him the 'lean-hawk face' his daughter Marris described many years later.[121] In 1881, aged seventeen, Murray moved from Alford to Aberdeen to begin his apprenticeship and by 1887 was a fully-fledged surveyor at Davidson & Garden. Troubled by a chest complaint, he was advised to look for lodgings out of town and came to Cults where he too, joined the Glee Society. When the gathering was at the Shepherds', young Murray, already an adept raconteur, would sit on and on till two in the morning, tales pouring from his lips, until Jeannie would eventually, laughingly remonstrate: 'Charlie Murray, go home and let's get to our beds!'[122]

Neither Frank nor Nan was born when in 1888, Charles Murray left Scotland for South Africa. There he spent the remainder of his working life, initially as surveyor in the Transvaal, ending up in Government service in 1910 as Secretary for Public Works. He and his wife Edith holidayed in Scotland over the years, but it was not until his retirement in 1924 that he returned permanently. Many years later he would recall the Shepherds' kindness to him during his time in Cults, but what the story illustrates is that in those days, Jeannie was perfectly able to stay up talking late into the night.

In photographs we have of Jeannie taken from 1893 onwards, she is usually pictured either seated or lying down. In only two is she standing and in both she is either holding on to or leaning on another person. In a photograph of John, Jane, Frank and Nan Shepherd taken around 1902 her husband has his arm around her shoulder, not bringing her close, but outstretched, as if supporting her and her hands grip Nan's shoulders. The same photograph also reveals Jeannie Shepherd to be at least the same height as her husband, if not slightly taller, which, of course, might also account for the reason she is so often pictured seated in family groups.

John, Jeannie, Nan and Frank Shepherd c.1900.

A rare picture of Jeannie Shepherd (in the background) smiling.

Over the years, the images of her show her gradually wasting away, her large dark eyes grow shadowed, sunken into a face which is gaunt, hollow-cheeked and unsmiling—except in one. Here she is shown lying in the 'sit-ooterie' in the garden at Dunvegan, two unnamed children crouched in front of her playing with a set of wooden skittles. In this photograph, she is beaming.

Clearly, Jeannie Shepherd loved children. In her will she left sizeable bequests of £200 each (around £4,500 in today's money) to Aberdeen's Shelter for Children as well as its Hospital for Sick Children. It is perfectly possible she had wanted more of her own. The fact that she and John did not share a bedroom is not an indicator—separate bedrooms were commonplace in Victorian marriages. Hers was at the front of the house overlooking the Dee valley and the addition of the turreted bay was probably because she spent so much of her time in it. Until his death in 1925, John's bedroom was adjacent, his window looking on to the back garden leading up to the road.

The Shepherds may have had no more children of their own but from 1918, the patter of Sheila Roger's tiny feet was heard regularly at Dunvegan. Sheila's grandparents, John and Isabella Grant, lived a few doors down from Dunvegan at The Elms in Bieldside and were friends of the Shepherds. Neither of the Grants lived to see the birth of their grand-daughter on 2nd February 1917, but when their daughter Mary went off to sea with her Master Mariner husband George Roger, John and Jeannie Shepherd stepped into the role of grandparents and Sheila came to stay at Dunvegan—so often, in fact, it became like a second home to her.

From 1918, Nan kept a baby book for Sheila. As a commentary on her early years it must have been fascinating for Sheila to read in adulthood. It is as proud as any parent's. Recording her height annually until 1921, the little book is filled with the tiny Sheila's funny sayings written phonetically, comic anecdotes and meticulous observations of Sheila's growing command of language. The stories involving 'Maymama', as she called Jeannie Shepherd, are interesting.

On rare days, it seems Jeannie felt well enough to venture downstairs. More often than not, though, she did not leave her bedroom. The fire was kept stoked in there all day and Sheila would happily help by taking up sticks from the scullery one at a time in a little basket. She was not always so helpful. One morning, asked by Jeannie to fetch her bedsheets, Sheila retorted 'aim not going to trail downstairs for sheets—aim going to look at this book'. Asked again, she said 'Oo can go 'ooself'.

'Oh, but Maymama isn't well', Jeannie replied.

'Oo said 'oo was better today'.

'Not well enough to go out of my room', came the answer.

Yet on another occasion, when little Sheila was dancing a Highland Fling, Jeannie joined in. 'Such a disgusted face went on—"You can't do it Maymama, you needn't try!" '[123] There might well have been some basis for talk in the village that there was not much wrong with Jeannie Shepherd.

In 1905, Dr David Rorie took over as village GP. One of Cults's most colourful characters he was often to be seen out makings his rounds in the village, immaculately dressed in his chauffeur-driven French Dion Bouton. Remembered now for his poems and songs,[124] he was essentially a medical man with 'a sardonic view of medicine as part of a wider human comedy in which he himself had an active and not always dignified role' and was not averse to whipping out a child's tonsils on the kitchen table.[125] 'Dr Rorie in his car' paid regular house-calls to Jeannie Shepherd[126] but other than the good doctor, she entertained few guests. 'Does Maymama not like peoples?' young Sheila asked Mary Lawson, housekeeper at Dunvegan from 1907. 'They don't like her', came the response.[127]

Jeannie did lock horns with some in Cults—Euphemia Cruden for one. The two women fell out over a pair of lace knickers. A tiny Nan, the story goes, was invited to Euphemia's daughter Hilda's birthday party at their home just below the old primary school in Cults. Deposited at the Cruden's house that afternoon, Nan was wearing a pair of fancy lace knickers beneath her party frock. On her return home, she was minus the knickers. A search party was sent out to retrieve them, but they were never found. Jeannie decided Euphemia had availed herself of the knickers. What Nan actually did with them, nobody knows.[128]

The picture being constructed of Jeannie Shepherd here is of a woman who, possibly as a result of a little-understood illness which debilitated her physically and tired her mentally, like Lang Leeb Craigmyle, matriarch of *The Weatherhouse,* simply 'detached herself from active living'. Despite her slow deterioration, like the elderly Mrs Craigmyle, in old age Jeannie retained her erect carriage and delicate hands. She still had 'straight high shoulders and legs of swinging length' although they look bony beneath her long, full skirts. Her Glee Society days long gone, whether or not Jeannie still sang, we do not know. It's somehow hard to imagine her crooning in the corner like Lang Leeb.

What we do know is that on those rare occasions Jeannie Shepherd did make an appearance in company at Dunvegan, she was a silent presence. 'All this time Mrs Shepherd sat listening', remarked Robert Dunnett, who interviewed Nan in the garden for an article published in the summer of 1933. However, when pressed for an opinion on the subject of modern books, Jeannie gave one. She confessed there were a good many 'she disliked and some which seemed unnecessarily taken up with the less pleasant aspects of life'. "But things have changed very much in the last thirty years" she said, "and I suppose one changes with them. You see I've got a daughter who educates me in the new ways"'.[129] In Jeannie's response, there is a hint of Lang Leeb's ironic commentary on life: 'Life is an entertainment hard to beat when one's affections are not engaged.'[130]

A family portrait of the Shepherds taken in the summer 1894 is revealing. Quite how Jeannie felt about her mother-in-law's presence at Dunvegan and whether it had any bearing on her withdrawal to her bedroom, can only be conjectured. But in the photograph, there is old Mrs Shepherd, dressed in the requisite formal, if somewhat voluminous, black of mourning. John, behind her, leans towards her protectively, suggesting their closeness. A sailor-suited, four year old Frank sits in a wicker pram and behind him is Isabella Morrison, the Shepherd's live-in maid, crisply turned out in her black uniform and white, starched apron.

Grannie (Ann) Shepherd in black, behind her John Shepherd, Isabella Morrison, Frank Shepherd and, in the centre of the photograph, the first we have of her, an eighteen month Nan with her mother, Jeannie.

month old Nan Shepherd. Frowning at the camera, she is wriggling on Jeannie's lap. Already, you can see that compared to her mother, who had by then begun to disengage herself from active living and whose sedentary lifestyle took place mostly indoors, Nan Shepherd could not have been more different.

★ ★ ★

In 1981 Nan wrote to Barbara Balmer: 'I have been looking at a photograph of myself at eighteen months, a family group in which I am held on my mother's knee. I say <u>held</u> because my eighteen month old person is all movement, legs and arms flailing as though I were demanding to get at life—I swear those limbs move as you look at them.'[131]

They do. Limbs blurred, it looks very much as though Nan's toddler self, in tight-puffed sleeves, pinafore and thick woollen stockings, is being forced to sit still for the camera and is trying to escape her mother's grip, slide off her lap and be off and away. Later images of Nan as a child, reinforce this. Unlike her mother who smiles rarely for the camera, Nan is a grinning girl, her freckled face framed by waywardly curling hair. Of typically Nor-east stock, she is hazel-eyed and red-headed, to be sure. 'But', as Nan wrote in *Descent from the Cross*, a short story published in 1943, 'red heads kept you out of languor'[132]

There is mischief in Nan's face, an exuberance being suppressed for the camera's shutter, that is bursting to be re-released. It's an energy her mother seems often, in photographs, to be physically trying to contain. Perhaps she was anxious for her daughter to at least appear as though she were conforming to society's expectations of late-Victorian, middle-class girls as demure, decorous and deferential. Another family portrait shows her father, brother and Nan, distracted, smirking at something off-screen. Jeannie holds her daughter firmly by the shoulders as if worried she might run off. Nan Shepherd *was* 'all movement'. Those few periods of forced inactivity which would occur during her life, she found frustrating. She liked to be busy, to do things with her hands as well as with her head.

Learning young that 'hands have an infinity of pleasure in them' she loved to hold her fingers over the tap at full cock, pressing with all her puny strength until the water defeated her, spurting all over her freshly-laundered frock.[133] Visiting the country home of a friend, about to head out for a walk, Nan went to fetch her gloves from the hall table where she had left them before lunch. Her friend's aunt took them from her. Laying them back on the table she said, 'You don't need these. A lot of strength comes to us through the hands'.[134] Her words left an indelible impression on Shepherd. The feel of things: surfaces; rough like cone and bark or scratchy lichen; smooth like stalks, feathers and pebbles rounded by water; the teasing of gossamer; the delicate tickle of a caterpillar; all these textures she fingered, relished, stored and recounted years later in *The Living Mountain*.

Juniper she particularly savoured, perhaps because it is as reticent about its scent as Nan was about herself. Noticing that the shrub has a peculiar habit of dying in patches, she snapped off a dead branch. Surprised by the spicy smell it suddenly released, she took to carrying a piece of Juniper wood in her pocket for months, breaking it again every so often, to refresh its spice.[135]

As her mother was house-bound, it was her father and brother Frank, with whom Nan went for long walks and it was John Shepherd who instilled early in her a love of the natural world. Having taught himself botany during his Sunday morning walks around Drumoak in the days before he was married, John Shepherd passed on his knowledge to his children. It was John who instructed Nan in the art of picking toadstails, the fuzzy stagmoss that grows in heather. Together, they would lie side by side on the heather while he showed her how to feel her way with her fingers along each separate trail and side branch, carefully detaching each tiny root until they had thick bunchy pieces many yards long. It was a good art to teach a child, she said. And though Nan didn't know it then, as she acknowledged later, she was 'learning her way in, through her own fingers, to the secret of growth'.[136]

One of the rites of early summer was a visit to Lupin Island which lay across the river from Dunvegan, off the south bank of the Dee, halfway between Ardoe and the Shakkin' Brigie. In the late nineteenth and early twentieth century it was carpeted end to end with blue lupins carried downstream, it was supposed, by seed throw-outs from Balmoral and Borrowstone. That was until the ferocious spate of October 1920 scalped the islet of its eponymous flowers. 'When the water fell, every lupin had been swept away, and not one ever grew again', Nan wrote mournfully in 1966. [137]

Lupins were a favourite of Nan's. Visitors to Dunvegan arriving at the green gate from the Deeside road would wander down the sloping garden on the little path running alongside the hedge to reach the back door. It was not an orderly garden. There was no pattern or stiff arrangement, no rigidly imposed boundaries between beds. Instead it was a riot of scent and colour. In the summer, as well as lupins, there were Sweet Williams, rosemary, white peonies, poppies and lavender. The garden was her father's joy and Nan's too.

Every morning, John Shepherd rose with the dawn—in the summer months as early as 4am—to work in the garden before breakfast. After a cold bath, he would head off down the garden towards the railway line, disappearing through the gate at the bottom on his way to West Cults station to catch the 'subbie' to work. Once home again, he would eat, then work in the garden—on those evenings when it was light for long enough—and on Saturday afternoons too. Out at work and when at home, out in the garden as much as possible, while his wife lay upstairs in bed, the picture being constructed of the Shepherd's marriage here is one of separate lives lived in separate spheres. One outside, one in; disconnected from each other, or so it seems from the outside.

What Nan thought of her parents' relationship while she was growing up, is difficult to discern. She left little behind to help. All we have is refracted from behind the mask of her novels and, autobiographical as they all are to a greater or lesser extent, any insight they might give is constructed from her adult perspective. Perhaps, in the way that small children do, she never really questioned their relationship but just accepted it, viewing her parents, like Edwin Muir: 'as allegorical figures in a timeless landscape'.[138] Certainly Nan's portrait of her father in *The Weatherhouse* borders on the hagiographic. But as she wrote the novel

John Shepherd.

three years after his death, this is perhaps to be expected.

John Shepherd was apparently tireless in the garden long after retirement and into old age:

> Sometimes, as he crawled weeding among the beds, in his old garments that had turned the colour of earth itself, with his hands earth-encrusted, he seemed older than human—some antique embodiment of earth…Steady and happy. Absorbed. Like a part of what he worked in, and yet beyond it. The immanent presence.[139]

However, as well as providing a description of the elderly John Shepherd for us, there is much here already in Nan's writing of her philosophy on life. He seems part of the earth itself, 'an embodiment', 'absorbed' which can be taken to mean 'part of' as well as 'focussed on his task', part of his garden and yet beyond it. 'Immanent': the use of that word suggests that observing him working in the earth, seeming part of the earth, was to realise that ultimate reality was right there, in all things, not elsewhere or distant—a philosophy that is Eastern rather than Western in its origin.

It is not hard to imagine John Shepherd, like John Grey in *The Weatherhouse,* crawling on all fours weeding his flowerbeds and afterwards, nodding off in the sun. After his death Charles Murray described him as kind and generous—ever hospitable,[140] adjectives often applied to Nan Shepherd, too. He had an Edwardian, rather than Victorian, attitude to children. In John Shepherd's presence children were both seen *and* heard. He was approachable and could clearly take a joke in the form of a child's reprimand. On his way out for dinner one evening seeing his suit was airing at Jeannie's bedroom fire he said 'I'll take the breeks' and was 'gravely reproved' by little Sheila Roger, 'It is exceedingly rude to say breeks, say knickers!'[141] And in photographs of John Shepherd sitting on the lawn, pipe in his hand, a child playing nearby, there is an air of calm forbearance about him. He looks a kind, comforting and steady presence. But while his mouth is hard to distinguish buried behind the bushy beard that he wore all his life, the gleam in his dark, deep-set eyes beneath that broad, high forehead with those shaggy brows suggests, too, that laughter might at any moment erupt and apparently often did.

Playing 'animals' with Nan and little Sheila, 'Nan was a fearsome kangaroo and 'Uncle John' ran from her & covered his head with a shawl. "Come to me, Uncle John, A'll save you"', was Sheila's cry until 'Uncle John' was 'weeping with laughter'.[142] The Shepherds, it seems, were a laughing family and if John made time to play with his own children the way he played with little Sheila, he will have been a loving and patient father.

But it was not just John Shepherd's merriment and manner that made him popular with children. It seems there was nothing he could not make or mend. In an entry in the *Sheila Book* Nan records that the little girl's doll's cot had broken. 'There was talk about how it could be mended. "Just wait ain' a'll see what my uncle Don says about it"'[143] the child said confidently, testimony once again, to the description of John Shepherd as John Grey in *The Weatherhouse*:

"The eyes came out, said John Grey as he lifted the toy and examined it with care, and her little mistress brought her to me. She believes I can mend everything that breaks, but this was hard a task as I have tried. I have had to work the eyes back into place and fill the head up with cement to keep them fixed. See, it has set".

The bookcases, bursting with books, glimpsed behind him in a photograph taken in the drawing room at Dunvegan, were made by him.

So, most probably, was the 'sit-ooterie' which appears in several family photographs. There, within its curtained alcove, Jeannie Shepherd is sometimes pictured lying, on a wooden bed with an adjustable back, a thick rug laid over her legs.

The hen-house in the back garden was also his handiwork. Jeannie Shepherd liked an egg every morning. But 'Highstepper' and 'Grannie' (for the hens, of course, had names) were reared not just for their eggs, but for eating too. The fowls were Nan's domain. She fed, hatched, dispatched, plucked and ate them,[144] cleaned out the henhouse and shooed them from the flower beds. They were part of Dunvegan life at least until the late 1940s. After that, even though the birds were gone, the henhouse found new purpose as a playhouse for neighbours' children who on summer afternoons would hide inside begging Nan in her floppy straw sunhat and flowery frock to march around singing 'Ten o'clock, all's well, ten o'clock, all's well, Town crier calling, swinging his bell'. Which, of course, she did.[145]

The Dunvegan hens appear in Nan's writing. Geordie's line in *The Quarry Wood*, 'It's a grand thing to get leave'[146] comes just as he has wrung a chicken's neck, ending its life. The irony, of course, is deliberate. The recurrent theme of Nan's novels, *how* to get leave to live within a society so strict in its conventions, is explored through many of her female characters. Lang Leeb gets leave by disengaging herself from active living. Aunt Josephine on the other hand, actively engages. She will interrupt a game of cards at the sound of a scraping of a hen and won't fence in her chickens because 'deep within herself she felt obscurely the contrast between the lifeless propriety of a fence and the lively interest of shooing a hen; and Aunt Josephine at every turn chose instinctively the way of life'.[147] The hens are as symbolic as they are necessary, part of life and yet beyond it, like John Grey in his flower bed. They escape over their boundary as a reminder that animate and inanimate are interrelated, the boundaries blurred, not easily defined.

In around 1918, Nan wrote 'Pixies and Or'nary Peoples' for Aberdeen High School's magazine. In storytelling, she observed, there is a divide, between the ordinary and the magical: 'the sea-coast of Bohemia and Main Street, Prometheus and Soames Forsyte'. From time immemorial, she explains, the storyteller is listened to because he tells his audience what they already know as well as what may not be known. 'Both are necessary—both mystery and certitude', she says:

> I love a broom-stick and also a walking stick. I want the moon and the Pleiades and buttons to fasten my coat…Are the supreme moments of human experience, very strange or very

simple? I think both. We classify, but there is no real dividing line…There is a pixie element in the plainest life.[148]

The ordinary and the mystical were of equal importance to Nan Shepherd. 'I have a keen relish of the coarse, salty vulgar life about me' she wrote to Neil Gunn in 1930, 'and at the same time an intolerable intolerance of it…if one could combine the two—? irradiate the common? That should make something universal.'[149]

In 1930, Nan was writing poetry in a flurry of activity she likened to 'the hens of *Saint Joan*[150], laying like mad!'[151] 'I don't know whether the results are any more valuable than eggs—it's nothing great after all to produce an egg (not if you are a hen anyhow) especially when what you want to produce is rather to be figured as a Taj Mahal'[152] she continued. As it happens, according to the critics, Nan had already 'irradiated the common' and made something universal in her novels. She of course, would never have said this, because her novels, to her, were never the 'Taj Mahal'. It would be another fifteen years before she began the writing she felt was truly worthy of the title.

About Nan's brother as a child, testimony is scant. Frank, too, was a red-head and in *The Weatherhouse* he is turned into John Grey's son, David: 'Tall, red-headed, fiery tempered, wild and splendid', he was 'a brilliant boy who had inherited and intensified his father's genius.'[153] The brainy and inventive Frank also had creative talent. Charles Murray, writing to Nan after a holiday in Scotland when he spent time with the Shepherd offspring, mentions their poetry:

> I was much interested in your lecture, but more in your own verses & your brother's. I liked his picture of farm life in winter immensely & would like to see his other bit you mentioned when you can lay your hands on it…tell your brother that I smacked my lips over his 'Days Darg'. When he can make a picture like that he ought to turn out more of them.[154]

As for Frank and Nan's relationship, a photograph taken around 1905 shows the two of them in Dunvegan's front garden. An adolescent Frank, tall, in peaked cap, Norfolk-suited and booted, gazes over the fence dividing Dunvegan from its neighbour. His little sister, in ruffled pinafore and black stockings, stands nearer the house looking towards him. That Nan would have looked up to Frank, seems reasonable to suppose, in the way younger siblings look up to their elders, especially when there are only two of them, and that their relationship was close is obvious from a scrap of letter Nan kept. The last leaf of a ten page epistle, it is affectionately teasing.

The only other letter of Frank's we have is one he wrote aged six to his other Grannie, Jeannie Tough Kelly, written on 4th April 1896, the day his grandfather, Francis Kelly died, saying he and Anna wanted her to come and live with them at Dunvegan. Perhaps he thought that as they already had one 'Grannie' living with them, there was no reason why she should not move in too. Roomy as it now was though, there was no vacancy at Dunvegan. Jeannie Kelly remained living in Rubislaw in Aberdeen,[155] amply provided for by her late husband's will, until her death in 1915.

Until the 1960s, the Quarry Wood of Nan Shepherd's first novel, and part of the woods from which Cults took its name, rose up towards Blacktop Hill behind the houses ranged along the North Deeside Road. Today, the only suggestion of the quarry itself is 'Quarry Road' diagonally opposite Dunvegan. Known as 'Bramble Brae' during Nan's childhood, it still leads upwards past West Cults Church. In all seasons, Nan haunted the Quarry Wood. Up the brae she would climb, to her left, Braemar-way, lay Clachnaben and Cairnmon-Earn and the passes over the hills through which Macbeth and Montrose led their armies—those symbolic gateways that star in her third novel, *A Pass in the Grampians*. On mist-free days, she might even have glimpsed Lochnagar.

The woods were Nan's playground and her inspiration. It is not hard to imagine her, clouds of dust puffing from her boots, as she ploughed her way along a cart-rut before scrambling over the granite dyke into her 'enchanted wood'. Once inside, there were many paths to choose from. Rearing on either side of these paths, tall firs swayed and in later years, when some of the trees were cleared, grass was allowed to grow, spreading a carpet of pale bloom, bracken all around. For Nan, crawling through the bracken, finding the 'unpath' was always best. She would spend hours roaming the woods, exploring its nooks and recesses, learning how to read the light so she would know when it was time to wander home through the fields again for tea. And so, long before she reached womanhood and the Cairngorms became her road to knowledge, she was learning her way into the woods.

Little of Nan's childhood playground remains today. Most of the wood is long gone, but glimpses of it can be seen still in the occasional sagging remains of a wall, or a 'consumption' dyke, built of stones gathered from the fields. Until the 1960s, successive generations of children growing up in Cults played in the Quarry Wood. At the end of the nineteenth century, when Nan was wandering the woods, quarrying was still going on but during the Second World War the great conifers beyond the wood were felled and quarrying stopped. Much of the equipment, the ladders and great solid horse-drawn sledges were left abandoned. It was as though the quarrymen simply downed tools and went to war. The quarries were not deep. At around twenty-five feet, they were more like scratchings, so that the ground looked pockmarked, like the surface of the moon. But it was still a grand place to play, as the roe deer flitted among the trees. From the 1960s, though, the area was being used as a tip. The flies were terrible and it was filled in.[156]

As buses took over from rail transport, a steady influx of incomers to Cults meant that land near the station was no longer so sought after. Houses were needed elsewhere and much of the wood was cleared for development including a new Primary School, the old one too small to cope with the rapidly rising numbers of pupils. A series of sprawling, interlocking, low-rise brick buildings set in green playing fields, including a man-made, adventure playground, the school, which opened in 1974, now has over five hundred pupils. In its grounds was a cairn[157] which, when excavated, yielded a cist[158] and human remains.

Part of the new school's grounds includes land at Hillhead, where the quarrymen's cottages stood as empty shells for years after quarrying stopped. They were undoubtedly borrowed for the Ironside's home in *The Quarry Wood*. Nan knew the cairn well:

> A field's breadth from these cottages, where two dykes intersected, was piled a great cairn of stones. They had lain there so long that no one troubled to remember their purpose or origin. Gathered from the surrounding soil, they had resumed a sort of unity with it. The cairn had settled back into the landscape, like a dark outcrop of rock.[159]

It was here nine-year old Martha 'was dwelling on a planet of her own' when Aunt Josephine marched over and took her by the shoulders, as Emmeline announced she would be taken away from school. That was when Martha kicked Aunt Josephine and is the point at which the novel begins:

> School for Martha was escape into a magic world where people knew things. Already she dreamed passionately of knowing all there was to know in the universe: not that she expressed it so, even to herself. She had no idea of the spaciousness of her own desires; but she knew very fervently that she was in love with school. Her reaction to the news she had just heard, therefore, was in the nature of protest—swift and thorough.[160]

Whether or not Nan herself loved school, given her subsequent academic career, she excelled there. In the 1970s, she gave a talk at Cults Primary regaling pupils with stories of what school was like in her day. Unfortunately it was not recorded nor notes taken, but Nan's primary school experience would have been very different.

Scotland had a reputation for being one of the best educated societies in the world, a reputation founded in the seventeenth century Calvinists' insistence on bible reading. Putting people in touch with the 'word of God' was paramount—and to do that they needed to be able to read. Open to boys and girls regardless of social status, schools paid for by the Church of Scotland and local landowners were established in rural areas by an Act of Parliament in 1696 and run by the church. By the early eighteenth century, so impressed was the writer Daniel Defoe by the democratic Scottish system, he remarked that while England was a land 'full of ignorance', in Scotland the 'poorest people have their children taught and instructed.'[161]

'Grinning girl':
Nan c. 1900.

This was not strictly true. As we know, John Shepherd and his brothers attended school only when they could be spared from work on the farm. They were not unique. Many children forced to work to support their impoverished families received scant education. As a result, while most male adults could read, few could write and the number of females able to do so was even fewer. Schools' emphasis was on the 3 R's—reading, writing and arithmetic—and while boys received tuition in foreign and ancient languages, teaching classics to girls was considered a waste of time. Only boys were considered worth educating beyond elementary level. Girls received a second-class education and domestic training designed to fit them for life as domestic servants or wives and mothers.[162]

By the time Nan reached primary school age, things were changing. The 1872 Education Act shook up the Scottish school system. Schooling became compulsory for children between the ages of five and thirteen[163] and a new system of education run by School Boards was put in place. The old Endowed school in Cults, in line with the Education Act, was taken over from the church by the Peterculter School Board in 1891.

By the late nineteenth century Cults had grown from what had been a small farming community fifty years earlier to a thriving, bustling village. The old school where Frank began his education three years earlier was now considered quite behind the times. Into one large schoolroom a hundred children were being crammed and its desks and interior furnishing were deemed simply not fit for purpose. A new one was built.[164]

Turning five in February 1898, Nan started at West Cults Primary that August,[165] a year after its official opening. An outburst of Jubilee splendour, the new school's rather elegant, Rubislaw granite facade was a stark contrast to the sombre, stone buildings surrounding it.

On two acres of land beside the North Deeside Road, just west of the village centre, it was well sited, with ample playgrounds. Boys and girls, separated at break times, also had their own entrances—girls on the west, boys, the east, with a fence down the middle of the playing fields to enforce this segregation. Inside, six classrooms opened off a large central hall, with a pitch-pine floor that survived sixty years of children's boots before it succumbed and splintered.

When Nan started school there was a new Dominie. As a non-graduate, the previous headmaster, the much-loved Mr Donald, no longer met the government's criteria. His enthusiastic replacement, Mr Croll, M.A., keen to equip the school with the latest equipment, ordered pointers, moveable alphabets, maps and a cabinet of specimens for object lessons. Science, of a sort, was taught too: during object lessons, seeds and rocks were placed on each desk and the pupils tasked to make observations on them. At the school's first inspection, however, the only subjects reported to be excellent were singing, sewing (taught to the girls while the boys were learning woodworking) and drill.[166]

Drill (which involved exercises such as jogging on the spot, marching, stretching and lifting weights in the playground) was pretty much the only form of P.E. in schools then. Britain's poor performance in the first Boer War[167] was blamed on the failure of schools to provide proper physical training. Working-class soldiers, particularly, were declared unfit. Barrack-style drilling and marching were introduced to increase fitness levels and instil obedience and discipline into the children. It's no wonder Nan detested playing most sports.

The Second Boer War, the background to Nan's primary school years, rumbled on from 1899 until the last of the Boers surrendered in May 1902. The First Boer War may have shown Britain how few European friends it really had, but the country then seemed at the height of its power, as invincible as the Queen. Few could imagine life without her on the throne. Aged four, Nan stood in the flag-waving, crowded Aberdeen streets for Victoria's Diamond Jubilee procession on 22nd June 1897. Jingoism, along with the British Empire, had reached its peak and the aged, arthritic Queen ruled a quarter of the world's population.

The Queen had been a regular Deeside visitor until November 1900 and Nan, along with the other Cults bairns, would run excitedly to West Cults station to see the royal train pass by, hoping to catch a glimpse of Her Royal Highness en route to Balmoral. More often than not, though, the blinds of the Royal Saloon were firmly drawn. Then, in January 1901, the Queen died. The nation went into mourning.

Chapter Three

1903-1910

Christmas 1903 was a black one for the Shepherds. Grannie Shepherd, died just a few days before. Hers was a drawn-out death. On 6th December a stroke caused paralysis down one side of her body and for more than two weeks she lay in this state, incontinent, with difficulty swallowing and possibly unconscious. Aged nine, Nan would have been old enough to have been aware of Ann Shepherd's drawn-out dying and of the atmosphere at Dunvegan that December of 1903, which, for days, would have been one of waiting.[168]

Eventually, the end came, long before it was light, at 4.45 am on 17th December. Aged eighty-seven, Ann Shepherd was three years older than Queen Victoria and had survived her too. She had also outlived her husband and two of her children.[169] For Nan, who would not have known life at Dunvegan without her grandmother, the house must have seemed strangely empty in the absence of Ann Shepherd in her billowing, black bombazine—for she was rarely out of mourning in her final years, what with the deaths of her husband, her oldest son and then the Queen.

But it was not too long before Grannie's room was occupied again. When Nan was around fourteen, Mary Lawson joined the Shepherd household as housekeeper. Maimie, as the family called her, arrived in 1907,[170] with a trunk containing all her worldly goods. As it was being carried upstairs there was some difficulty with its rounding the tight bend at the top of the first flight: 'Never-mind, it'll never have to come down again', said Mary.[171] It never did. Twenty-three years old when she first came to Dunvegan, Mary Lawson died there some sixty years later at the age of ninety two.

Just how quickly and efficiently she took over the running of the household, while Jeannie Shepherd lay upstairs, is suggested in *The Quarry Wood:*

A raw country lass, high-cheeked, with crude red features and sucked and swollen hands, she managed Drocherty and his household to the manner born. Mrs Glennie, Drocherty's feeble wife, lay upstairs in her bed and *worritted*... But she need not have *worritted*, for Clemmie, though she came only at last November term, had the whole establishment, master and mistress, kitchen and byre and *chau'mer,* securely under her *chappit* thumb.[172]

The repetition of 'worritted' implies that there may have been some basis to the opinion of many in Cults that there was nothing wrong with Jeannie Shepherd—that she *was,* as Euphemia Cruden dubbed her, one of the 'worrit well'. The setting and names may be different, but the situation is unmistakably the one in which Mary Lawson found herself on arrival and the portrait of 'Clemmie' describes her down to her *chappit* thumb and swollen hands. A hard-worker, Mary washed all the linen and clothes by hand, putting them through the mangle in the outhouse. 'Mary had been putting clothes out in the front—& was making v. funny noises over the pain in her cracked hands', Nan records in the *Sheila Book.* Young Sheila had toddled downstairs 'to see what was up—"Mawy, don't go out in the cold—you know Jackie Frost bites 'oss fingers" and offered her muff for Mary to put her hands into, one at a time.'[173]

Mary Lawson was the inspiration not just for 'Clemmie' but for a number of other characters in Nan Shepherd's novels. Nan was no prig, nor was she narrow minded, Jessie Kesson said.[174] Mary Lawson was illegitimate and that Nan knew of the circumstances of her birth and upbringing is obvious: she uses this knowledge in *The Quarry Wood* and in doing so criticises late-Victorian society.

Born in Echt in 1884 to unmarried parents, Jane McGhie, a domestic servant, and George Lawson, an agricultural labourer, Mary Lawson was brought up by her grandmother (herself a domestic servant, widow of a farm servant and also named Jane McGhie). With no effective contraception available and abortion illegal, this in itself was not unusual although having a child out of wedlock still carried social stigma. In nineteenth century Scotland, unmarried motherhood was particularly prevalent among farm and domestic servants. The support and care given by grandparents and relatives was thus paramount.[175]

Like most Victorian domestic servants, Mary's mother Jane, lived in at her employers. Forced to move back to her mother's during her confinement, after a short weaning spell, Jane McGhie then returned to work, leaving baby Mary in her grandmother's care. She saw little of her daughter growing up. By the time Mary was seven, her mother was living over in Dyce, some fourteen miles from Echt, where she was employed by James Hendry, a widower with three girls under the age of ten, the youngest of whom was seven, the same age as her daughter.

Mary's was not a solitary childhood however. In 1891, also living with her grandmother were five other children aged eleven and under—the youngest only a year old. All these children, bar one, were born in Echt and all of them are described on that year's Census as 'grandchildren'. It's quite possible they were. Each has a different surname, which could mean they were all illegitimate and, like Mary, patronymically named. Only sixty-three year old Jane McGhie appears to be living with these children. There is no sign of any other adult occupant in the tiny cottage in Echt.

A survey of parishes conducted in 1881 found that nearly eighty percent of illegitimate children lived in households headed by grandparents—infants who might otherwise have been aborted, adopted or become dependent on the Poor Law.[176] But for Mrs McGhie to have quite so many illegitimate grandchildren seems highly unlikely. It is more probable that some, if not all the other six children were 'fostered'. The only relatives Mary Lawson was known to have were Nelly[177] and Gordon Dick who lived with their two children in the countryside, north of Aberdeen.[178] Neither are amongst those 'grandchildren' living with Mrs McGhie.[179]

Nan Shepherd re-imagines the scenario in The Quarry Wood: what it would be like to live in the cramped conditions of a minute cottage with the constant flow of other children coming and going. She even gives 'Emmeline' an agricultural labourer for a husband:

> Emmeline would undertake any expedition to mother a child for gain. She liked the fuss and the pack in her two-roomed stone-floored cottage. The stress of numbers excused her huddery ways. Some of the babies died, some were reclaimed, some taken to other homes. Martha accepted them as dumbly as her father, brooding a little—but only a little—on the peculiarities of a changing population. Other people's families were more or less stationary. Martha's fluctuated. [180]

Fostering was not uncommon in the Victorian era, when proper adoption agencies and social services did not exist.[181] Instead, often untrained women offered fostering and adoption services to unmarried mothers who would hand over a sum of cash and their baby in the hope it would be re-homed. Most of the babies were, in one way or another. By 1901, all but two of Mrs McGhie's 'grandchildren' had gone, Mary included. She had found a live-in situation as general domestic servant with the Ferres family in South Kirktown. Her appointment by the

Shepherds some eight years later as Housekeeper at Dunvegan, was a not-inconsiderable step-up.

The linchpin of Dunvegan's domestic wheel, as her job description implies, Mary Lawson was indeed 'keeper of the house'. But she was much more than a retainer. After Jeannie Shepherd's death in 1950, she stayed on. Nan's middle-class upbringing precluded housework—just as well, as 'she disliked the petty drubs of housework'[182]—but that Mary's position by the end was as a companion, is made clear on her death certificate. Signed by Nan, her relationship to 'Mary Lawson, Retired Housekeeper' is given as 'friend'.

A slight, bony woman, with narrow, blue eyes that missed nothing, Mary Lawson had a 'soul of gold' and a tongue that would 'clip clouts'.[183] She was also a regular Doric spitfire. Nan may well have picked up some Doric from her cottar classmates in the school playground (only English was meant to be spoken during lessons).[184] But it was Mary Lawson, Nan said, who supplied her with salty, Aberdeenshire phrases for her work—and with some of the stories, too.[186]

Popular in the village, Mary had her enemies too. 'She was couthy',[187] a neighbour described her, 'but she was no soft touch, you would not mess her about'.[188] According to Jessie Kesson, 'if Mary Lawson liked you, it was all right. But visitors had to get past her'.[189] Mary Lawson liked Jessie. She was not so keen on her writing, however. Nan admitted this in a letter to Jessie written in 1963, which reveals the double standards still prevalent, even then, in Aberdeen society and of which Nan was only too aware:

> Mary was charmed to get your letter and intended to answer, but her letter-writing always gets put off! And now that she has read your book [*Glitter of Mica*] I don't believe she'll write at all, for she didn't like the book, oh no, she didn't like it at all. Swearing and sex, when seen in cold print, seem to her inexpressibly evil—though she'll tell a story (in Scots of course) with as good a damn in it as the next man's![190]

Much, if not all, of this social hypocrisy was effected by the Church. Mary, a keen churchgoer, was a member of the United Free Church at Cults East. The Reverend Kenneth Elder, minister there for forty years, recalled the 'outrageous scandals' that sprang from Mary's lips as she washed the Communion Cups with his wife'.[191] She was once overheard relaying some scandalous episode to Jeannie Shepherd by a young Sheila Roger, who, of course, repeated it. 'He's adjust a hypolitte', little Sheila finished, 'I don't like him myself, he's sweaty hands'.[192]

Until 1844, there were no church buildings in Cults. The only kirk in the parish[193] was St Devenick's on the south side of the Dee and the only way across the river was by ferry—and that was a rowing boat. During rough weather, this could be a somewhat hazardous journey. In 1837, the Reverend Morison, who couldn't help noticing that the size of his congregation fluctuated with the weather, paid for a bridge to be built across the river. Morison's Bridge it was called, but because of its flexible, timber decking, it was always known locally, and rather irreverently, as the 'Shakkin Briggie'. Quite a spectacle it must have been, seven hundred or so villagers from Cults and Murtle on their walk of faith across the footbridge in their Sunday best, its boards quivering beneath their feet.

By the time John and Jeannie Shepherd moved to Cults there were two kirks to choose from: the Church of Cults[194] and the Free Church on Kirk Brae. Scotland's Free Church was a result of a wave of mid-nine-teenth century evangelical fervour which led to a schism in the Church of Scotland known as the 1843 Disruption,[195] when elders staged a walk out and set up a church free from Westminster's intervention. The Free Church was popular with Cults parishioners, many of whom threw in their lot with the Dissenters. More receptive to Gaelic language and culture it was funded by merchants and storekeepers, who were elected as elders rather than chosen by landowners and the Crown, and quickly became identified as the middle-class church.

The Church of Cults, which was just a stroll across the road from Dunvegan, might have been a more convenient place of worship, but the Shepherds were Free Church people.[196] So, turning their middle-class backs on the Church of Cults,[197] they headed east up the road to the Kirk on the Brae. Services were conducted in the open-air to begin with. But by 1902, the congregation had swelled to over 200 and the Kirk had its own building. It was described as 'one of the finest ecclesiastical edifices'[198] around Aberdeen and famed for its stained glass—until it burnt down in 1941—not, as it was thought at the time, as a result of enemy fire but because of a faulty boiler vent. Now, only the spire and stair tower remain.

Kirk attendance in late Victorian Scotland, whatever your beliefs, was a matter of keeping up appearances. In *The Weatherhouse,* Ellen Falconer stops going to church. ' "You might at least keep it up for appearance sake," Theresa hectored. "We've been a kirk-going family all our days. There's no need to be kirk-greedy to do the respectable thing. A pretty story they'll make of it, a Craigmyle and left the kirk" '.[199] ' "We should all go to church as long's we're able" ' Annie says, but it is hard to imagine Jeannie Shepherd, like Miss Annie, 'crippled and serene', setting out alone each Sunday morning, an hour before the service was due to start to make her 'slow laborious journey' to the Kirk and as Jeannie was never seen out and about in her wicker chair, it is highly unlikely she ever went post-1893.

During the First World War Nan had her own rupture with the church and, while she may have kept up appearances until her father died in 1925, by the 1930s she was definitely not kirk-going. Malcolm Sutherland, a friend from those years, recalls her missing Sunday services to go and talk politics with his father instead. 'Nan was a leftie' as Malcolm puts it. His father was a staunch Tory and they enjoyed sparring with one another. But conscious of community convention, rather than appear to be flagrantly disrespectful, Nan would make Malcolm wait up the lane to watch for people coming out of church so she could skedaddle back to Dunvegan without being seen.

As a child, however, Nan was devout, attending services with her father and brother (and later Mary Lawson) as well as Sunday school. The Authorised Version of the Bible was as familiar to her as the Scotch porridge she ate daily for breakfast (milk in a separate bowl on the side). 'Miss Anna Shepherd, Cults', appears regularly among the top scorers of the Sabbath-school Welfare of Youth examinations. In the years 1907-1909 she was a prizewinner in the New Testament and Catechism papers.[200]

The English Bible was considered the most important textbook and the Welfare of Youth exams were designed to ensure that young people were kept on intimate terms with the good book: 'It would be an ill day for Scotland when the Church was content to leave to other agencies, or none, the duty of training her young men and women and testing their knowledge of Scripture on which her existence so largely depended'.[201]

Kirk was no laughing matter. Pious young Martha is shocked at her father's irreverence during a service in *The Quarry Wood:*

> Some weeks later Geordie had a shaking and shuffle of excitement in the middle of the kirk. He nudged Martha with signs and whispers she could not understand. She held her eyes straight forward and a prim little mouth, pretending not to see or hear. It was dreadful of her father to behave like that in church.[202]

More overt criticism of the kirk comes in Nan's third novel, *A Pass in the Grampians.* Alison tells Kilgour about the lace collar she bought for herself aged twelve and which she was wearing proudly on her way to church when:

> 'some speirin' body told it to my mother—not in any ill spirit, but turning the matter over as they will do where there's little to think about. So my mother hid herself by a broom rush, as I came paidlin' on through the dust of the road to Kirk, and out she flies and grabs the collar off my neck and says, "For shame to you. I'll have no daughter of mine stravaigin' the roads like a Jezebel. The Kingdom of God is not to be won by scarlet and fine linen but by the subjugation of the flesh."[203]

In Kilgour's response is Nan's comment on the oppressive culture created by the Evangelical fervour of the Free Church: 'A lace tippet surely could never stand between you and your salvation'.[204] According to Evangelists, it could. *The Christian*, a kind of biblical *News of the World*, dubbed late-Victorians a prudish, hypocritical lot. Capitalists and moralists, they were hidden adulterers with the devil of lust inside them. Moody and Sankey were the pop stars of the era, with hits like 'I am redeemed', 'O Jesus I have promised', 'Kept for Jesus' and 'Lamb of God'. It was faith in Jesus Christ, evangelicals believed, that would redeem you from sin. In the Mansion of the Sky, Jesus Christ featured as Lord of all—above God and the archangels. To be saved required intense bible study, almost perpetual prayer and constant self-examination so as not to give into temptation. You were expected to spend your free time doing good works and visiting the poor, rather than undertaking any activity purely for your own pleasure. Sunday was a day strictly reserved for observing the Lord: children's toys locked were away, libraries, parks and sports grounds closed. On top of this, entrance into heaven required you to worry not just about the state of your own soul, but other peoples' too.

"Have you given your heart to Jesus, Nobby?" Betty Macmurray's mother would regularly ask the postman. Betty, a friend of Nan's from her secondary school days who lived not far from Cults in Inchmarlo, near Banchory, grew up in this atmosphere of evangelical fervour. Her mother, who spent much of her time writing religious tracts and had a great way with bereavements, believed her pen to be the 'instrument of the Holy Ghost,'[205] and 'transformed everything into Holy Significance'.[206]

It must all have felt quite suffocating. It's no wonder that under a heading 'The Lord is my Shepherd' in Nan's *Gleanings* book, two pages are left completely blank.

* * *

Nan c. 1900.

Aged twelve, Nan's world began to widen. In May 1905 she sat the qualifying examination required by the Scottish Education Board for entry into secondary school, passed, and was enrolled in the Intermediate Department of Aberdeen's High School for Girls at the start of its next session on 29th August. The Shepherds' choice of school for their daughter was a sign that she was set on a different course to her mother and grandmother.

The late nineteenth century society into which Nan was born was still one that conspired to push women firmly down the aisle. The only reason for bothering to educate them was to make them more interesting to their husbands. The prevailing attitude was summed up in 1890 by the Reverend James Wilson in his public address to 'Girls at School': 'Who could bear to live with a thoroughly uneducated woman? She would bore one to death in a week'.[207] It would take the First World War for such patriarchal attitudes to be corroded, but Nan was luckier than her female forbears. Not only had universities started accepting women (Aberdeen was one of the first to open its doors to them in 1892) but the Intermediate and Leaving Certificates which were introduced at the same level as the universities' new entrance examination in the late nineteenth and early twentieth centuries, dramatically improved the standard of secondary school education in Scotland.

Nan was lucky too, that the Shepherds were among the more progressive of middle-class, Aberdonian parents, keen that their daughter should have the benefit of a decent, complete education and that her father could afford to pay for it. As the 1872 Education (Scotland) Act made no provision for secondary schooling, private, day school education was the rule among the professional classes in Scotland. Boarding school was alien to the Scottish ethos—even now it is not considered a true part of the Scottish education system and boarding schools remain few in number. In any case, there was no need to send Nan away to school. Thanks to the 'subbies', the High School for Girls was almost on their doorstep in Aberdeen.

Emblazoned beneath the High School's badge with its tulip and open book between two castles, the school's motto to this day remains 'By Learning and Courtesy'. Its aim was 'to provide a liberal education to equip its students for home life or for those professions open to women'.[208] Importantly for Nan, ever since the universities had started accepting women, the High School had been supplying a steady stream of its scholars not only to Aberdeen's university but further south as well, to Cambridge's Newnham and Girton Colleges. The school remains proud of its pioneering attitude:

These days it may be difficult to understand how significant

Aberdeen High School for Girls was in its early days. At a point in history when women still did not have the vote, the school aided the cause of education for women in the North East of Scotland, affording its students an excellent education and giving many of the students of their day the opportunity to achieve University education at a time when only a small number of women had the chance at all. The High School's former pupils[209] were to take their learning and courtesy out into their own worlds, whether family and domestic or far reaching, and achieved much that was worthwhile, often in the professions of education, law and medicine.[210]

Now Harlaw Academy, a co-educational comprehensive with over a 1,000 pupils, Aberdeen's High School has had several incarnations. It began its life as Little Belmont Public School, 'an academy for girls' at elementary level run with the aid of a government grant, according to its 1874 prospectus. Despite its rather humble beginnings, its headmaster, John McBain, was sure it would develop into 'a great and prosperous school' but even he was taken aback by how quickly it took off. Early on he was struck by the number of 'earnest, capable girls' in its classes 'and the all but universal desire on the part of parents for a thorough and complete education for their girls'.[211]

During the school's first session, there were forty pupils. In its second year, pupil numbers trebled and by the start of its third, all the rooms in the Little Belmont Street building were occupied. Demand for places at the school was so high that by its fourth session in 1881, the Board, in line with the 1872 Education (Scotland) Act, declared the academy a 'higher class school', changed its name to the High School for Girls and gave up the government funding, raising the fees and extending the school building at the rear. But it was not long until it was again overflowing, forcing the use of nearby church halls. These were hardly suitable—there were no desks. Thankfully, in 1891, the School Board was able to purchase new premises in Albyn Place to house the school's by then five hundred or so pupils, ranging in age from five to nineteen.

Set back behind iron railings fronting a wide semi-circular sweep of drive, in a two acre site landscaped with trees and shrubs, 19 Albyn Place is on the south side of the street, two hundred yards or so from the junction of Union Street and Holburn Street in Aberdeen's West End. It was designed in 1840 by Archibald Simpson, who was the Architect responsible for many of the city's municipal buildings, including the Assembly Rooms and the fairytale-turreted Marischal College. Simpson had 'a perfect horror of all that was incongruous or contrary to good taste'. He was incapable, apparently, of turning out an 'inelegant design'.[212]

'The High School stands proudly at No 19, Its wa's built o'granite, its woodwork sae green',[213] Dorothy Kidd began a poem she wrote in her second year at the High School in 1929 and Simpson's design of 19 Albyn Place, described in 1893 as 'at once graceful and effective… entirely in chaste outline and exquisite proportions',[214] remains even today an imposing and still graceful, pale granite edifice, its outline still intact. The woodwork is now white and the city has built itself up around it, but back in the early 1900s Aberdeen was still filling out into its green spaces. A photograph from its early days shows it surrounded by countryside and, behind the school, hills rear in the distance. It is not so surprising to learn, then, that an albatross landed from the roof during Nan's time there.[215]

Until its purchase by the School Board in 1891, 19 Albyn Place had been home for fifty years to Miss Emslie's Orphan Asylum[216] which trained girls for domestic service and the building needed some interior alterations before it was deemed fit for the school's use. Adapted and enlarged, it was reopened in 1893 with numerous class-rooms all of which were 'fitted up with many modern conveniences for teaching purposes', as well as Art Rooms, a Lantern Room and a Library of some 2,000 volumes 'at the disposal of senior pupils and teachers lending and consultation purposes'.[217]

According to Mary Clarke, a pupil from 1894, the new school building was well-adapted to its purpose. Except, that is, for its venti-lation system. Fans in the basement pumped fresh air in and out of the classrooms, but as none of the windows could be opened, a generation of white-faced schoolgirls suffered appalling headaches. Fortunately, by the time Nan arrived at the High School, the windows had been fixed so that fresh air filtered into the classrooms during lessons—although the noise from traffic passing outside in the street made it harder to concentrate. In 1904, the year before Nan's arrival, there were further extensions, including 'an Assembly Hall, spacious Cookery and Laundry rooms and a suite of laboratories of the most approved description for the teaching of Physics, Chemistry, and Biology'.[218] According to the Chairman's report, by 1906 the High School was flourishing both numerically and educationally, the Board 'having spared the ratepayer no expense in order to equip it'.[219]

So began a new stage in Nan Shepherd's life, one with a little more independence although not as much as she might have liked. The bicycle possibly did more to emancipate pre-1914 woman than any other machine,[220] except perhaps the typewriter. Not only did a bicycle make a woman mobile at minimum cost, it enabled her to roam on her own, away from the watchful eyes of parents and neighbours. A bicycle would have given Nan more freedom and it was certainly one enjoyed by many of her school friends. From the 1890s, for tuppence a week, the High School proved it was thoroughly modern by allowing girls to park bicycles in a purpose-built shed. In *The Quarry Wood,* Nan gives Martha the independence of a bicycle. The Ironsides do not have the money to spare for daily train fares and so travelling the four and a half miles to school by train was a luxury afforded to Martha only when the weather was at its worst. 'In most weathers she cycled back and fore to town night and morning'.[221]

But Nan Shepherd's childhood was never penurious. Unlike Martha, she did not have to worry about the extra cost to her parents of purchasing the vast numbers of school text books required (although these were stocked at Alexander Murray's in Union Street who helpfully gave a discount for cash of three pence in the shilling). She did not have to ration her pencils, or save candle stumps so she had light enough to do her homework. And there was certainly the money for train fares. So Nan travelled each weekday to and from school on the 'subbie' with Frank who was a pupil at Robert Gordon's College.

The choice of schools for boys in Aberdeen was straightforward: between the Grammar School (Lord Byron's Alma Mater—a fact which pupils were never allowed to forget) and Robert Gordon's on Schoolhill.[222] The oldest school in Aberdeen, founded in around 1257, the Grammar had a somewhat upper-crust image. The rather more academically high-powered Robert Gordon's, which prepared its students for the Bursary Competition and University, provided a better social balance, mixing 'clever laddies from working class city homes and the affluence of west-end fish and granite with the plain dyst of country loons'.[223]

Established in 1732 as a charitable hospital for the poor boys of his hometown by Robert Gordon, (one of Aberdeen's many wealthy merchants), the school opened in 1750. From 1881 it was was fee paying—an injection of cash which no doubt helped finance the addition to the 'Auld Hoose' of two smart new wings designed by John Adam.[224] Other than that, the school itself was little changed when Frank started there in 1904. Up Schoolhill, past the statue of Robert Gordon in Khartoum, he strolled each weekday morning during term time, under the vaulted gateway and along the avenue flanked by lawns to the Auld Hoose and into the school's black-gowned, musty corridors. As it turned out, Frank's was less of a stroll and more of a triumphal march through school although his younger sister's academic career was no less illustrious.

Emerging into Aberdeen from the old Suburban train station at the foot of Bridge Street with her brother on school mornings, how noisy and dirty the town must have seemed to Nan after the the clean sweep of countryside around Cults—and how shiny. 'Silver-veined city', 'town of pure crystal', its buildings a-glitter with mica in its windy corners, 'silver' is one of the epithets most applied to Aberdeen. Its origins were humble, from twin, but initially very discrete settlements, which had grown out of twin rivers, the Don and the Dee. During the nineteenth century when the great granite pits were quarried, rival architects Archibald Simpson and John Smith used the stone with reckless abandon, filling the town with towers, spires and vast municipal buildings—until the money ran out. By the time Nan started school there in 1905, Aberdeen's greatest physical flowering was over, leaving a city that shines in the sun after rain.

But Nan Shepherd was no sentimentalist and relished the evidence that, despite its granite grandeur, Aberdeen was still firmly yoked to the countryside around it. Railways ran through it, its streets, criss-crossed by tramcars, were hazy with the smoke of innumerable coal fires, but the shriek of seagulls, the fishy whiff in the wind from the harbour and the parade of livestock at Kittybrewster were all very much part of its bustle. Pigs stampeding in the Great Northern Road had been known to hold up the trams. 'It is the only big town I know,' John Allan was to say of Aberdeen 'where, instinctively and without surprise, a gentleman will step off the pavement to make way for a cow, as he would do for any lady.'[225]

At Union Street Nan and Frank's routes diverged, as he headed off to Schoolhill and she turned left to walk, or take the tramcar, swaying and jolting along Union Street, all shops and offices, to reach Albyn Place. Either way, it would not do to be late for school. Except for Tuesdays, when lessons finished at 1.15pm, school hours were from 9 am to 3.45 pm with an hour and half's break for lunch.[226] The High School set high standards in matters such as behaviour, etiquette and uniform. Tardiness was frowned upon. A prize of a book was given annually to the pupil whose time-keeping and attendance was deemed most excellent and academic prizes were awarded only if the pupil had been 'punctual and regular in their attendance' and their behaviour and conduct satisfactory.

It would have been natural for Nan, pristine in her uniform of white jabot (frilled blouse) and dark, ankle-length skirt, mounting the stone steps to the arched, double-doored entrance on her first day at school that August of 1905, to have felt nervous. She needn't have been. Grey-bearded, John McBain with his twitching winged eyebrows, was a 'grandfatherly figure'[227] who watched over his pupils with the most 'anxious solicitude and care' according to the Chairman's report of 1906.[228] 'Kind' was the adjective most used by his pupils to describe him. Mary Esslemont, a High School pupil two years above Nan, remembers no unpleasantness, even when, as the greatest punishment for some misdemeanour, she was sent to Mr McBain's room.[229] So much loved was their headmaster that on his retirement in 1912 his former pupils clubbed together and presented him with a diamond ring.[230]

It was not unusual in those days for a school to have a male head. More surprising for a Scottish school, was that its Head Elf (senior mistress) was an Englishwoman, Lucy Ward, B.A., who went on to become the school's first female superintendent, replacing McBain in 1912—a year after Nan left.[231] A progressive, who expanded the High School considerably from the few hundred pupils there during Nan's time to nine hundred by her retirement in 1929, Ward considered the higher education of women at Aberdeen's High School for Girls her life's work.[232] On her retirement she was still fervent on the subject of the value of women's education:

> Any education which was given or received with a view to individual improvement or success only was stunted. It was for the good of the community that a great school like [the High School for Girls] should exist, sending out year by year women of good education, women with well-balanced minds, large-hearted, interested in their fellows, with broad sympathies, and ready, if need be, to make some sacrifice in order to serve the community.[233]

The bespectacled Lucy Ward, her dark hair plaited around her head, was the first of a series of teachers to inspire Nan Shepherd. Like her English mistress, Nan's flyaway auburn hair was braided in a halo around her head throughout her life—although this may also have had something to do with her phobia about hairs falling on to tablecloths, or worse, into food. More important was her teacher's intellectual influence. A philosopher, with high ideals, Ward was also a realist who 'could keep her hand to the plough of ordinary, everyday life'.[234] Nan, too, would admit years later that 'There's a great big bit of me detached and amused, and quite often cynical, that weights the wind of the spirit with the weights for corn and potatoes and things'. Art mattered supremely to her, but not so much the craftsmanship as 'the thing inside, that is part of living just as is eating one's porridge and loving one's wife and getting excited over one's holiday—the grasp of the essential meaning and nature and being of whatever one turns into art, I mean'.[235]

Lucy Ward's influence can also be seen, in some of the earlier extracts Nan copied into *Gleanings*. Nan was an insatiable reader. *Gleanings,* the first of her commonplace books, reveals the astonishing breadth of her reading—much wider than those texts prescribed by the school, suggesting she made good use of its library of 2,000 volumes. Early entries, made while she was a pupil at the High School are in slanted un-joined handwriting, unlike her later, cursive, upright script. Early on, she favours poetry using metaphors of nature and landscape and of working on the land, like the American clergyman and writer Maltby Davenport Babcock's: 'My life is but a field,/stretched out beneath God's sky/ Where grows the golden grain?/Where faith? Where sympathy?/In a furrow cut by pain'. During her schooldays, Nan was still a devout Christian, so it comes as no surprise to find several excerpts with a religious bent: hymns and psalms mingle on the pages with Sidney Lanier's *A Ballad of Trees and the Master.*

The Intermediate Course, which Nan began aged twelve, lasted over three or four years, ending in an examination for which only those pupils considered likely to pass in all the subjects were entered. The curriculum concentrated on English (with History and Geography) French, Mathematics, Experimental Science and Drawing. As it was a prerequisite for entrance to university, those pupils intending to go learnt Latin which they began in the second intermediate year at the High School. Those who were not were offered extra tuition in cookery or needlework. After all, the High School's aim in providing a liberal education for its pupils was to 'fit them for home life or for any profession open to women'. One of the only professions open to women of pre-war Britain was teaching and there were two routes into this profession. You could either go straight from school to the Training Centre's two year course, or you could opt for a university degree followed by a year's teacher training.

Nan, who could not have cared less for extra tuition in sewing or cooking, already had her sights set on a place at university. In her second year, she began Latin. She describes in *The Quarry Wood* the feeling of becoming saturated in Latin prose, the precision required to turn 'flighty little English sentences into one rolling Latin period': 'Words, phrases, turns of speech, alert and eager in her brain, drumming at her ears, clamouring in an exultant chaos. And that last triumphant mastery, forcing on the chaos order and a purpose'.[236] Finding precisely the right word to translate meaning was something for which Nan strove all her writing career and in that description is the satisfaction gained when it all came together.

In the late 1890s Mary Clarke was disappointed by the standard of education at the High School:

> French, Mathematics and Latin were in the hands of those who could not impart the knowledge they presumably possessed... Science was only a name...once a week we watched the master set up experiments in physics which invariably failed.

It would have made no difference to the pupils if they had succeeded as no coherent explanation was ever given.[237]

By Nan's era, the quality of teaching had improved considerably. The mixed staff of about forty men and women at the High School were picked for their zeal as well as their academic achievement. The teaching of experimental science was dramatically improved by the appointment, in 1906, of Elsie Fyfe Findlay to assist Miss Philip. A photograph in the school's prospectus shows off the new Science Room, 'the lab where we make a' the queer smellin gases' of Dorothy Kidd's poem. Patiently expectant girls sit on stools at vast wooden workbenches fitted with individual sinks and shiny brass gas taps. In front of each pupil sits a bunsen burner below its tripod and alongside there are racks of labelled glass bottles filled with chemicals. Glass-blowing, water distillation, artificial freezing and the dissection of an ox's eye were among their experiments. There were also detailed, illustrated surveys of plant life with drawings taken weekly of a plant's growth and notes on development as well as a herbarium filled with dried plants. Nan's passion for botany, inspired by her father, flourished here.

Geography, too, had come on in leaps and bounds since Mary Clarke's day. It was considered an 'English' subject and taught by Lucy Ward, who encouraged her pupils to use theodolites and make clay-modelled contour maps. As for History, the British Empire having reached its zenith under Queen Victoria's rule, it seemed as though everything that mattered took place under the British flag. Current Events did not yet feature on school timetables and while the names of foreign countries might be familiar from the study of maps in geography lessons, unless British armies had fought battles there, their histories were a blank.

In *The Quarry Wood* Nan describes how this rote-learning and gaps in Scottish education resulted in confusion and misinformation being passed from generation to generation. Geordie, Martha's father, has little knowledge of Scotland's actual geographical location. One January evening, wresting Martha and Dussie from their homework, he takes them outside to see the Aurora Borealis. Watching 'the north on fire' Dussie asks questions which Geordie struggles to answer. 'I min' fan I was a laddie there was a bit screed I used to ken. It was some like the geography' Geordie says. 'On the sooth o' Scotland there's England, on the north the Arory-bory—Alice; on the east—fat's on the east o't?' Martha eventually supplies the answer—'It's the Atlantic Ocean'. But Geordie is not satisfied with this and some weeks later, after a moment of epiphany in church, triumphantly informs Martha: ' "Eternity. That's fat wast o' Scotland." '

Martha repeats it to herself over and over: '*Scotland is bounded on the south by England, on the east by the rising sun, on the north by the Arory-bory-Alice, and on the west by Eternity.* Eternity did not seem to be in any of her maps: but neither was Aurora. She accepted that negligence of the map-makers as she accepted so much else in life…She repeated the boundaries of Scotland with the same satisfaction as she repeated the rivers in Spain. Up to her University days she carried the conviction that there was something about Scotland in the Bible.[238]

The importance of Empire was still being drilled into pupils, literally. 'In view of the importance of the subject, *Drill* is taught throughout the school,' reads the High School prospectus. Every pupil was expected to attend Drill classes, unless she brought in a medical certificate saying she was unfit to do so. For the 'correct performance of the exercises', done to music with dumb-bells, bar bells and Indian clubs, pupils were required 'to wear a dress that did not interfere with their movements'.[239] For Nan, the exercises would have been almost identical to those performed at Cults primary and just as tedious.

Less tedious for her was drawing, which was taught by a middle-aged drawing master 'imbued with the most advanced methods', according to the school's prospectus. The reality was that art lessons were devoted to drawing, freehand, copies of plaster casts of flowers or raw-faced, earthen pots. Anyone whose sketching did not conform and resemble the still-life model was severely criticised.[240] Nan enjoyed drawing even much later in life. Sheila Roger's daughter, Deirdre Burton, remembers Nan's letters to her were always adorned with illustrations of flowers and cottages. Clearly the drawing master's so-called 'advanced methods' paid off. In 1906, Nan won fourth prize at the Aberdeen Flower Show for the best painting of a flower in a competition for which guidelines were so strict they even included the size of the paper and style of illustration to be used.[241]

In the 1930s, Nan, as a former pupil and, by then, a published author, was invited to the High School's Junior Department prize-giving when she gave 'a delightful little talk to the girls based on the idea of wearing uniform'.[242] Pointing out that postmen, policemen, Girl Guides and Boy Scouts all dressed the same and punctuating her talk with anecdotes, Nan said that 'people who dressed alike were all trying to do the same thing and that the girls all dressed alike in their school uniform were all trying to learn as much as they could'.[243]

Whether or not that was still the case in the 1930s, certainly in

Nan's era most of the girls were studious and motivated. So much so, it was a question not of inciting pupils to work but of trying to prevent them overworking. 'Preparation', in the intermediate years was meant to be no more than two hours and in the post-intermediate (sixth form classes) a maximum of three. The girls did much more than this. When exam time came, signs they were burning the candle at both ends were especially visible.[244]

There may be no school reports or records[245] from Nan's time at Aberdeen High School, but there is no doubt she flourished intellectually in its academic atmosphere. In 1907, she won one of two Aberdeen Town Council Scholarships available, halving her school fees of forty shillings a term for the next three years.[246]

Not all the High School pupils found the intellectual atmosphere as stimulating as Nan, though. Elizabeth Hyde Campbell thought the teachers terrifying. They were a straight-laced and staid lot, she said, and the curriculum was indigestible:

> The unceasing regularity of lesson after lesson irked her, thirty minutes' algebra, thirty minutes' geography…ticked off with brutal definiteness. She became dyspeptic and constipated, unable to digest or get rid of so many courses in this complicated menu of Secondary Education.[247]

★ ★ ★

'Hydie',[248] as Elizabeth Hyde Campbell was known to friends in her youth (and 'Betty' later on) moved to the High School after an unsatisfactory year at Aberdeen's Central School, where 'cleverness didn't always meet with the approbation of teachers' who often thought the brighter pupils were 'taking the mickey'.[249] Thirteen months older than Nan, she was in the year above her at school, but the two girls travelled to and from Aberdeen on the train together every day, although Betty's round trip was longer. Five days a week, she would cycle the three miles from her Inchmarlo home to Banchory station to catch the Deeside line train into Aberdeen, reversing the journey in the evenings.

No doubt there were gaggles of High School girls hurrying to make it on time for its 9 o'clock start every morning but, when school was out, they could dawdle past shop windows in Union Street on their way to the station. At the time, electricity was a novelty in Scotland. A reflection of social status, it was found only in the houses of the wealthy and important, or in hotels. As the academic year advanced with the seasons, it would soon be dark by the closing of afternoon school and in the glow of the gas-lamps the girls could slide their way along frosty pavements to the train. Then, when the weather warmed again, before they broke up at the end of June for the summer vacation, there was the beach to tempt them before they headed home.

Aberdeen, Silver City by the Sea, was advertised as one of the 'most beautiful resorts in Britain'—although it would surely take a hardy person to swim in the North East's chilly coastal waters. Fierce winds blowing off the North Sea regularly sent everyone running for cover, but photographs from the period show the beach thronged with people, crowds of them 'promenading' along the sea front. Whether Nan actually braved the water or not, the ocean drew her during after-school hours. A photograph of her in school uniform shows her sitting at the water's edge, gazing out to sea. Hair loosened, thick black stockings and buttoned boots discarded, one rather elegant, long, bare foot can be glimpsed below her skirt. Seated on a boulder below her, you can just make out another girl, her dark hair loose too, flowing over one shoulder. It might be Betty. If so, her toes would be in the water.[250]

Nan, in school uniform, gazing out to sea.

The two girls were very different looking. Long-limbed Nan was already tall for her age and slender. Fair and freckled, with tawny hair down to her waist, later, colour photographs show her hazel eyes like Martha's in *The Quarry Wood*, had 'something in them of Nature's greens that have gone brown, of grass fields before the freshening of spring'.[251] Small, sleek and dark, Betty is unmistakably the 'tiny', 'radiant' Dussie, Martha's closest friend in *The Quarry Wood,* down to her piano-playing, and 'burnished' hair. [252]

Dussie thinks herself a dunce and is 'dreadfully unhappy about it'. 'I once tried to make myself literate. I read and read at your books—I thought you'd hate me for being ignorant' she says in *The Quarry Wood.*[253] And through Betty's autobiographical writing runs a similar refrain. 'What a pity…that I was not more intellectual' she says. Taken into the garden one evening by her father-in-law and asked to identify the stars, she could not, 'not even the good old 'plough''.[254] It can't have helped that her older brother Duncan (who becomes 'George' in *Out of the Earth)* had walked 'leisurely to the top of his class with the hearts of masters and classmates slung carelessly round his neck'. Within a year at Robert Gordon's, 'the school had bet its well-polished boots on his achieving first place in the Bursary competition'.[255]

Just as Betty is turned into 'Dussie' in Nan's *The Quarry Wood*, Nan is cast as 'Maribel' in Betty's novel, *Out of the Earth*. For reasons which will become clear, Betty's description of Nan as a schoolgirl is less than flattering, 'Like a swallow with her smooth white jabot and long slim lines'. She describes Maribel flitting in and out of the desks on her way to her place as dux of the class. The class was split into two in its opinion of her: 'one side hero-worshipping, the other hating jealously'.[256] Whether class opinion was really so polarised, there is no way of knowing. No other testimony from Nan's time at school has so far come to light. But Nan was certainly top of the class in her third year, earning her the Town Council scholarship.

Betty loathed school. She went only to please her father, who was so keen his children should have a decent education that he would wake in the middle of the night to build up the fire in the study so that they could revise at exam time. Farm manager of the Inchmarlo estate, owned in the late nineteenth century by the Davidsons, George Campbell was a retired missionary. 'Six foot three of warm human earth baked brown by a tropical sun,'[257] Bety describes him on his return from Africa. He was only six months a widower when he met his second wife, the plump, diminutive and devout Miss Betsy Wyse.[258]

A mile from the Dee and a retirement village since 1987, the plain, pale pink, Georgian facade of Inchmarlo House in its hundred acres of fir and pine studded parkland still looks much the same as it did in Betty's childhood. Home Farm, which came with George Campbell's appointment, was not really a house, but more of a series of interlocking rooms adjacent to the byre. The smell of horse and stench of ammonia seeped through the walls. This did not bother Betsy Campbell, who was indifferent to the setting, certain she would eventually be in a 'higher place'.

In evangelical circles, she was thought a gifted woman. Betsy thought so too; 'but with humility, giving God the praise'.[259] Her articles, which were mostly on bereavement, were published weekly in magazines like *The Christian*. But as a result of her mother's preoccupation, the Holy Trinity occupied a lot of space in Betty's childhood and even accompanied them on holiday. Growing up convinced the Holy Ghost was always whisking around in trees, hiding behind a bush, or swinging on the clothesline, as a schoolgirl, Betty, unsurprisingly, confesses to being something of an 'ersatz prig', 'enveloped in a cloak of piety'.[260] During her schooldays, Nan, too, was still 'pi'. But she would soon become conflicted on the subject of religion and ultimately reject it, a change in her beliefs wrought in the critical, intellectual atmosphere of university which coincided with the First World War.

Nan's last three years at the High School were spent preparing for the School Leaving Certificate Examination, a prerequisite for university entrance. Her cousins William and Francis Kelly and her older brother Frank went to university, but Nan was the first woman in the family to go.

Aberdeen's university had existed for four hundred years before it began admitting women. In July 1892, a motion to admit women in all Faculties was sanctioned and by the end of October 1892 the 'first Eleven' came careering over to King's on bicycles. As Nan said in an article she wrote in 1942 for the university's *Review* celebrating fifty years of women in the university,[261] this event, so exciting to its participants locally, was not, of course, local but the result of a movement in history which resulted in the 1889 Universities (Scotland) Act. The world was altering and women's demand for admission to the Universities was 'merely a part of the developing and outreaching liberalism of the century and already, when the Scottish Universities admitted them, the demand was old.'[262]

All of those first eleven came from cultured, city homes. None had entered for a degree, a fact which may have prompted jibes about King's being turned into a finishing school. 'Do you know what I saw as I came through the Quad? I—saw—six—hags,' said Keith Leask,

who was described by Nan as 'that calcified rock of learning and preju-
dice'.[263] One of these 'hags' was Rachel Annand Taylor. A feminist and
poet, the colourful and glamorous, Annand Taylor, although brilliant
academically, never obtained a degree. Her ode to her university days in
Aberdeen reflects the atmosphere of mockery and ridicule encountered
by the first female students:

> What marvellous mad hopes were cherished
> In Aberdeen!
> Oh, that's a city to be born in.
> The pure air kindles you, and witty
> Your mind goes dancing. To learn scorn in
> Oh, that's a city!
> Under the Crown that dreams of Flodden[264]
> And Borgia,[265] in a scarlet gown
> Youth lightly treads where youth has trodden
> Under the Crown.[266]

By October 1894, however, the first genuine 'lady undergraduates'
appeared and having been placed in the Bursary Competition, came
not solely from Aberdeen but from outlying districts such as Fyvie
and Portsoy. Twenty-strong, they began to infiltrate the societies.
But despite grumbling that half their common room was given to
women, the male undergraduates were friendly.

Then there was the question of academic attire: should women be
permitted to wear the 'buttonless garment and comfortless platter'?
On a February day in 1895 women appeared in the Latin class in
trencher and gown only to be gently 'reminded' by the Professor that
trenchers were not millinery and must be removed.

Always topical, the student show that year was titled 'The Sweet
Girl Undergraduate' and offered women a wide choice of new
subjects from Double Dutch to Archaeological Cookery. Around
this time the Senatus met to discuss how these new students should
best be officially referred to: female, women or lady students. 'Lady
students', it was decided, although Professor Terry was later to say
that the word should have been 'fillies'.

But beneath all this froth ran a steady stream of achievement.
The first four women to graduate did so in 1898 (two with Honours)
there were five the next year and by 1901 there were female graduates in Medicine and Science.[267] Although one woman complained
in the *Alma Mater*: 'when will men remove from my name the incor-
rect and insulting adjective *new*', by the century's turn, the novelty

of women in the university was wearing off. 'Sometimes,' wrote another, 'it even happens that all the students do not turn to look at us when we cross the quadrangle'.[268]

There were few substantial scholarships to be had at Aberdeen University[269] and none geared to women students, but there was some funding available. As well as bursaries, there was the 'Carnegie money'—around £15 a year paid to those deemed eligible. Nan needed neither of these to fund her university education[270] and as she lived at home rather than in lodgings like most of the other women students, her parents only had to find her tuition fees. Betty, however, *did* need financial help: the year before she went up to King's, her father died on 7th May 1910.[271]

The effect of George Campbell's death on his family was a catastrophic, financially as well as emotionally. Within a month, Duncan, Betty and their mother found themselves homeless. Turfed out of Home Farm so the next Farm Manager could move in with his family and on the promise made by the Laird of a pension of fifty pounds a year (which he paid only for six months[272]) they took a tiny flat on the top floor of a tenement at 54, Forest Avenue, Aberdeen.

After the freedom of the countryside, the lack of space irked all three, although it was Mrs Campbell who particularly felt it. For Betsy Campbell, who had so long considered herself 'an emissary of God, every moment on hand to receive his messages',[273] lost her faith when she lost her husband and her religion failed to bring the solace she'd expected. In Aberdeen, she began to wither. Slowly it dawned on her children that their mother had stopped smiling. She stopped writing too. There were no more religious articles or comforting messages on bereavement. Her memory went, dissolving into fantasy and vagueness. Then, in October 1911, she took an overdose, leaving a note for her children saying that she wanted to be with their father. Her life was saved by a stomach pump and on doctor's orders she was removed to an asylum where she lingered on for a few years more.

Without their mother's meagre income and with no further pension payment from Laird Davidson apparently forthcoming, money was tight. Duncan had been intent on university. But with his mother and sister now dependent on him he was forced to apprentice himself to solicitors in Aberdeen. Betty was luckier. After her father's death, Lady Davidson suggested to Betsy Campbell that her daughter should give up her idea of a university education and work as a governess. Instead, thanks to Betty's godmother's financial help and a grant from the Carnegie, Betty was enrolled for King's College. With their mother in the asylum though, for the next few years Betty was housekeeper and cook as well as student. They were lean days. [274]

Chapter Four

1911-1913

John Macmurray comes into the story in August 1911, the summer he fell in love with Elizabeth Hyde Campbell. Not that he had confessed his feelings to her: 'With Hydie—if there was any doubt of it before, there is none now—I have fallen in love, but dare not tell her so. I am not worthy to blacken her shoes', he wrote in his journal on 12th August'.[275]

Although not widely recognised as such during his lifetime, John Macmurray would become one of Scotland's most original thinkers. Considered a maverick by the academic world which found him difficult to pigeonhole, he was concerned that philosophy should deal with issues of real, 'living' importance. While he was influenced by Kant and Marx amongst others, rather than sift or synthesise the work of previous philosophers, he explored new territory, working from his own radical ideas.

More contemporary to twenty first century thinking, Macmurray's pioneering 'philosophy of the personal' (to use his own description) rejected the mind/body dualism of Descartes and others of his ilk. Instead of differentiating between the objective and subjective, thought and feeling, the individual and the communal, public and private, science and religion, Macmurray proposed 'a unity in human action and relationship'.[276] He published fifteen books and over two hundred articles and contributions to publications from the 1930s until his death in 1976, yet references to Macmurray in contemporary writing are scant and his work still little known.[277]

Macmurray's intellectual precocity showed on his arrival at school for the first time in 1896 when it became obvious he had already read all the books provided, even those for the highest class. Astounded, his teacher asked him what he wanted to be when he grew up. 'A man of knowledge', he replied.[278] Born in Maxwelltown, Kirkcudbrightshire[279]in 1891, John was raised in an atmosphere of devout Presbyterianism. His civil servant father, James and his mother Mary, shared strong religious ideals. Family prayers were held daily in the parlour, when John, his three younger sisters, Ella, Lilias and Mary and their younger brother Joseph, each read a Bible verse. They were strict Sabbatarians; outbursts of merriment on Sunday were sternly rebuked. Sunday school or bible class followed morning kirk, evenings were for family prayers or another service.

It was his upbringing, John said years later, that provided the foundation for his thinking. Although he became critical of institutionalised religion, a religious impulse, he believed, was fundamental to the fabric of human beings. It was this religious impulse, he argued, that makes us seek out friendship and through friendship, in community with others, we discover who we really are. 'Freedom, and the secret of it lies in our capacity for friendship', he claimed. 'It is only in friendship that we are completely ourselves, completely free'.[280] Betty is more succinct: 'My philosopher husband says we can only know ourselves through other people'.[281]

After botched surgery in childhood to remove a tubercular lump on John's neck left an ugly scar, the surgeon asked what the boy's ambition was. His parents said he would be a missionary. "Oh that's alright then" was the response. Apparently a disfigurement would not matter in a life of holiness'.[282]

There is no doubt of his piety. In December 1908, aged seventeen, John began a journal:

This book is intended as a personal record of daily life and conduct, ever to keep before me the object of life, the goal of the race, "that I might know Him". On bended knee I spread it before thee, dear Master. Use it Thyself to keep my wandering mind, to stay my wandering thoughts and to remind me of Thyself and Thy coming again.[283]

He then outlines his proposed timetable of bible study and prayer—rigorous enough, frankly, to challenge a monk.

A university education was denied to James Macmurray. Determined his clever oldest son should have one, in 1899 he moved his family from Maxwelltown to Aberdeen where the standard of schooling was much higher. After two years at the Grammar School, John won a scholarship to the more academically-challenging Robert Gordon's College. His years there from 1905 to 1909 overlapped with Frank Shepherd's,[284] but it was Duncan Campbell, Betty's older brother, who was his closest schoolfriend.

Duncan talked often and glowingly about John to his sister, of his devout evangelical faith so similar to the Campbells' and of his genius. He was convinced John might one day become prime minister. On the wall at Home Farm, alongside Queen Victoria in a fat meringue of a dress, hung two portraits of prime ministers. 'I didn't fancy them very much, not even Gladstone, who was quite cosy looking. I couldn't imagine John hanging on my bedroom wall at some future time', Betty said.[285]

Macmurray was a good-looking man. According to Joyce Campbell (who was married to Betty's nephew, Duncan) he was very attractive to women. 'They loved him! He was very attentive. He never talked down to people'.[286] Tallish and athletic, in the late 1920s when he grew a beard to hide the scar on his neck he was sometimes mistaken for DH Lawrence. But in 1907, when Betty first clapped eyes on him, he was not so prepossessing.

John's parents' austere Presbyterianism had softened somewhat after their introduction to the American evangelists, Moody and Sankey. Most Sundays the Macmurrays now worshipped at the Gordon Mission and during his summer holidays John helped out at the 'clouty kirk', as their travelling tent meetings were affectionately known. One Sunday evening, Betty turned up to one of these gatherings.

Standing in the entrance to the tent was a lanky young man of about sixteen, dressed in a badly fitting tweed suit with a highly starched collar and cuffs. His dark hair combed straight back from his high forehead, furrowed with concentration, blue eyes grave, short-nosed and full-lipped, he was singing loudly and unselfconsciously from a hymn book. 'Safe from corroding care',[287] he boomed, too absorbed, apparently, to notice Betty on that occasion. A few weeks later, their paths crossed again.

During her year at Central School, Betty was in the same class as Macmurray's sister Ella. The two girls stayed friends after Betty changed schools and one afternoon Ella invited her to supper at their home in Aberdeen at 31 Mile End Road. Betty was nervous. Her brother had built up John to such a degree that, on speaking to him, she worried he would think her a fool. John was equally intimidated. Quietly spoken and shy in social situations, he had no idea how to talk to girls. Betty and Ella were playing the piano when he made his appearance in the parlour:

> Very shy he was. He asked if he might play. I found his playing
> shattering. I hated it. He had just taught himself from scratch
> to play his first piece, Moonlight Sonata. John always believed
> a man's reach must be beyond his grasp. It was. His fingers

galloped up the second movement, sometimes halting to begin over again. His face, contorted into scissor-like movements, seemed funny to me, and I laughed. The music stopped. I don't believe he had ever been laughed at before. He stopped playing. His family were very serious and respectful of each other. To laugh at him was hitting below the belt. He shut the piano lid, looked at me gravely, and asked his sister if his mother had the tea ready.[288]

John does not mention this meeting in his journal. It is not until some time later 'Hydie' begins to appear regularly. For the next year and a half, in the hope of seeing John again, Betty would call on Ella at home as often as she could. On these occasions, she recalls the pink, plump James Macmurray, quizzing her to assess her intelligence. Betty, dreaded these moments almost as much as when it was her turn to read aloud bible verses during family prayers in the parlour.

John too, would often make the trip from Aberdeen on the train out to Inchmarlo. Ostensibly, of course, this was to see Duncan but as he and Betty both admit, his ulterior motive was to snatch moments alone with her. Often, they contrived to slip away on walks together. 'Occasionally we touched hands', she recalled in her memoirs. 'Later he told me he thought I was too pure and holy, and was ashamed to show how he felt…I sat beside him in the woods while he read poetry aloud, often Browning, who I came to detest. He didn't seem to notice.' Any relationship between them could not even be hinted at for years. 'We had to weave through all the subtleties of Victorian courtship, where even coquetry was frowned upon'. [289]

Not long after George Campbell's death had forced Betty, Duncan and Betsy to find lodgings in Aberdeen, John Macmurray won a bursary to the University of Glasgow to read Classics and Geology and in April 1909, the Macmurrays left Aberdeen. Their move came as a great blow to Betty. John had not yet proposed to her, but she said, 'we both knew we had an unspoken agreement'.[290]

From his journals, you can see what a devout, inhibited, young man John Macmurray was. Subjecting himself to the constant self-scrutiny expected of an evangelist, he was a perfectionist in his faith. Striving to overcome sexual urges normal in a young man he was often frustrated at not being able to live chastely without succumbing to them: 'I have gone down twice under temptation', he writes on 31 January 1911 adding 'yet today I feel that I am stronger than when the year began. Life has a deeper meaning; a higher goal'.[291]

The summer of 1911 was a scorcher. Temperatures topped 100

degrees in some parts of Britain. It must have been sweltering under canvas. Nevertheless the 'clouty kirk' was on its mission in the North East. Shortly after term ended at Glasgow University, in mid-June 1911, John returned to Aberdeen to earn some money helping out with the Gordon Mission services. He had been writing poetry with religious themes in his journal, but that summer he wrote his first love poem. Dedicated to 'H' it begins: 'Love shall I unlock my heart and bid thee enter here?', ending:

> Come, oh! come; I am weary of waiting for thee
> And the roses are blown.
> Come, love, come with a kiss on thy lips for me
> And my heart is thine own.[292]

His declaration of love, which at that point was still unconfessed to Betty herself, appears on 12th August followed by several poems addressed to 'Agnes' (his codename for Betty and the name she gave to the heroine of her autobiographical novel, *Out of the Earth*). Despite enjoying an 'enchanted week' at the Campbell's flat in early October and being able to spend time alone on walks with her while Duncan was at work, John was still reserved towards Betty—which irritated her. His outpourings were saved for his journal, from which it appears his feelings have deepened to worship: 'I dare not say as once I rashly said, that I love Betty in the full sense of that deep word; I reverence her rather'.[293]

John's diffidence diminished only after Betty's mother's mental decay reached the point where she attempted suicide and was removed to Aberdeen's Royal Asylum, a few days after he had returned to Glasgow for the start of his university term. That Christmas of 1911 Betty spent with the Macmurrays in Glasgow. It was there, according to Betty's memoirs, that John finally proposed and it was then that she received her first kiss. 'We were on the road to matrimony'.[294]

John's version of events that Christmas is more implicit on the subject of a proposal: 'I told the story of my love, and heard from Betty's lips the sweet confession of her own'. They played the piano together and then he 'knelt at her side...and told of the dawning and the deepening of my love for her, and how my whole being lay as an offering at her feet.'[295]

Whether Nan knew at the time what was going on between her friend and John Macmurray is moot. John breathed not a word of their relationship to anyone except his sister Ella. There is no mention in his journal of Betty until 18th July 1911, where he described playing golf on the links with Duncan and his sister as 'a forenoon whose pure pleasure will not soon be forgotten', before proudly recording her coming 68th in the University Bursary competition.[296] But whenever he had time off from the Gordon mission, he spent his weekends with the Campbells at their Aberdeen flat, as well with friends, picnicking in the surrounding countryside. Exactly when Nan Shepherd first met John we do not know. It is quite possible they encountered one another that searing summer of 1911.

In more than one of her works Nan based a character on John Macmurray.[297] In *The Quarry Wood,* he makes his entrance in Chapter Five: 'Luke came in on a day in August...lanky and sober-suited, a plain unsmiling youth'.[298] While his physical appearance is eerily resonant of Betty's description of the young John, Nan's disguise of his personality is a good one, even to those who knew him in person. To camouflage John in her text, Nan makes 'Luke' a composite character, a combination of the personalities of John Macmurray and Betty's brother, Duncan Campbell. Jocelyn Campbell, who knew John Macmurray very well, often thought 'Luke' might be modelled on John. It was just that some of 'Luke's' characteristics did not match the modest, self-effacing man she knew. 'I do not see the self-confident young student, conscious of his own intellectual power that Nan offers', she said, agreeing that this aspect of his personality is more like Betty's brother Duncan, who she described as 'a very complex character, quite charismatic'.[299]

In *The Quarry Wood,* when Martha first meets Luke, he and Dussie are already married and living, to her surprise, in a flat 'right on the top...above the shops and offices' on Union Street. '"You can get out on the leads"—Luke added his touch to the picture—"grand view. All up and down Union Street." ' Martha 'went to tea four stairs up...and Luke showed her his row of books'. She takes home as many of them as she can carry.[300]

The Forest Avenue flat Betty and Duncan shared was also on the top floor and was filled with books and reproduction art. In her memoirs, Betty recounts how Duncan's 'enthusiasms led him to buy books and pictures' a few reproductions by Corot and Burne Jones. 'Culture is what we are seeking, he said, "We must be connoisseurs of life and Art'.[301] The same words and almost identical description of the flat, its paintings and her brother's 'helter-skelter enthusiasms', appear too in Betty's *Out of the Earth.*

Effectively, what Nan has done is take Betty's and Duncan's life in Aberdeen and reconstruct it as Dussie's and Luke's in *The Quarry Wood.* John Macmurray was at Glasgow University, in her novel, Luke is a student at Aberdeen. This, of course, is to suit the narrative, but is also a way to disguise John Macmurray's identity. After Betsy Campbell was dispatched to the asylum, times were tough for Betty and Duncan. Without any income from their mother's writings, nor the promised pension from Laird Davidson, they were dependent on what Duncan could earn from his legal apprenticeship.[302] This, too, is reflected in *The Quarry Wood*: 'They lived on little...Dussie played eagerly at economy'.[303] Then there is the timing, which fits with when we know John Macmurray was in Aberdeenshire—in the summer of 1911— spending as much time as he could with Betty and her friends. ' "You must be our guest next coronation procession" ,'[304] Luke says to Martha: George V was crowned on 22nd June that year.

Close reading of *The Quarry Wood* armed with what we know of Nan's life and of her friends', along with analysis of Betty and John's autobiographical writings, makes it possible to penetrate the layers of camouflage in Nan's fiction and try to provide some insight into her emotions. What is clear from the narrative of *The Quarry Wood* is that during the first few years she knew John, he was no more than a friend, someone who was her intellectual equal, with whom she could spar and who could challenge her enquiring mind. 'For Martha, she was happy in the possession of books and gave no thought to the owner'.[305]

As for John, it is obvious from the journals he kept from 1908 to 1913 and from copies of his letters made by Betty (the Macmurrays destroyed most of their correspondence from this time when they left for South Africa in 1921) that at the time, he had eyes only for Betty. This, too, is acknowledged in *The Quarry Wood*:

> He had no more desire to offer love to a woman other than Dussie than to offer her a used teacup; but with his avidity for exploring other people's minds, he wanted as much intellectual comradeship as he could obtain, from men and women alike. He wanted to go on talking philosophy.[306]

There is no mention of Nan in John's journal entries. In Betty's memoirs, written when she was an elderly woman, Nan Shepherd's name is made conspicuous by its absence. In fact, only once is she referred to, along with May Anderson, as Betty's friend from her Aberdeen days. This is odd, given that over the years Nan often holidayed with the Macmurrays and even went out to visit them while they were living in South Africa. The two women were in touch until the end of their lives. Not long before Nan's death Betty visited Nan at Dunvegan. Betty herself died the following year in 1982.

John Macmurray's thinking, however, appears in *The Quarry*

Wood. Luke may have had eyes only for Dussie, but as an intellectual comrade, Martha, he declares '"was worth the knowing…She's so absolutely herself…so still and self-contained too. She's like—a crystal flame. Perfectly rigid in its own shape, but with all the play and life of flame"'.[307] To explain his ground-breaking philosophy, in *Freedom in the Modern World* John clarifies what he means by the difference between an 'unreal' and a 'real person'. An unreal person, he says, is one who tends to be overlooked in company, chatters a lot and thrusts himself forward, and all his talking makes him a bore. 'He is often, I find, highly intellectual but…for all his brilliance he always seems to be somehow up in the air, out of touch.' Unreal people, he continues, 'are vague, shadowy and indefinite, like ghosts when you get behind their defences'. Of a person who is 'real', however, he goes on:

> There is a wholeness or a completeness about him that I sense… he is very much himself…There is always a curious simplicity and definiteness about him—a quietness which is sure of itself…the quietness of a steady flame…A very real person seems to have a flame in him, as it were, that shines through and makes him transparent…He is significant, and significant just by being himself…because he is vital…It is rather a fullness of life, a completeness of life, an inherent livingness about him. Then I know I am dealing with a real person.[308]

While this first book of John's appeared in 1935 and included much of the content of his popular radio broadcasts of the early 1930s, its subject matter was the result of years of thought. The inclusion of such a similar description in *The Quarry Wood* suggests that not only was Nan aware of John's thinking during the years leading up to the publication of his book, but that she had discussed it with him.

Of course, we can only speculate as to whether or not John thought Nan was a 'real person', but his description of an 'unreal person' does not fit Nan's personality. Reticent, enigmatic, she never pushed herself forward. In company, she was a listener rather than a talker; yet she had presence, as Erlend Clouston says:

> What I remember most about Nan, I think what everybody would remember most about her, was her presence. There is a wonderful description in *The Living Mountain* of an eagle hovering imperceptibly on the thermals, vibrating with an energy but without really moving. Nan was a lot like that. She had this terrific presence, without forcing herself on you.[309]

Nan clearly worried that her own life experiences were not sufficiently camouflaged in her first novel. This is obvious from a letter of Mure Mackenzie's in which she tried to reassure her: 'Don't get the wind up: it doesn't look too much like personal experience—for one thing the most personal parts are fairly universal: for another, you have blended them very skilfully'.[310] In an unpublished poem of Nan's, written in May 1921, the effect of any revelation is made transparent: 'I tremble with fear that thou/Utter the secret that clarifies./O, I could watch my world blaze up and perish/As price of that dread knowledge!'[311] Nan's concern that her own life should not be discernible in her fiction was not just because she was a private person, it was also because of a fear of censure. As she said, not long before she died in that letter to Barbara Balmer, if she were to write about her life recognisably—she *would* have been 'for it'.[312]

The Quarry Wood was published in 1928 when Aberdeen society, unlike that of the more liberated, bohemian London, was judgmental and critical. 'I hear Aberdeen considers my books are "naughty"', Mure Mackenzie exclaimed in a letter to Nan written in around 1933, adding sarcastically, 'What's their adjective for Aldous Huxley??'[313] Nan could not afford a whiff of scandal—it would have affected her career as well as her family. It was imperative, therefore, that she at least appeared to conform to the role of respectable, modest, middle-class woman, foisted on her by society.

Prim and proper Aberdeen relished scandal. Gossip, and its effect on individuals living in small communities, is something Nan returns to time and again in her fiction. In *The Quarry Wood,* Stoddart Semple is 'greedy after the secrets of his neighbours; and loved his own importance when he could divulge what others did not know'.[314] The victim of Stoddart's tale-telling, poor Martha is horrified at the prospect of something she supposed 'as secret and self-contained' as her adventure with Luke being 'bounced and bandied in plain daylight'.[315]

For someone as private as Nan, too, the idea would have been abhorrent. And her relationship with Betty and John would become complicated: not long after their marriage she realised she was in love with her friend's husband. In the meantime, in October 1912, she went up to King's.

★ ★ ★

The imperial crown on the tower of King's College Chapel, built on the east side of College Bounds in the early sixteenth century, is a potent symbol. Feted by poets and revered by Aberdonians, for centuries it has symbolised the pursuit of knowledge—and Nan Shepherd who, like young Martha Ironside in *The Quarry Wood*, had yet to apprehend that man does not learn from books alone, was in passionate pursuit of all the knowledge the university had to offer.

King's College was built to house the university founded by Bishop Elphinstone in 1495 in Old Aberdeen. The city of Aberdeen as we now know it, developed from twin settlements which grew up around the Dee and Don rivers. One was famous for its commerce, the other for its learning. Quite separate from 'new Aberdeen', Aulton was a community of students, professors and cathedral clergy, all its houses owned by King's College. Despite being surrounded now by high-rise flats and some rather futuristic departmental blocks—including the turquoise-glassed statement that is the Norman Foster designed new library—it has managed to retain the atmosphere of a tiny university city.

When Nan arrived for her first term at university in 1912, Aulton's skyline, with its two historic symbols, the twin towers of St Machar Cathedral and the Imperial Crown of King's College, could still be seen from the northern end of Aberdeen's seafront promenade. Although little of Aulton remains today, those buildings which have survived are all safely preserved within a conservation area. What is left is College Bounds, the narrow street that runs into the High Street up to the Town House where it divides into the tree-lined Chanonry leading to St Machar Cathedral, and Don Street, which takes you to the Brig o'Balgownie over the river. The professor's houses, still stand too, gable-end to the road and among them little lanes of cottages, trees overhanging their low garden walls.

Two miles out from the centre of 'new' Aberdeen, there was still a lot of country in Aulton at the turn of the twentieth century. Surrounded by green fields, at least one town dairy still existed then. Somewhere in the huddle of houses behind the Town House and at the top of School Road you would invariably find a cow or two. Twice a day in summer the 'town cows' were driven through Aulton on their way to 'exercise' in nearby pasture. Udders swinging, tails twitching away flies, snorting breath and slavering on the pavements, they would appear round the front of the Town House and tangle with the procession of professors on their way home along the Chanonry for lunch. Heads down, tails up, the cows would empty themselves in the road, causing much disgusted umbrella waving and muttering amongst the professors.

King's College itself stands back from the road. In front of it is a green expanse of lawn and around it are buildings in Scottish Gothic style begun back in 1500 and completed in the second half of the nineteenth century. Passing through the archway and into the Quadrangle, in the

Nan during her undergraduate years.

angle of the south-east corner of the Chapel with its brightly coloured coats of arms, is the massive and rather ugly Cromwell tower. Six storeys high, square with a flat roof, it looks more like a Norman keep. Much more handsome is College Library, added after the merger of King's and Marischal's Colleges in 1860.[316]

Standing on the site of the ancient college kitchen the library was begun in 1870 and took fifteen years to complete. Extending eastwards for over two hundred feet, on its front is a sculptured unicorn, symbol of immaculate virtue and divine wisdom. Inside, its oak-arched lofty hall is impressive. 'No library in Scotland is so magnificently housed',[317] declared Sir Robert Rait, historiographer of Scotland and graduate of Aberdeen in 1894.

High and long, the narrow room lined with shelves housed an enormous collection of books, numbering hundreds of thousands, which spilled from the main hall into the stack room behind. With its sub-tropical temperature and general mustiness, King's College Library had its own unique atmosphere. A sort of 'fertile climate of the mind', John Allan describes it. The great library of King's remained for him a 'high-arched gate out of childhood to the living world'.[318] Its effect on Nan was no less profound:

In the long Library, too, with the coloured light filtering through its great end window, and its dim recesses among the laden shelves—where thought, the enquiring experiencing spirit, the essence of man's long tussle with his destiny, was captured and preserved: a desiccated powder, dusted across innumerable leaves, and set free, volatile, live spirit again at the touch of a living mind—she learned to be quiet…She stood a long time in a dark corner, watching the people come and go, touch books, open them, read them, replace them, carry them away: and at every contact she thrilled. "Spirit is released." The great room tingled with it.[319]

Now a young woman, her hair up for the first time (if constantly escaping its umpteen hairpins) and her skirts lengthened, it is not difficult to imagine Nan Shepherd at King's College, sitting beside the sundial or under the old trees, her nose in a library book, whiling away summer afternoons, the passing hours chimed by the college bell and answered, more punctually then, by the cathedral's. Or to picture her, a tall, slim figure, hat perched atop what would become her trademark halo of auburn plaits, walking across the Quadrangle carrying her bulging, leather dispatch case, lifting a hand to return old Dankester the Sacrist's wave of greeting.

An image of Nan as an undergraduate shows her, hat thrown off, dispatch case discarded, happy and relaxed, her legs outstretched on the grass—although it looks as if she was caught by surprise by the photographer (who was female, judging by the other hat and dispatch case). But if little seemed altered in the four hundred-odd years of the university's life, in terms of its buildings and its atmosphere of learning, by the time Nan started there in 1912, there had been changes at the University—all of which she was able to take advantage.

The opening of its doors to women in 1892 was the most momentous change at the university. Bajan, Semi, Tertian and Magistrar, the names given to first, second, third and fourth year male students, were adapted for the females—albeit half-mockingly. Twenty years later, when Nan arrived as a Bajanella,[320] the novelty of women in the university was wearing off. Mercifully, she and her female peers did not, unlike Myra Mackenzie,[321] have to endure the rather pitiless ribbing by male students and professors alike. At lectures, Myra sat at the front, properly dressed, of course, hat on head. The professors regaled the class with their dirtiest stories while the male students sitting behind Myra clapped and cheered, delighted by the blush gradually rising from the nape of her neck to her hairline. But her 'sheer pluck' eventually won their respect: Myra went on to be the first female graduate in medicine. 'By the end, there wasn't one of us who wouldn't have died for her' those same men said later, ashamed of their behaviour.[322]

At Aberdeen, the number of female students rose faster than in any of the other Scottish universities. By 1899 a quarter of the Arts students were women and by the time Nan was a Semilina in 1913, they formed almost half the faculty.[323] There were few student facilities in either King's or Marischal College then, but as most of the women were taking Arts courses they were based at King's, where their rapidly increasing numbers caused problems. A new sports pavilion opened in 1908 providing a meeting place for male students between lectures. But there was nowhere except the Ladies' Room for the women to gather together. This was a rather depressing place, the only place to sit was on a hideous crimson divan with broken springs, or hard, straight backed chairs. Nicknamed The Refrigerator, the room set aside for women at Marischal, known as The Coffin, sounds equally dismal.

In other universities, halls of residence were built which gave women students a social outlet (as well as presumably a 'safe, domestic' environment protecting them from any unchaste association with male students). But an attempt to set up a university hall of residence in 1898 proved disastrous: Castleton House, near King's, attracted few students and lasted only one session. Aberdeen women students apparently preferred the independence of living in lodgings, although it was not an independence enjoyed by Nan who remained living at home with her parents, commuting into Aberdeen daily for classes. If she minded, we do not know, but it would be hard not to, when your peers and friends were all enjoying this freedom. But as Betty was living with her brother in a flat in 'new' Aberdeen, Nan often went to tea there, mingling with other students at Duncan's 'salons', as he called them, gatherings which bear a remarkable resemblance to Luke's 'sky-highs' in *The Quarry Wood*.

On Friday evenings there were opportunities to socialise at the Society meetings, held at Marischal College. Not all the university societies were open to women. The Debating Society was not. Undeterred, the women set up their own and it was this Women's Debating Society, with its jolly sing-songs and informal 'At Homes', that became the focal point for the female students to mix with one another. Although, as the meetings were once a week, this had its limitations. Nan joined the Women's Debating Society and was a member, too, of the 'Sociolog'.[324] Both launched her into a maelstrom of new ways of thinking, but it is doubtful that she ever headed the debates;

Nan was never one to seek the spotlight. Her political stance was very much on the left, but she was quietly, rather than overtly, anarchic.

On the surface, Nan appeared every inch the lady. It is easy to spot her in group portraits, because she never crossed her legs, nor did she wear anything but skirts or dresses. Underneath, however, she was a mass of ideas—the sociolog personified—she was just less voluble than some of her peers. She was also still finding her feet. Nan has been described as diffident in her youth and although it is hard to reconcile this with the bubbling vivacity of her childhood photographs, if her portrait of Martha Ironside is anything to go by, there may be some truth in this.

Aberdonian café society was hardly Parisian. There was Kennaways at the top of Bridge Street, a cafe with rooms where societies held their annual dances, and 'Jack's', the Aul Toun Cafe, where hungry arts students could buy a bun. But aside from the university's societies, the only other occasions male and female students mixed were the annual picnics and the 'At Homes' at Marischal's Mitchell hall run by the professor's wives. Known as 'Cinderellas' (they ended before midnight) these happened two or three times a year—although anything as risqué as a tango was banned and chaperonage was strict. If you did manage to escape to the seating areas outside the hall in the adjacent natural history museums, romance had to be conducted in front of an audience of hollow-eyed, leering skulls. To go to a Cinderella, though, you had to be invited by a male student and the men often took a girl from outside the university instead.[325]

To begin with, Nan was not so much interested in socialising as the pursuit of knowledge. At learning, she shone. Top of the class at the High School, she excelled, too, at University. When the students gathered in the quadrangle around the glass cases displaying lists of their essay marks, her name was often at, or near, the top. 'Anna Shepherd, West Cults' appeared just as regularly topping the pass lists published annually in the local papers. She scooped first prize in subjects as diverse as Roman History and Zoology, as well as English and French and seventh prize for Latin.[326]

Of the characters Nan came across at university, there were three who stood out and to each she pays tribute in *The Quarry Wood*. There was Dankester, Sacrist of King's from 1891-1916[327], 'Daxter' as she rechristens him, is the 'old campaigner, like Odysseus full of wiles from warfare in the East'[328] who would wave to her as she crossed the Quadrangle each day. Nan was honoured by being admitted into his den, 'a narrow room at one corner of the quadrangle, the walls and table of which were covered with photographs'.[329] From the photographs

'Daxy' could reconstruct the inner history of the University since he had become Sacrist, and it was from him Nan learned the secrets of King's; tales which appeared in no official record and which she would use years later to inform her articles for the *Aberdeen University Review*.

Then there was Professor Thomson who taught Natural History, the only class for which arts students had to traipse to Marischal (which most of them did, to save the halfpenny tram fare). Many of them took his course, even those who weren't particularly interested in the subject, because Professor Thomson was renowned for the quality of his lectures. Everyone turned out for his first lecture of the season.[330] Nan's portrait of him in *The Quarry Wood* is reverent:

> The Professor, in a quiet voice that he never raised nor quick-ened, peopled for her the airs, glancing waters and grassblades, and the cold dark grave profundities of the sea. He had the tongue of a poet and of a humorist:…[Martha] lunched between her two diets of worship, between King's in the morning and Marischal in the afternoon.[331]

Professor Herbert Grierson.

Inspired as she was by Professor Thomson—and she clearly thrived on his lectures, earning herself First Prize in Zoology—most idolised by Nan was Herbert J. C. Grierson, immortalised as Professor Gregory in *The Quarrie Wood*.

Grierson, who took over from the beloved Professor Minto,[332] was made Chair of English Literature in 1894. As an undergraduate at King's he had studied English for a term and while he won a prize for the final examination, he had no qualifications in English Literature—but then at the time, few did. The first time Nan heard him lecture, she reconstructs in *The Quarry Wood*, describing it as one of those 'moments of apocalypse by which life is dated'.

The presence of women in the university had diminished some of the rougher university rituals, like ragging and gown-tearing (any student wearing a pristine scarlet gown or toga as they were known, would be teased mercilessly, their gown torn by others until it was antiqued into more respectable tatters). It had also inhibited some of the rowdiness in lectures, although foot-stamping to show students' appreciation continued. Everyone went to hear Professor Grierson's opening lecture too and the old Logic class-room was filled with students' voices 'and then two hundred pairs of feet were pounding the floor' as in came 'a long lean man, spectacled with a smile running up his face that drove the flesh into furrows'.

When Grierson smiled, his face became corrugated, there was not a smooth space left anywhere. Then he began to speak. 'He spoke like a torrent. He digressed, recovered himself, shot straight ahead, digressed again. He forgot his audience, turning farther and farther round till he stood side on to them, gazing through a window and washing his hands with a continually reiterated motion while he spoke his monologue. Then suddenly he would turn back upon the class with a wrinkling smile and swift amused aside; and a roar of laughter would rise to the roof, while the feet thundered on the floor'.[333]

Writing in 1960 after Grierson's death, Nan saw that intellectual ardour was something Grierson inspired in his students and that he shared:

He understood intellectual passion. It was the wide-ranging quality of his mind that caught us first: from the beginning he made us share his own exhilaration over the sheer abundance of knowledge. Later we came to understand how minute, precise and particularised knowledge had to be, and then saw to our delight that it need not cease to exhilarate.[334]

And she could still vividly recall not only Grierson's mannerisms but the content of his lectures too:

> how fresh our memories of him have remained…his ways—washing his hands as he spoke, turning gradually away from his audience till he was declaiming to the windows—and his voice, unlike any other voice one had ever heard, swaying and sonorous, chanting *Tears, idle tears,* or *Timor mortis conturbat me.* None of those who sat under him can hear those strains without his accent. Abundantly living with the peculiar life of a legend;[335]

In 1911, the year before Nan went up to King's, Grierson along with Professor W M Dixon of Glasgow University, had published *The English Parnassus,* which warrants a mention in *The Quarry Wood* and which Martha apparently devours from cover to cover. Then in 1912, Grierson published *Metaphysical Lyrics and Poems of the Seventeenth Century.* This, although she did not realise it at the time, was to prove a seminal influence on Nan's own writing and poetry. With hindsight, she recognised this:

> No Aberdeen student could leave his care without having undergone the impact of Donne, though we did not then realise what we were able to see later, that in his work on Donne and the Metaphysical Poets he was putting into the hands of generations to follow the material for a new approach to poetry. The influence of the seventeenth century metaphysicals on the poets of the 1920s was possible partly because Sir Herbert Grierson gave them a new approach to forgotten texts.[336]

The English Literature course at Aberdeen may have broadened Nan's reading and influenced her thinking but it did little to help, practically, with her creative writing. Save for contributions to the student rag, *Alma Mater,* there was no creative platform for her either. Cultivating a good, literary style, was part of the essay-writing process, but creatively, it constrained, as the poet Flora Garry, a student from 1918, says: 'You were inhibited all the time…[by] criticism of other people's writing… you were made to feel very self-conscious and self-critical…and there I was writing in a strange language all the time'.[337]

Like school, at university Scots was not tolerated. You might think in Scots, but essays were written in English; lectures were on English, not Scottish, Literature. When it came to a lecture on ballads, Scottish ones were included in the selection discussed, but as a nod, rather than a focus. Nan's genteel, middle-class background may have meant she was 'well-spoken' but it did not mean she was oblivious to these cultural concerns of identity in Scotland. Far from it. She drew attention to them in her novels and redressed the balance for her own pupils when she herself became a Lecturer in English Literature, as we will see. 'There is something to be said', she wrote to Christopher Grieve in 1938, 'for seeing to it that the droves of youngsters who descend on the schools have at least heard that Scotland has a literature, and that a country's poets are much more significant than her press'.[338]

Chapter Five

1913-1917

In 1913 the Irish question dominated the news. Ireland was still British-ruled but the threat of civil war festered. Europe was in the melting pot too; the Balkan situation causing unease. Christmas came and in Aberdeen, it was a white one: the fairy-tale kind, with snow and frost. Shops stayed open till ten on Christmas Eve and last-minute shoppers on Union Street mingled with people making their way to church services. Aberdeen's middle and upper class were spending the festive season as they always did: black-tied, young men escorting lustre-frocked women were out in force at all the usual balls and dances. A year later all the young men would be in khaki.

One morning, not long before the summer break of 1914, Nan was sitting in Professor Grierson's English class listening to him describe 'with a sort of chuckling gusto' how Hamlet had behaved as a university student. 'The bell rang—he laughed and desisted. And of course at the next lecture he had forgotten his sally. The war came rather like the ringing of that bell'.[339] On 4th August 1914, Britain declared war on Germany. By the end of September, a train carrying around a hundred casualties steamed into Aberdeen. It was the first of many.

The war's impact was felt by the university almost immediately. Men disappeared in droves. The Aberdeen University Corps was mobilised at once—half of them killed within the year. The only male students who remained were either below military age, medically unfit for service, studying medicine or, later on, those who had returned, wounded in action. Very quickly, the university became an almost women-only institution. The 'Cinders' and other forms of entertainment were dropped almost immediately in 1914. Sporting activity ceased and the athletic field was leased for grazing.

Nan was twenty one years old, a 'magistrella', in her third and final year[340] at King's when term began again on 18th October. Denuded of men, the university's women assumed responsibility for the running of student life. Nan took over editorship of *Alma Mater,*[341] which though slimmer, and fortnightly rather than weekly, continued to appear and was regularly dispatched to Aberdeen's student soldiers at the front. In December 1917, when she handed over the editorship to Isabella Smith, the magazine printed a tribute to Nan:

> *Alma Mater* is justly proud that it is one of the few British University magazines to survive in these troubled days, and it is to Miss Nan Shepherd that our thanks for this are greatly due. She has taken control in many emergencies. We owe her for much of the more difficult Editorial work. Miss Shepherd is not one of that nowadays too numerous body who forget that the welfare of *universitas nostrum* is the work of separate individuals.[342]

It was not only for Nan's administrative work as the 'business-like lady of galley slips and make-ups' however, that *Alma Mater* was grateful. A glance through its issues during those years shows she was a regular contributor to the magazine, not only providing 'some delightful and very personal prose' but much verse, too, 'some of it of great strength and beauty'.[343] (Although Nan was apparently not proud enough of any of it to keep it as the first poem in her manuscript notebook is dated February 1918.)

In the meantime, the war dragged on. As the backdrop for Nan's second novel, *The Weatherhouse,* the lexicon of war pervades her imagery. There are 'roads like mortar';[344] 'the shriek of wind' is like 'minesweepers riding the storm'; men are 'like machines walking'.[345] She forces Garry Forbes to spend a day and a night in a shell-hole with the body of another soldier and her graphic narrative of his twenty-four hours there, plunges the reader into the grim horror of war alongside him:

> The other fellow had died where he stood, slithered through his fingers and doubled over into the filth, and Garry was violently sick. He stared at the horror beside him, and now he saw that blood had coagulated in the pit between the man's knees and his abdomen. Poor beggar, he must have had another wound...He must get out of sight of that, but his feet were stuck, they would never pull free again. He stooped, plunging his arm in the slimy water. Branches came up, dripping long strings of ooze. Now he had detached the other man's feet; the body canted over, a shapeless rigid mass, and he saw the glaring eyes, the open mouth out of which slime was oozing...Rain fell, sullen single drops, that burrowed into the surface of the slime and sent oily purplish bubbles floating among the ends of branch that were

not submerged. Clots of blood appeared, washed out from the body. 'A wound I didn't know of" he thought. " A wound you couldn't see." Perhaps his own abdomen was like that—black with blood. Squandered blood'. Perhaps he too was wounded and did not know it…Delirium came on him[346]

The waste of war, the 'squandered blood' as well as the less obvious psychological wounds inflicted by war are all revealed here. Garry Forbes embraces the 'shapeless horror' of war embodied in the unidentified corpse and brings it out of the shell-hole with him. But so many men did not come home.

★ ★ ★

In 1915 Nan graduated M.A. The ceremony, held at noon on Saturday 10th July, was one of the quietest ever witnessed beneath the vaulted roof of Mitchell Hall[347] at Marischal College. Many of the undergraduates were in khaki. Service uniform was worn, too, by members of the university staff and glimpsed here and there among the audience filling the hall and galleries to overflowing. Dankester's mace was draped in crepe. [348]

Britain was now in its twelfth month of war and in Principal George Adam Smith's address, which was interrupted continuously by bursts of applause, he talked with pride of Aberdeen's contribution to the war effort.[349] The university's response to the war's call for recruits had been immediate, increasing steadily from week to week. Already the conflict had taken its toll; much of it on the 4th Gordons fighting in Flanders. Never in the university's history had there been such a drop in the numbers of matriculating students.[350] The names of the fallen were read out; among them were more than twenty of Nan's Arts Class of 1912. After prayers for the university's 'martyrs in a sacred cause' the degrees were conferred.[351]

Nan had won prizes once again that year: First in Roman History and French and Second prize in Systematic Zoology. Up she went, onto the stage below the massive, stained glass window to be 'capped', dismissed into the world with a little tap on the head to signify there was learning there. *'Initium sapientiae'*,[352] the Latin motto of Aberdeen University begins: 'the beginning of wisdom'. But there was still much for Nan to learn—and not just from books. So if, like Martha in *The Quarry Wood*, she thought that graduation was 'after all not very exciting but ordinary and inevitable, like stepping out of a train when you reach your destination',[353] there was always the possibility that her world might widen further and become less ordinary, through work.

Employment opportunities for educated, middle-class women were still limited in the early twentieth century. The only jobs open to them were teaching, nursing or secretarial work. Medicine appealed to a minority, but its training was expensive and not many could afford it. Unsurprisingly then, while a handful took up journalism, librarianship or secretarial and civil service posts, between 1901 and 1925 most of Aberdeen University's female graduates went into teaching.[354]

Immediately after graduation, Nan found work writing occasional pieces for Dr James Hastings, the editor of *Encyclopaedia of Religion and Ethics*[355] based in King's Gate, Aberdeen. A thirteen-volume work compiled between 1908 and 1927, the Encyclopaedia's goal was to cover the latest developments in knowledge and scientific thinking of the early twentieth century. Folklore, myth, ritual, anthropology and psychology were all included. Hastings was keen for Nan to go full time, but 'it was not a life that drew me', she said.[356] Teaching did not appeal to her either. What drew Nan, it turned out, was a life as a teacher of teachers—or more precisely, a lecturer of teachers—at the Training Centre in Aberdeen.[357]

Housed in a substantial, Victorian building[358] on St Andrew Street, the pride of the Training Centre was its Demonstration School[359] in John Street, where students could put teaching theory into practice. Lecture-rooms and school-rooms were already crowded by October 1915, when, fresh from university Nan joined the Training Centre—part-time to begin with, her duties mostly just essay-marking. That same year, demand for places at the college rose again when the government decreed that all teachers in Scotland's state schools were required to possess a 'parchment' (Teaching Certificate) and those teachers who were un-certificated either had to undergo a training programme or lose their status.

All students who intended to become secondary school teachers needed a decent Honours degree as well as a year-long professional training course. However, until the late 1920s, most of the Training Centre students were non-graduates who, on successful completion of its two-year course, could go on to teach at primary school level. It was these non-graduate students who came under Nan's tuition when she was taken on full-time as Lecturer in English in 1919.

The quality of teaching at the Training Centre during the 1920s was sub-standard according to Flora Garry and Winifred Black, both Aberdeen graduates taking its year long training course, and neither of whom felt they learned anything at all. 'I thought the lecturers were a waste of time. They were up in the air, they hadn't their feet on the good solid ground at all. I learned all my teaching from watching good teachers being actually in the classroom with class contact',[360] Flora Garry said. As a Lecturer in English, it was not Nan's job to train students in teaching techniques, and as graduates, neither Flora Garry nor Winifred Black would anyway have been taught by Nan.

In the 1940s, though, Grace Law was, and while, according to her, the standard of teaching wasn't much improved, Nan's lectures stood out. 'Other Training Centre lectures were boring', Grace recalled. 'The other staff weren't a happy lot.' 'Logic Annie', for example, shuffled about the classroom with a chair in her hand, set the chair down, then picked it up and shuffled along again holding it, over and over again. Rusk, the Education Lecturer had no originality, just read straight from a book. Nan was different'.[361] Grace, a gifted artist, would keep a sketchpad and pencil to hand so she could draw when the other lectures grew tedious. During Nan's, her sketchpad remained untouched.

Whether Nan was aware of the other staff members' lacklustre approach, we do not know. But as she was fresh out of university, the voices of Thomson and Grierson still ringing in her ears, she was no doubt fired with enthusiasm for her new role. We do have her views on lecturing though, voiced by Martha, in *The Quarry Wood*. During her year at the Training Centre Martha is taught by Lucy Warrender, 'A mine of information' she may have been, but she could not impart it:

> No doubt but that Miss Warrender knew her subject and lectured, as she talked, brilliantly and with authority; but she had no power to fuse the errant enthusiasms of the young minds before her, to startle them from their preoccupations and smite them to a common ardour to which all contributed and by which all were set alight. She had not discovered that lecturing is a communal activity.[362]

'She was the most fascinating teacher I have ever known' said Mary Gall, a student of Nan's in 1955 not long before she retired and proving that her enthusiasm never waned. 'Such insight she gave us. She often used a book when reading poetry aloud, but never any notes. She was witty, a great one for throwaway one-liners. Her comments on our essays were always encouraging, constructive, never unkind. She was a legend',[363] Mary continued, echoing Nan's own description of the inspirational Professor Grierson.

Lecturing, for Nan, was very much a communal activity. 'Technically I am Lecturer on Literature', she said, 'but I lecture as little as possible! I teach by reading and informal discussion.[364] During anyone else's classes, students never dared open their mouths. But Nan asked and invited questions; she expected students' active participation in class. She even set out her classroom differently to other lecturers, making her pupils the focus. Opening the door to Nan's classroom, facing you was a bank of three large windows. Nan positioned her desk diagonally across the room, so that the sun poured into it from behind her, lighting her students' faces. And always, perched on the corner of her desk was a vase filled with whatever was in season, brought from her garden: a christmas rose, a posy of primroses, a huge bowl of autumn leaves and chrysanthemums,

Although they were reinstated later, during her early years at the Training Centre, Nan discarded examinations. They were superfluous, she thought, an unreliable gauge of her students' achievements. At a party given by senior students for their lecturers, each of the guests was asked to wear or carry the clue to a famous book title. Nan chose Shakespeare's *Midsummer Night's Dream* and displayed the pass-list of her literature class with 99% passes for everyone.[365]

Nan's passion for literature was infectious. To feel this, you only have to listen to the one surviving recording of her talk on Charles Murray's poetry. Liberally sprinkled with quotations and injected with humour it provokes outbursts of laughter from her audience:

> Now Charles Murray was a man of the world, widely travelled, widely read, friend of all sorts of high and important people, advisor to a government but as a poet he is exactly right when he says that the Vale of Alford was "a' the warl" to him. It was his one theme. There's practically none of his verse that isn't about Alford. Even when he translates Horace, and he translates Horace quite frequently, "drift oxter deep hap Bennachie", although Horace poor fellow never heard of Bennachie, [laughter] I don't think you can get a better translation.[366]

She had a way of inflecting words and an ear for rhythm that you can imagine being very well the reason students of hers still hear the poems she recited to them echoing in their heads years later.

Nan's lectures were not confined to the Training Centre, however. From the late 1920s until long after her retirement 'Miss Shepherd' was in constant demand by local societies for lectures on literary topics ranging from Ballads to Burns to the Bard. After her talk to the Aberdeen Branch of the British Empire Shakespeare Society in 1935, a local reporter who was in the audience declared:

> I have seldom heard a speaker more fluent than Miss Nan
> Shepherd, who spoke for an hour and a quarter in a clear,
> incisive style, without a single reference to notes and she had
> memorised long quotations from Shakespeare which she
> recited with a fine sense of their dramatic value.[367]

But for every student at the Training Centre who was enthralled by
Nan's classes, there were some for whom they were way above their
heads[368]—and Nan had little patience for stupidity. She was never
mild, according to Jessie Kesson. 'She didn't suffer fools gladly. Not
being a fool, I didn't irritate her, but I remember her reaction to
someone who did. "Stupid woman", she snorted, "describing me as
a Wonderful Old Lady. *I* am an old Woman" '.[369] Malcolm Sutherland agrees: 'Always fun, she could be abrasive'. 'Joe, Joe. Don't be
mundane', she once ticked off Malcolm's older brother who had to
go home and look up the word in the dictionary.[370]

Nan's role, as she saw it, was to open and enrich her students'
minds by introducing them to writers, past and present—those
who had ideas to spread.[371] And it was not just English Literature
she covered. During her own education, scant attention was paid to
Scottish works. She set about redressing the balance, devoting at least
a term to Scottish Literature. 'From William Dunbar, Scottish makar
of the late fifteenth century to Perth-born poet William Soutar of the
early twentieth, 'Nan S' as we nicknamed her, took us through them
all right up to the modern day', Mary Gall recalls, adding, 'Edwin
Muir, Helen Cruickshank, Violet Jacob and Douglas Young were
favourites'.[372] At the end of the spring term, Nan earmarked a whole
day for Scottish culture. Then, says Mary, 'she would pick people
to sing, sometimes unaccompanied—from Burns's to Hebridean
work songs'. The summer term was devoted to modernist poetry, by
Scottish poets too, some of whose work was unpopular or misunderstood in their time.

One such controversial twentieth century writer was Christopher Grieve, mover and shaker of the so-called 'Scottish Literary
Renaissance' of the 1920s and 30s, whose vernacular verse under
his pseudonym, 'Hugh MacDiarmid', tended to polarise opinion. A
champion of MacDiarmid's work, in 1938 Nan wrote an article for
the *Aberdeen University Review* revealing an extraordinary insight into
his poetry at a time when it was being much maligned and miscon-
strued. Finding that the Training Centre library held some, but not
all, of MacDiarmid's volumes, she arranged for a number of his other
poems to be typed up for her students' use. As she said in a letter to

Grieve in January 1938, none of the students who passed through her classes at the Training Centre left without having read at least some of his work. She was realistic about its retention though, adding 'Heaven knows how much abides. One always hopes a little'.[373] Clearly, given ex-students' accounts of Nan's lectures, more than a little abides of their content. 'MacDiarmid's Little White Rose of Scotland, she loved that', remembers Mary Gall who then immediately quoted the last line of the verse: 'That smells sharp and sweet—and breaks the heart'.[374]

'You never associated a fanfare with her', Mary Gall goes on, 'she was always quiet and dignified'.[375] However, like all the best-remembered teachers, Nan had her eccentricities. In the 1950s, Jessie Davidson was the class mimic. Nan loved the Brontës' work and while explaining their biographies, to add context, would recite (a sigh after each sentence) 'and then Branwell died. And then Emily died. And then Ann died'. Then she would turn to gaze out of the window. Jessie Davidson, had this down pat, apparently. Sadly, nowadays, Jessie's memory is unmoored by Alzheimer's. But the impact Nan made on her as a student was illustrated by a recent episode when she was summoned back, briefly, by Nan's image. On a trip to the Makar's Museum in Edinburgh, arriving at the top of the spiral staircase where there is a photograph of Nan Shepherd on the wall, she stopped short before it. 'Nan S', she pronounced, and was suddenly present, the old Jessie again.[376]

According to Georgie Meldrum, a colleague who lectured in Home Economics, Nan had other idiosyncrasies, like 'a strange hessian dress' and 'an appalling brown coat which would go on in October and stay on till March'.[377] 'With her auburn hair, flecked with grey, neatly tied back, sometimes you'd think she was a flapper girl', Mary Gall chuckled. 'She had a penchant for shoes, not particularly fashionable then, the ones with a King Louis heel.'[378] There was also an extraordinary frock, which appeared to have been made out of two different patterned ones sewn together. But this *was* in the late 1940s when clothing was still hard to come by and as Grace Law says, it made a welcome change from the other staff whose clothing was boring, 'their dull outfits down to their ankles—never anything different'.[379] But Nan Shepherd was never one to follow 'the tricksey wiles of fashion'.[380] She never bobbed her long, auburn hair nor did she adopt the 1920s trend for trouser-wearing, even when walking in the hills. And despite the invention of the bra in 1914, Nan went without one long before the bra-burning seventies. She was unconventional in other ways too.

In the early twentieth century when it was a taboo topic both at home and in the classroom, Nan was unusually candid about sex.

Refusing to teach her Training Centre students Hardy's bowdlerised version of *Tess of the D'Urbervilles*[381] (produced in 1891, when the novel was refused for publication and from which Tess's seduction and rape were cut) Nan taught instead the full, unexpurgated version. 'She was no prude', Malcolm Sutherland confirms. 'Tell her a good, earthy story and she laughed her head off'. [382]

Not long after Nan became a full-time member of staff, the Training Centre and its methods came under attack by Duncan Clarke, an ex-teacher who had connections with the college and claimed he 'knew the ropes well'. In an article printed in 1922 in the *Aberdeen Journal*, Clarke suggested that the Training Centre was failing to weed out 'the tares from the wheat' and turn out men and women as efficient and capable of maintaining the traditions of the teaching profession as those who had qualified in the 'good old days'. The system was too slack, he went on, because the majority of students passing through the college were non-graduate men and women, some of whom had only intermediate and junior student certificates. His most scathing comments, however, he reserved for the women: in his opinion, the majority of women students 'make teaching only a half-way house to matrimony...some of them, at least, come to the Training Centre with the idea of having two years of a good time more than anything else.'[383]

1919, during which the Training Centre employed Nan full-time, was the same year the Sex Disqualification (Removal) Act declared that 'a person shall not be exempted by sex or marriage from the exercise of any public function, the holding of civil or judicial office or the carrying on of any civil profession'. The Act made it illegal for women to be excluded from most jobs, allowing them to hold judicial office and enter the professions. Women could now become magistrates, solicitors or barristers. But the reality was that upon marriage, many women still lost their jobs. Even those who defied these 'unofficial rules' found it hard to continue working once they had children. Out of over a thousand women graduating from Aberdeen University between 1901 and 1925 who were employed as teachers, by 1935 42% had 'retired' on marriage. In the 1930s only one tenth of married women worked. Society, predominantly, still saw women's work as 'in the home', caring, cooking and cleaning.

How incensed Nan must have been, then, by Duncan Clarke's comment which suggested that women had a choice; that they could marry and still hold on to their careers. As we know, Nan never married. This may well have been deliberate. As a full-time lecturer in 1919 she was on a salary of around £12 per month,[384] a not-inconsiderable sum in those days and as she had no overheads while she was living still at home, financially, she was pretty well-off. Why give that up? It was not just about the money though.

From correspondence, it is obvious Nan loved her job and was committed to her students. In the 1930s, when she was already a well-known author and poet, Nan told a journalist she thought more of her lectureship than she did of her work as a writer.[385] It was more than just a job, it was a vocation. In a letter to Neil Gunn in 1930 Nan described her role at the Training College as her 'heaven appointed task of trying to prevent a few of the students who pass through our institution from conforming altogether to the approved patterns'.[386]

Ruth Fletcher, a former student who went on to become Head of a London comprehensive, a magistrate and a lecturer herself, described Nan's lectures as revealing a feminist approach ahead of her time.[387] As Nan claimed to write no notes for her lectures,[388] we have no evidence to confirm this, but other ex-students agree that she was certainly feminist in her thinking. According to Grace Law, she encouraged women to just do things—hill walking, for example. 'She said women had a place doing that too, not just sitting by the fire knitting'.[389] She often took groups of her students hill-walking and inspired Grace Law to start up a hill-walking club of her own in Banff.

She also took a keen interest in her students once they had left the Training Centre. Long into her retirement she was invited to stay with numerous former students and did so, claiming later that she had learnt the geography of Scotland over the years by visiting them in one-teacher schools from Shetland to Galloway.[390]

In the summer of 1931, while Mary Lawson went on a conducted tour of Paris, Nan travelled all over Shetland on holiday, in the sidecar of one ex-student's motorcycle. To reach another, Nan tramped five miles up the glen, knapsack on her back, to sleep on a makeshift bed in the parlour. The next morning Nan went with her to the school, told some stories to her pupils and tramped the twelve miles across the hills to the railway line.[391]

Right up to retirement, Nan's interest in and commitment to her students was fervent. Unwell for four weeks in the Autumn of 1955, she asked her class of thirty five to write short essays on themselves, not just about their literary tastes, but about their personal likes and dislikes. She wanted to get to know them, so that on her return she would have some insight into them all. When Nan did retire, Mrs Balneazes, who eventually took over from her, was a very different proposition. You sat up straight, you did not open your mouth in lectures and there was never a posy on *her* desk.[392]

Frank Shepherd in his
early twenties.

Mary Lawson.

★★★

Both Shepherd children were bright, ambitious and hard-working. In 1915, the same year Nan graduated from King's, Frank graduated with a B.Sc., in Engineering from the University of Glasgow. Frank's school career had been as exceptional as his younger sister's. He left Robert Gordon's College in 1908 with 'Highers'[393] in Chemistry and Physics, Higher English, Maths and Science and Latin, as well as passing the University prelims. In April 1908 he began a four year apprenticeship at James Abernethy & Co in Ferryhill, and like his father (who was by then Works Manager) he took evening classes.

From then on he was hardly seen or heard of in Cults. In 1912 he moved to Glasgow to start at the Royal Technical College, lodging with his uncle, the Reverend Andrew Shepherd, his wife Jane Ann and their three daughters at the Manse in Chryston. During the summer vacations, rather than coming home, he found work as a draughtsman, first at the Coventry Ordnance Co, then with Grice's Gas Engine Co in Carnoustie and lastly with the Singer Sewing Machine Co., in Clydebank. In 1913 he was admitted to the Institute of Mechanical Engineers and was awarded the Neilson Gold Medal at the same time as his degree.

It was from Glasgow that Frank sent the one surviving letter we have of his to Nan. It was written in his final year at college, just before exams: 'I hope you don't faint when you get this newspaper', he teased. 'It's quite the longest letter I ever wrote in my life, so you may think yourself highly honoured, my lady. My news has run dry now, so I'm going to bed. Tata, FJS'.[394] Frank's handwriting is upright, exuberant, the words joined and running into one another, suggesting he was writing quickly, his thoughts tumbling on to paper. What came before in this 'newspaper' as he calls it, can only be speculated.

Beneath his signature—enormous, shaded and calligraphic initials—Frank has added a stick-figure drawing of a tall man wearing a hat, embracing and kissing the much smaller figure of a woman. In fact, so much smaller is the female figure that she has either been placed on a step or lifted into the air in order to expedite the kiss. Next to it, Frank has written, 'What I'll be seeing at our front gate (perhaps)' and below this the initials 'A.S.' with a scribble the other side of his sketch which reads: 'sorry I had to tilt the noses so far up but they would have jammed each other'. 'A.S.' might stand for Anna Shepherd. However, aside from the kiss (which does not look filial) Nan was tall like her brother, ruling her out as the diminutive stick-figure of Frank's drawing. Given the timing of the letter, the tiny woman was someone else, someone whose initials would be 'A.S.' on marriage to Frank.

In *The Weatherhouse* Nan's picture of her tall, red-headed brother (disguised as David Grey) is of a wild and fiery-tempered young man who had inherited his father's capacity for engineering and his power over those who worked for him. 'John Grey saw his own dreams fulfilled in his son. Proud of his achievements, his father kept himself abreast of modern engineering developments and together they amassed a library of professional books on the subject'.[395] Frank, with his apprenticeship, experience and academic qualifications behind him, looked set for a bright future. He would have been quite a catch. He might have married anyone he pleased. He chose the girl-next-door. On 12th December 1916 at Cults's United Free Church, twenty-six year old Frank Shepherd married Alice Margaret Thomson, four days before her twenty-sixth birthday. Along with Alice's younger sister Harriet, Nan is recorded as a witness on their marriage certificate.

After the death of her merchant father, George Thomson, in December 1902, Alice, her mother Isabella and three of her sisters, Janet, Harriet and Jennie, moved thirty miles south from the family home in Longside to 'Briars', a large, granite detached house flanking Dunvegan's east side. The Thomson marriage, George's second,[396] produced eight children in all, six of whom were girls.[397] Isabella Thomson the oldest of the six daughters, born in 1885, died two years before her father aged fifteen. Charlotte, the youngest of the Thomson brood was born in 1903, a couple of months after her father's death. Marriage for her remaining five daughters,[398] in 'Mrs Bennett' fashion, must have been on high on Mrs Thomson's agenda.

Separated only by a garden wall for years, the Thomson and Shepherd children grew up together. Frank and Alice were close in age and Harriet, born in 1893, was Nan's contemporary, too. In the only photograph we have of her, a smiling Alice looks impish, a good match perhaps for the fiery Frank. Fine-boned, her dark hair in untidy waves around her face, she is astonishingly pretty—and petite, at least a head smaller than Nan. But from 1912, Frank had hardly been at Dunvegan. If we can speculate that his long letter to Nan was on the subject of his plans to propose to Alice, he came home only briefly to do so, before heading off again.

The war was in full swing by the time Frank graduated. He did not enlist. Instead he put his skills and training to use at the Royal Arsenal in Woolwich. Dedicated to the delivery of death, the Royal Arsenal also killed off many of its workers—although this was kept quiet so as not to discourage the war effort. It was a factory like no other. Just a piece of open ground in South-East London for gun-testing in the

1600s, by the time war broke out in 1914, the Arsenal was a sprawling mass of different, semi-independent departments desperately in need of modernisation.

The Arsenal's stock of artillery shells, designed for use against armies in the open, were pretty much useless in the trench warfare of WW1. Bigger and better guns were needed. Supplies of high explosive shells ran low and of those that did reach the front, a third were dud. Minister of Munitions from May 1915, David Lloyd George sprang into action. Money was pumped into the Arsenal and thousands more workers were employed—thirty thousand of whom were women brought in on war-only contracts to work in the less highly-skilled areas, supervised by men.

Working conditions at the Arsenal were ghastly. Hours were long: a thirteen day stint from 7am till 7pm was followed by another from 7pm till 7am, with only one day off in between. Conditions were overcrowded and the ventilation was poor; it was either too hot or too well-ventilated making it freezing cold. Shortly after Frank joined the Arsenal, in August 1915, the first workers became ill, among them the 'canaries' whose skin turned yellow from handling the particularly hazardous TNT. The deaths began the following year in March 1916. From then on, there were two fatalities a week. [399]

The increased workforce meant more housing was needed and in 1915 the government built the Progress Estate, as well as large swathes of temporary hutments. Frank, however, had found lodgings on the nearby Corbett estate and by February 1916[400] was living at in a red brick, bay-windowed three bedroom terraced house in Earlshall Road, Eltham.

The Eltham Park Estate was bought by Archibald Cameron Corbett in 1900 when it was little more than a village street in an area still rural, surrounded by woodland. In the middle of it all, not far from the railway station was the stately, if somewhat dilapidated, Well Hall House.[401] A temperance reformer, Corbett spent fourteen years developing the estate to provide neat rows of well-built, solid suburban housing aimed at skilled working and middle class tenants. Corbett was Glaswegian and many of the estate's road names are Scottish.[402] Perhaps this made Frank feel more at home. Two streets away, running parallel to Earlshall Road was Dunvegan Road.

Keen to promote healthy living, Corbett allocated space on his estates for churches, schools and shopping parades, as well as gardens to the front and back of his houses. At Eltham, he also earmarked forty-one acres of public parkland.[403] Most of the front gardens are now turned to off-street parking, but the integrity of Corbett's Eltham estate remains.

The terraced houses were built in pairs, each the mirror of its adjacent twin, so that the front doors were next to each other, sharing chimney stacks with their neighbours on the other side. The low brick, white-capped walls, topped with iron railings, border wide pavements. A tree is planted in each front garden and the black and white tiled path to the front door in many cases remains intact. Corbett's estate today is an affluent-looking place, the houses are well-maintained, clean-bricked, their white framed windows pristine and it is still a relatively peaceful, leafy, residential area—no doubt effected by the numerous speed bumps on its wide streets.

Sometime later in 1916, Frank leased another house in the adjacent street. 156 Greenvale Road was much bigger. With four bedrooms, an upstairs bathroom, a top floor for nurseries and staff, its wide hallway leading to the parlour, kitchen and sculleries behind, this was very much a family house. Marriage and children were on Frank's mind. At one end of Greenvale Road lay the woods and at the other, Craigton Road, which led, after a conveniently short walk, to Well Hall Station.[404] No doubt Frank commuted by train on the South-Eastern railway to the Royal Arsenal. But given the long working hours and the thirteen-day shifts with only one day off in between, he would had little time to enjoy Corbett's recreational spaces or his own garden.

While we do not know what Frank's responsibilities were to begin with, by 1916 he had sufficiently impressed his employers to earn a promotion to night superintendent (or 'shop manager' as he described it)[405] in the new fuse factory, where several thousand women were employed. During the night shift, the place was poorly lit. White aproned, their hair gathered into matching white caps, the women sat on wooden chairs at low tables. One lamp, hung low, at head level, afforded them just enough light to see what they were doing. As super-intendent, Frank had his own office on the shop floor, coming out at regular intervals to patrol the lines of 'munitionettes' and oversee their work.

By 8th November 2016, concerns about the working conditions in the new fuse factory were raised with the Minister of Munitions. Replying on behalf of Lloyd George, Mr Primrose said it was regret-table but inevitable owing to the crowded state of the Arsenal and that every effort was being made to provide better lighting and relieve the congestion.[406]

Consumption (tuberculosis) was rampant. The coughing went on and on. It was such a problem in the early twentieth century that sanitariums were built in the countryside with huts in the grounds so patients could gather to breathe fresh air into their damaged lungs.

Still, death claimed rich and poor alike. On top of that, the amount of asbestos used in the factories was so great it lay in carpets so thick on the floors you could see your footprints in it. Asbestos and a smoking habit were sure to bring death and in almost every photograph of Frank, his pipe is clenched between his teeth. Predictably, Frank's health began to fail.

From July to November of 1916, over four hundred thousand British soldiers were lost during the Somme during a battle that, in all, saw over a million casualties. Scarcely a family in the land was unaffected by loss. The Shepherds must have been thankful they were still intact. In December, Frank came home to Cults to marry his childhood sweetheart and he and Alice returned to South-East London, setting up home together in their big, family house in Greenvale Road.

Their wedded bliss was short-lived. Frank was probably already unwell when he and Alice married. Tuberculosis is an insidious disease which can go undetected for some time. One of the first of its symptoms is significant weight loss, but of course, this could have been put down to the stress of Frank's long working hours and little time to eat. If Frank already had T.B. by the time he started work at the Arsenal, his illness would only have been exacerbated by the appalling working conditions there.

As we know, the Shepherds had connections in South Africa— descendants of Jeannie's grandmother on the Smith side of the family. Several of them had emigrated there and they hoped that in its warmer, drier climate, Frank would recuperate. On 28th February 1917, Frank and Alice boarded the '*Norman*', a Union-Mail steamship bound for Cape Town from where they journeyed inland to Bloemfontein.

Nicknamed 'city of roses', Bloemfontein[407] sits in central South Africa on the southern edge of the Highveld, bordering the Karoo. In the 1900s it was quite a substantial settlement, its houses clustered either side of a long, wide, sandy road. Snow is rare. The winters are cool and dry, summers blisteringly hot relieved by afternoon thunderstorms. It should have been the ideal climate for Frank's lungs to heal. Instead, he died on 19th May 1917 and was buried in Bloemfontein's cemetery.

The telegram arrived soon after at Dunvegan. From out of his leather bag, the little post-office boy, smart in his uniform, his belt and his badge, delivered Frank's death to the Shepherds. Nan gives us an idea of how the news might have affected her father in *The Weatherhouse:*

His only son, a brilliant boy, unlike his father in appearance and temperament, had inherited and intensified his genius...John Grey saw his own dreams fulfilled in his son. The boy marched

triumphantly through school and college, and, entering
Woolwich Arsenal in the war, became night manager of a
new fuse factory. His work was his passion. Brilliant, inventive, steady in work as his father, he lacked the older man's
composed serenity. The artist's sensibility, the lover's exaltation,
went into his work; and broke him. He developed tuberculosis, and in three months' time was dead.

John Grey took the blow in silence. He spoke to no-one of his
son, but went on his steady quiet way. Only the professional
books that he and the boy together had amassed ceased to
interest him. He never read them again, and his tired mind had
no further concern with the modern developments of which,
for the boy's sake, he had kept himself informed.[408]

It's not a surprising reaction. The Shepherds' loss was not unusual. So
many men did not come home from the war and in those days, rather
than show weakness, you kept that upper lip stiff. Frank's death was not
discussed outside the family. Even in the 1950s when Nan was close to
retirement from the Training Centre, former students say that although
she never revealed anything about her own family life, she was fond of
the First World War poets, Owen and Sassoon in particular. Relaying the
moment Wilfred Owen's mother received the telegram informing her
that her son had died on Armistice Day, Nan's voice would crack and
she would turn to the window, looking towards Robert Gordon's on the
street opposite.[409]

Forced to suppress her grief in life, Nan expressed it in her fiction.
Of her three novels, *The Weatherhouse* is the one most heavily shadowed
by the war. Wounded in the trenches, a traumatised Garry Forbes returns
to Fetter-Rothnie and learns that Louie Morgan is claiming to have
been engaged to David Grey, his engineer friend, who had died of T.B.
Through Garry Forbes, Nan voices her anger and resentment over the
way her brother died: '[He] was the cleanest thing on God's earth. And
not killed, you know. Not a clean, sharp death. Rotted off. Diseased. To
die like that! It's an insult. A stupid, senseless, dirty joke…'.[410] Brooding,
strong, with more than a hint of irony in his expression, Frank stares back
at us from the few remaining photographs of him. His death, along with
so many others in WW1, was such a waste.

John Shepherd's hopes and dreams, which he thought would be
fulfilled in the son whose experience had escaped beyond his father's
at so many points, were dashed. He put his energies into his garden and
into his work, which, since his retirement from the Ferryhill Foundry
in 1914, was for the Munitions Department in Aberdeen as a voluntary,

unpaid Inspector of Shells. At night he toiled home exhausted only to be up with the light the following morning to work in the garden. He took on more land to grow more vegetables, distributing them among the local hospitals. He kept himself busy. But John's own strength was beginning to fail and in what seems an eery coincidence he would die in 1925, eight years after his son, on the very same date: 19th May.

And what of Alice, Frank's bride, widowed so soon after their marriage? Travel during the war was difficult. The Armistice was signed in November 1918 and Alice remained in South Africa for a few months more before returning to Britain. On the 8 April 1919 in Durban, Alice boarded the '*Saxon*', another of the Union-Castle mail steamships bound for Plymouth. Her occupation is given as 'housewife' on the ship's passenger list, a first glance at which suggests Alice was travelling alone. Closer scrutiny reveals she was not. It turns out that after Frank's death, she had given birth to a child, a daughter born sometime between September 1917 and February 1918.

Alice Shepherd (back row, second from left, kneeling behind her daughter). Next to her, clockwise, are Mary Lawson, Nan, Euphemia Cruden, Jeannie Shepherd and Sheila Roger.

One photograph exists of Alice and her daughter, a group shot on the lawn at Dunvegan taken around 1921. A healthy-looking, tanned Alice kneels in the back row, alongside Mary Lawson and Nan. Sitting on the ground in the front row is Jeannie Shepherd, her arm around a four year old Sheila. Next to Sheila and in front of Alice, is a small girl, white-socked legs stuck out straight in front of her, frowning into the sun. She might be a little younger than Sheila, or she might just be petite like her mother, but she is all glossy bob and fringe and already has Frank's fierceness about her. Rather than at the camera, Nan, Jeannie and Alice all gaze at her.[411] Absent from the photograph, perhaps because he was the one taking it, is John Shepherd. It's a happy image. Having their grand-daughter back in Scotland may have gone some way towards making up for the loss of their son. If so, it was short-lived. She died aged six.[412]

Poor Alice. After the death of her husband and then their daughter, life must have looked bleak.[413] But Alice did not remain a widow, or childless, for too long afterwards. On 23rd April 1927, she married George Wilson, a banker in Torphins. Twenty-one years her senior, George was a widower. His first wife, Rebecca Rillet Eno, had died in Balgownie Nursing Home in Aberdeen in March 1923 leaving him with a son, Andrew, who was fifteen when his father married Alice, their housekeeper.[414]

An imposing, detached, granite villa, Bank House on St Marnan Road in Torphins, is substantial. George Wilson was clearly a man of means. Whether this was a marriage of convenience can, of course, only be conjectured, nor do we know how long Alice was working at Bank House prior to marrying George. It is possible that she was housekeeper there before his wife died and that she stayed on, running the household and helping with Andrew. However, a daughter, May, was born to them in 1928, a year after their marriage which was to last twenty years until George's death in 1949. Alice herself lived to be seventy-two before dying on 1st October 1963 in Woodend Hospital, Aberdeen. After George's death she had moved to a bungalow in Cairns Road, Peterculter only 4 miles up the road from Cults. But how close Nan and Alice were is not known. Nor do we know if they kept in touch after she remarried.

On 27 December 1918, Nan penned 'Lux Perpetua'.[415] First published in the *Scots Magazine* in August 1929, it was included, too, in *In the Cairngorms*. In printed form, the poem appeared as follows:

Lux Perpetua

Nobis cum semel occidis brevis lux ...
A sweep of sky went round and round the place;
  The land ran sloping away to the left and right
And the hills looked low across that width of space,
  The sea, blue-white.

O clarity, colour, the height of a winter noon,
  The flocking of stormy gulls in the stormy sky,
The flocking of winds together, the flight, the croon
  Of their passing by,

And a hush behind them that lay on the wood like a spell,
  A hush that was quick with the underthrob of sound.
After, to south-south-west through asphodel
  The sun slid round.

Last, the dark; and out of the jewel-blue east
  Sudden the first full star, the oft-approved,
That with the tranquil motion of a priest,
  Somewhat removed.

Above the restless turmoil earth must know,
  Gazing through clear aerial lucency,
Looks on the face of light, until the glow
  Perceptibly

Shines from his own devoted countenance;
  So mediates the evening star, so keeps
The sun, and prophesies the lights that glance
  Through vaster deeps.

And we returning take the star of eve,
  We mortal and our sun how soon gone down,
For proclamation, and thereby believe
  The wild renown

Of life whose long potentialities
  Quicken, like flame from perishing star to star
Through unimagined primal silences
  And vaults afar,

New revelations of the only Light,
  Illumining awhile again returning
Within the unbroken splendour infinite,
  The always[416] burning.

A lament for the fleeting life ended and a reminder that death comes
to us all: 'We mortal and our sun how soon gone down,' the poem
works on a universal level—a comfort to the bereaved. The Latin
sub-heading is Catullus's[417] which can be translated: 'as for us, once
our brief light sets … ', the ellipsis suggesting what is not said or what
follows on. The next line of Catullus's verse is 'we must sleep a never
ending night'. And it could be anywhere, this sweep of sky around
the hill, the sea blue-white in the distance. Some verses sing, some,
it has to be said, are a little lumpy in their rhythm. This may have
been deliberate, of course, to unsettle the reader. But amongst all the
repetition, the 'flocking of stormy gulls', 'the flocking of winds', there
is a sense of anger in the repeated 'ck' and at the same time a soothing
underlined in the repeated 'hush'.

The metaphors used to symbolise the transition from life to
death, the earth's turn from light to dark and day to night, are universally recognised, traditional elegiac devices. So, too, is the lily, which
Nan has dressed in more Eurasian garb as the asphodel, an allusion
to the everlasting flower said to grow in the Elysian fields where
ordinary souls were sent to live after death.

There is a sense here, that life has gone beyond and goes on,
repeating its pattern in the stars, flickering and extinguished again.
The priest appears to be the only religious allusion, followed by
'somewhat removed', as though faith is being questioned, replaced
by a belief in the landscape and the eternal vault of sky. The last short
line of each stanza leaves its own haunting, an enforced pause before
leading on to the next. By the last line there is some resolution, too,
as well as a return to the poem's title in the flame 'alway burning', a
perpetual light.

Nan's manuscript version of the poem is interesting. Not only
was the poem several verses longer originally, but there is a dedication: 'To A.M.S. In Memoriam' and beneath this, the following:

At the monument of one Boswell, of whom be it said, as of
Cestius:

'Boswell in life maybe
Slew, breathed out threatening;

I know not. This I know: in death all silently
He does a rarer thing
"In beckoning pilgrim feet
With granite finger high
To where from sea and stream the moors rush up to meet
The silence of the sky."

> (With apologies to Thomas Hardy.
> Also to Shelley and Keats.
> Also to Boswell, whose tablet
> proclaims him a model laird.)

Is it too much of a stretch to think the poem was written as consolation for a grieving Alice Margaret Shepherd? The monument in question is a circular tower of granite ashlar with a crown spire (now collapsing inwards on itself). Boswell's monument was erected by his grieving widow, Margaret, 'as solace in her bitter bereavement' after John Irvine Boswell's death in 1860. It is a well known local landmark sitting on the top of Auchlee Hill, west of Portlethen and not far from Cults. No doubt Nan and her brother had often walked there and as Alice, too, lived in Cults, she may well have accompanied them. Knowing this, the poem becomes more personal, the hill and sweep of land easier to locate and the poem, with its universal imagery, more private than public. Which is probably why its 'preface' was left out in the printed version.

The apology to Boswell is for infusing him with Frank's fiery temperament in the first stanza. The inscription carved on one side of the monument's octagonal base gives a short biography of the laird who does indeed sound a model one, responsible for making the fields more productive, blowing up rocks, fallowing and dunging the land on his Kingcausie estate. Hardy and the Romantics, Shelley and Keats are clearly influences, hence Nan's humble apology, as well as nods to previous famed elegists. The Pyramid of Cestius, a funeral monument in Rome built into the Aurelian walls, like Shelley's Ozymandias, is Nan's satirical allusion to the ruins of a great civilisation, symbolic of man's short-lived existence and nature's perennial power. Nan's elegy, of course, serves as its own monument. Whether or not it was written as solace for Alice, it was probably cathartic for Nan to write.

After Frank's death, Nan consoled herself by reading poetry. Emily Dickinson's, in particular, seems to have helped. 'We never know when we are going/We jest and shut the door—/Fate following behind us bolt it/And we accost no more', she copied into *Gleanings* on a couple of pages devoted to Dickinson snippets which included, 'Each that we lose takes part of us;/A crescent still abides,/Which like the moon, some turbid night/Is summoned by the tides', and the following verse, which seems somehow the most conspicuous of the Dickinson extracts:

> The going from a world we know
> To one a wonder still
> Is like the child's adversity
> Whose vista is a hill,
> Behind the hill is sorcery
> And everything unknown,
> But will the secret compensate
> For climbing it alone?[418]

Death is inevitable, Dickinson's poem says and then uses the analogy of a child's excitement on approaching a hill, not knowing what lies beyond it. It ends with a question, whether the knowledge of what wonders lie on the other side make the journey any less lonely. But the use of 'sorcery' is interesting. An afterlife seems here to be suggested, not so much in a religious context, but in the realm of magic.

It is not hard to see why this poem of Dickinson's appealed to Nan. It chimed with her own experience of loss, her thoughts on an afterlife and it employs a hill climb as metaphor. She knew all about the secret that was worth the solitary climb, too. When she was not much more than a child she had toiled alone up Creagh Dubh to find the glittering white Cairngorm plateau spread out before her.[419] But Dickinson's poem would also have had a deeper significance for Nan, whose faith in Christianity during the First World War and after the death of her brother, was wavering. She began to search for answers outside institutional religion.

Chapter Six

1917-1919

Nan was not alone in her religious about-turn. For many, the war triggered religious questioning. While she continued to attend the Cults Free Kirk services for a while—and perhaps until her father's death in 1925—she went out of respect, not because of any religious belief. Seeking answers elsewhere, she discovered them—in alternative philosophies not found within the Free Kirk's granite walls. In 1917, it was not just Lafcadio Hearn's writing on Eastern philosophy that intrigued her. Around the same time she discovered George William Russell's work.

Better known by his spiritual name 'AE',[420] George Russell was also an active Irish nationalist, a painter and writer as well as a poet and a key figure of the 'Celtic Twilight', the Irish Literary Renaissance. From 1870 until the end of World War 1, Ireland was blasted by a wave of fierce, political nationalism. Home Rule was the country's focus, but in 1891, when Parnell fell from power, a disillusioned and embittered Ireland turned away from parliamentary politics and the modern literature of Ireland began. Closely linked to a revival of interest in all things Gaelic, the Celtic Twilight gathered strength, becoming a vigorous literary force centred around William Butler Yeats.

Yeats initially started the movement in English, 'the language in which Modern Ireland thinks and does its business'. But discovering that the Irish people had become inured to language by endless political speech-making and as a result, read little, he found a more effective way to reach them, establishing the Abbey Theatre with the help of the writers Lady Augusta Gregory and John Millington Synge. Yeats's plays were in English but Gregory's dramas were in the English spoken by the working class people on her family's Irish estates, a form of English which owed much of its syntax to Gaelic and much of its vocabulary to Tudor English. Synge's mature works, too, were cadenced with the language of the 'peasants' as Yeats puts it. This use of language became a powerful instrument.[421]

Finding (and agreeing on) a language for a Scottish literature was one of the central issues of the 1920s Scottish Literary Renaissance in which Nan was to play a part. And although he would change his tune, in 1921 when the movement was in its infancy, the poet Hugh MacDiarmid argued that a modern Scottish literature would need to be in English. Scots had declined since Burns, he said, and was not suitable for the ambitious literary aims he had in mind and used the work of the Irish revivalists to support his argument. 'Synge, Yeats and other great Irish writers found no difficulty in expressing themselves in an English which they yet made distinctively Irish'.[422]

Nan's slant on the use of Scots to create a national literature we will come to later, because in 1917 it was not the Irish revivalists' use of language that intrigued her. There is a nod to Yeats in *Gleanings*,[423] but it was AE's take on Theosophy and his poetry that excited her most and to which she devoted several pages. She had got hold of a volume of his collected poems published in 1913 and copied six of them into her notebook. Aside from Rabindranath Tagore, she privileges no other writer with so much space.

When AE developed an interest in Theosophy it was a relatively new philosophical movement. Not a religion in the ordinary sense any more than the Theosophical Society was a Church in the ordinary sense, the movement began in 1888 with the publication in New York of Helena Blavatsky's *Secret Doctrine*. Blavatsky was a high-ranking, plump, dark, Russian woman with unsettling pale eyes. She may well have been a charlatan. Apparently, in order to gain converts to Theosophy she felt obliged to perform miracles which on several occasions were proved to be fake. Yet despite this, she attracted quite a following.

Rooted in the universal laws of nature, Theosophy was a not new idea. Blavatsky herself described it as an archaic wisdom-religion known for centuries by any country with an ancient civilisation. It was defined by de Purucker (fourth leader of the Theosophical Society) as 'the formulation of the truths of Nature—not of outer Nature alone… but more particularly of the vast causal realms behind the outer Nature which our senses know—behind the outer veil of Reality; for these inner and causal realms are the inner Heart of Things.[424]

Fundamental to Theosophy's teaching is man's oneness with the universe. In simple terms, Theosophists believe there is one infinite Life, without beginning or end. To them, no such thing as dead matter exists in nature, instead every atom is a spark of the one Life and the Divine unity behind this spirit and matter, which some call God and others call That,[425] is so beyond comprehension, that human beings can only stand in awe of it, let alone describe it. Man on earth, then, is the life-atom of this Divine unity. Immersed in matter, man can be seen as a pilgrim seeking a way back to the source and at a certain point in man's experience an inner awakening occurs. Then, it becomes possible for him or her to step knowingly on what is called 'the path'. [426]

There are obvious parallels with the Eastern philosophies Nan was exploring through Hearn around the same time. But then Theosophy was just a new name for a belief system which had been around for centuries and Blavatsky even claimed to have been trained by members of the Tibetan Lodge. Theosophy was the message of the 'great Sages and Seers of all the ages' and importantly for Nan, it was not for Sundays alone, but needed to be lived and experienced. It was innate in all human beings; it just required self-examination and awakening. 'Examine yourselves;' Theosophists urged. 'Realise that there is divinity within you, call it by what name you please. . . . Examine your own inner movements of consciousness, and you will know that these things of glory are in you. They are the working in you of your inner god, your spiritual inner sun'. [427]

AE has been described as a mystic, 'an arch-visionary' [428] according to Yeats, and the terms 'Seer' and 'part-time mystic' have been applied to Nan, too. [429] In *The Living Mountain* she recounts several dream-like, visionary moments. Long-sighted (she wore specs for reading) she 'looked often at distances' [430] and long before her Cairngorm-walking years, believed she had caught glimpses of what she thought was another realm, an 'other' landscape. One clear, midsummer day, she thought she could see from out past Ben Nevis to Morar and had to be persuaded she was not seeing even further: 'I could have sworn I saw a shape, distinct and blue, very clear and small, further off than any hill the chart recorded. The chart was against me, my companions were against me'. She decided she must be imagining it and blamed it on the altitude. [431]

It would be over ten years before Nan set foot on a Cairngorm and some fifteen or more before she began recounting those moments of perceptual shift in *The Living Mountain,* but in 1917, she was withdrawing from organised religion, opening her mind to other ideas. AE's poetry was another step on from what is implied in Emily Dickinson's 'sorcery' behind the hill. Whether or not Blavatsky was a charlatan, AE's brand of theosophy appealed to Nan. [432]

For AE, religious experience was not something to be found through worship within church, but in nature.

> I think of earth as the floor of a cathedral where altar and
> Presence are everywhere. This reverence came to me as a boy
> listening to the voice of birds one coloured evening in summer,
> when suddenly birds and trees and grass and tinted air and

myself seemed but one mood or companionship, and I felt a
certitude that the same spirit was in all. A little breaking of the
barriers and being would mingle with being.[433]

The landscape—woods, hills, bird and plant life were his source of spiritual energy. Nature was what pagans and early Christians worshipped and it is to nature AE exhorts his readers to return.

There are close to two hundred poems in AE's 1913 collection—a lot to wade through. Nan always had a book about her, but it's hard to imagine her popping AE's tome in her pocket. From his works, she selected the poems, 'Epigram', 'The Place of Rest', 'Desire', 'Frolic', 'Immortality' and 'Dana: The Mother of Gods',[434] all of which share a common theme—the religion of nature.

In early 1918, influenced by her reading of AE's works and Hearn's *Gleanings in Buddha Fields,* Nan wrote some verses of her own. Six in all: four written in three days towards the end of February and another two in May of that year. Not all these poems, Nan decided, merited inclusion in *In the Cairngorms,* published in 1934. Those that did not, however, act as a kind of pre-writing. In them, you can see she is playing with diction, style and structure. Occasionally, too, a phrase find its way into some of her later poetry.

February 1918 was an exceptionally mild month. Little snow fell and there was hardly any frost.[435] By the 19th February when the rain stopped and the days were quiet and fine, Nan went 'out on the tramp', as she called it, . What she saw inspired her verses. Unsurprisingly given the amount of rain that had fallen that February, the first poem is 'Flood', which did make it into *In the Cairngorms*—with a couple of alterations. 'The pools came over the brim at night/And the river silently', it begins and works its way through a description of the flooded landscape. 'How the sober flats grew/Elfin, uncertain, half like dew/And half like light withdrawn,' the poem ends with a dream-like vision reminiscent of AE's, as though in that moment the narrator sees, through half-closed eyes, into another dimension:

> And all of a sudden the world was strange
> With the strangeness of things that seem
> Familiar the more they change,
> The queer, familiar forms that range
> Through the wide land of dream.[436]

This dream-state comes again in 'Between Lights': 'Early, early came the light…when the sun comes up I forget quite/ something in the dark that was throbbing, throbbing/ that I half remember in the light, but not quite. In 'Alienation', the earth does not speak, seems estranged and as a result the narrator feels alienated rather than connected. 'Rest' which follows this, portrays the earth, made anthropomorphous, as mother:

> And there is nothing, nothing at all
> To beat the blood from the earth's own pace—
> Only her bosom's rhythmic fall—
> The moving of worlds' processional—
> The heave of space.[437]

In April 1918, Nan was out again, walking on her own among the larch and rowan trees in Hazelhead Woods, about two and a half miles from Dunvegan. Now a park with formal gardens and golf course, a giant maze, pets corner, a play park and café, Nan would hardly have recognised the place, but the paths still run between the tall trees and there are traces of the forgotten, half-quarried lumps of stone she describes. There she had an unnerving experience, provoking 'The Trees' written on 5th May. She was unsure at the time whether the experience was pagan, or just uncanny, but there is in her poem an element of AE's 'super-nature'.

That April was windy, days were dulled by overcast skies. Mist and haze hung around like the war, which still showed no signs of ending. Who knows whether Nan really saw anything, or whether it was a case of having read so much of AE's work, she *wanted* to see. Either way, what she describes is a sensation anyone who has walked at dusk in the mist, on a path between wind-blown trees, would recognise:

The Trees

> Forgotten temples in forgotten lands,
> Half quarried stone forbidden to achieve
> The form some master-thought had asked to leave
> Cut on it—and reflected there it stands,
> Lichened and frustrate—columns that the sands
> Have long since quilted and cities that the heave
> Of earth's cramped body carelessly did thieve
> Of fame, and halls both raided and ruined by hands:
>
> All these I thought on—all the dead done world
> Deliberate things and things without desire.
> For it was April, and I dared not look
> Save furtively upon the trees, that whirled

And fled and followed my path. And one was fire
One laughed and mocked; one melted while
I swore she shook.[438]

Once seen, it is hard to un-see in Nan's writing (both prose and poetry) these new ways of thinking she was working through in her head while out on the tramp. And of course, out walking in the landscape was to immerse herself into nature, to put philosophy into practice. Her novels were all written before that momentous Loch Avon encounter in July 1934 when everything crystallised, but her perspective on nature and its interrelation with man had already shifted.

In *The Weatherhouse* Garry Forbes is out one evening when he has a moment of realisation, a perceptual shift giving a glimpse of the infinite, something primeval, known but unknowable. 'Primordial' is used twice in as many paragraphs:

> The sky, still dark, brooded upon a darker earth, but with no sense of oppression. Rather both sky and earth rolled way, were lost in a primordial darkness whence they had but half emerged. Garry felt himself fall, ages of time gave way, and he too, was a creature only half set free from the primordial dark…A sound broke the stillness, faint bubble of a stream, the eternal mystery of moving water; and now the darkness, to his accustomed eyes, was no longer a covering, but a quality of what he looked upon. Waste land and the fields, in common with the arch of sky, and now a grandeur unsuspected in the day. Light showed them as they were at a moment of time, but the dark revealed their timeless attributes, reducing the particular to accident and hinting at a sublimer truth than the eye could distinguish. Garry felt for a moment as though he had ceased to live at the point in time where all his experience had hitherto amassed.[439]

The Weatherhouse was published in 1931 and followed in 1933, by *A Pass in the Grampians*. In this, man's oneness with the universe is explored. Durno and Kilgour stand side by side at the grey stone dyke:

> These two old men…were ribs of the earth. The land made men like these because she needed them; and made them in her own image because she knew no other way…The earth become conscious as it were in Andrew Kilgour, so fully were her qualities embodied in him—her strength, patience, faith-

fulness, her wholesome vigour and enchanting peace, her heavy
reiterations and profound satisfaction in herself, knowing that
she was good—the earth, embodied in Andrew Kilgour, stood
watching.[440]

The last poem in the series Nan wrote in early 1918 is 'Underground'
which is worth seeing in its entirety.

> What passionate tumult tore this black disturbance
> Out of the rugged heart of the obstinate rock
> Fixing secure a thousand-age-old shock
> Beneath the quiet country's imperturbance,
> I have no wit to utter, nor what breath
> Blew like a bubble that flees through water this
> Chasm in the bowels of earth where dark streams kiss
> In guilty dark slant shores they will kiss till death
>
> And never look on: but I give my thanks
> Tonight to that antique destructive whim
> That so the risen and torrential flood
> That else had burst all measure and drowned the banks
> And swamped my life, may pour along those grim
> And secret caves, and none discern its thud.[441]

Theosophy's tenet, that man's oneness with the universe is something
known since ancient times, is there in the 'thousand age-old shock'
and the 'antique destructive whim' which has caused this underground
flood and has 'swamped' the narrator's life. Here too is AE's idea of the
breaking of barriers between human beings and their natural surround-
ings. Nature's state, is humans' state. But all this is going on under the
quiet, unperturbed surface.

There is also the suggestion that this knowledge is to remain secret,
so that 'none discern its thud'. Secret, perhaps, because few would
understand or be able to grasp this philosophy. Or secret because of the
atmosphere of religious fervour of the era.

In 1917 Nan was as reticent about her inner life as she was in 1981
when she died. There were few people to whom she could talk about
her changing views on religion. With the exception of Neil Gunn, she
also kept quiet about her 'secret life'. But the use of 'guilty' suggests this
poem is about something else, some undisclosed, inner turmoil in the
narrator. In that 'thud' is heartbeat and the second stanza implies that
whatever has erupted and engulfed the speaker needs to be kept hidden,

below the surface.

Several of the women in her fictions, seem to be incarnations or projections of Nan at different ages. Aunt Josephine in *The Quarry Wood* is one, Ellen Falconer in *The Weatherhouse* another, and Mary Kilgour too, in *A Pass in the Grampians*. The closest we come to Nan herself, however, is Martha in *The Quarry Wood*. To read 'Underground' alongside a passage from her first novel, gives some insight into what the poem might also be examining: 'Martha was undergoing at the moment one of her fierce revulsions from a bout of passion. She wanted to dash up out of the waters that had engulfed her, to stand high and dry on common ground'.[442]

Martha is in love:

> One loves, the books had taught her, though she had given the theme but little attention—as one must, perhaps against one's will and inclination: but she, sucked under without aware-ness, had loved the greatest man she knew. Judgment approved. She counted herself among the blest. Besides, this secret and impossible love had a wild sweetness, flavoured and heady, luscious upon the palate, a draught for gods. It was eternal, set beyond the shadow of alteration in an ideal sphere.[443]

Nan too, it seems, was in love. But by the time she appears to have realised that her feelings for John Macmurray had grown beyond mere friendship, he was already married.

★ ★ ★

In 1913, having graduated First Class from Glasgow, John Macmurray enrolled at Balliol College, Oxford, to read Classics. For the first time he was studying philosophy. Betty, proud to have a fiancé at Oxford, was still living in Aberdeen with her brother Duncan while she finished her own degree.

When war was declared in August 1914, John was still at Oxford. He was in a quandary: 'exercised about pacifism, but never having decided whether he should stand as a conscientious objector or not', according to Betty.[444] Eventually, he compromised, joined the Royal Army Medical Corps and in 1915 was shipped to the front.[445] By June the following year, John decided he might as well pursue a commission. In the Medical Corps, he felt, in a way, that he was already fighting by helping men to return to active service. Transferred to the Queen's

Own Cameron Highlanders as Second Lieutenant, he was dispatched immediately to the Somme.

Four months later, on 9th October 1916, John was granted a three day leave and in secret, he and Betty married at the registry office in Westminster. Betty, who was now teaching at a private girls' school in the south of England,[446] fearing she might lose her job if the school found out she was now married, took off her ring and hung it round her neck. After a honeymoon night spent at The Randolph in Oxford, she went with John to break the news to his parents.[447] There was no need to tell Betty's own mother: Betsy Campbell had died in hospital in Aberdeen earlier that year. The following day, John Macmurray rushed back to France to join his men fighting on the Somme.

As no correspondence between the Macmurrays and Nan remains, it is uncertain whether she was privy to their secret marriage. John's sister Lilias is recorded as witness on the Macmurray's marriage certificate.[448] Most likely, Nan found out afterwards. In *The Quarry Wood*, Luke and Dussie's marriage is presented as a *fait accompli*.

In December 1916 John was sent home with a broken ankle and spent his convalescence in Stonehaven. Quiet and grey with its picture-perfect little harbour, Stonehaven was a northern fishing village that grew into a small, county town and remains a popular resort—although its harbour nowadays is filled with pleasure cruisers rather than the red and brown sailed fishing fleet. Nearby, on the cliffs, sits Dunnottar Castle ruined and roofless. Carmont Cottage, where John was staying from late 1916 to early 1917, was a little way out of town, set back in cliff-top country. It was home then to Duncan Campbell, his wife Mary and their newborn son, Duncan Ian, and belonged to Mary's mother.

Duncan had his eye on Mary Beedie from around 1911. A little older than him, for some years Mary had been the Campbell's maid at Home Farm, Inchmarlo.[449] It was not until 1916, though, that Duncan was financially in a position to marry Mary, which he did, before promptly enlisting. So when John was recuperating at Carmont Cottage, Duncan was away fighting in France. Betty was not there either, she was too busy teaching in the south of England to join her husband, leaving John with Mary, her mother and the baby for company.

January 1917 was cold, but dry. Dull elsewhere in Britain, Scotland's start to the year was a sunny one.[450] John would not have been able to put weight on his ankle for some time and even then would have had crutches. How galling it must have been to watch the sun light the landscape through the cottage windows and not be able to spend time outdoors. Without Betty or Duncan's company and with Mary distracted by the demands of a small baby, he spent much time alone and used this time to read and think. He was also writing poetry again. Having not written any verse since 1913 he wrote two poems during this period, as well as an article on 'Trench Religion' provoked by his experiences at the front.

John might have known no-one else locally, but he was not without visitors. In 1917, Nan was still part-time at the Training Centre. It would have been easy for her to take the train from Aberdeen along the east coast to Stonehaven to call in on John. It is also apparent from *Gleanings* that she did. Into the book she transcribed a series of his poems. The earliest is dated 1st September 1911 and the two latest, written while he was on convalescent leave, are dated 27 December 1916 and 11 February 1917. The dates are confusing at first, until it becomes clear from the entries either side of John's verses, that all the poems were copied into *Gleanings* in 1917. As none of his poetry was ever published, Nan could only have been shown them by John or Betty and as we know, Betty was working in the south during John's convalescence.

In her autobiographical writings, Betty often remarks on the fundamental difference between herself and John: 'I live by sensation, not by the intellect'.[451] As a result, she sometimes felt isolated by the incessant 'chatter, chatter, chatter' as she put it, during the 'sky-highs' of those university years in Aberdeen. Sitting by the fire in the Forest Avenue flat, with John, Nan and Duncan, the conversations would become heated. Duncan enjoyed baiting John, trying to pierce the 'armour of idealism' which was upholstered by his devout religious beliefs and would 'bully and batter home his ideas'. She just wished they would all be quiet. 'The mind makes monkeys of us all', she said. To Betty, it was life that mattered.[452]

Life mattered to Nan too, but she also relished a good debate and she and John had much to discuss during those Stonehaven pow-wows. Both, at the time, were questioning institutionalised religion and she was eager, too, for John's thoughts on the war. She was also interested in his poetry, although unlike the ebullient Luke in *The Quarry Wood* 'who had none of your young poet's diffidence in showing them off',[453] John would have been shy about showing Nan his verses.

On John's first day as an officer at the Somme, he survived a shell blast that killed two out of the three men with whom, seconds earlier, he had been sitting in an angle of a trench, drinking tea. One minute they were drinking tea and joking, the next they heard the whine of a shell which exploded near John. When the smoke cleared he saw one of his men lying cut in two by a flying shard, the other, bleeding copiously, looked as though he would not make it. As an introduction to life in the trenches, it was a huge shock, he said, recalling the moment over fifty years later. 'But very soon that sort of thing was common-place—part of the routine of daily life'.[454]

The soldier's catchphrase, 'if there is a bullet with your name on it, you'll get it' did not come out of nowhere. Faced with this arbitrary, daily doling out of death, many of the men had become fatalists. Every-thing out in the battle zone seemed to be in the hands of fate. Soldiers did their duty and put their faith in luck. Caught in a tight corner or faced with a terrifying battle, they would fall back on some 'Being' they called 'God' to get them through, but it was not generally a particula-rised god and to some perhaps simply a habit borne of Sunday school teaching and understandable in moments of paralysing fear.

The article on 'trench religion' John wrote during his convales-cence was published in 1919 in *The Army and Religion*. The soldiers' fatalism, John believed, stemmed from the overwhelming sense of 'man's littleness' in the face of a 'terrific display of mechanical force':

> Nowhere, as in a great army, does a man's littleness and unimpor-tance stare on him so startlingly. Nowhere, as on a battlefield, is there such evidence of the powerlessness of the mightiest human organisation to protect his own small individuality. A millimetre's deflection in the laying of a gun is the difference between life and death to him. He knows how a shell will burst between two men, blowing one to pieces, yet leaving the other unhurt and amazed. He has crouched in holes in the earth, with earthy smells in his nostrils, and listened to the hum of a thousand unseen menaces under the placid stars. What eats his soul is the knowledge that all violence is blind. Chance rules as an autocrat in the metropolis of our most perfect mechanism…
> The solder's prayer is for protection, for strength, for peren-nial spring of inspiration to courage. His God is one who can supply all these.[455]

Nan listened carefully to John's experiences at the Front and its effect on the religious life of the men. Vividly reconstructed, much of this found its way into *The Weatherhouse*. 'A wind roared hideously. He knew it was an advancing shell…again the rushing mighty wind'. There are two, not four men in Gary Forbes's shell hole, but the ratio is the same. So, too, is this sense of the arbitrary, picking-off of men, that creates a 'comradeship with Death' and causes Garry's identification with his fallen comrade. It was just fate or luck that killed one soldier and spared another. Survivor's guilt, too, perhaps, makes Garry drag that body out with him. He is found next morning, a corpse bumping at his heels like a shadow, that he insisted was himself and wouldn't leave. Through Garry, Nan Shepherd also voices the sense of 'man's littleness'. Lying in his hospital bed Garry tries to explain this sensation to one of the nurses: ' "It's because it's so big". "Yes I know", she answered pressing his hand. But of course she didn't know'. [456]

Nan depicts too, the gulf between what went on in the trenches and life back home. Convalescing in 'Fetter-Rothnie', Garry feels that the war he has left behind, despite all its accompanying death, is more vital than the life in Scotland to which he has returned, which seems petty and small-minded:

> Over there one felt oneself part of something big. One was making the earth. Here there were men, no doubt, leading their hapless, misdirected, individual lives…too far from life… this dead world annoyed him. The reconstruction of the universe would not begin in this dark hole, inhabited by old wives and ploughmen. [457]

Garry begins to yearn to return to the trenches, 'It's a battle about something and I must get back'. [458]

John's attitude towards religion altered while he was on leave. It seemed everywhere you looked there were posters emotionally black-mailing those men not yet in khaki with questions like 'Daddy what did *you* do in the war?' and demonising the Germans as 'Barbarians'. 'Enlist today', they counselled, to show these barbarians Britain is not afraid. He had been shocked to see the random pinning of white feathers (often by women) on unsuspecting men not wearing uniform. To him the practice underlined the enormous gulf between trench life and civilian life. The latter seemed infected, inflamed no doubt by the government's propaganda, as much as through incomprehension, as with small-minded malice:

> It was, I think, the ignorant and superstitious hatred of the Germans, and the equally ignorant and unreal glorification of us, in the trenches, as heroes that had this effect. In France we were not heroes..and we do not hate Germans, at least not the Germans in the trenches opposite. We understood them and they understood us. We were sharing the same spurious and obscene life, no doubt with the same feelings. [459]

Like Garry Forbes in *The Weatherhouse,* John became anxious to get back to the trenches, 'where for all the misery and destruction, the spiritual atmosphere was relatively clean'. Before he rejoined his regiment in France though, he gave a sermon in which he urged the congregation, instead of wreaking vengeance, to seek a more Christian reconciliation with the enemy. It did not go down well. In truth, the response was so hostile that no-one spoke to him after the service. John did not take it personally. It was not a rejection of him, he decided, but a rejection of Christian doctrine and the embrace instead of a ghastly, self-righteous patriotism. 'I spoke and wrote thereafter in defence of religion and Christianity;' he said, but I thought of the churches as the various national religions of Europe.'[460]

So while John did not abandon religion, he was no longer keen to parade what he felt was a spurious kind of Christianity. He maintained this view until 1959 after he retired from the University of Edinburgh and he and Betty moved to Jordans in Buckinghamshire and joined the Quakers. In the meantime, even if it meant walking alone, like Nan, John chose his own path. He was unconventional, not only in the way he lived his life, but in his approach to philosophy—which is why he was considered such a maverick.

In the summer of 1917 John returned to active service in France. Just over a year later, on 28th March 1918, the war was over for him. The only one of his company to survive the bombardment which wiped out all three of the battalion's companies, he was severely injured in the attack which annihilated the rest of his men, his face and body pierced by several pieces of shrapnel. After surgery to remove what the doctors could of the shrapnel, in April he was invalided back to Scotland again, to convalesce in a military hospital near Inverlochy. This time Betty did join him and by January 1919 John was fully recovered and back at Balliol and graduated MA with distinction that September. From there he and Betty moved to Manchester where he was Lecturer in Philosophy at the University and there they remained until 1921.

Given the dates of her entries in *Gleanings,* it seems it was around 1917 that Nan realised her feelings for John had deepened. For the next fourteen years she loved him,[461] which is perhaps why the eleven sonnets included at the end of *In the Cairngorms* are grouped under the heading 'Fourteen Years'. It seems most likely that it was for John the sonnets were written (as well as other verses, some of which also ended up in the collection). We know the man for whom they were written read them, because Nan admitted it in an interview in 1976. 'Very few people will understand these poems', he told her, which made her feel better. In December 1976 when she gave this interview, John Macmurray was dead. Still she did not name him; just smiled her enigmatic smile and let the rumours persist that the sonnets were addressed to Rupert Brooke or Charles Murray.[462]

As Ali Smith says, as well as 'oblique' the sonnets are 'bruised'.[463] Nan, who would turn twenty four in February 1917, was mature intellectually, but not emotionally. That tap on her head she received on graduation two years earlier signified that learning was there, but as the University's motto, *Initium sapientiae,* warned, this was only the beginning of wisdom. Emotional maturity would come with experience; and like most experiences that bring real growth, it was painful.

The next fourteen years were an emotionally turbulent period for Nan. The situation was made more complex not just because John Macmurray was married—and to her close friend—but because his 'philosophy of the personal'—to know yourself through others—was a lived reality. From the mid 1920s, the Macmurrays' marriage was an open one. 'We agreed', Betty said in her memoirs, 'to share the love we had for each other with others too. No easy task, but a rewarding one' that she believes 'only increased and released our everlasting affinity'. She went on to admit, however, 'I don't think we really ever played fair in our adventures into friendships involving sex outside marriage… John, with such disciplined emotions, true or false, I sometimes felt underestimated the fiendish power of sex to defeat all judgement'. What she also said is that all the time they were living out 'John's belief in Freedom, we always knew that we belonged, and always would, to each other. This could be hard on others'.[464]

Betty was always foremost in John's affection. He reassured his wife of this several times in correspondence over the years, lines from which she copied out on a separate sheet marked 'special letters to keep'. In 1923 he wrote:

> I feel I could love multitudes of women without ever being unfaithful to my love for you. It is so fixed & central and eternal. It isn't a feeling of mine. This centring of life in you, nor an activity, nor an idea—far less a duty or an obligation. It is me.[465]

Open marriages were not such an issue in 1920s bohemian London where John and Betty lived from 1928. The Bloomsbury crowd, 'who lived in squares, painted in circles and loved in triangles',[466] made no secret of their unconventional attitudes. But prim and proper Aberdeen could not have been further from Bloomsbury in its outlook. If Aberdonians loved in triangles, they kept it to themselves.

But this was all in the future. In 1917, John was still newly married and soon to be returning to the Front. Although it can't have been easy for her, Nan kept her feelings to herself. She did, perhaps, allow herself to vent through Mary Kilgour in *A Pass in the Grampians*: 'How could he have married her? How could he?' Gib Munro, who used to sit in the barn with her and 'philosophize' married Bella Cassie instead of Mary. She puts on a cheerful front, but inwardly she seethes: 'Mary's face remained smiling and her voice light; but something darkened far within'.[467]

Nan hid her feelings well—John was apparently oblivious. During those Stonehaven weeks John, it seems, still saw Nan as a friend, albeit a good one, whose intellectual precocity he respected. What is apparent from its recurrence as an issue explored in Nan's poetry and in *The Quarry Wood*, is that she started to see that John loved her, not as a woman, but as an idealised vision. 'She began to understand that she was for him an earnest of the spiritual world; its ministrant; his Beatrice.'[468] It is no coincidence that references to Dante's beloved keep appearing in *The Quarry Wood*. Dante, who also studied philosophy of course, loved Beatrice from a distance; they had very little contact. She is an idealised love, of the kind that transcends physicality.

The Dante connection appears elsewhere too. Nan borrowed the title of the poet's autobiography *La Vita Nuova* (The New Life) for the second in her sonnet series. 'I have been dumb these many days since knowing/the power of that which once I did deride',[469] the poem starts. And life is indeed made new by the power of this love. Until 1917, no man had captured Nan's romantic interest. Scathing on the subject of love, the speaker is taken by surprise by the strength of the emotion.

In 'Snow', too, the narrator voices amazement: 'I did not know. How could I understand,/I, who had scorned the very name of love?… And now—and now—I am mazed to find my world/Sore altered in the passing of a night…no proclamation…Of haunting prophecy came… But at morn the earth was strange, a blur, white'.[470] Both these poems speak of the shock of revelation and an inability, or refusal, to voice it.

In 1923, when Nan was writing *The Quarry Wood* she and Mure Mackenzie were discussing Dante. Mure thought it quite possible that Dante's wife, Gemma Donati, 'understood about Beatrice—and that Dante knew it'. 'He had a very real love for Gemma', she went on, 'and knew it not disloyal to Beatrice—and could trust her comprehension. Of course its—'.[471] The rest of the letter has been cut off mid-sentence, presumably by Nan who lodged Mure's letters in the archives. Perhaps Nan was pondering whether her Dante allusions worked within the scope of her novel. If Mure then went on to discuss the Betty/John/

Nan triangle we cannot know but it seems possible and given Nan's concern for privacy, it is not surprising that the rest of the letter is missing.

What is extraordinary in *The Quarry Wood,* is that Martha feels no guilt over Dussie. Of course, the novel was written in hindsight. Nan's perspective is from her older, wiser self and because of this, the story has more of a bite of honesty about it. It would have been easy to make Martha overcome with shame, wracked with guilt over falling in love with her best friend's husband. Nan doesn't. She neither excuses or condones Martha's behaviour and actually succeeds in making Martha seem self-absorbed and rather unlike-able at this juncture. In fact, she depicts Dussie as the bigger of the two. It is not Dussie who inspires Martha's jealousy, but the intellectual Lucy Warrender who she hears has also been talking philosophy with Luke. After Martha's jealous outburst over this, 'it dawned on Dussie that Martha was in love with Luke...she was moved with a grave pity for her friend. "How unhappy she must be"'.[472]

But Martha isn't unhappy. 'She had her paradise within herself and it sufficed her', because to begin with her love for Luke is also an idealised one, and not possessive:

> It was eternal, set beyond the shadow of alteration in an ideal sphere...it would satisfy her eternally. There was nothing possessive in her love; or rather she possessed already all that she desired in him—those far shining, terribly intimate moments of spiritual communion.[473]

It is soon clear, however, that this 'spiritual communion' is not enough, and that Martha, 'wanted Luke. All of him, and to be her own. And the torrent of her passion, sweeping headlong, bore her on in imagination past every obstacle between her and her desire'. The thought of Dussie 'was like a straw tumbled in a cataract'.[474]

In Betty's own autobiographical novel, *Out of the Earth,* in which she casts herself as 'Agnes', John as 'David', and Nan as 'Maribel', Maribel is not let off so lightly: 'Maribel realised she had only looked one way, towards David. She hadn't thought of Agnes at all except as an intrusion and this had caused her to humiliate her in word and in action'.[475]

The second stanza of 'Without My Right', which in Nan's notebook is titled 'Illicit Love', is a dark version of this longing:

Love, love, I have no mind for sane respect
I crave too long thy presence to abhor
For thee rape's dark dishonour. Without my right
I draw thee on toward me and infect
My being with thine.[476]

The sonnet, which is included in *In the Cairngorms,* is one of the most oblique in the series, but its meaning is explained in *The Quarry Wood:* 'Love's imperative demand was now to take. She wanted Luke, his presence, his life, his laughing vitality; and it seemed to her…that reaching him she could draw his very life away and take it for her own. I mustn't, I mustn't'. Martha struggles with herself like the speaker of the sonnet struggling all night with the war raging within her:

> It was like rape. And her exultant clutching was followed by an agony of shame…There had been nothing illicit in her loving Luke, nor in the outpouring of her spirit upon him; but this reckless grabbing was like a shameful and beloved vice. She fought frantically against it, only to succumb to a blacker and more gluttonous debauchery.[477]

Given her emotional state, it seems somewhat masochistic of Nan to have carefully copied John's poetry into *Gleanings*—they are all love poems to Betty. In all these verses, there is more than a nod to Browning, whose work John greatly admired. As Betty says when she described first hearing John play the piano and laughed at him because it was so awful, John always believed man's reach should exceed his grasp—a direct quotation from Browning's 'Andrea del Sarto' which continues: '…or what's a heaven for?'[478] During their courting days when John's physical restraint towards her was wearing her down (it was only after he proposed in December 1911, that they finally kissed[479]) she says he would draw away from her and read Browning aloud instead. The Victorian poet left Betty cold. 'I haven't got a head for that sort of thing',[480] she said, although it was probably not so much the poetry as John's self-control that irked her.

Browning, so popular in the nineteenth century, had rather fallen out of favour by the early twentieth. Ezra Pound might have hailed him as one of his 'literary fathers', but other Modernists like T S Eliot were critical. Judging by Nan's notebooks, Browning was not a favourite of hers either.[481] Whether she copied John's poems into *Gleanings* because she admired them or because, like Martha in *The Quarry Wood,* they spoke to 'some tune within her own being',[482] or because, secretly, she wanted to imagine they were written for her, we can only speculate. But coming just before John's poems in *Gleanings* are pages of extracts, in the same handwriting and the same coloured ink suggesting they were written during the same period, from Tagore's lyrics of 'love and life', *The Gardener*.[483]

Nan first came across Rabindranath Tagore at university, a matter of months after he had won the Nobel prize in Literature in October 1913[484]—the first non-European to do so. On 5th February 1914 Betty gave a talk on his work to the University's Literary Society[485] in Marischal's Botany Classroom. It was a refreshing departure for the Lit Soc's talks that year which included Keats, Blake, J M Barrie, Lady Gregory and Irish Theatre, *Peer Gynt* and the *Humour of Wells,* among other topics. Tagore's work struck Nan. As well as the extracts in *Gleanings,* she also wrote some notes on him in her *Medley Book* including the resignation of his knighthood in protest at the 'measure of suppression of the Punjab disorders'.[486]

Although Nan has not numbered the Tagore extracts, comparing them with his original translation from Bengali, you can see she has placed them in a different order. As such, they create a narrative similar to those of *The Quarry Wood* and the early sonnets, read as a series. The narrative (necessarily abbreviated here) begins with a refusal to acknowledge love: 'Trust love even if it brings sorrow, Do not close up your heart/Ah no my friend your words are dark, I cannot understand them', 'the last cowardice, the fear of love' of Nan's 'La Vita Nuova'. This is followed by: 'Why did he choose to come to my door, the wandering youth…I know not if I should speak to him or keep silent'. In 1917, Nan kept silent. Then we have, 'Your questioning eyes are sad. They seek to know my meanings' followed by, 'I paint you and fashion you ever with my longings' and, 'my heart longs day and night for the meeting with you'. Then, in a reversal of the 'rape' of Nan's 'Without my right' there comes, 'Sweep break open my sleep and plunder my dreams… let us become one in beauty'. The last of these extracts is number 16: 'No mystery beyond the present; no striving for the impossible;…This love between you and me is simple as a song'.

It was not simple though. Tagore's 'Traveller must you go' is included after the extracts from *The Gardener*. And Betty and John did go, to Manchester, where John was to Lecture in Philosophy. In *The Quarry Wood,* Manchester is swapped for Liverpool where Luke is to be a GP 'So it's a P after all', says Martha. 'Remember all the P's we planned you were to be? Philosopher, Poet, Professor [487]—John Macmurray was all three.

When Luke and Dussie go, Martha is relieved: 'so that's over', she thinks, believing 'she had only to exercise her will to be again what she was before, passionless, possessed only of herself'. But of course it wasn't over. 'The waters were loosened and not to be gathered back'. [488]

Chapter Seven

1919-1922

Nan threw herself into her work. By 1919 she was full-time at the Training Centre and committed to trying to prevent at least a few of the students who passed through its doors from conforming altogether to 'the approved patterns'. Education was one of the very few ways a girl could gain freedom and be upwardly mobile. If marriage to a higher status male was not an option, a clever working class girl whose family was prepared to go without the wages she might have earned for five years or so could penetrate the middle classes by becoming a schoolmistress. Enter Martha Ironside in *The Quarry Wood* who does exactly this.

Like Nan, many of these female teachers proved vital to the women's movement, which then, despite the vote (which in 1918 was only extended to women over thirty who met a property qualification) was still in its infancy. A woman with a working identity, instead of a family one—as mother, daughter, wife or aunt, or one created by her class—was a new model of woman. Pupils' married mothers might snigger over the 'spinster' label, but they could not escape the fact that many of these women were better educated, more independent and often better off than they themselves were. Post-war, those men who *had*

Agnes Mure Mackenzie.

come back, were preferred for all the good posts. The only professions open to women then were teaching and nursing—but they could offer a path to independence and financial freedom. Nan enjoyed this freedom because she was still living at home. Her father, always frugal, had saved for his retirement and even after his death had left sufficient to maintain the house, so that her income from the Training Centre was her own. For Nan's friend Mure Mackenzie, making ends meet while living away from home, was a struggle.

Agnes Mure Mackenzie first came into Nan's orbit at King's. She was a year ahead of Nan at university but had stayed on post-graduation, as Junior Assistant in the English department after the previous incumbent enlisted. Keen to contribute in a practical way to the war effort, Mure started a club to darn socks for the men stationed in Aberdeen and Nan joined—although she was not at its first meeting. Some miscommunication over the date meant no-one turned up to darn an enormous pile of socks which needed returning the next morning as the men were under orders to move. Mure sat down and darned. She darned all night and in the morning, bleary-eyed and blinking, returned the bundle. When she got to know Mure, the story did not come as a surprise to Nan, it was typical of her 'pluck', she said. But it is a story made all the more extraordinary when you realise Mure could hardly see.

From left to right:
Nan, Jeannie Shepherd and Agnes Mure Mackenzie in the garden at Dunvegan.

Mure Mackenzie was an Isleswoman, from Stornoway. A bout of scarlet fever when she was eight destroyed one of her eardrums completely and severely damaged the other. For a while, she was totally deaf and although treatment restored some hearing to her right ear, she was never able to hear from her left. 'I cannot imagine what bi-aural hearing feels like' she said, 'if I try, it feels as confusing as having three legs'. [489] The scarlet fever also left her extremely short-sighted. A fervent feminist, during her suffrage years she admitted to Nan that her one real fear was of being involved in a scuffle in which her glasses would be knocked off.

Growing up in Stornoway, Mure was pretty much isolated from the outside world. To her parents Mure was delicate, damaged and needed protection. Had they known then, that her death in 1955 would be described as 'a loss to the nation'; that by 1926 she would be listed in *Who's Who;* that she would go on to publish volume after volume of historical works, novels, literary criticism;[490] and that after her name she would write the letters C.B.E. (for services to Scottish literature and history) and LL.D, they would have been astonished. But Mure's mettle manifested early. On her seventeenth birthday she decided that she must go to university. As Nan said in her portrait of Mure published in the *Aberdeen University Review* in 1955, in view of her disabilities, and remembering that Mure came from a remote island during, and that the time was the 1900s, when university women were still a novelty, 'one does not wonder that she had to fight for what she needed'.[491]

At King's, Mure was a favourite of Dankester's who would set out a chair for her under the Professors' noses. Despite this, she was still unable to hear many of the lectures and as her sight was so poor she could not lip-read. A slight, nimble little figure, her trademark dark-rimmed, round spectacles lent her the intelligent, if somewhat abstracted, look of a young barn owl. 'I'm an ugly divil' Mure once wrote in a letter to Nan,[492] but photographs of her later in life reveal her snowy-haired and rather distinguished-looking. Her 'deaf eyes', as Nan described them, however, could make Mure seem a little vague in company. 'That queer friend of yours—do you think she's all there?' a relative of Nan's once asked her. Mure, she says, would have met the remark with a quip. Any outrage or hurt she felt would have been 'because of the stigma unimaginative people set on the deaf these days'.[493]

Mure was very much all there. Highly intellectual, she was a stellar student who made the most of her university years. She was the first woman editor of the students' university rag, *Alma Mater,* (Nan was the second) and had a reputation as an undergraduate for her dancing, her 'pungent wit' and for her suffrage activities. A member of the National Union of Women's Suffrage, she walked alone one night to tie suffrage slogans on the bridge in the middle of the Deeside Golf course and threw a hammer wrapped in a huge cabbage of red, white and blue ribbons on to the lawn of a suburban opponent.

'I may add that there is some little suspicion of you as an ardent suffragette.' Professor Grierson wrote to Mure in January 1914 in response to her request for help finding employment post-graduation. 'I suppose you have too much sense to let your ardour for the cause interfere with the work or make you an anxiety to the authorities',[494] he continued. Disabled as she was, successful professional opportunities for Mure were limited and her father, a country doctor with two younger children still at home, could not afford to support his daughter outside Stornoway. Despite his concern over Mure's 'ardour for the cause' (and in any case, suffragism and political activities were suspended during the war[495]) Grierson did help. He found her a job at the Training College tutoring and correcting essays, which, of course, is where she and Nan came across one another again.

It is no accident that Nan, always so careful with her words, describes Mure as 'a comrade' in the portrait of her friend she wrote after her sudden death in 1955.[496] An outspoken critic who once compared John Knox to Adolf Hitler, Mure 'bore her learning less like a scholar's robes than as a fiery cross with which to rouse even the indifferent, the illiterate and the ineffective to some sense of their abiding obligation as citizens of the future, to the undying past'.[497] Most of the brightest university students in Nan's era were Socialists, even the middle class ones who had little first-hand experience of working class life. 'We wanted a better world, with better opportunities for all', said Winifred Hodgkiss, a Cambridge-educated, middle-class contemporary of Nan's who, like her, became a lecturer. 'Mine was an intellectual rather than a practical conversion to Socialism', she explained, 'but I have never gone back on it.'[498] Neither did Nan, who, like Mure, was left wing. Not that either of them were open about their political proclivities at the Training Centre. If they wanted to keep their jobs, teachers and their families could have no taint of political affiliation (hence Grierson's concern).

'She could not be niggard', Nan says in her memoir of Mure. Although the same is true of Nan herself; both women were generous friends. It was Mure who worked tirelessly on Nan's behalf to secure a publisher for *The Quarry Wood* and Nan who helped Mure when her job prospects looked bleak at the end of her three year stint as Junior Assistant at King's. Mure's work at the Training Centre was only part-time and so Nan, deciding Hasting's *Encyclopaedia* was not for her, suggested Mure for the post. Nan found her lodgings near Dunvegan in Lower Deeside and from July 1917, outside of work hours, the two spent hours in each other's company.

Mure looked back on those years as a vividly happy time. Out walking with Nan, she learned to listen, isolating sounds, turning her good ear towards them. Nan watched as Mure's '*gamin* grin' lit up her face when for the first time she heard a blackbird or the 'skirl of a railway train'. In 1921, by which time Mure had left Aberdeenshire, she wrote to Nan of her longing for the 'face of the hills in the sunlight when we halted on the heather and the moon standing on Craignorrie, the smell of myrtle under those little birches'. 'Remember me to Clachnaben',[499] she added, ' & the little woods, and the path down the line'.[500]

In 1920, post-war difficulties meant the publishers financing Dr Hasting's *Encyclopaedia* withdrew much of their support; Mure had to go. Eventually, she found work as a Lecturer in English Literature at Birkbeck College. There she remained for the next five years. But while Mure's removal from Deeside was a considerable blow to Nan, it marked the start of a lively, affectionate correspondence between the two women. To read their letters is to see just how close they had become during those Deeside years. 'Dear Muriel-through-the Mica', Nan begins one of her letters in 1928. Dear 'Nancy' or 'Nannickie', Mure replies—a nickname which, it seems, was reserved only for her use.

Few of Nan's letters to Mure are extant. Only three are held in Mure's archive at Scotland's National Library. Nan herself lodged Mure's letters to her in the Aberdeen University archives, providing dates where there were none. It is not a complete collection. There are gaps, and, typically, Nan has made heavy crossings out and excisions in places where the content becomes too personal—aware, as ever, of the need to avoid censure.

Judging by a letter of Mure's dated 12th July 1927, it seems Nan has raised the issue of the gossipy Aberdonians. In Mure's reply, she is quick to point out their paradoxical nature:

> I don't know if Aberdeen is really much worse than other places but I do know that I never believe anything the Aberdonian tells me about another…We're a queer country… the Aberdonian who is running to her neighbour to embellish some virulent scandal about me (and I've no doubt there are a few by this time!) would stop and help me with both

hands and her bank balance if she came on me in trouble by the way.[501]

Mure's Lower Deeside years coincided with the beginning of Nan's period of spiritual and emotional turmoil which began in 1917 and continued after Mure left for London. There is nothing in their extant correspondence to suggest that Nan shared with Mure her growing scepticism for Christianity. This is probably because, whatever her own religious standpoint might be, Nan was respectful, always, of others' beliefs and Mure was a devout Episcopalian. Mure's letters are littered with references to her unwavering faith along with the assumption that Nan's was no less solid:

> I shall be making my communion at midnight. Think of me then Nancy & put in a bit prayer for my bairns at Coll. so I won't let them down. God seems curiously close—or I suppose its true to say his closeness is vivider than usual.[502]

Nan's spirituality aside, however, she must have confided in her friend to some extent on the subject of her emotional state because Mure was able to recognise just how autobiographical *The Quarry Wood* was.

Like Nan, Mure never married—something she attributed to her disabilities: 'It's not humility that has made me refuse to pray that any man should come true, at all events in my sober senses…I couldn't pray for it without praying at the same time for my own sufficeingness [sic] and I know too well what that involves to pray for it'.[503] Which is sad, but probably realistic. Competition was fierce in the 1920s marriage market. With sinister regularity the war had killed off men of marriageable age and the 'problem' of Britain's 'surplus women' was rarely out of the news after the publication of the 1921 census. The press whipped up a frenzy. Hysterical headlines like 'Two million who can Never Become Wives' were followed later by worse: 'the superfluous women are a disaster to the human race'.[504] The 25-35 year old age group was the most affected—Nan's. In 1921 she was twenty-eight.[505]

'So many nicely brought up girls were withering into virginity', Winifred Hodgkiss said in her memoirs. The general consensus was that if you hadn't had a man by your thirties, it was too late. You just became frustrated and unhappy. 'Husbands are scarce' a friend told Winifred 'but lovers grow on trees'. Winifred took a lover. 'We weren't in love' she admitted, 'but we enjoyed each other's company…I hadn't any feelings of guilt. I thought, "I have become a woman" '.[506]

Nan herself once hinted, to a class of rather shocked eighteen year olds in the Training Centre during the 1950s, that married women didn't have *all* the fun. But in the 1920s, having an affair was risky. Society was, at least outwardly, strictly moral. Chaperones were still *de rigeur* for any entertainment that included men other than fathers, brothers, guardians or married uncles. The discovery of an affair, or worse, of a resulting pregnancy, brought disgrace.

John Macmurray may have been out of sight in Manchester, but Nan was unable to put him out of her mind, at least not all the time. 'Busy, practical and gay, prodigal of herself in good works, like a little hill pony for sturdy strength, she lived on the solid earth and loved her life', she describes Elizabeth in *Descent from the Cross*. Then, in a line reminiscent of the floods of 'Underground', she adds, 'yet sometimes she had dreams; she dreamed of engulfing seas'.[507]

In 1922 Nan would turn twenty-nine. She was not going to let her virginity wither. A year earlier, the Macmurrays had sailed for South Africa. While John was in his second year at Manchester, he heard from Jan Hofmeyr, a friend from his Balliol days who had returned to South Africa post-graduation). In Hofmeyr's letter was the offer of the Chair of Philosophy at the University of Witwatersrand in Johannesburg: 'There was no two ways about it. The answer was "Yes"', Betty recalled in her memoirs. She was excited: 'we were setting sail into the unknown'.[508] Friends and relatives, however, were dismayed. Manchester was far enough, but South Africa, in those days, was a very long way away.

★ ★ ★

Travel in the 1920s wasn't easy. There were no package tours; you found your own way around. 'To South Africa in Seventeen Days', the Union-Castle Line advertised its weekly mail service to South Africa in travel agents throughout the country. On the poster, one of its steamships, smart in its livery—a lavender grey hull topped with two red funnels—sits sleek in Cape Town harbour. Behind it rises Table Mountain, its summit hung with cloud. Nan was enticed. Not only would a trip to South Africa give her the opportunity to visit Betty and John, she could also catch up with Charles Murray and, probably most importantly, see her brother Frank's final resting place in Bloemfontein. On a cool and rainy Friday, the 23rd June 1922, the RMS Kenilworth Castle slipped out of Southampton Docks bound for Cape Town with Nan on board. For the first time, Nan left Scotland.

As First Class set you back £100, Nan was travelling in Second, along with most of the professional classes, immigrants and budget tourists. The ship's passenger log reveals Nan was travelling unaccompanied, but there were plenty of other women her age on board, also crossing solo to South Africa. Typists, teachers, students, clerks—many of them were emigrating. Not Nan though, her country of intended permanent residence is marked Scotland.

Nan would have been in lively company. Amongst the doctors and dentists, merchants and storekeepers, there were actors and artists on board too, as well as a couple of Cambridge scholars to keep Nan's brain engaged. Dinner-table discussions were likely to have been a little more stimulating than Betty found them on her voyage the year before. 'The talk at meals has been gossipy & doubtless therefore of much human value', she wrote scornfully in a journal she kept of her journey out to South Africa.

> We learn that Mrs X wears a jersey too squeamish for words. Miss J dances beautifully, but is rather short "don't you think?" & the gentleman with the grey hair—prematurely so, of course as my confidante assures me (unlike the peroxide-haired lady who is conversely preternaturally young) has lovely eyes and is worthy of notice, & so on.

There was much musing on the matrimonial too: 'How to retain a husband's love (by being skittish) and other remarks on the fickleness of man in general, lack edification. People seem to be more body than soul in an Atlantic liner'.[509]

But if the company was not, after all, so edifying, after four days the Kenilworth Castle dropped anchor in the bay of Funchal, on the southern coast of Madeira. How different and exotic it must have seemed to Aberdonian eyes. The second class deck was transformed into a market, hung with heavily embroidered linens and swarming with hucksters, chattering in Portuguese, holding out little baskets of oranges and dates, bananas and walnuts and thrusting sunny-scented violets and pink camellias into the passengers' hands. 'Halloos' rose from boats filled with naked youngsters who splashed into the sea after coins thrown for them.

And in the background, away from the all the noise and bustle on the boat, rose the island itself, its conical peaks draped in mist, the mountainside studded with red and yellow homesteads, each surrounded with terraces of vivid green and purple bougainvillea and here and there the white tower of a church. Those passengers who wanted to explore the sights in and around the town were taken over by steam launch. Having wandered its streets, stepping aside for the ox-pulled toboggans, they could then head up to the Fort. There, soldiers leaning lazily on their rifles in the heat, snapped to attention at the sight of a camera and marched up and down for the tourists.

Excursion over, its passengers stowed safely back on board, the liner steamed on, through the equator along Africa's west coast, towards Cape Town. To entertain passengers during the remaining thirteen days' voyage, activities were organised on deck which sound rather like nursery school sports days now. Among these were a 'driving competition' (in which ladies drove blindfolded gentleman in and out of rows of bottles) an egg and spoon and a potato race. Although she might well have been a wry observer, it's hard to imagine Nan taking part in any of these. According to Betty, people were shy on board and apt to be cliquey. Nan was far more likely to be found, a book in her hand, settled on a steamer chair in some quiet corner under the awnings, or standing at the rail as the 'ship tossed on billows', watching the 'flying fish skimming the surface of the sea like swallows',[510] a memory which finds its way into *The Quarry Wood*.

The cold and wet of Britain left far behind, on 10th July the Kenilworth arrived in Cape Town, where most of the passengers, Nan included, were disembarking. When it rains in the tropics, it rains, but June to September is South Africa's winter and its dry season. The days are bright and warm, heating up in the afternoons to the balmy temperatures of a British summer. Charles Murray was there to meet her from the boat. Leaning over the deck-rail she spied him, standing, still tall and spare, among the crowd waiting on the dockside, in his shabby coat full of tobacco holes—he had a tendency, absentmindedly, to shove a still burning pipe into his pocket. Murray was delighted, some forty years on, to be able to repay some of her parents' hospitality during his apprentice days in Cults by showing Nan around the Cape and Pretoria. 'Her parents were so good to me in the Cults days, it is a pleasure to be able to show her some small attention', he wrote to his friend George Walker in August 1922.[511]

Charles Murray was now sixty one. His hair was receding, greying like his moustache and bushy brows, and his 'lean hawk face' was a little more lined, but his lips were still quick to twitch with mirth. For the past couple of years, his health had been a worry and he was leading a quieter life, looking forward to retirement from his post as Secretary for Public Works. Two years before, he and Edith had celebrated their silver wedding anniversary. He remained as devoted to her as he was in the early days of their marriage when he was 'jealous of the heather-scented breezes that take liberties with your hair—my hair'. '

Nan and Dr Charles Murray in the Aberdeen Art gallery,
September 1934.

Yes, my wife, 25 years ago was a lucky date for me', he wrote to Edith,
adding 'there is one thing I have always felt grateful to you for—that is the
way you put up with my Scots leanings and hobby'.[512]

That hobby, as he called his vernacular verse-writing, in 1920 resulted
in an LL.D., conferred on him for his services to literature and his contribution to Scottish poetry. But since then his pen had grown idle. Apart
from some Greek translations of the *Epigrams* he had written no poems
for some time, but he was still keen to talk poetry with Nan. He had been

reading work by the avant-garde poet Edith Sitwell and wanted to know what was happening to poetry back in Britain.[513]

For the first few days Nan stayed with Charles and Edith at the comfortable, if rather expensive, seafront hotel where they spent half the year. As the Union Government's parliamentary session sat for six months in Cape Town and six in Pretoria, the Murrays, too, were forced divide their time between the hotel and their home over a day's journey north-east.

After a couple of days in the Cape they headed to Pretoria, stopping en-route in Bloemfontein so Nan could visit Frank's grave. Lying some thirty-seven miles north-east of Johannesburg in the Sunnyside district of Pretoria the Murray's home, 'The Willows' was a white, square house in the colonial style. A large, creeper-covered stoep[514] running round the ground floor on the front was echoed by a smaller, roofed balcony above. On humid South African summer nights, you could sleep semi-outdoors under mosquito nets—which would have appealed to Nan who, even in Scotland's summer, regularly took her bed outside.

In July, when South African nights are cooler than its days, no doubt Charles Murray's company made up for the evening's chill. A photograph of Nan sitting next to him in around 1912 shows her radiant, laughing. 'Charles Murray was a man one could not miss in a company', she said. 'He had presence: not self-assertive, but dynamic—one felt more alive from being with him. When he spoke, he had compulsive listeners. Droll, witty, solemn, seemingly nonchalant but with a delighted relish in what he related he was a raconteur of genius'.[515]

It was with the same relish he regaled Nan with 'the tale of the master mason', as he showed her round the vast new Union buildings, Parliament's official seat in Pretoria. The construction of these new government buildings was Murray's responsibility and between 1910 and 1913, when they were going up, he was there to supervise on a regular basis. One day, he sat himself down next to a stonemason, who asked, eyeing the rather rough-looking man who had sat down on a stone and newsed with him in his own North East dialect:

"Was ye wantin' a job?"

"I've gotten a job"

"Ye're lucky."

Discovering some time later who Charles Murray was, the stonemason was mortified, exclaiming, 'It was me that speired if ye was wantin' a job'. It was an encounter that went straight to Charlie Murray's heart, Nan said.[516] Illustrating he was company for 'Duke or ditcher alike' and imperturbably himself with either, the story went straight to hers too.

She retold it, almost word for word, in *A Pass in the Grampians* where the stonemason becomes a sheep farmer and Charles Murray, David Kilgour. The third of the Kilgour sons, David taught in a Colonial University in the Antipodes, declaimed Latin in a Scots accent and 'fell readily into the Doric, loving to recount a good Scots story'. 'Once he chanced upon a sheep farmer by the roadside and fell into talk. "Youre' frae the Nor-East" he said. And they talked of sheep and the ways of farmers. After a while the man eyed the Professor's clothes and said:

"Was ye wanting a job?"

"I've got a job."

"Ye're lucky"'.[517]

Towards the end of July, Nan headed back to Johannesburg, where the Macmurrays were renting a bungalow just around the corner from the city's zoo on Jan Smuts Avenue. The roars of lions regularly rent the afternoon air as they sat in wicker chairs on the brick-walled stoep drinking cups of tea served by the Macmurray's houseboy Kubugwami. 'Kubugwami was an imp, a sinner', Betty said. 'Full of peccadilloes, he had an infectious smile and a great sense of humour. Naughty, he was not vicious'—although he nearly poisoned them once, mistaking ant powder for pepper and shaking it liberally into their soup. Telling him she would box his ears if anything should happen to their little white terrier, Jessica, and her newborn pups,[518] Betty, John and Nan then took off for a holiday in Delagoa Bay.[519]

Betty's account of the holiday is curt.[520] They didn't much enjoy it. They had hoped to see crocodiles and didn't, and during an outing in the bay, their motor launch stalled leaving them becalmed for an hour in blistering sun.[521] For Nan, used to looking at the panorama of her native Deeside, the view of the Low Veld as the train hurried them from Delagoa was something else. It left its imprint in her fiction. 'Distance upon distance. Wouldn't you think it would never end?' Martha says to Roy Foubister in *The Quarry Wood,* having dragged him outside to look at the view of Lochnagar from her garden gate. 'Wait till you've seen the Veld", he responds, 'You won't talk about distances then. Or going down to Delagoa—the Low Veld. You look down and down and down and there's always more of it. You begin to think it must be the sea, and it isn't. It's always more earth'.[522]

'Earth' is the watchword linking Nan and the Macmurrays. Beneath her dedication to them in *In the Cairngorms* is the epigraph, 'Islands are united by the bottom of the sea'—the earth, in other words. In *The Weatherhouse,* there is an explanation. 'The sea was, after all, not so very wide; and earth, primitive, shapeless intractable was everywhere about one, & could not be ignored. Roots, if one thought of it, must grow somewhere—in the customary earth'.[523] Betty makes the meaning more explicit in her own novel, which even headlines the axiom in its title, *Out of the Earth:* 'You are the earth. I am planted in you already', David says to Agnes. Betty's title, of course, refers to the creation of man and woman in Genesis and in the copy she signed and gave to John she has written 'Wouldn't Adam be disgusted if his rib produced such a female?'[524] But her book also exudes D H Lawrence—which is not surprising as both Betty and John were disciples of his.

To Betty, Lawrence's appeal lay in his representation of sensuality in what she, like him, considered an over-intellectualised world. Underneath all the metaphysical idealism, to Lawrence, part-time anti-metaphysicist, lies the earth. In his introduction to the unexpurgated edition of *Pansies* (1929) he explains what he means and in doing so, clarifies what the word meant to these three, loving in a triangle:

> The fairest thing in nature, the flower, still has its roots in the earth and manure; and in the perfume there hovers still the faint strange scent of earth, the under-earth in all its heavy humidity and darkness. Certainly it is so in pansy-scent, and in violet-scent; mingled with the blue of the morning the black of the corrosive humus. Else the scent would be just sickly sweet. So it is: we all have our roots in earth…We have roots, and our roots are in the sensual, instinctive and intuitive body; and it is here we need fresh air of open consciousness.[525]

Lawrence, John is supposed to have said, meant more to him than anybody,[526] a description which sounds rather exaggerated—Betty was the only person who meant more to John than anybody. Once John recovered from the shock of Lawrence's freedom of expression over the body and sex, he decided this was the one modern writer from whom he could learn. Lawrence, he thought, was conscious of life in a way he was not, a consciousness he wanted to explore, through 'passionate friendships' with others. In dialogue which sounds as though it might have been a conversation that actually took place (perhaps on several occasions over the years) Betty explains John's thinking in *Out of the Earth:* "You are so glib in theory", Maribel says to David "Do you really need people except in vague general terms—aren't you sufficient in yourself?" "What a question to ask a married man", David responds, before continuing:

> "If I'm sufficient in myself where does Agnes come in, and all my friends—you, for example? Don't you think that friend-

ship is the biggest thing on earth?"

"You mean intellectual friendships?"

"You can't separate emotion and intellect. Why should the intercourse of friends be intellectual only? Friendship without emotion isn't friendship."

"But if emotion comes in isn't it love? Wouldn't it get you into an awful hole?"

"It's worth risking." David answers and smiling, kisses her on the cheek. [527]

In South Africa in 1922, however, this was still a theory which had yet to be put into practice.

Perhaps the reason for Betty's terse description of their Delagoa holiday and the fact she makes no mention in her memoirs of Nan's stay with them out in South Africa, is because what seems to have happened during that time was fraught, emotionally, for all three. 'One can't preach freedom without trying to test it out, and as I know, enjoying it' Betty wrote years later in her memoirs. But as she was to discover, she could be 'a vicious and jealous little cat', [528] and on the crossing from Britain to South Africa over a year and a half earlier, she had a premonition: 'The query arises, do climactic conditions change character? If so, what will J.M. become? At the moment of writing the cock from the upper deck crows: 'Surely if omens are worthy of regard, a timely warning that he will betray me!' [529]

In *Out of the Earth* David tells Agnes he wants to have 'many friends for your love to reach through me!' Agnes tries to grasp what he means and finds it is beyond her. Then she thinks of Maribel. David 'evidently, was tremendously attractive to her' and so she invites her to stay with them in Oxford. [530] After the Macmurray's South African sojourn was cut unexpectedly short in November 1922, they moved to Oxford. Much to Betty's sadness, they had to leave Jessica behind. In her memoirs she recalled the heart-rending sight of a bewildered Jessica chasing their train as it pulled out of Johannesburg. But in her novel, while Betty locates Maribel's visit to them in Oxford, Jessica (who, coincidentally, is described as 'soon to become a mother to little mongrel pups') makes several appearances—bounding onto Maribel's bed and upsetting her morning breakfast tray, for one. In the absence of any concrete evidence, to compare Betty's memoirs, *The Quarry Wood* and *Out of the Earth* side by side, is to unravel what seems to have happened in South Africa.

There is also, of course, Nan's poetry. As Robert Macfarlane says, we must be wary of identifying the narrator of the sonnets as Nan herself, 'yet it is clear' he adds, 'that she used them in some way to dramatise personal experience'.[531] And it is, indeed, hard to imagine they were written from second-hand experience, or constructed solely from her imagination— they are too intensely realised, too powerful, too raw. Their first-person narration also brings them closer to a more confessional reading. Not that Nan's poetry, any more than her prose, limits itself to a single interpreta- tion. But, if we go carefully, an examination of Nan's poetry may also add some insight, if only as a working-through of emotion.

While the Macmurrays were far away in Manchester, Nan perhaps thought she could shut away her secret yearning and let it rot. But like the narrator of 'Half Love' she may inwardly have been in torment, troubled still with longing, loving from afar. The second stanza runs:

> So coward I cried, broken and spent with loving,
> Broken and spent with half-fulfilled desire.
> I am too weak and mortal for your having
> Who fear to flare not burnish in your fire.[532]

Fire is an image often used to evoke strong emotion and sexual desire. The imagery recurs in 'A Girl in Love': 'we did not know/How fair she was, nor how her ways/That we had thought dull earth could burn…Her woods are shapes of ire, her frame/Is haloed with a fiery ring./Her rocks, her hills, are kindled now.[533] What is implied here, is a change, and the narrative constructed in her entries in *Gleanings,* which is echoed in the sequence of poems in her manuscript book, suggests that Nan too, underwent a change.

The trouble, it seems, was that this change was not immediately recognised and came as a shock during confrontation. Because at some point, Nan must have confronted John. We know from *Gleanings* that she was reading Sappho and the extracts she has written in Greek and translated on the opposite page reveal agitation and the realisation that silence is no longer an option: 'I am paler than grass, and seem in my madness little better than one dead. But I must dare all…'. In *Out of the Earth,* Betty constructs a confrontation, making it clear from David's reaction that his vision of Maribel until then remained an idealised one: '"But Maribel, I don't understand, I've never really thought of you that way at all. I've never wanted to make love to you, not because you're not desirable, but simply because you didn't seem to exist for me that way, at least I don't know. I never thought of it.'"

Maribel is more than a little frustrated by his response: 'You make love to a woman with your head, tearing aside all her reserves and then when you're confronted with the woman herself—naked of thought— you don't recognise her! "I don't love this woman, you say, I loved the thing, the mental thing she was" '.[534] For a time, David cannot decide whether or not he loves Maribel and treats her like an abstract problem while he makes up his mind.[535] Eventually, as he confesses to Agnes, he told Maribel he loved her, 'but that I did not know how much, nor what I wanted of her love',[536] which must have been both confusing and humiliating.

It is clear from her poetry that for Nan love was not something to be intellectualised; it was felt, furiously. And while we cannot be absolutely sure of the timing, it was, at some point, physically expressed. In *The Quarry Wood* Luke and Martha's 'moment of exquisite communion', takes place in the 'glimmering gloom' of the woods, where she 'offers herself', her whole being crying 'take me, take me'. The moment of 'communion' is made deliberately ambiguous as if it were spiritual rather than physical, but there is in Nan's use of language a hint that there was, in fact, more than she will let on in phrases like 'afterglow and the promise of dawning dissolved together in one soft lustre'.[537] With the censure of her readers in mind, Nan cannot be explicit so she implies instead.[538]

In her *Medley Book,* Nan copied out Kathleen Raine's 'He married me with a ring, a ring of bright water, whose ripples travel from the heart of the sea',[539] underlining the last three words. The quotation is followed by an extract from L MacNally's *Highland Years* '…that lovely delicate green nimbus, a shimmering mistiness rather than a tangible reality, enshrouding the earliest birch trees…' Betty sets David and Maribel's 'moment' beside a pool, which she employs to represent secrets 'like a stilled memory'.[540] Nan goes further, linking trees and water together into an image (which may well have been rooted in fact) that seems symbolic for the act of consummation and which, for years, 'shimmered' in her memory. The pool beside the birches, trees symbolic of rebirth, passion and growth, and the pool's associated imagery of reflection, hidden depths—a secret place—haunts her writing.

Pools and naked birches recur in 'An Ecstasy Remembered' as the setting for 'our moment of amazed beatitude': 'A shining group, the bare wet birches stood,/Their trunks like glass, their thousand rain-drops caught'.[541] And again in *The Weatherhouse:* 'Birches were like tangles of shining hair,' Garry thought, 'insubstantial, floating like shredded light above the soil'.[542] Ellen Falconer, too, sees the annunciation of Spring, 'a wood of naked birches hanging on the hillside like a cloud of heather, so deep is the glow of purple in their boughs'.[543] The sensuality in the Lawrentian-style language is palpable, its meaning explicit. And then, in *Gleanings* Nan's Catullus translation ends: 'Maidenhood, maidenhood, whither art thou gone away from me?

Never again will I come to thee, never again'. [544]

In 1931 Nan sent Neil Gunn several poems. Among them was 'Union', a sonnet which appears neither in *In the Cairngorms* nor in Nan's poetry manuscript book. Too personal, too revelatory perhaps, because here the act of consummation or 'surrender' is less oblique:

> Dear, I have kept not back, though I made my boast,
> Once, to have dark reserves and hidden store
> Of mine own intimate self: but now no more
> I am afraid to offer the uttermost
> And come all naked to thee: yet thou Know'st
> Though more, still less of me than e'er before.
> Seeing that the giver gives and the gift is o'er.
> But when giver and gift are one, to the end thou ow'st.
>
> Ah love, surrender could not be more complete!
> But in the very surrender I discover
> New intimacies to show to thee my love
> And showing, yet newer privacies secrete,
> Till ever upon the marge of oneness we hover,
> Yet ever, O love, from lonelier travelling meet. [545]

The sextet, particularly, has an intricate metaphysical quality that Neil Gunn recognised, 'hovering on the marge of oneness' suggesting that shimmering 'other landscape', but it is also, sensually suggestive. The holding back is over, and there is a vulnerability in the speaker, 'naked' their 'intimate self' exposed.

Post-consummation, however, there seems still no real comprehension by the recipient of the enormity of this gift of surrender in 'Union'. The line, 'yet thou Knows't/Though more, still less of me than e'er before', might even be read as a cynical rebuttal of the theory about only knowing oneself through passionate friendship with others. Afterwards, the breaking of 'vows I never swore' and 'shame for deeds I disallow' of the sonnet 'Growth', speaks to both the covenant of marriage and of friendship. 'Pardon', too, reveals the aftermath:

> And after, no beatitude for us,
> But hatred, shame, contempt, disgust, despair,
> Estrangement and unsanctified remorse
> And black self-knowledge eating like a curse'. [546]

'The inexpiable wrong' remained between them, 'unredeemed, pure pain, pure loss, destructive, sore'. 'Without expiation',[547] written in March 1933, reeks of bitterness. The lines in the third stanza 'No reparation can be made./Put all pretence away, and meet/The consequences unafraid', suggest that damage has been done, it can not be undone and honesty is now paramount.

Two years before her death, Nan wrote to Jessie Kesson, 'giving up to someone else what one has held inside one for a lifetime is a queer experience & one may suffer revulsion against oneself. But that does pass. And perhaps one gains new light on one's experience'.[548] Nan was writing then with knowledge gleaned from hindsight. It would take some time for her to gain new light on the experience, but she would eventually come to terms with it at least.

On the 8th September 1922, Nan shoved the rather large water-pot she had bought during the trip into her hat box and boarded the Balmoral Castle bound for Southampton. 'You see I didn't care what happened to my hats on the way home', she said, smiling.[549]

Chapter Eight

1923-1928

Nan Shepherd never wanted or intended to write a novel, she said in an interview in 1933 adding, 'I can't tell you why I did it'.[550] She also said, however, that she wrote only when there was something which simply had to be written.[551] *The Quarry Wood* simply had to be written. She began it not long after she returned from South Africa.

Some insight into what prompted the novel is given in the book itself: 'I am an uncompleted work of art. My creator has flung me aside', Martha thinks to herself. 'But stung suddenly by the admission the thought implied, "Good Lord!" she exclaimed. "Am I such a slave as that? Dependent on a man to complete me! I thought I couldn't be anything without him—I can be my own creator".[552]

With the press furore over the 'surplus women' and the complicated situation surrounding the man she loved, Nan uses Martha as a vehicle to vent. But at the same time, instead of the route to fulfilment that post war society still insisted on imposing on women, she offers an alternative. The First World War may have deprived many women of potential mates, but it enabled a pioneering few to establish careers and to remain financially independent. Spinsterhood could be a deliberate choice. In many ways, Nan's progressive choice for her heroine anticipates the one made by Toni Morrison's, Sula, in her novel written some fifty years later: 'When you gone to get married? You need to have some babies. It'll settle you', she is asked and replies, 'I don't want to make somebody else—I want to make myself'.[553]

By the end of *The Quarry Wood*, Martha has found in little Robin an outlet for her maternal urge and is fulfilled by her work. She has 'acquiesced in her destiny and so delivered herself from the insecurity of the adventurer'.[554] Nan, as we know from the *Sheila Book,* devoted herself to Sheila Roger. She also had her work. She was lucky to have it.

The post-war years were grim. The euphoria of victory quickly dissipated in the face of unemployment and inflation. By 1923 the number of 'idle' in Aberdeen alone had jumped from below two thousand to almost eight, many of them ex-servicemen. To compound the misery, there were endless flu epidemics, and outbreaks of dysentery closed schools and claimed lives. Strike followed strike. Even the weather matched the mood. In the wettest February for fifty years, nine inches of rain fell on Deeside and salmon swam in flooded fields.[555]

No doubt the writing of *The Quarry Wood* provided a relief from all this misery and was cathartic to some extent, but Nan would continue to work through her feelings for some years yet—albeit not so much in her prose as in her poetry. She wrote in snatches. Whenever she could find time to spare between work at the Training Centre and its endless round of marking, Nan drafted fragments of her novel which she intended later to weave into a more coherent narrative. Mure Mackenzie was sceptical about this approach: 'I wonder which really is the best way— your writing bits to be co-ordinated later or my solemn march along the road. I doubt if I tried your way, though, I should find I'd anything left for the connective tissue.' Nevertheless, she was encouraging: 'I'll be pleased to meet Maggie Hunter; even in bits…although "Maggie" is a name I love not'.[556]

As there are no manuscripts of Nan's novels extant, it is hard to know exactly when 'Maggie' was changed to 'Martha'. On publication there were, inevitably, comparisons made with George Eliot's, also autobiographical, *The Mill on the Floss*. Nan's novel is as thoroughly Scottish as George Eliot's is English, but aside from both works being their authors' most autobiographical, they are both, too, about bookish girls with intellectual ambitions growing up in an atmosphere of little encouragement, whose most valuable lessons are learned outside of education. Whether or not Nan wished to discourage further comparison to *Mill on the Floss*—Eliot's heroine is called Maggie Tulliver—or because Mure disliked the name, 'Maggie' went. In any case the etymology of 'Martha' is polysemous which no doubt appealed to Nan.[557] From the Aramaic 'marta' signifying a lady or mistress, as well as its biblical association as Lazarus's sister and Mary of Bethany, known for her obsession with housework (a foil for the slovenly Emmeline, although Martha has to be angry to be intolerant of dirt) 'Martha' was better suited to the plot. In Hebrew, the name means 'bitter', which, post-South Africa, Nan was.

During the writing process, Nan's female protagonist also underwent a surname change, from 'Hunter' to 'Ironside', probably in 1925. Adjacent to the Shepherd family lair at Springbank Cemetery in Countesswell's Road, Aberdeen, is the Ironside's. Coming from an Aberdeenshire family, Ann Ironside who died in 1922, had outlived her three sons (one of whom is buried in South Africa). The name of her youngest son 'George' may even have been borrowed for Martha's father, Geordie. It could be pure coincidence, but Nan, with her ever-seeing eye can hardly have failed to notice the inscription on the gravestone next door to her family's. And in 1925 she would have cause to be there, at the burial of her father.

The winter of 1924 was harassed and laborious. Without being officially recognised as Head of Department, Nan had taken on more responsibility at the Training Centre, dramatically increasing her workload. She was still writing her novel and on top of this was working on a study of Rupert Brooke's poetry. Then, in what seems a bizarre coincidence, John Shepherd died on the morning of the eighth anniversary of Frank's death, the 19th May 1925. He suffered a cerebral haemorrhage and by 7.25 am he was gone, slipping away unobtrusively in his sleep at the age of seventy-two.

Towards the end of his life, John's intensely black hair, brows and beard had turned white. Much of his hair receded from his forehead and temples giving him a more noble appearance than he had in his youth. Always a small man, he grew slighter, more hunched around the shoulders and somewhat weary-looking in old age. Frank's death had knocked the stuffing out of him. He never mentioned it, just carried on in his own quiet way. But he long since stopped bothering to keep himself abreast of the latest engineering news; with Frank gone he had no-one with whom he could discuss and debate them.

Whether or not it was Nan who found her father dead that morning, it was she who signed his death certificate. With both the Shepherd men gone, Dunvegan was now a house of three women. Nan was still only thirty two. The freedom she had tasted fleetingly on her South African adventure only three years earlier was still fresh, and until John Shepherd died, she may well have entertained thoughts that she might one day leave home. His death now made that an impossibility. In the will John Shepherd made in 1919 he left his estate in trust to Jeannie, bequeathing Dunvegan and its contents to his wife for life rent (meaning she could live there but not dispose of the property) and to his daughter in fee. Always careful with his salary, John left enough money too for the repair and maintenance of the house, making Nan's position easier, but without his pension she was now the sole bread-winner. Like Martha in *The Quarry Wood* there would be no sailing beyond the Pillars of Hercules. 'Life was bounded again in its exter-nals'[558] by the domestic responsibilities at Dunvegan and by her invalid mother.

Once again, Nan threw herself into her work. But if, on the surface, she seemed acquiescent to her destiny, she was determined others would not share the same fate:'I did this, don't you do the same', she is reported to have been overheard saying to one of her students, making it sound as though she had a choice in the matter—which, realistically, she did not. Society expected Nan to remain at home and look after her mother and remain she did. But it was a difficult period of adjustment, exacerbated by grief for her father, who along with her brother, she later brought back to life in *The Weatherhouse* as John and David Grey.

'A gey quiet missy—terrible keep-yersel'—tae—yersel-kin' the folk at school said of Martha.[559] At the Training Centre Nan's colleagues would have thought, if not said, the same. If her inner life was turbulent and if, as she said many years later in her letter to Jessie Kesson, she was suffering revulsion against herself, Nan would have kept it to herself. Poetry, it seems, was her outlet, a way to order her emotions. In July 1926 she wrote 'Love Eternal':

There are two ways of loving. One must own:
Jealous, exclusive, careless of the event,
Abandoned, rash, superbly insolent,
That having has the world and to atone
For theft so huge, were other worlds but known
Would have them too in having its content;
That having not has all of punishment,
Yet will not have except it have alone.[560]

The first stanza admits the single-minded pursuit that is articulated in Betty's *Out of the Earth,* 'she had only looked one way'.[561] 'Jealous, exclusive, careless, abandoned, rash, insolent'. In an echo of the sonnet, 'Without my Right', having stolen what was desired may have felt like having the world, but it was at some cost to all parties. The line, 'were other worlds but known' is explained in *The Quarry Wood*. 'She saw that Luke had broken her integrity, and by not loving her had put a larger wholeness beyond her reach. "He had no right," she cried savagely to herself'.[562]

But the phrase also lifts the sonnet onto a more metaphysical plane, an 'other' dimension is suggested here, which could be toying with the idea of man's oneness with the universe as well as with each other and links, too, with John Macmurray's philosophy of knowing oneself through others as an infinite not definite idea. 'Having not' is the punishment, the speaker says. This kind of loving will only accept exclusivity.

The sonnet is ambiguous, layers of meaning woven through its lines.

Going forward, the Macmurrays' agreement to experiment with John's philosophy of personal freedom within their marriage meant that all involved parties had to manage their jealousy. None can be exclusive. In her memoirs, Betty said that in London in the late 1920s when she and John finally threw off convention, both 'had to go through much suffering when it seems it wasn't worth a candle'. 'But,' as she acknowledged, 'one can't preach freedom without trying to test it out, and as I know, enjoying it.'[563]

The second stanza of Nan's sonnet, 'Love Eternal', attempts some form of understanding of this freedom—'And one is free and unconcerned as air…it seeketh not but is already there'. The symbolic waters of 'Underground', that broke open and swamped her, resurface. Here, Nan uses the strength and eternal mystery of water to symbolise this sharing: 'It flee through space, they rove upon the ground' the sonnet ends. Loving like this, liberates rather than imprisons.

It is not surprising that around this time Nan became ill and stopped work on *The Quarry Wood*. 'Poor Lassie', wrote Mure, who had developed a passion for oranges and was downing them at all times, so that her letter was liberally spattered with their juice, 'I'm awfully sorry Brother Ass[564] has gone down again…I hope it's only a temporary out-of-gearness…I'm sorry about *The Quarry Wood*. But you simply aren't fit for the strain right now. I'm different—my Coll. work this year and last is indecently light…you <u>couldn't</u> work on top of your heavy Training Centre work. Have some sense wummmaan!… get yourself better…Oh dear, let's go and get drunk!'[565]

It *was* a temporary out-of-gearness. Nan rallied and began writing again. Mure, reading the novel in instalments as they were written, was anxious to see the end. She was already thinking about the book's reception on publication:

I'm afraid you'll be in for a lot of the irrelevant—both praise & blame. Superficially in the QW is what has been done often & often, though luckily for you the biography from infancy to first love-affair is still very fashionable…The fact of its fundamental originality will only strike the better people.[566]

Whatever the critics thought, Mure anticipated fat sales and a print run of at least a thousand.

By late 1925, Mure had seen the complete novel and wrote to congratulate Nan. 'Nancy wuuummman, you've done it with a vengeance', she applauded, immediately recognising the parallels with *The Mill on the Floss*. In her opinion *The Quarry Wood* was the better of the two: 'It has George Eliot's qualities and avoids her lack', she said, before going on to lay a heavy, critical hand on the book:

> There's nothing wrong in the <u>stuff</u> of it. That is first-rate: the thing is a great book, if there's any meaning in the adjective. And the general layout is all right [sic]. The argument is logical & inevitable. What's wrong is in the actual writing. I fancy the root of it is the habit of lecturing—& I fancy of lecturing without notes, too. The dialogue is excellent all through—the Scots especially, though I think you'll be wise to give the book a glossary. <u>Most</u> of the landscape is singularly lovely: and <u>most</u> of the narrative is clear enough. There's one passage ... of the coming on of autumn. That's a rare bit of work.[567]

Mure is talking about Chapter 14. Beginning 'At the turn of July there was already a hint of autumn', a long, lyrical paragraph follows, filled with acute observation:

> Birds gathered; suddenly on a still day a tree would heave and *reeshle* with their movement, a flock dart out and swoop, to settle black and serried on the telegraph wires [ ] a roaring and a rustle and a creak was everywhere; and dust and dead leaves eddied in the gateways.[568]

But there were other parts that suffered from what Mure considered Nan's most dangerous failing, a common one she felt (although she was surprised to find it in Nan's work): 'Every now and then the words so to speak <u>clot</u> (they cease to be transparent) on top of the meaning: one is conscious of them and not of their significance'. [569] Mure goes on to explain that this is not just carelessness, more often it is that having expressed something fully, Nan then proceeds to repeat it, cheapening the idea. 'You've even used the very word that crystallises your idea. Why do you want to go and spoil a good effect???' Coming from Mure, who by this time had published *Without Conditions* and *The Half Loaf*, it was the kind of constructive criticism for which every aspiring writer is grateful (as well as something battered home nowadays in creative writing classes).

Nan took Mure's criticism on board and acted on it. This we know, because the examples Mure used to show Nan where there were 'clots' are no longer to be found in the published version of *The Quarry Wood*. Apart from the sometimes careless and clumsy prose, however, Mure found the book 'excellent reading'. So good, that for the most part, she said, her 'mind swiftly accepted the content of the narration & went no further—a sincere compliment to an MS with slabs of a not very familiar dialect in it.'

She went on to discuss the characters. Martha, she thought first-rate. Luke and Dussie she felt were merely adequate and while she thought Dussie charming, she disliked Luke (although the touch of astringency in later chapters saved him as a character). As for the others, Aunt Josephine, Clemmie and Mary Annie, Mure declared to be on a par with Scott. She had been prepared for something great to come out of her friend, 'but it's bigger than I was expecting'.

In 1925, Mure is cheerfully confident that *The Quarry Wood* will be taken on immediately. Having already told C. S. Evans at Heinemann about it, Mure suggests sending the manuscript to Evans himself with a letter reminding him of the fact. 'I don't think there's any good asking for a fixed sum in advance on this one. Anyhow, you aren't hard up, so it doesn't matter.'[570] Nan was not hard up. Her salary by then was keeping her mother, Mary and herself comfortably, which was just as well, because her novel was refused by thirteen publishing houses before it finally appeared in print in 1928.

★ ★ ★

Those who refused it, did not quite know what to make of it. *The Quarry Wood* did not conform to the perception, at the time, of what a Scottish novel should be. Nor could it be shoe-horned into one of the categories then available: 'Kailyard', 'Scots Romantic' or the antithesis of 'Kailyard', like George Douglas Brown's *The House with Green Shutters*. 'Kailyard'[571] (cabbage patch) was a dismissive term used to describe sentimental, rural Scottish tales. It had fallen from favour at home, but at the turn of the twentieth century 'Kailyard' works by the likes of J M Barrie were still popular internationally. Nan, of course, cannot resist an irreverent mention of 'Kail' which slips in several times in her first two novels. 'You don't get the like of that at Knapperley', Theresa says, slapping pancakes down on the tea-table. 'It's aye the same thing with Bawbie, a stovie or a sup kail'.[572] *The Quarry Wood* was difficult to categorise because, like Theresa's pancakes, it was something new.

Never one to mince her words, Nan felt strongly on the subject of labelling, the tendency to shove a writer's work into one category or another and leave it there, without subjecting it to further scrutiny:

All categories are absurd where art is concerned. I don't believe in categories but in individualities. It's just the slack-thinking that is one of the curses of our hurried and mass-producing age that makes lazy people love to label things and think they have understood them. Mental inertia makes one flick a book into a category and then suppose that is all there is to it. Whereas what there is to it is an individual mind, a mode of experience, a whole universe, one unique vision of truth. Or should be.[573]

However, whether she liked categorisation or not, Nan's novels were intrinsically modern. Exploring female identity, their geographical location and use of dialect also binds them with the issue of Scottish nationalism during the period which was manifesting itself in a debate over language and a discrete national literature. When *The Quarry Wood* eventually appeared in 1928, those hoping for a renaissance in Scottish letters at last felt their hopes had not been in vain 'and that granted another writer or two of the same power and originality as that possessed by Nan Shepherd…Scotland might yet make her mark upon the world of literature and art which is too often prone to leave her in the rear'.[574]

The context out of which Nan Shepherd's novels were written, the 'Scottish Renaissance', for her, was not just background noise. Like fellow Scottish women writers of the period, among them Lorna Moon, Willa Muir, Catherine Carswell and Naomi Mitchison, she was very much part of the movement which began in the inter-war years.

A new-found nationalism provoked by the First World War made Scottish writers returning from the battlefields look closely at what was happening in their homeland. What they saw was a Scotland being Anglicised. Along with the speaking of Scots language in classrooms, Scottish history and literature had been banished from school curriculums. This was compounded by the fact that, in order to reach a larger audience, Scottish writers were having to write in English and that what was being written was 'romantic tartan', reinforcing a culturally unhealthy stereotype of rural Scotland and its inhabitants.

Scotland, the revivalists decided, was culturally bankrupt, its own national identity being subsumed into the larger one of Great Britain. The impetus of the 'Renaissance' movement was a desire to overturn the perception of Scotland merely as 'North Britain', to create a discrete, national identity and to place Scotland firmly on the European literary map.[575]

1922 is the year generally considered the starting block of literary modernism[576] and that summer, while Nan was away in South Africa, Scotland's literati were stirring. Ezra Pound's modernist war-cry, 'Make it new', was heard, adopted and adapted to suit his purpose by Christopher Grieve, then a young journalist in Montrose. 'Il far un libro meno e che niente se il libro fatto non rifa la gente' ('To make a book is less than nothing unless the book, when made, makes people anew') he wrote in August 1922, in the inaugural issue of his Scottish *Chapbook.*

Grieve's was arguably the loudest voice of the early Scottish Renaissance movement. A colourful character, 'in some quarters', Nan said, he was regarded 'as an unmannerly tub-thumper'.[577] Straw-haired and fidgety-eyed, pugnacious in person and on paper, Grieve was as idiosyncratic as Ezra Pound and a more entertaining drinker than Dylan Thomas.[578]

Aware of the activities of small, avant-garde publications in London, Grieve wanted a similar platform for Scotland, a forum for debate about matters national and cultural, and a place to experiment with new ideas on creative writing. 'Not Traditions—Precedents' proclaimed the lion rampant image emblazoned on the flame-red cover of *The Chapbook* and inside, in true avant-garde spirit, Grieve outlined his manifesto: a campaign for the revival of Doric; to support the movement for a Scots National Theatre; to support encourage and publish the work of contemporary Scottish writers, poets and dramatists, whether in English, Gaelic or Braid Scots; to insist on truer evaluations of the work of Scottish writers by British literary critics and develop a distinctively Scottish range of values; to bring Scottish Literature closer in touch with European techniques and ideas or concepts; to cultivate 'the lovely virtue'; and generally, to 'meddle wi' the thistle and pick the figs'.[579]

Debate about language became central to Scotland's literary 'Renaissance' movement. The problem was Scotland's linguistic diversity. In *The Athenaeum* in 1919, T S Eliot, having asked, 'Was there a Scottish Literature?' decided there was not, because Scotland had neither a single language nor a coherent literary history.[580] Scots dialects, pre-renaissance, were not seen as a serious literary tool— if anything there was a view that Scots as a literary language was inferior to English. Having initially argued, using the work of Irish Revivalists like Yeats as an example, that any modern Scottish Literature would have to be in English, Grieve then changed his tune. As issues of the *Chapbook* progressed, so did Grieve's contention that the Scots language was not purely something to be encouraged alongside Gaelic in Scottish literature, it was fundamental to the Scottish literary revival.[581]

In 1922, however, he decided that Doric was simply not up to the task. 'A modern consciousness cannot fully express itself in the Doric as it exists',[582] he said and finding a copy of James Wilson's *Lowland Scotch* lurking on his own bookshelf was delighted to discover words, some by then obsolete, that were resolutely local, unusual and idiomatic. Poems by 'Hugh MacDiarmid' then began to appear in the *Chapbook*.

Many of MacDiarmid's early lyrics were written in a language which has been described as 'synthetic Scots',[583] but which is, according to David Murison of *The Scottish National Dictionary,* 'by and large, the equivalent of 'Lallans', the language of the Lowlands of Scotland.[584] However, in his attempt to develop and extend literary Scots, MacDiarmid had a habit of random dictionary-dredging and sprinkled into his verse, words which had become largely obsolete through disuse. Murison, for one, did not think this was the right way to go about developing a literary language for Scotland.

Grieve defended the use of these words:'They serve a useful purpose, I think, in rescuing from oblivion and restoring to literary use, forgotten words that have a descriptive potency unavailable elsewhere'.[585] Some sixteen years later, Nan would defend MacDiarmid's use of what had also been called 'a private vocabulary':

> Private words are a revolt against conventional emotion. If in using them the poet repudiates all those overtones and under-tones of suggestion and association on which poetic effect depends...—this is exactly his purpose, a gain and not a loss. For he sees words, as well as phrases, sickle o'er, made senti-mental through an excess of sentiment...Let us have new words, therefore, to give our stark clean exact meaning, words not yet saturated with other people's meanings so that we have no guarantee at all that our readers will take our meaning from them'. [586]

It was nothing new after all. Wordsworth had been doing much the same thing over a century before. Using words which had become obsolete, to Nan, seemed sensible:

> It is the endless spiral of expression; and as slow time revolves, the past soaks out of the older words and we can use them again: even, if we have wit enough for new meanings. After all, why should new words for new modes of experience be denied to the pioneer yet allowed to scientists?[586]

The *Chapbook* was the first of a series of periodicals established and edited by Grieve during the 1920s. Most of these were short-lived, but all of them had an impact and far-reaching influence. Eventually, they had the desired effect.[587] By 1925, when MacDiarmid published *Sangschaw*, his first anthology of Scots lyrics, Scottish newspapers had begun to feature articles on Scottish literature and culture and were using the term 'Scottish Renaissance' to describe this new movement. But it was not until MacDiarmid's *Penny Wheep*[588] and *A Drunk Man Looks at the Thistle* were published in 1926, that the press outside Scotland began to pay attention to what was going on there. His works were reviewed in the *Times Literary Supplement* and America's *Saturday Review of Literature* amongst others, and from then on, despite the controversy he caused (or perhaps because of it) he remained very much a headline of the 'Scottish Renaissance'.

Nan's own thoughts on Scotland's literary language were clarified in 1933. It was a natural, unforced use of dialect and a typically Scottish syntax that was important. Her inclusion of the Aberdeenshire dialect in her own novels, she said, was because it came naturally to her. She never forced a word into its context. The word had to be there:

'Whenever a suitable dialect word offers itself in a piece of description or narrative I use it without hesitation' she said. 'And then, of course, there's another thing. Scottish speech has a rhythm of its own; a quite distinctive rhythm. These two things—dialect and that typically Scottish arrangement of words—seem likely to be two of the most important features of any national literature Scotland may produce.'[589]

The problem with this, (despite the fact that English papers were beginning to notice and report what was going on in Scotland's literary scene) was that like most new and unknown Scottish writers Nan had been forced to look to England to sell her work. 'Scots publishers', as Lewis Grassic Gibbon said, 'are surely amongst the sorriest thing that can enter hell'. New Scottish writers therefore had to 'consign their manuscripts to alien publishers and the consideration of largely alien readers'. [590] And these 'alien readers'—the English—were put off by works using Scots language.

In May 1926, Evans was still deliberating over *The Quarry Wood*. He recognised its merit, but the book's length would make it expensive to print. He was also concerned that the amount of dialect in the text would limit sales: and as this was Nan's first novel, she had no reputation as an established author to help increase them. He suggested cutting some of the early parts of the book, particularly the opening and some of the descriptive passages which he felt were too long. Mure Mackenzie also felt that architecturally the book would benefit from some compression. What Nan thought about this, we do not know. Before she could respond, Heinemann rejected *The Quarry Wood* on the advice of one of its readers.[591] Mure saw the reader's report and described it as 'thoroughly cheap' but was unable to persuade Evans to change his mind.[592] Dents, Cassells and then Blackwood also turned down the novel. Like Evans at Heinemann, Blackwood decided that the work was too Scottish for English readers and therefore not worth risking the heavy cost of printing.

Eventually, things began to happen. After an hour's talk with Otto Kyllman, Senior Partner at Constable & Co,[593] Mure dashed off a letter to Nan telling her it looked as though *The Quarry Wood* was going to be accepted. She had provisionally agreed terms on Nan's behalf (10% to five thousand, then 15%) which, although not high, were better than she had expected. It was better to accept low terms, Mure counselled, and benefit from good advertising and a decent imprint.

Founded 1795 in Edinburgh, Constable & Co opened a London office at 10 & 12 Orange Street, Leicester Square, WC2 in 1890. By the early 1900s it was one of the leading publishing houses in England, with authors such as George Bernard Shaw, Damon Runyon, Theodore Dreiser, Dorothy Sayers and James Bridie. Nan was lucky: its three main directors, Otto Kyllman, William Meredith and James Sadleir, were friend, confidant and literary advisor to their clients.

Echoing Evans, Kyllman thought the book could stand some cutting. The opening was too slow, he said and he was concerned readers would be put off by too many patches of Doric. He also thought a glossary might be sensible and Mure offered to compile one (although as she came from Stornoway, the dialect was no more her native speech than Kyllman's). The consensus was that Luke was the weakest element of the book and needed pruning, that in places the connective tissue needed compression and some of the landscape descriptions needed condensing. Martha, however, needed no revision.[594] Constable was number fourteen on the list of publishers to try. If Nan had not been prepared to cut the book for Heinemann, several rejections later, she now was. She set about revising it as quickly as possible.

However, even with a revised manuscript, a contract was not guaranteed. 'If a Scot had said what he had, I should consider the contract as good as signed,' Mure remarked, 'but with an Englishman one has to make a considerable discount'.[595] Nationality aside, however, Constable came good. In July, Kyllman was drawing up the contract and by September 1927, Nan was awaiting proofs. Finally, in February 1928, *The Quarry Wood* was published. She dedicated it to her mother.

The morning after the book was published, her students showed their appreciation: Nan entered her classroom at the Training Centre to the thunder of stamping feet. Holding up her hand for silence, she sat down at her desk and went straight into her lecture as though nothing had happened.[596] Being a perfectionist, Nan's silence on the subject of her novel may well have been because the end result had not met her own expectations. Jessie Kesson thought so. 'I could only deduce' she said in 1990, 'that the book did not, in her opinion, come up to the standard of her *mind's* conception. I know the feeling well. Nothing I have written ever comes up to that flawless work my 'mind' conceived.'[597]

Mure Mackenzie, whose third novel, *Lost Kinellan,* had been published the year before *The Quarry Wood* in 1927, also understood the 'horrible differences between the original idea & accomplished fact'. 'It's not the feeling of having "made oneself a motley to the view"—though you'll probably have that worse than I have', Mure went on:

> It's beyond the egotism. It's the sheer deadly terror of having failed to make the thing intelligible, of not having translated the idea into comprehensible language, or at least into a language that will carry it without falsifying it. It's beyond even the feel or fear of wasted labour. Of having suffered for something still-born. [598]

In Mure's opinion, 'Any sort of tripe gets praise from a reviewer & you can never know if your work is positively good until you've been dead a century or so',[599] which is ironic really, given the attention Nan Shepherd's work is now receiving.

On the whole, reviews of *The Quarry Wood* were good. A glance at the sheaf of press cuttings kept by a proud Jeannie Shepherd reveals there was certainly praise:

> 'Her novel is the greatest even in Scottish Letters of recent years.'[600] 'Miss Shepherd can reveal personality in a single, vivid phrase…Here for once is a realistic treatment of a Scottish village (recognisable as West Cults) far removed from the mawkishness of the 'Kailyard' school..it rings true, sometimes terribly so.'[601] 'A book of rare and unescapable fascination… *The Quarry Wood* has, indeed, every mark of literature of high quality.'[602] 'A first novel that is a distinguished achievement rather than a promise. There are no crude infidelities to life and experience, no shoddy places in the writing. It is mature,

and exceptionally fine work. Miss Shepherd has become, with her first novel, an author of unusual importance, a novelist to put alongside…Virginia Woolf.[603]

In 1933, Lewis Grassic Gibbon thought it would be another fifty years or so before a Scots Virginia Woolf would astound the Scottish scene, but as we will see, he was not a fan of Nan Shepherd's work.

Opinion was divided on the use of Doric in the novel. To the *Scots Observer,* 'her Scots is a sheer delight',[604] while an American reviewer went further, declaring that in her 'effortless handling of dialect and the saltiness of phrase and word native to the Scotch men and women she portrays … one is reminded of the incomparable Hardy'.[605] Another critic, however, pronounced her dialogue 'illegitimate', continuing, 'there are more snags called words in this book than in any book I have ever tried to read in the Scottish'.[606]

Constable's first edition of *The Quarry Wood* included a two and a half page glossary at the back of the book. This, too, had polarised opinion. The 'phonetic transcription of the racy Deeside idiom may occasionally prove a stumbling block to the impatient Sassenach, but a glossary is provided and the effort is decidedly worth making',[607] said one reviewer. The novelist Hugh Walpole disagreed. While he praised *The Quarry Wood* for its 'honesty, courage and un-sentimentality', he felt it was hampered by the glossary. 'Let novelists avoid glossaries at every cost', he warned, 'a reader shrinks and rightly shrinks, from any such compulsory education.'[608]

What Nan thought of the reviews, or if she even read them, we do not know. But she was clearly proud enough of *The Quarry Wood* to give a copy to her uncle. On his retirement from the Chryston Church in Glasgow, the Reverend Andrew Shepherd had moved to Cults with his wife Jane and their three daughters, Evelyn, Dorothy and Isobel.[609] Their house, 'Dumbreck' was diagonally opposite Dunvegan, making them almost neighbours of Nan's and remains today, somewhat enlarged, just the other side of the North Deeside Road.

The Reverend Shepherd's reaction to his niece's work was far from favourable. He had read only as far as page fourteen when he came across the passage where Martha goes home to find 'her father was alone by the fire, in shirt sleeves, his sweaty socks thrust up against the mantel'. Disgusted, he threw down the book saying, 'I'm not having anything to do with this dirty rubbish'.[610] Clearly he failed to realise the novel's symbolism and was reading it 'photographically' so that the 'pool beside the birches' episode would have escaped him (along with much else) and his reaction shows him still firmly entrenched in middle-class snobbery.

Nan may have been middle-class, but as Jean Roger said, she was very different to your average Aberdonian: 'They were very prim and proper in Aberdeen in those days, and they thought, 'that funny woman', and 'those funny clothes', writing these very odd novels. And they didn't quite approve'. Jean Roger was of the opinion that Nan never mentioned her novels because 'nobody approved of them'.[611] Given the Reverend Shepherd's reaction to *The Quarry Wood*, it seems she had a point.

In the meantime, Nan's second novel, was already underway. She had begun writing it in 1927 while still in negotiations with Constable over the publication of her first. 'I shall be interested in *The Weatherhouse'*, Mure wrote to Nan in July 1927,

> So much autobiographical stuff went into *The Quarry Wood* that it will take a second book to show what you really can do creatively and I want to see. You can transcribe the life about you and your own personal experience with rich vigour…But I want to see what you can do beyond transcription. I don't mean that what you have done is small. It isn't—far from that. To transcribe with so much insight and rich vigour is a very considerable thing. Your danger is that the range may make the transcription narrow & that you may fall into mechanical reproduction.[612]

★ ★ ★

In the summer of 1927, Aberdeenshire was having stirring weather. It even made the London papers. By July, the storms had hit the capital. Traffic was disrupted as torrential rain flooded the streets up to two-feet deep in places. What would be the wettest summer so far recorded in the twentieth century was the one when Nan began writing *The Weatherhouse*.

From July to September, Nan completed seven chapters of the new book. In October she laid the manuscript aside. Throughout the winter, although she wasn't writing, the characters of *The Weatherhouse* were often in her head. 'New layers of experience within the story came into my ken', she told Mure Mackenzie, and gradually, while the plot did not alter, a new theme began to emerge.[613] The following summer, armed with this new theme Nan sat down and, beginning at the beginning, rewrote the whole novel. Only some six pages of her original manuscript remained, and while its synopsis stayed much the same, it had become quite a different book. But she had not gone far in the new writing, she said, when she realised that what had emerged in the end was her original, first image: 'the true theme was what I had seen it to be at the beginning.'[614]

The Weatherhouse was Nan Shepherd's most ambitious and complex novel. As Mure Mackenzie had hoped, her second book revealed what she could really do creatively. Although she certainly drew on family members for some of her characters, such as Lang Leeb Craigmyle and John and David Grey, she had indeed progressed from the intensely autobiographical *The Quarry Wood*. She also moved away from the genre of the '*Bildungsroman*' with its trajectory of education, escape and self-discovery.[615] And while you might expect her second novel to be a sequel to her first—a case of 'what Martha did next'—it is not.

Like *The Quarry Wood,* however (and *A Pass in the Grampians* which followed it) *The Weatherhouse* is decidedly local. It is set geographically in the North East of Scotland, against the backdrop of 'Fetter-Rothnie', 'a land denuded of its men' during the First World War. On the surface, it appears to be just another story about a small, rural community and the Chekhovian tangle of intricate family ties and gossip binding it together. The novel's parochial setting and its use of the vernacular might also make *The Weatherhouse* seem concerned only with issues of Scottish national identity. After all, it combines those two features Nan identified as being the most important to any national literature Scotland might produce—dialect and a typically Scottish arrangement of words.[616]

Equally important to her, though was that a novel should be universal in its reach. 'As a matter of fact, I read few novels. They bore me', she announced to the writer, Elizabeth Kyle, in June 1931. 'Fiction without imagination, no matter how clever or witty, how "true to life" (in the misleading cliché) leaves me cold', she said. Those novels she did read and which excited her, because it was what she was trying to do, were the ones in which she found, 'the raw material of life as we all know it, transfigured and irradiated and given significance by the impact of a mind'. [617]

Its theme is what lifts *The Weatherhouse* to the universal. It was inspired by the weather (prompted, perhaps, by that stormy summer of 1927 when she began writing the novel). To Nan, the weather can be unsettling as well as stabilising. It offers a variety of perspectives. It can shadow, slant, soften, dim, distort and obscure, as well as crystallise, bringing details into sharp relief. It was this Nan wanted to explore. The vagaries of the weather gave her a kaleidoscopic lens through which she could examine human nature and the complex relationship of 'truth' to fiction. The weatherhouse itself acts as a kaleidoscope. With its 'glass door to the garden; and between the two cottages…a quaint irregular hexagon, with an upper storey that contained one plain bedroom and one that was all corners and windows… The room seemed not to end with itself, but through its protruding windows became part of the infinite world,'[618] offering a series of different ever-shifting perspectives on the world outside.

In *The Quarry Wood,* Nan's theme is contained in her opening paragraph, 'man does not learn from books alone'. In her second novel it comes towards the end. Lindsay remembers Louie Morgan having a dog, Demon:

> "Nonsense!" rapped Miss Theresa. "Louie never had a dog."
> "But I remember. I can see him. A whippet hound he was."
> "Nonsense! She hadn't a dog. She wanted one…But old Mrs Morgan wouldn't have an animal about the place… after a while she used to pretend she had it—made on to be stroking it, spoke to it and all. A palavering craitur."

Theresa's answer floors Lindsay. She doubts her own memory, unsure whether what she thought she saw was real or fiction:

> I know [Louie] pretended a lot of things. But Demon—?
> He seemed so real when I look back. Did she only make me think I saw him? He used to go on our walks with us. We called to him—*Demon, Demon*—loud out, I know that.'
> She pondered. The dog, bounding among the pines, had in her memory the compelling insistence of imaginative art'.

Lindsay feels angry at Louie, 'as though by her own discovery of Demon's non-existence Louie had defrauded her of a recollected joy'.[619]

The fallibility of memory reveals 'truth' to be subjective, as Lindsay realises. Individuals remember events differently and reconstruct them 'as imaginative art' with their own slant. Theresa says the dog did not exist; Lindsay remembers it as a vivid reality and is destabilised by this new knowledge. The reader is destabilised too, not sure who is telling the 'truth' here. Which, of course, is the point.

The summer of 1928, when she was rewriting *The Weatherhouse,* Nan began walking in the Cairngorms. Up on the plateau where the weather is so unpredictable, the effect this could have on her vision was really brought home to her. In *The Living Mountain* she describes how mist shifts perspective:

> Such illusions, depending on how the eye is placed and used,
> drive home the truth that our habitual vision of things is not
> necessarily right: it is only one of an infinite number, and to
> glimpse an unfamiliar one, even for a moment, unmakes us, but
> steadies us again.[620]

But in *The Weatherhouse,* written over a decade earlier, she is already
exploring this idea of perspective.

The novel is not just about man's relationship with the universe,
but man's relationship with man: how much humans need each other
and yet how little we really know one another—let alone ourselves.
As well as exploring how our habitual vision of things is only one
perspective and not necessarily right, the novel is about perception
and delusion: how as humans we like to be perceived and how we
perceive ourselves; and the narratives we tell ourselves in which our
egos have the starring role. Here again, Nan is already Zennish. Ellen
Falconer tells herself stories, 'it might be wicked but it made life
radiant. Concerning Charley Falconer she told herself an endless
story. The tragedy of her brief married life lay in the clash between
her story and the truth'.[621]

While the plot of *The Weatherhouse* revolves around nineteen
year old Lindsey Lorimer's engagement to Garry Forbes, no single
character has a starring role. Yet each of the characters is memorable,
drawn vividly, sometimes in no more than half a dozen strokes. While
Jake's wife cut a whole loaf into slices for a visitor, with the gener-
osity inherent in her kind, Jake 'remained with his worried eyes fixed
on the table. A lifetime of laborious need was in the look he bent
upon the piles of bread.'[622]

The plot is slight, it must be said. Garry Forbes, on sick-leave
from the front, arrives home at Fetter-Rothnie to discover that the
rather shallow and artificial Louie Morgan is claiming she was secretly
engaged to his dead friend, David Grey. Certain this cannot be true and
determined to vindicate David, Garry sets out to prove Louie is lying.
The story develops around the effect of his exposure of Louie Morgan's
deception on each of Nan's cast of characters. But for Nan, the plot is
merely a tool through which she can reveal her characters and bring
them into conflict to create drama. That this is intentional, is spelled out
in the novel's architecture. A 'List of Characters' is given at the outset,
followed by 'The Drama', as it is titled, which is neatly sandwiched
between an explanatory Prologue and Epilogue.

The text is also about the nature of writing itself. Nan was concerned right up to the end of her life with the difficulty of translating felt experience into language. She wrote to Neil Gunn on several occasions about this, admiring his capacity to put into words moments that for her dissolved 'one's being'. In *The Weatherhouse* Shepherd's characters often encounter these moments of dissolution—a place beyond language, beyond scientific or religious explanation where nothing is black and white; there is no simple distinction between right and wrong, true or false. Garry Forbes, who Nan casts as an engineer, symbol of scientific thinking, has such a moment:

> ...right and wrong were as separate as the bridges he had helped to build and the waters over which he built them... limits had shifted, boundaries been dissolved. Nothing ended in itself, but flowed over into something else. [623]

Constable published *The Weatherhouse* in February 1930. A review in the *Scots Observer* described it as a work of genius,

> a far greater novel than *The Quarry Wood*, great as that first novel was. Enriched again from the stores of the Aberdeenshire tongue, its prose has become still more pliable and expressive, the unusual word has become apparently inevitable, and the dialect more full of savour. [624]

Nan had indeed honed her use of dialect in her second novel which, after the criticism of *The Quarry Wood,* was printed without a glossary. Inevitably, there was still some dissent over this. 'A glossary would have been useful for this Lowlander' said a critic in *The Scotsman,* whose review missed much in the novel and went on: 'Miss Shepherd has a fault. She crowds her stage with too many characters...it's a little annoying to have to turn back to work out who's who'.[625] To Leonora Eykes writing for the *Illustrated London News*, the novel was like Marmite: 'Either you will like *The Weatherhouse* immensely or you will not like it at all' but ends, '*The Weatherhouse* is no common novel and Miss Shepherd is no trivial novelist'.[626]

Although Nan knew there were good things in the book, she was not particularly proud of *The Weatherhouse* as a whole. In the 1950s, when a friend mentioned that she was unable to lay her hands on a copy, Nan pulled a face. 'It was dreadful' she said, 'I'm glad you can't get it'.[627] But in March 1930 shortly after *The Weatherhouse* was published, Nan was writhing beneath what she felt were the 'too-flattering ejaculations of the Scots press'. 'Don't you loathe having your work over-praised?' she complained in a letter to Neil Gunn, 'it makes me feel positively nasty towards the praiser'.[628]

Neil had returned from a few weeks holiday early in March 1930 eager to give himself the pleasure of reading Nan's latest work. While there was, he felt, some 'extraordinarily fine work' in the book, his immediate concern was how *The Weatherhouse* would be received by the general public, the less discerning reader. 'Have you done us too great an honour?' he wrote to Nan on the 10th March, 'your feel for character is so sure that you positively do sleight-of-hand with it.' Her landscapes and background he described as, 'vivid and shining, solid and yet translated to fiery particles'.

> This is magical, illuminating, but how shall I say? The least trifle sudden! I am thinking more of the normal reader. (Of whom, of course, I never think when I am underway myself!…) Possibly I am merely moved by the very commonplace desire to see work that I like successful—at least in the sense of attracting many readers. [629]

He was right, of course, as some of the reviews reveal. Much of what was in *The Weatherhouse* sailed straight over readers' heads.

Nan wrote back to Neil by return on 14th March:

> Yes, I know *The Weatherhouse* demands closer reading than many of its readers will give it. And I know also that that is partly due to bad craftsmanship, and partly to good! There are a lot of subtleties of character presentation that wouldn't strike the average reader, at any rate at a first reading; and equally there are a lot of blurred effects, where I haven't really got the meaning through.[630]

Neil guessed she might have no interest in how the book fared commercially and he was right. Creatively, Nan was done with it. She had already, mentally, moved on from her second novel. But what is obvious from this exchange of letters between the two writers is a mutual understanding and insight into each others' work.

★ ★ ★

Neil Gunn in the 1920s.

Born two years earlier than Nan in 1891, in Dunbeath on the east coast of Caithness, Neil Miller Gunn was the seventh of nine children born to James Gunn, a herring boat captain and his wife Isabella, a domestic servant. Isabella Gunn was ambitious for her seven sons and determined that they should not go to sea like their father and in 1907 Neil followed his older brother, James, into the Civil Service in London. By 1910 he had been posted back to northern Scotland as a Customs and Excise Officer. Married in 1921 to Jessie Frew (known as Daisy), Neil was appointed Excise officer at the Glen Mhor Distillery in the summer of 1923 and the Gunns moved to Inverness.

Remembered chiefly for his writing, Neil Gunn was a socialist who was passionate about Scottish Nationalism and a strong supporter of the National Party of Scotland.[631] A regular contributor to the *Chapbook,* Neil met Christopher Grieve, the man behind it, around 1924. Initially, the two men found they had a great deal in common, aside from a taste for whisky and a love of literary conversation, and became staunch comrades. Although they later became alienated, their opinions on literature, politics and philosophy of life diverging, Grieve said of those early days 'in the twenties, when the ideas of a Scottish Literary Renaissance were first being canvassed, there was no one in Scotland with whom I was in closer touch'.[632] Grieve was an ardent supporter of Neil's writing, declaring him 'the only Scottish prose-writer of promise, that is to say, in relation to that which is distinctively Scottish.'[633] Neil returned the compliment, describing Grieve (in his guise as Hugh MacDiarmid) as 'Scotland's Greatest Poet of Today'.[634]

Neil Gunn, who delighted in this sort of literary comradeship, kept up a correspondence over the years with various movers and shakers of the 'Scottish Renaissance' movement, male and female. From his novels though, it is clear that Neil instinctively understood women and wrote with sensitivity about the way women felt. A literary idol of Jessie Kesson's, she described it as 'almost a tenderness' towards them'.[635]

Tall and spare, with his strong-boned face, unruly thatch of dark hair and a hint of a dimple in his chin, Neil Gunn was an attractive man. In a photograph taken in the 1920s he is astride a motorcycle. In his long, waxed coat, cap crammed on his head and a cigarette clamped between his lips there is more than a suggestion of the brooding, young Brando's sexuality over thirty years later in *The Wild One*. It is not surprising Neil was popular with women, but while he could be flirtatious and sometimes teasing, he was never condescending.

Naomi Mitchison and Agnes Mure Mackenzie were among the other women writers with whom he was in touch, but it was Nan Shepherd's sensitive, supportive and insightful letters about his work he particularly relished. After his death in 1973, in a letter to Gunn's biographers, Nan explained why she thought this was:

> I think he valued my remarks on his books because from the first I had apprehended that inner awareness which his early critics were blind to. He said he never felt a book of his was properly published till I had had my say. But that, you know, was because we felt the same way about life and loved the same things in the world.[636]

It was on 19th August 1929 that Nan first wrote to Neil Gunn via The Porpoise Press:[637]

> May a stranger be allowed to thank you for the pleasure she has had in reading *Hidden Doors?* There are things in it so imaginatively fine that they haunt the memory like great poetry: in particular the conclusion of Symbolical which seems to me definitely to achieve greatness. In the old man frozen to his spade beyond the last dyke he had built against the moor, you have summed up generations of our Scottish life. I have read the last page of that tale many times, yet one reading was all that was required to fix it ineradicably in my mind.—It is also very finely written, with an economy of wording that gives me a keen pleasure.

She goes on to praise and quote 'for sheer delight in quoting' from Neil's work, ending sympathetically over the difficulty she heard he was experiencing finding a publisher for his second novel, *The Lost Glen.*[638]

Nan's first letter to Neil, with its insight, praise and obvious delight in his writing, reached him at just the right moment. Although in his reply to Nan, he characteristically brushed off the uncertainty he was feeling over his writing, pretending instead that he was just 'being lazy', the truth was Neil was frustrated at not being able to find a publisher for *The Lost Glen,* which had been rejected by several, including The Porpoise Press. *The Poaching at Grianan,* a sixty thousand word story which appeared in eight instalments, serialised from September 1929 in the *Scots Magazine,* was another false start and never materialised into a book. *Hidden Doors,* his collection of short stories, had been a modest success, but the novel, for Neil, seemed to be a non-starter. He turned his attention to drama.

As it turns out, the novel *was* Neil Gunn's medium. He would become a prolific novelist, and a heavy-weight of the 'Scottish Renaissance', who was rated alongside Lewis Grassic Gibbon as one of the two most important Scottish authors of the first half of the twentieth century. Although real success did not come until the publication of *Highland River* in 1937, enabling him to take early retirement from Customs and Excise and write full-time, Neil had actually begun writing during the 1920s. *The Grey Coast* appeared first in 1926 and was well-received, some critics going so far as to describe it as the best Scottish novel since *The House with the Green Shutters*—another nail in the Kailyard coffin. It was followed by a second novel, *The Lost Glen* which appeared initially in serialised form in the *Scots Magazine*.[639]

Nan had come across the first instalment of *The Lost Glen* in April 1928. But she loathed serialised novels and with a month's hiatus between magazine issues her interest waned. She hadn't bothered to read any more, thinking she would wait and read the novel when it appeared in complete form. However, as Neil couldn't find anyone willing to publish it, she would have quite a wait.

Neil's reply to Hodder and Stoughton, one of those publishers who rejected *The Lost Glen,* shows just what new Scottish writers were up against:

> Those of us who are interested in what is sometimes called the Scottish Renaissance Movement must, I suppose, be sanguine enough to keep looking for the publisher who is prepared to take risks! Though why we should expect him to, heaven knows! for we are aware how comparatively easy...it would be to supply the staple fare of kilts, sporrans, and Romance, in island dawns and Celtic twilights—not omitting a helping of cabbage from the 'Kailyard'!...Possibly, it is the only merit of *The Lost Glen* that it stands for the first honest attempt, as far as I know, at introducing the Highlands as they are today.[640]

Neil wrote back to Nan on 26th August 1929, the day he received her letter:

> Dear Miss Shepherd,
> Your letter has today reached me from the Porpoise Press. Being so sensible of the value of your own work, I appreciate it very highly. Indeed, I have discussed *The Quarry Wood* with men like C M Grieve & *The Scots Magazine* editor,[641] etc., frequently, and would have written you personally were it not that I found more public ways of expression—as for a broadcast talk from

Glasgow on modern Scottish letters, where I gave it as my opinion that your work is more significant than all the novels of 'the Glasgow School' put together. Had there been—there wasn't—a lingering doubt in my mind, your first poem in *The Scots Magazine* ['Lux Perpetua'] would have dissipated it. For we have got to that stage where we need something more than a realism which is often little more than a species of reporting designed to attract at all costs.

The Lost Glen, he said, was still in his drawer where it would stay for some time. It was too political, he explained, 'a trifle too concerned with the Highlands as they are; not enough romantic tartan. It is so easy to dish up precisely what is wanted! Meanwhile my interest has turned to drama'.[642]

In Dublin, Irish national life was so strong, according to Neil, 'that it created a drama out of itself…It said: We will show you your own life translated into drama, and make you sit up and look at it, and realise it as you have never done before!' He had seen many of the Abbey plays and the shock of hearing Irish voices coming over the footlights towards the audience was vivid. 'I had forgotten,' he said, 'if I had even known, that contemporary drama could act on one like this.'[643]

Stimulated by the work of the Irish revivalists, a new movement in Scottish drama began in the early 1920s and in February 1922 the Scottish National Theatre Society was formed to run the Scottish National Players, an amateur organisation founded in Glasgow aiming to develop Scottish Drama. The Players were putting on Gunn's drama, *The Ancient Fire* that October, he told Nan, adding: 'I'm afraid it won't do them any good' (He was right, the production was badly received.) He was optimistic, though, that 'our forces are beginning to make a slight impression. But,' he ended the letter, 'the real pleasure in the fight comes from the exquisite understanding of what Whitman would call a comrade. Yours very sincerely Neil Gunn.'[644]

★ ★ ★

The comrades did not meet often over the years and, according to Nan, when they did, they were 'not putting the world to rights, or even pronouncing on Scotland and her literature, but just enjoying each other's company and the beauty of the earth. 'He was the sort of man you could be silent with', she said.[645] But Neil was also a great talker. A dram at his elbow, he could talk into the night. He much preferred to discuss a question in depth, face to face. In his first letter to Nan he invited her to stay, suggesting they 'could have a useful talk about literary affairs in Scotland today'.[646] It was a while before she took him up on it.

In the meantime, Neil hoped they might have a chance to chat at a PEN meeting in Aberdeen early in 1930. In the event, however, he was frustrated:

> I was disappointed that the PEN function broke up without our having a talk. In talk you can get down to things. And I'm afraid I was prepared for an all-night sitting! Instead of which I was compelled to go solitarily aloft about midnight! It was too bad. Positively without even a good night to the one or two whom I was interested in![647]

Nan, was also disappointed. 'I too was sorry that there was so little chance to talk at the PEN dinner', she wrote back, 'but a massed affair of that kind isn't really the place for talking is it? Someday I hope we shall have opportunity and leisure for something more satisfying than set speeches'.[648]

PEN International was founded in London in 1921 by the Cornish novelist Catharine Amy Dawson Scott, with the support of John Galsworthy, the organisation's first president. A reaction to the devastation of the First World War, the idea behind it initially was simply 'to unite and foster friendship and understanding between writers' and at first PEN was nothing more than a dining club; a space for writers to share ideas and socialise. But Galsworthy's idea of a 'League of Nations for Men and Women of Letters' took hold and four years after its inception there were twenty-five PEN centres in Europe.[649]

That soggy summer of 1927, when Nan was busy writing *The Weatherhouse,* Christopher Grieve founded a Scottish Branch of the international PEN.[650] 'No politics in PEN Clubs—under any circumstances' was one of the founding principles. A non-racial, non-political and non-sectarian organisation, PEN saw itself as standing for freedom of expression, peace and friendship, not political debate. But by the time the Scottish PEN was founded, the political climate was changing, tension was rising between the German PEN Club and the rest of the PEN community and by 1926 the club could no longer ignore politics.

Strong nationalistic feelings were often the mainspring of PEN's various centres and Scotland was no exception. Many in Scotland felt that there was not enough knowledge of its cultural heritage and there is no doubt that the rising tide of national Scottish sentiment brought many members into the movement.[651] Among them were Edwin and Willa Muir, Catherine and Donald Carswell, A J Cronin, George

Malcolm Thomson, Naomi Mitchison, Rachel Annand Taylor, R B Cunningham Grahame, William Soutar, Lewis Grassic Gibbon and Compton Mackenzie.[652]

Along with poets Alexander Gray and Marion Angus, Nan joined the Aberdeen branch. She wrote to invite Mure Mackenzie to become a member. Mure was not convinced. 'I'll join the PEN with pleasure,' she said:

> IF you can muster a reason why I should. (a) my joining wouldn't help the PEN cause…if I have a reputation of sorts by now it's a London one. In fact, you can buy my stuff more easily in Paris than in Edinburgh. (b)—and more important, how does the PEN help Scots letters? No doubt it helps amateurs to feel they are WRITERS and those professionals that like to play to admiring minnows… I feel I can do more in any degree by my firm than either my tongue or stomach. And one doesn't write books at a public meeting.[653]

True. One doesn't. But the PEN was still a draw for writers, particularly those concerned with the state of Scottish Letters.

Often described as a sort of 'handmaid to the Renaissance' (a label she disliked and which seriously downplays her role as one of its key campaigners) Helen Cruickshank probably did more to publicise and chronicle the movement than anyone else involved in it. Although as a civil servant Helen could not take an active role in politics, she was a member of the British Socialist Party and a suffragette. But when votes were awarded to women over thirty, she needed another cause and found it—in her country. In the 1920s all her spare time was absorbed in Scotland, 'her problems and potentialities, and especially her position in the world of art and letters.' She 'read voraciously, and wrote reams of verse' which she says she had no intention of publishing.[654]

Honorary Secretary of the Scottish PEN from 1928 to 1935, Helen acted as a catalyst, making sure that writers and publishers attended the same gatherings. Most of these PEN meetings were informal and sometimes impromptu and were often held at Helen's own home, 'Dinnieduff', her modest, semi-detached villa on Edinburgh's Corstorphine Hill. But on Helen's civil service salary, liquid refreshment other than tea or coffee was not an option and as hard liquor, as she said, was 'sine qua non' in those days, the Dinnieduff gatherings tended to be more sedate than the ones at Arthur Lodge. The home of W G Burns Murdoch, who threw open his doors to the PEN at Christmas or Burns-tide, Arthur Lodge was adorned with his paintings of Arctic icebergs and souvenirs of his expeditions which included a stuffed penguin. There were always pipers and a sword dance in the great hall and it was here, on one occasion, that Naomi Mitchison reportedly scandalised another guest by dancing with her plaited hair down.[655]

As well as hosting her more dignified 'Dinnieduff' meetings, Helen Cruickshank often provided accommodation for her 'distinguished authors'. Among these were Christopher Grieve,[656] Edwin and Willa Muir, Catherine and Donald Carswell, Lewis Grassic Gibbon and Nan Shepherd. All of whom, at one time or another, had slept in what was christened 'The Prophet's Chamber',[657] her tiny guest room with its sloping ceiling above the hall.

The PEN brought Helen Cruickshank and Nan Shepherd together. They met for the first time at an Aberdeen meeting one Sunday afternoon in 1928.[658] It would have been a lively gathering. It was hosted by the poet Marion Angus at her little cottage in Hazelhead in her low-ceilinged sitting-room brimming with books, flowers, faded chintz and china and its quirky fireplace in the corner. 'A room with personality',[659] Nan described it—much like its owner.

'A wilding slip...Marion Angus was not wholly human', Nan wrote in an article for the *Scots Magazine* in 1947, a year after her death. A vigorous intellectual, Marion was as self-effacing as Nan, but besides her talent, what Nan revelled in was her friend's mischief: the jokes that would prick. She could do disconcerting things, 'like tearing a few pages from a book to indicate that it was poor stuff, or deliberately under-stamping a letter to a pompous dame who was niggardly with her pence'. Growing deaf in old age, Marion had a tendency, in company, to describe the shortcomings of someone who was present, embarrassing listeners who excused her on the grounds of her deafness. Nan, however, suspected she knew very well how loud she was talking. And in this, Marion Angus bears more than a passing resemblance to Lang Leeb Craigmyle in *The Weatherhouse,* whose 'asides were stage asides, meant to penetrate the corners'.[660]

Nan and Marion were old friends. Their paths first crossed in 1902 when after her father's death, Marion, her mother and sisters moved from Arbroath to Cults, renting Inchgower, a handsome granite house just below the railway station. Old Mrs Angus died in 1914 and Marion moved away for a time, returning in 1921 when, on an impulse she bought the little cottage in Hazelhead, a couple of miles away from Nan in Cults.

Grey-eyed, with bobbed hair that curled around her ears, Marion had an elfin quality about her—a 'gnomic charm' Helen Cruickshank described it. She could be diffident among strangers, but she was eager to meet others interested in writing and to discuss the state of poetry in Scotland.[661] In the late 1920s Marion was writing and publishing her own vernacular verse and, like Nan, was very much engaged in the language debate. While the use of Scots was not a guarantee of poetic excellence, she was adamant that its extinction should not be allowed and was vocal on the subject. 'Our Scottish poets are using the old speech somewhat timorously and tentatively', she said, 'it is like an old gown which becomes us very well but is going out of fashion'.[662]

Marion Angus's vernacular verses are heavily influenced by the Scottish ballads and more traditional, but her work is now seen as a precursor to MacDiarmid's. At the time, critics like Grierson, tended to sentimentalise her poetry which was rather unfairly defined by her private life. In 'Waater o'Dye' Marion is explicit: she has 'niver kent… the luve o'men.' Yet despite this confession, in Nan's opinion, she knew a great deal about human nature in love beyond the limits of her own experience. 'Her themes may be few and her range narrow…[but] she has the power—and what is that abut creation?—to experience the things that did not happen to her. There is here a consummation of a very rare order'.[663] Nan saw this in 1947. It is only recently, however, that Angus's work has finally begun to be recognised.

Many of the Scottish literary elite were PEN Club members and many were members of the Nationalist movement which was rapidly gaining ground. Not so much in Aberdeen, according to the poet Alexander Gray who was also at the PEN meeting that Sunday afternoon in 1928, and who admitted: 'the waves of Nationalism beat idly against us here. The Aberdonian is unperturbed about it'.[664] Marion Angus certainly took a chilly stance towards it and Nan's job, as we know, precluded her from taking an active role in politics. While she certainly considered herself a Socialist, there is nothing in her extant correspondence to suggest she was a member of the Nationalist party. It is more likely that as far as political organisations were concerned she was a non-joiner. But, like Helen Cruickshank, she was very much engaged with what was going on in Scotland at the time—politically and culturally.

Even without that common interest, you can see why they liked each other. A precociously bright child whose parents couldn't afford to send her to university, dark-haired, dark-eyed Helen was vivacious, and a great talker. Passionate about gardening, like Nan, Helen was an avid walker, 'never happier than when scaling some mountain peak to see what was in the next valley round the bend or following old drove roads from glen to glen'.[665]

Her solitary rambles on foot, rucksack on her back, wearing boys' boots, map and compass in her pocket with a poetry book somewhere about her, have a ring of Nan Shepherd about them. But there was another parallel between them that cemented their friendship: both women had done their daughterly duty and in the process, lost their freedom. After her father's death in 1924, Helen had been forced to give up her beloved studio flat in Edinburgh's Shandwick Place—and the free and easy bohemian lifestyle that went with it—to buy somewhere larger, with room for her mother. She had brothers, but 'everyone, including my mother, assumed that the only daughter would provide a home for her in Edinburgh and so it turned out'.[666] Buying 'Dinnieduff' meant taking out a large mortgage. It also meant she was forced to say goodbye to any chance of marrying the penniless artist with whom she was in love. On marriage, female civil servants were required to resign their posts and Helen needed to work to support her mother, pay the mortgage and run the house. On top of that, Mrs Cruickshank lived for another twenty years and for the last ten years of her life, as could not be left alone during the day, Helen had to employ a live-in housekeeper.

Helen Cruickshank (front row, far right) and guests in the garden at 'Dinnieduff' in 1931.

Nan, as she herself acknowledged, was the more fortunate of the two. It might have been her income that fed and clothed the Dunvegan women, but on her father's death she had inherited a debt-free house with enough money to maintain it and pay rates and duty.

Over the years, 'Dinnieduff' became a regular meeting place for the Scottish Revivalists. At parties, as many as forty would turn up and friends often dropped in on Sunday evenings, when Helen's mother, who despite being almost completely deaf, 'wasna' blate'[667] would join in, reciting Scots poems and acting out parts. A photograph taken in 1931 in Helen's garden shows the sort of literary company typical of those PEN gatherings.[668] Christopher Grieve stands at the edge of the group, his arm around old Mrs Cruickshank's shoulder, pushing her gently forward into the picture. Standing on Helen's crazy-paving the guests that day were Marian McNeill, Jamieson (he of the Scottish Dictionary) J H Whyte, founder of *The Modern Scot,* Professor Otto Schlaff, John Rafferty, J Tonge. In the foreground, beside the stone bird bath, sits Scottish Nationalist and poet Nannie K Wells,[669] elegant and seated while the others are all standing. It's as if she seeks to diminish herself and yet she draws attention, head tilted, looking sideways and up at the camera. Helen sent a copy of this photograph to Nan who commented: 'Oh I relished the group photograph taken in your garden. Isn't Nannie Wells characteristic—coy and self-conscious!'[670]

The first wave of the 'Scottish Renaissance' in the post-war years and into the 1920s was a ferment of activity steered by Grieve. But the movement was supported by many others, all keen to engage in the debate about national identity he started and all of whom were contributing to it with creative and critical writing of their own. These were not just men. Busy writing and working for the 'cause' were women like Helen Cruickshank and Nan Shepherd. They might not have been able to be too vocal politically, but there were others who were—Naomi Mitchison, Catherine Carswell and Nannie Wells to name just a few. Until recently, the role played by Scottish women writers in the 'Renaissance' has been overshadowed by the men's. But as well as offering support, encouragement and friendship, a glance at their correspondence shows just how much interaction they had with their male counterparts on literary and political matters. Grieve's periodicals had as many women contributors as men.

Willa Muir was the powerhouse behind her husband Edwin's career as journalist and critic. Originally from Orkney, by 1919 Edwin Muir (who had little in the way of a formal education) was assistant editor on *New Age* magazine, to which he also contributed poetry and reviewed books. That same year he married teacher and linguistics expert Wilhelmina Anderson and by the early 1920s, the Muirs had left London for Europe on the back of Muir's first book *We Moderns,* which had secured him a contract with *The Free Man* magazine.[671] The publication of works such as *Latitudes* and *The Structure of the Novel* during the 1920s cemented Edwin Muir's reputation as a critic and he began a series of collaborations with Willa translating texts by Hauptmann and Kafka, among others, as well as writing poetry collected in two volumes published by the Hogarth Press.[672]

Willa, too, was a translator and writer. In 1925 the Hogarth Press published her essay *Women: An Inquiry.* 'I was thinking out the implications of my inability to detach myself from emotions, which I suspected might be not only a peculiarity of mine but a characteristic of most women' she wrote in her memoir, *Belonging.*[673] The essay was the result of her thinking on the subject.

The Muirs may have been living abroad but they kept a close eye on what was going on at home and it was not long before Edwin began contributing to Grieve's magazines. In Europe, they began to feel homesick. As Willa had grown up in Montrose in July 1924, they settled back there and while Edwin began working on his essays on 'contemporary literature in an age of transition', Willa followed up on her Inquiry into the nature of Women. It was in Montrose that the Muirs first encountered Christopher Grieve.

When he first met the Muirs, while Grieve was still editor of the local weekly, the *Montrose Review,* he was engaged with fellow-borderer Francis George (F.G.) Scott on the 'ferment of poetry and music with which they meant to regenerate Scotland' which they felt was slipping into 'a moribund provincialism'.[674] Grieve wrote Scots lyrics set to music by the ebullient Scott which Grieve then set about publicising in his magazines. In 1923 Edwin Muir had already contributed three Scottish Ballads and some verse to Grieve's *Chapbook* but fond as he was of Scott, his interest in the 'Scottish Renaissance' was lukewarm. Lallans, the vernacular of the Lowlands, was not Muir's vernacular; his was Orkney. And in any case, he preferred to write his poetry in his adopted language, which was English.

Muir felt that Grieve and Scott's attempts to make the Scottish vernacular central to the Scots literary revival could never be anything more than marginal. Grieve, 'true to Border feeling, blamed the "Eng-glish" for the whole of Scotland's backwardness in the arts. Edwin only smiled kindly as if at a little boy squaring up to a bogey',[675] according to Willa Muir. It was not just a difference in agreement over the use of English language, it was also the difference in temperament between the two that would separate Edwin from Grieve's campaign.

Grieve, the fighter and show-off, keen to score points over others was the opposite of Muir with his unassuming, quiet passion. But as Willa said, when they first met Grieve in 1924 in Montrose, neither she nor Edwin could have predicted the influence he would wield as political agitator and poet of Scottish Nationalism.

To begin the process of changing the perception of Scotland as 'North-Britain' and a land without a literature, the 'Renaissance' writers toppled Burns and Scott from their pedestals. Scott was taken down for his support of the Union and for his historical novels. The Revivalists could see no vision of a future in what they described as his 'harking back to the past' and 'a curious emptiness…behind the wealth of his imagination'.[676] Then in 1930, Grieve denounced Burns, castigating him for the sentimental legacy he left behind.[677] Catherine Carswell fired back, making mincemeat of his criticism of Burns yet managing, at the same time, to demonstrate she was firmly on the side of the Revivalists.

Nan was a fan of MacDiarmid's poetry from the outset. 'There are things in his *Cencrastus*[678] that would make me die of envy if I hadn't already died of sheer joy at their discovery', she admitted in a letter to Neil Gunn written in March 1930. For her, Burns and MacDiarmid represented two opposite sides of the Scottish genius:

> and both so tremendously <u>real</u>. I suppose one might say the difference is much the difference between Chaucer and Shelley—the man who glories in every manifestation of the actual, relishing common life with a divine gusto—and the man who strikes upward out of the mess and stultifying inertia of the head, sword-sharp and flashing, to the cold shining heights of the intellect and spirit.[679]

'Some day', she went on, 'I should like to work out a contract between him and Burns (not on paper, I'm too indolent—but perhaps I'll do it some day as a talk to one or other of the Literary Societies that keep asking me to "favour" them)'.[680] A few years later, she did, and the article provoked by the talk was published in the *Aberdeen University Review*. As few understood MacDiarmid's work at the time like Nan Shepherd, it's not surprising he then 'borrowed' it for his autobiography.

In the meantime, in 1934, she gave what was described in the press as 'an utterly original' speech at the annual Burns supper of the Scottish Women's Club in Edinburgh (of which Helen Cruickshank too was a member). Ignoring MacDiarmid's attack on Burns's sentimentality, she took another tack. 'To celebrate the past is dangerous;' she began, 'if we were are assembled here to celebrate only a memory and not something present, immediate, and vital, we might just as well go home again and drink in secret'. Grieve's *Chapbook* may have brandished the slogan 'Not Traditions—Precedents' on its cover, but many modernist authors in Scotland were in fact adapting and creatively transforming traditional techniques of past authors to reflect ideas of the time. What Nan suggested was that as well as employing the same creative gusto Burns applied to his writing, all modern writers should be adopting his way of seeing to the essence of things.

What they were there to celebrate that evening, she felt, was not the past, but a matter more immediate to themselves, 'creative energy':

> Robert Burns had it—or it had him; which was the reason they chose his birthday for the celebration. But creative energy was a force that no people abundantly alive could do without. It was the only force that carried them anywhere. The forms in which it expressed itself were enormously varied. It might manifest itself in architecture or in religion, in education or government, which might be the expression of a living creative genius as well as an empty formalism.

One of the most urgent tasks of 1934 Nan believed, was to discover a creative energy whose expression would accord with 'the real needs of our living'. 'The past', she said 'served to discern something of the nature of this force, and the genius of Burns was useful for this', but what modern literature needed first was to articulate things so that their essence was apparent:

> This involves, of course, the power to perceive, to see beyond inessentials to the essential. Many can perceive without the further power of expressing their perceptions so that they are self-evident. They might say, in a cold, abstract fashion, that carousal was good, had its own value and right to exist: Burns said 'Tam O'Shanter'. He created a man and in creating Tam he had done what Shakespeare did in creating Falstaff and Sir Toby Belch—made a value in human life self-evident.

It was the gusto with which Burns wrote, tears of joy pouring down his face as he composed 'Tam', the elemental energy he poured into his creative writing, Nan believed was what was now needed by the world in the 1930s.[681]

Nan's contribution to the Scottish Renaissance movement is evident, not just from her narrative experimentation with the Scots speech and idiom of her novels, but from her correspondence with others involved in the movement as encourager, supporter and as friend. From her Burns talk, as well as from other interviews she gave during that period, it is clear, however, that she was not solely interested in 'making it new' for Scotland by attempting to elevate the country from its position as district of North Britain and giving it a literature of its own; hers was a wider, still thoroughly modern, but global concern.

Nan, 'on the tramp'.

For many of the Scottish women writers of the 1920s and 30s, Pound's war-cry meant exploring their identity and new position in society, post-vote. In Nan's three novels she explores the implications of this through many of her female characters, young and old, but particularly through her female protagonists. Alongside Lindsay in *The Weatherhouse* the other women in the cast try to position themselves somewhere either within the community or beyond it. And then there are those like Nan herself, who position themselves at some point halfway between both poles.

On the surface, Nan appeared content to live within the confines of community and to accept the domestic, female-centric environment of Dunvegan. And during the early 1920s she was kept busy. Not only did she have her career, her writing and Sheila Roger to 'mother', as well as keeping abreast of the activities of the Scottish Revivalists and the PEN club, she had a prolific correspondence to maintain. But from 1928, while she was *in* that life, she was not *of* it, much of the time she was somewhere else—on a mountain.

Chapter Nine

1928-1932

Nan Shepherd was resilient. At the age of thirty-five she had been knocked down—in love and in life. After her father's death in 1925, Nan was firmly shackled to Dunvegan, as house-bound, in effect, as her mother. Getting beyond that 'Pass' now seemed improbable and while she might love the 'greatest man she ever knew',[682] John Macmurray was unavailable. In 1928, he and Betty were still very much married and living in London where, after the constraints of Oxford, they were enjoying a more unconventional life, both experimenting with John's 'philosophy of freedom'.[683]

'To create', Nan said in her Burns talk, 'the creator must be in naked touch with experience. He must know his material in the raw, not canned in books or the experience of others. Burns knew his raw material in the raw and transmuted his experience with elemental energy, tears pouring down his face as he wrote'. [684] Elemental energy was what was needed in creative writing, she said, and naturally, she was talking, too, about her own writing. First though, she needed to know her material in the raw.

Kierkegaard expressed this for her succinctly and she copied a quotation from his *Diary* into her *Medley Book*. 'If a person does not become what he understands, he does not really understand it'. Nan needed knowledge and not just the knowledge she had so far gleaned from books.

In the late 1920s, Nan wrote an extract from Edward Thomas's *Cloud Castle* into the *Medley Book:*

> …He went up into the tower, that he had built upon a rock in his own mountains to think about life before he began to live…He desired to learn to see in human life, as we see in the life of bees, the unity which perhaps some higher order of living beings can easily see through the complexity that confuses us. He had set out to seek at first by means of science…For a hundred years men had been reading science

and experimenting, as they had been reading history, with the result that they knew—some science and some history. So he went up into his bright Tower.[685]

Of course this resonated for her. Nan's spirituality was still in the process of becoming apprehended as felt experience. She had so far sought knowledge through reading. The works of Hearn and AE had given her insight and altered her perception of the 'higher order of living beings' Edward Thomas talks about. But the knowledge Nan was after, was still rumour; it did not yet live in the muscle.[686] The Cairngorms[687] were her road to knowledge. Through sensation, through its seasons and through experience, she learned 'her mountain' until, finally, she was ready to transmute this knowledge creatively through her writing.

From childhood Nan had been *thirled* to the mountain, haunted by that 'stormy violet of a gully on the back of Sgoran Dubh'. As a child, the Cairngorms were forbidden territory. To climb them had seemed to Nan then, 'a legendary task, one that heroes, not men, accomplished and certainly not children'.[688]

Mountaineering, which developed as a sport during the Victorian era, had long been considered the domain of men. The golden age of Alpine mountaineering in the mid-nineteenth century had made heroes of climbers like Edward Wymper and Leslie Stephen. Measured by their successes and failures, the British public was alternately thrilled and horrified by their exploits. 'There is no manlier sport in the world than mountaineering...', wrote Aubrey Le Blond in his wife Elizabeth's book, *True Tales of Mountain Adventure* published in 1903. 'A mountaineer sets his skill and his strength against the difficulty of getting to the top of a steep peak. Either he conquers the mountain or it conquers him.'[689]

Truth was, women were jockeying for position with men to take their places alongside them in many pursuits—not just mountaineering. Fanny Bullock Workman made a record-breaking first ascent of the Himalayan Pinnacle Peak in the Nun Kun Massif which was estimated in 1906 to be 23,264 feet[690] while British climbers Lily Bristow and Lucy Walker were among many Victorian and Edwardian women who hitched their skirts and took to the ropes for adventure in the Alps.

As only the wealthy could afford an annual Alpine trip, by the turn of the twentieth century, Scotland was becoming a serious climbing playground. The Cairngorm Club was founded in 1887, followed in 1889 by The Scottish Mountaineering Club and then, two years later Sir Hugh Munro compiled his famous list of Scottish mountains over 3000 feet.[691] Not to be outdone, the women founded their own society. In April 1908, a year after the Ladies' Alpine Club was formed, Jane

Inglis Clark, her daughter Mabel and friend Lucy Smith, established the Ladies' Scottish Climbing Club (LSCC). It was a bold move. These women had years of experience from climbing with their husbands and brothers, but it was testament to their determination and pioneering spirit that they asserted their right to be different, to defy middle-class convention and climb independently of the men.

In those days, sportswear for women did not exist. As suitable boots were hard to come by, most, like Helen Cruickshank, wore boy's boots. Women climbers were hampered by petticoated-layers beneath long skirts that trailed in the dust or mud and hats that did not fit and often had to be held on firmly—sometimes with both hands. As 'Ladies' dared not walk around the villages skirt-less, breeches were often worn beneath their billowy skirts which could then be removed and hidden behind a convenient boulder while their owners made their ascents. 'Aye, ye'll have come back for your wee bits o'decency' was the (probably apocryphal) remark of a pipe-smoking shepherd found standing guard over the 'ladies' modesty' with his dog, on one occasion.[692] Better that than leave it at the summit though, as Elizabeth Le Blond, matriarch of Edwardian mountaineering did. To guard her 'modesty' she had no choice but to ascend it once again.

In its early days the LSCC issued new members with a leaflet describing suitable winter mountain attire which included thick stockings; puttees or gaiters to keep out snow, tweed knickers, woollen underwear, woollen blouse, slouch felt hat, woollen cap or Shetland helmet, woollen gloves with fingers and a pattern for snow gloves as well as a jacket, golf jersey, Shetland muffler and waterproof cape or 'Wettermantel'. By the time Nan began walking in the Cairngorms in 1928, attitudes to women's mountain-wear had changed too. A well turned out women climber in the late 1920s wore a tailored jacket with belt and breeches to match. Breeches were not for Nan. In all the photographs taken of her out on the tramp, she is wearing a skirt.

During Nan's hill-walking years it was not unusual for mixed and single groups of women to head to the Cairngorms. Their names appear in the 'visitor' books wrapped in waterproof covering which were left in the cave of the Shelter Stone above Loch Avon. Netta Dick, Helen Smith, Lena Dunbar and Biddy Noble, women belonging to the Aberdeen University Open Air Club are listed in 1930. Then in 1931, Helen Mennie (poet and friend of Nan's) and three other women were Cairngorm-walking with some male friends who 'also <u>ran</u> up—we do not think!' Nan's name, too, appears in a long list of Aberdeen women walking together in October 1931. Leafing through the books there are fewer females than males listed, but there are more women than you might think, often in all-female groups.[693] What was much more unusual, was Nan's habit of walking alone.

'A mass of granite, thrust up through the schists and gneiss forming the lower surrounding hills, planed down by the ice cap, and split, shattered and scooped by frost, glaciers and the strength of running water', the Cairngorm range of North East Scotland is an Arctic plateau, lethal to the careless. It is a place of extremes. As Nan says in the opening to *The Living Mountain*: 'Summer on the high plateau may be as delectable as honey; it can also be a roaring scourge'.[694]

Most years the Cairngorms are the snowiest of the Scottish hills.[695] Snow can fall here all year round and lies permanently in its deepest, coldest recesses. In winter, the plateau is whipped by winds which can reach hurricane force—gales which pluck out plants by their roots and gust with enough force to blow you over, battering till you're crawling on all fours. Wind-speeds of over 170 miles an hour have been recorded as well as the lowest ever temperatures anywhere in Britain: −27.2 degrees centigrade in Braemar.[696] When gales strike and bring storms of ground drift, or in heavy-falling blizzards made more perilous by mist, conditions become extremely dangerous. It is difficult to breathe, to open your eyes and next to impossible to communicate. Blizzards in the Cairngorms can be as bad as anywhere in the world.

The sheer scale of the Cairngorms is breathtaking. There is no other part of Britain so high over such a vast area—which makes it unique. A colossal expanse of granite landmass larger than Luxembourg[697] it has five of the six highest peaks in Britain. To see the entire Cairngorm range from ground level is impossible, as Nan recounts in *The Living Mountain*:

> From below, oddly enough they are not so majestic. There is something in their lift, their proportions and bearing, that can only be seen when one is somewhere near their own size. Seeing the Cairngorms from other mountains, Lochnagar or the Glen Lyon Heights emphasises them as a group. It is worth climbing unexciting heights if only to see the higher ones from nearer their own level.[698]

And while she was still not much more than a child, this is exactly what Nan Shepherd did.

One cold, blue, brilliant October day after heavy snow, Nan was alone, climbing Creagh Dhubh above Loch an Eilein. Excited, but with no real idea just how close she actually was, she toiled up the last slope until she came out above Glen Einich:

> Then I gulped the frosty air—I could not contain myself, I
> jumped up and down, I laughed and shouted. There was the
> whole plateau, glittering white, within reach of my fingers, an
> immaculate vision, sun-struck, lifting against a sky of dazzling
> blue. I drank and drank. I have not yet done drinking that
> draught. From that hour I belonged to the Cairngorms.[699]

It was in that moment Nan saw that the hills are not several, but one,
a plateau:

> The plateau is the true summit of these mountains. They must
> be seen as a single mountain, and the individual tops, Ben
> MacDhui, Braeriach and the rest, though sundered from one
> another by fissures and deep descents, are no more than eddies
> on the plateau surface. One does not look upwards to spectac-
> ular peaks but downwards to spectacular chasms.[700]

A number of years were to pass before Nan actually climbed them,
but from the moment she first did, in April 1928, she was hooked.
It was an appetite that grew in feeding. 'Like drink and passion, it
intensifies life',[701] she wrote, comparing her lust for ice cold peaks to
addiction, which for Nan Shepherd, it was. It was also a release: physically, emotionally and spiritually.

At first, exhilarated by the 'tang of height', Nan climbed all six
summits—some twice over. Her first ascent, of course, was the highest
Cairngorm, Ben MacDhui, which stands at 1,309 metres in the centre
of the plateau. From that first climb, she gleaned two pieces of knowledge, both of which persisted. The first was of the inside of a cloud; the
second was that a mountain has an inside.

Nan's route that April in 1928 was the classic one via Coire
Etchachan. She and her two companions were only a little way above
Loch Etchachan, which stands at around 922 metres,[702] when they were
engulfed in a cloud so thick that when the man who was leading went
only an arm's length ahead, he vanished. With only the sound of his
whistle to guide them, Nan and the man's wife walked on in whiteness.
'We climbed an endless way,' she said, recounting the episode in *The
Living Mountain,* 'nothing altered'. At one point, wraith-like, the man
reappeared saying, 'That's Loch Etchachan down there'. They could see
nothing. If anything the whiteness seemed thicker. 'It was horrible to
stand and stare into that pot of whiteness,' Nan recalled. 'The path went

on. And now to the side of us there was a ghastlier white, spreading and swallowing even the grey-brown earth our minds had stood on. We had come to the snow. A white as of non-life'.

After that first ascent, Nan walked often in cloud. She learned quickly how they can drench. The cloud that day was 'wet but not wetting' until they had almost reached the summit when it broke into hard rain and at last they could see the corries, 'scarfed in mist'.[703]

Nan was no hill-walking novice. She was used to hills, having climbed them from childhood; and the end of an ascent for her had always meant a moment of elation at 'the opening of a spacious view over the world'. But the sight that greeted her that day astonished her. Toiling upwards, feeling the gradient slacken as the top drew closer, at the end of the Etchachan ascent Nan found, not spaciousness, but an interior:

> And what an interior! the boulder-strewn plain, the silent shining loch, the black overhang of its precipice, the drop to Loch Avon and the soaring barricade of Cairn Gorm beyond, and on every side, except where we had entered, towering mountain walls.[704]

She was transfixed. This was the perspective-altering second knowledge she retained from her first ascent, that the mountain has an inside.

Her first glimpse into the mountain, it was also Nan's first sight of Loch Avon where six years later she would experience that mind-stopping moment of enlightenment. In 1928, however, Nan was all about the bodily sensation of summit. She had discovered what most mountain lovers do:

> As they ascend, the air grows rarer and more stimulating, the body feels lighter and they climb with less effort, till Dante's law of ascent on the Mount of Purgation seems to become a physical truth: 'This mountain is such, that ever at the beginning below 'tis toilsome, and the more a man ascends the less it wearies'.[705]

At height, Nan's body was at peak performance. She was *fey*, she said, drunk on the 'joyous release of body that is engendered by climbing'.

Having thought hers was a universal reaction, Nan was surprised to learn that it was not something everyone feels but was to do with individual physiology. For some, the rarer mountain air brings lassitude, slowly stifling them—the same way she felt at sea-level. She realised, too, that first day that 'her delight in the expanse of space opened up from the mountain tops' was also down to a quirk of physiology, prompting her somewhat dismissively to remark in *The Living Mountain* that 'the short-sighted cannot love mountains as the long-sighted do'.[706] Nan, of course, was long-sighted.

Waiting to greet her on her return from her first Ben MacDhui climb was the short, sturdy figure of old James Downie. More than thirty years later she could still recall the moment. 'He doffed his bonnet and clasped my hand in a gesture that was pure ceremonial. I was initiate'.[707] James Downie of Braemar was one of the truest hill lovers Nan ever knew. Like his father, he was a crofter and a mountain guide. A stout teller of tales, some of the stories Downie told Nan were extremely funny:

> His tales had a delicious tang—like bog-myrtle or juniper, sharp and good; of ladies climbing Lochnagar in trailing skirts; of the Loch Callater shepherd who had provided shalts for them to ride and who hid in his bothy and wouldn't help to mount the ladies, saying later to Downie "I likit fine to see ye settin' them on the shalts'; of Gladstone, a guest at Balmoral and desiring to see the Pools of Dee, but refusing to go the half-mile beyond the Pools that would have led him to the summit of the Pass and the long view over the Spey, and Downie, true hillman, deprived of his view, bearing a grudge for fifty years after. [708]

But he was not one to laugh much himself. According to Nan, 'the stern grandeur of the corries had invaded his soul. There was nothing tender or domestic about him'.[709]

His parents, John and Catherine Downie, came from Corriemulzie to Tomintoul croft on Morrone, Braemar, in around 1840. They arrived with one son and over the next seventeen or so years crammed six more children into the little croft which is said to be the highest in Scotland. In ruins for years, it still sits to the hill on a corner of Morrone, just below where the Field Club indicator stands. When its current owners opened the door they found the croft exactly as it was when the last of the Downies died and it was closed up. Listed category A, it is now being painstakingly restored, at enormous cost to its new owners, as a holiday let.

As a girl, Nan knew the croft:

We never climbed Morrone but we stopped to look at its

ancient knobble of glass in one of the windows, to speak to the
old people and perhaps be allowed to peep in at the door of
the old house ('up-by' as it always was to us after we became
habituees of the new cottage lower down) and see the deas,[710]
the box-bed, the plate-rack reaching to the roof and gleaming
with flowered plates and bowls. [711]

If she had been allowed more than a peep through the door, Nan would
have seen the three further box beds needed to accommodate the
Downie brood. There was another downstairs and two more in the attic
where the walls, eaves, and even the doors are papered with layers of
magazine and newspaper cuttings dating from the early 1900s—presumably to keep the damp and draughts at bay. The box-bed Nan spied
would have been the one in the kitchen opposite the fireplace with its
timber 'hingin lum'.[712] And until restoration work began, the wooden
hanging chimney, the beams and the box-beds, with their mattresses
packed with straw, were blackened by the brook of years of open fires.
It's a wonder the place had never gone up in flames.

John, the oldest of the Downie's children, married and went to
shepherd at Invercauld. The other two sons, William and James, after
their father's death in 1879, took over the running of the croft. By 1928,
still master of the croft, old James Downie was living by himself in the
bothy, leaving the house 'up-by' to Jessie 'who was a little short of a
barrowful'[713] and his other sister Kate.

Kate Downie was one of the last of the Gaelic-speaking Catholic
residue of the Braemar folk and still spoke the language on an everyday
basis. Like Kate Falconer in *The Weatherhouse,* 'who deciding she must
earn her living took a Diploma in Domestic Science becoming a
cook',[714] for a time Kate Downie left Braemar, working in London as a
cook, leaving her son James in the care of his grandmother.

In Spring 1928, Nan was staying with Kate's son, James 'Jimmy'
MacGregor and his wife Amelia in 'Braeview', the home Jimmy built
for himself in 1926. On that April day when Nan first saw the 'doon-
by' house, she fell instantly in love with the place. 'Its diminutive size,
its compactness, the ingenuity with which it used every fraction of
its interior space, its stair that ran up straight and narrow like a ship's
companion-way, its gable window, its poised and groomed assurance,
stole my heart'.[715] And for years, at least until the 1960s, she went back
at least once, if not twice a year. She even joined Grant and Jean Roger
there on their honeymoon in 1944 when she heard it was where they
were going.

Grant, Sheila Roger's brother, was the 'rabid naturalist' of *The Living*

Mountain. It was from Grant that Nan gleaned much about the botany of the mountain. She learned, for example, how the alpine flora of the Scottish mountains is Arctic in origin—that these small plants have outlived the Glacial period and are the only vegetable life older than the Ice Age. But as Edward Thomas said, and Nan also understood, this is science. It doesn't explain them. The secret of growth is a humbling mystery; and no matter how often you go up into that bright tower, 'that secret the mountain never quite gives away'.[716]

Nan went often to the hills with Grant Roger and from the early 1940s, with his wife too. 'Of course, if you married my husband you had to go the Cairngorms', Jean Roger said. And when Nan came with them on their honeymoon, Jean gave the impression, in an interview, that she thought it was funny. Nan took herself off on walks alone, but there they were in 'this tiny wee house and she was about ten feet from us! Great fun! A threesome honeymoon!'[717] Despite what she said publicly, in private Jean admitted to her son Neil that it really wasn't appropriate.[718] It does sound pretty insensitive of Nan. Her lust for mountain-tops clearly clouded her judgement. A photograph taken in 1944 at the door of Braeview (presumably by Grant[719]) shows a beaming Nan standing behind Jimmy MacGregor and an aproned Amelia, Jean barelegged in kilt and boots and at Jimmy's feet, Conny, his collie.

One snowy January morning, when the land was 'gleaming white', the snow 'made up of a million sharp-edged atoms of ice' lifted by a furious wind and driven against them, Conny, who would not be kept off the hill, followed Nan up Morrone. Time and again, Nan stopped to free the dog's shaggy eyebrows of ice. Nan was wearing ridged rubber boots, to which the snow did not cling but Conny's paws became weighted with balls of ice. 'Go home, Conny', Nan told her as she held her paws in her bare hands and freed them. But Nan could not bear to turn back and the dog would not. 'Did she do it to you then? That bad woman. Poor lass, was that a way to treat my dog?', Jimmy teased once Nan and Conny were safely back at the fire. But he knew why Conny and Nan had to go on and listened attentively to her description of the strange columnar structure she found in the snow near the summit and of the hunting eagle she saw flying low up the valley.[720]

It was from Mure Mackenzie that Nan first heard about Braeview, the 'shanty on the edge of the Cairngorms where one lives and is', as she described it to Hugh MacDiarmid in 1938.[721] In 1927, Mure told Nan how she had been sleeping there in the little bedroom with the gable window and woken at dawn to see sixteen stags in the garden.

The MacGregors with their dog Conny, Nan (behind) and Jean
Roger (far right).

Her presence at the window startled them and like a wave, they flowed
over the containing wall. Later, Jimmy MacGregor broke new ground
for the garden, fencing it securely against deer and rabbit so that he and
Amelia could cultivate flowers. But what Nan loved best was the 'exquisite clump of bluebells' by the door, their 'slender stems and delicate
inflorescence' increasing at each of her visits, year by year. She loved,
too, the roebuck antlers, the milky quartz, the wind-chiselled pieces
of limestone from the streak running across Morrone and the stones
brought from the steading at Glen Ey from where old John Downie had
been evicted in 1840. 'All placed with natural rightness. Into the parcel
of land—house, fields and garden—was put the genius of this man', she
wrote, after Jimmy's death in 1962.[722]

Over fifty years on, the 'shanty' with its antlers over the door is still
there. The window-frames are white now and some of the clapboard
has been covered and painted green below the rust-coloured corrugated
roof. It may have been too early for the bluebells, but there is no sign

now of the MacGregor's carefully planted garden; just a few nodding daffodils here and there.

Known as 'Creeper' because of his telescope, the word in the village was that Jimmy MacGregor was illegitimate, which is probably true. Not everyone thought him as interesting as Nan. Adam Watson, guru of the Cairngorms, found him a rather dull character. Others found him sharp tongued. But that, according to Nan, was because, 'they did not recognise for what it was a little toss of the head that he had, which belied the stern face and sometimes almost angry voice in which he said the most preposterous things'. She enjoyed his quirky mind and shared his delight in the droll and absurd.

She also admired his tenacity and skill. He managed to make a living from the exposed and stony fields, supplementing his income working as a ghillie, a gardener, occasional postman 'up the glen'. He built 'Braeview', channelling water from the hill, had water on tap and 'flush sanitation'. He manufactured some sort of generator and even wired the house electrically (although the light produced was too dim to be much use). Yet he had little schooling and neither an apprenticeship nor any training. What Nan valued was how he drew in knowledge 'like breathing' and his endless curiosity. So quick was he, 'he would be up on you before you knew it' surprising the thoughts out of your head. With Jimmy MacGregor you never chatted, you conversed and 'no-one stayed in his house but he drew from their stores of knowledge, their peculiar lore,' she said.

Equally, Nan learned from him and each time she visited, she learned and liked him more. If she went up to Braemar for a few days by herself, wandering all day alone on the hills, seated by the fire in the evening, Nan would relate to Jimmy all that she had seen and heard, his comments intensifying her knowledge. He loved to catch her out in some stupidity too—sleeping out without a tent after a blazing day when he'd warned her (and she wouldn't listen) that there would be ground frost at night—and creeping in shivering to be gleefully mocked.[723] But Nan learnt from Jimmy MacGregor as she learnt from others she met and grew to know, people she described in *The Living Mountain,* who lived close to their wild land, subject to its weathers, something of its own nature permeating theirs.[724]

Many of these 'forceful and gnarled personalities', 'the bone of the mountain', as she called them, vanished during Nan's walking years. Among these were the indomitable Maggie Gruer at the Linn of Dee 'that granite boss, shapely in feature as a precipice' and on the Rothiemurchus side of the Cairngorms there was Sandy Mackenzie, gamekeeper and already a done old man when Nan knew him. After his death, Nan often stayed a few weeks of the year with his widow, Big Mary, 'tall, gaunt and stooped, her skin runkled, grey hair tousled in the wind who had an *eldritch* look on her', who knew Nan's habit of sleeping by the door and prowling at all sorts of hours. Speyside, too, there were the Sutherlands: Adam, who was the guard at Aviemore station and his wife, 'a woman generous as the sun'.[725]

Up on the plateau, Nan could walk all day and see no-one. But when she stopped to really look, she could see man's presence everywhere. It was there in the cairns, the paths, the stepping-stones over burns, the indicators, the roofless shepherds' huts and the bothies. All of these relayed man's 'persistent passage' of the hills and his interrelatedness with the landscape and its nature. But in April 1928 Nan had yet to apprehend all this and much more; she was only at the beginning of her journey.

She had still to discover that, for her, the peaks were not the point. Early on, she scaled all of the summits, some twice over, making it sound in as if it were easy:

> Given clear air, and the unending daylight of a Northern summer, there is not one of the summits but can be reached by a moderately strong walker without distress. A strong walker will take a couple of summits. Circus walkers will plant flags on all six summits in a matter of fourteen hours.[726]

To begin with, too, she went to the hills for fun, with no other motive beyond wanting to. At first, it was only 'sensuous gratification' she was after, the sensations of height, movement, speed, distance, effort and ease: 'the lust of the flesh, the lust of the eyes, the pride of life. I was not interested in the mountain for itself', she confessed, 'but for its effect upon me, as puss caresses not the man but herself against the man's trouser leg'.[727]

Which is why, on that spring afternoon in 1928, as soon as she had settled in at Braeview, she set off to climb Morrone—and so earned old James Downie's friendship on her first night. The last time Nan saw him, he insisted on carrying her bag all the way to the bus. She remonstrated but he would take no refusal, treating her, she supposed, the way he had treated all his lady climbers. 'I'll not see you again', he said.[728] He did not. He died the following year at the age of seventy-eight.

* * *

In the Spring of 1930, Nan was ill again and feeling miserable. A grumbling appendix was the cause. She was losing weight and feeling low. She escaped to the hills for the Easter break and wrote to Neil Gunn from there in March. The hills had revived her. It was not just physically that she felt stronger, as she told Gunn, it was as though her 'whole nature has suddenly leaped into life'. She was churning out poetry:

> I've been making poems at about the rate of one a day—almost effortlessly—and yet with sufficient detachment from any intoxication to recognise that they are really the product of a thousand efforts, of thoughts that have tormented me and emotions that have wrung and exalted, and things seen and heard long ago that suddenly slip into just the imagery to convey a whole complex of thought and feeling. And as each new poem wells up into being, it doesn't seem to matter what my critical judging self will think of it when the stirring of the wells is over.[729]

Neil Gunn claimed that he wrote in a state of possession. He was 'told', he said. He never had to wonder where his writing was going to go next. 'I had nothing to do with writing him at all' he admitted in a letter to Nan in 1940, discussing one of his characters.[730] For Nan in 1930, it was 'the producing that matters so gloriously'. 'But it's all a cold inhuman kind of poetry', she went on, 'about stars and mountains and light and that sort of thing. When I'm possessed that's the only kind of thing that comes out of me!'[731]

No poems in Nan's poetry notebook correspond with this period. In fact, there is no verse recorded there at all between April 1929 and January 1931. There is, however, a burst of poetry-writing activity in 1931, filled with the emotional torment and moments of exaltation she talks about, which suggests that the poems are mis-dated and were actually written the year before. It is a theory lent weight by Nan's quotation of a line from a poem dated 16th April 1931 in her notebook in a letter to Gunn written on 14th March 1930:

> My greatest friend told me years ago—he wanted me then to publish my verse and I refused—that not a dozen people would be able to understand it! Not that it is obscure, or symbolist, or anything of that sort—but "caulder than mou' can thole".[732]

Her 'greatest friend', John Macmurray, the man she had loved by now for almost fourteen years, was much on Nan's mind and the poems she was writing were, as she says, flooding out of her as she worked through her feelings. John and Betty were still living in London, but they had been up in Scotland on holiday and the three had gone walking together. A photograph Nan took at the time shows John and Betty picnicking on a rock-strewn hillside. Nan's coat is spread on the grass next to a muscular-looking John wearing a 1930s swimsuit. Betty sits on his other side, smart in her hat and summer dress. All three have kicked off their shoes and around them, their walking sticks lie scattered amongst thermos, wicker basket and unfolded maps. There is a relaxed intimacy about the scene. John, fork lifted half-way to his mouth, appears to be talking about the food on his plate. Betty, her face obscured by her cloche hat, is turned towards him. Nan is not in the picture and by then, she really wasn't.

John and Betty Macmurray in the 1930s.
Nan is not in the picture: she is the one taking it.

In the early 1930s John, Betty and their close friends, Irene and Donald Grant, were moving towards what John hoped would be a sort of communal living and a sexual sharing—the two families effectively marrying one another. 'His thoughts were in confusion. A thousand meanings were in the air and he dared grasp at none. The brightness of the blade turned him back', Luke is reported to be thinking in *The Quarry Wood*. If this was a reflection of John's state of mind post-South-Africa, the blade analogy is reminiscent of Nan's poem on two ways of loving. Nan's way was exclusive, involving a cutting of ties—and that was never going to happen.

The intervening years had been difficult for Nan, but by 1933 she was able to look back on this love with some sort of serenity and acceptance, and to see that, painful as it had been, she had grown from the experience. It seems most likely that the ending was brought about by the realisation that she and John had grown and changed during those years of separation. While Nan stayed in Scotland John and Betty were elsewhere, in Oxford and then London. Nan once said of her friend, the poet Marion Angus, that 'she knew the cold relief when a passion is dead'.[733] Nan knew it too, but as she also acknowledged in *Descent from the Cross,* 'life needs the dark, slow decay of countless myriad frustrations to provide a soil for growth.'[734] And 'Growth' was the title of the sonnet Nan wrote in the summer of 1932. 'This bitter wisdom is my strength to-night,' it opens and goes on to explore the idea that only the inanimate, things 'safe and mechanical' do not develop 'but keep their state'.[735]

It is an idea re-examined in 'A Dead Love' which she wrote the following February. Here 'love is stripped and cold' and the secret wood can now be looked back on with such clarity it is in sharp relief. 'Like the X-Ray that penetrates to the bone', now 'each sees the other, without desire or hope'.[736] In 'Growth', 'loving has no safety'—making oneself vulnerable is to risk potential hurt. But the 'you', to whom the sonnet is addressed, is now altered: 'I had not failed you had you been the same/As that old self that at my bidding came'. And as a result, seeing the change, the speaker's pain is deadened somewhat: 'So may I blunt the sharpness of the sore'. What is idealised in memory, the sextet concludes, does not account for growth and change in humans.[737]

Lovers who have grown and changed becomes a refrain in those poems and in Nan's prose, too. 'Gib had no more place in her life. He wasn't her kind after all' Mary Kilgour says of the man with whom she was in love before Bella Cassie made off with him in *A Pass in the Grampians*:

He wasn't like this once, she thought. He had ideals...A smoulder of shame ran through her—the old feeling of dull unreasoning shame that rose in her body every time she thought about Gib...Now as she met him again after fourteen years, she realized how right she was.[738]

Nan and John had both altered. Their philosophies had diverged too.

After a month in the hills, on 11th March Nan returned to Aberdeen. John, still on her mind, was soon in her ears too. On 28th April, John, who had by then held the Grote Chair of Philosophy of Mind and Logic at University College, London for almost a year, began a series of BBC Radio broadcasts. There were twelve in all, on the subject of 'Reality and Freedom' and which, almost overnight, made John Macmurray a household name, creating 'a miniature renaissance'[739] among thousands of listeners. Once a week, at eight o'clock on Monday evenings, John's quiet, Scottish brogue drifted over the airwaves. For many, John Macmurray was the first philosopher to talk on the wireless who spoke in a language they could understand.[740]

By the early 1930s Nan had long since severed ties with Christianity and while she clearly respected John's ideas, her philosophy on the inner significance of life was now more in tune with eastern thought. It was becoming more obvious to her, too, that it was more in harmony with Neil Gunn's. And as they both began to see just how much they were on each other's wavelength, their correspondence grew more intellectually ardent.

Neil's reply to Nan's long letter about her 'well-stirring' in the hills arrived towards the end of May 1930. He was keen to see some of her verse and offered to suggest publishers or try to place them himself. Poetry was not Neil's own medium, his was the novel, but his letter was full of empathy for Nan's efforts as well as teasing: 'How happy you make me when I think of your bedevilments! Poor girl, it must be hard on you'. He was daunted, though, by her 'austere conception' of poetry:

There are times, I suppose when even a best-seller is disturbed by a vision of a higher peak than his own. Ah, positively a peak that is other, with different rock and earth and air. It is not a peak of commerce. May the clouds cover it! An air that is caulder than mou' can thole.[741]

The subject matter of Nan's poetry, which he too was exploring in his fiction, even if it was comprehended, was not commercial, as both of them knew.'Caulder than mou' can thole' was a quotation he relished, repeating it back to her several times in his letter. 'Well-water' came to be a shorthand bandied between them. 'The world isn't ready for the well-water Nan', he would say some years later. What he meant is partly explained by Nan's poem:

> Caul', caul' as the wall
> That rins frae under the snaw
> On Ben a'Bhuird,
> And fierce, and bricht,
> This water's nae for ilka mou',
> But him that's had a waucht or noo,
> Nae wersh auld waters o' the plain
> Can sloke again,
> But aye he clim's the weary heicht
> To fin' the wall that loups like licht,
> Caulder than mou' can thole, and aye
> The warld cries oot on him for fey.

> [Cold, cold, as the well
> That runs from under the snow
> On Ben a'Bhuird,
> And fierce, and bright,
> This water's not for every mouth,
> But him that's had a draught or no,
> No tasteless waters of the plain
> Can quench again,
> But still he climbs the weary height
> To find the well that leaps like light,
> Colder than mouth can bear, and still
> The world cries out on him for fey]

The poem is all about poetry. In fact, in her manuscript version Nan even gives it the title 'Poetry' although it was published untitled in *In the Cairngorms*. The poem works on several levels. Few of Nan's verses are written in Doric. That this one is, is deliberately to foreground its inaccessibility to an English audience not acquainted with the dialect of the North East. As the speaker suggests, it makes it unpalatable, 'wersh', and difficult to decipher. 'This water's nae for ilka mou'— the water's not to every taste—because an English audience will not understand it without a glossary! But as John Macmurray suggested, the poem's meaning may be opaque even for those familiar with

Doric. Yet, comprehension aside, the rhythm of the unfamiliar words is haunting. It draws the reader back, to 'climb the weary height' again and again. Somehow no other words will do. The Doric suggested itself to Nan because it felt right and is appropriate.

The language used also speaks of the creative process which produced it. In March 1930 in the hills, the poems welled into being apparently effortlessly—fierce and bright, as Nan said in her letter to Neil Gunn, yet as austere and cold, she felt as the snowy landscape which inspired them. There is also more than a suggestion in the poem of the exhilaration of climbing, to the tang of height that Nan was experiencing and to which she was addicted during her early Cairngorm-walking years, as well as that *feyness,* the joyous release it brought on.

But it is also speaking about the eternal mystery of water, one of the four elemental mysteries, which wells from under the 'snaw' and flows away. Water, as she says in *The Living Mountain,* 'does nothing, absolutely nothing, but be itself'.[742] This connects with the Eastern philosophies with which Nan and Neil were engaging. *Fey* can mean: a disorder of the mind; clairvoyant; or *not oneself.* Nan and Neil understood that the perceptual shift that brought about a leap out of one's self and silencing of ego, ironically, is the most intense state of being. Like water it is a state of doing nothing but being. Nan and Neil both saw; the world on the whole, did not, at least not then.

'It's so good to have someone who talks one's own language',[743] Nan wrote, seeing the parallels in their thinking early on, recognising it in Neil's work when, at the time, most critics missed it. *Morning Tide,* published in 1930, was extremely successful. For the first time Neil was enjoying fame. Nan's, 'delicate insight' had inspired him. 'You at least saw what I was after, and you know how refreshing it is to find anyone who recognises what's ado', Neil answered in March 1931. James Whyte had reviewed *Morning Tide* in the *Modern Scot*[744]. Neil was scathing: 'His review shows that he simply had no idea of what I was trying to do. He represents the undergraduate type of mind to whom words like "intellectual" and "continental" are apocalyptic!'[745]

He was encouraged, however, by the activity going on in many parts of Scotland regarding Nationalism and the Party, particularly in the West, and was confident about the future. 'If only Nan Shepherd would now come away and give us her best we could feel that Scottish Literature was founded,' a Glasgow acquaintance had said to Neil and he passed on the compliment adding, 'which, I suppose is a sort of roundabout way on my part of wondering what you are at.'[746]

Nan was recuperating. The autumn of 1930 had brought blustering gales that went right through her body as though it were paper. She was still losing weight and by winter, the grumbling of her appendix became a piercing shriek. She underwent surgery. 'It gave me a shock to hear you were being reissued without notes or appendix', Mure wrote to her when she heard. 'I'm afraid you had had a rotten time, poor lassie, and am very glad to hear the creation is mending. But I have small doubt you'll be better for the revision: there was obviously something that wanted a good overhauling. Proceed to grow fat.'[747]

The overhaul might well have been necessary and Mure's comic, creative analogy no doubt made her smile, but Nan was skinny and exhausted. Her weight had dropped to a mere seven and a half stone and it sounds as though more than just the offending appendix had been removed. Keyhole surgery was not an option in 1930 and the recovery process would have been slow and frustrating. That winter was a dreary one and it was several months before Nan felt more like herself again. In May 1931 Helen Waddell wrote to Nan. She, too, was sympathetic: 'operations are grim things the body seems to remember long after the mind has forgotten and it won't hurry back to the old ways at once'. In a postscript, scribbled across the top corner of her letter, Waddell added: 'Sometimes being ill is good for one's mind. Did you get anything out of it?'[748]

But the same year the 'talkies' came to Aberdeen, Nan Shepherd lost her voice. 'I've gone dumb', she complained bleakly to Neil Gunn:

> It's partly a profound dissatisfaction with all I've hitherto written: more profoundly, a dissatisfaction with my own grip on life and assurance in its fundamentals. I make all sorts of excuses to myself for not going on with the book I began nearly two years ago. I want to write it. I know its people, its place, its theme. But I can't write it. I think I'm afraid. One reaches these dumb places in life. I suppose there's nothing for it but to go on living. Speech may come. Or it may not. And if it doesn't I suppose one has just to be content to be dumb. At least not shout for the mere sake of making noise.[749]

The book was *A Pass in the Grampians,* 'PIG', as Mure referred to it, which Nan had started writing in 1929. In it, she re-examines the issues raised in her first novel, this time considering what you take with you and what you leave behind on a journey, swapping the Pillars of Hercules for a Grampian pass. Both of course are symbolic, gateways to the world beyond adolescence. Unlike Martha, however, who stayed put, sixteen-year old Jenny Kilgour chooses to cross that pass. At the end of the book she decides to leave her grandfather's remote Kincardineshire hill farm and head for an entirely different society in London.

Nan's dissatisfaction with her own grip on life and assurance of its fundamentals, was being underscored by writing the book. Like Martha, Nan had stayed put. By 1931 her work at the Training Centre had finally been recognised and she had been promoted to Head of the Department. She had also found fulfilment in motherhood of a sort, by 'adopting' Sheila Roger. But to finish writing *A Pass in the Grampians* was to have to consider what, if any difference, crossing that pass would have made. Would things have been different? The novel's conclusion suggests perhaps not.

1931 was coloured by the realisation that after fourteen years of loving John Macmurray that part of her life was over too. Ellen Falconer of *The Weatherhouse,* who in some respects seems to be a projection of Nan, 'thought she was experienced in life, but in truth she had assimilated nothing from her suffering, only dismissed it and returned to her dreams.' The dreams were over. Two things restored Ellen Falconer—'her child and the country. It was a country that liberated. More than half the world was sky. The coastline vanished at one of the four corners of the earth, Ellen lost herself in its immensity. It wiled her from thought'.[750]

★ ★ ★

The 'what if' stalled PIG for several months. Nan had not entirely lost her voice though. She admitted to Neil Gunn that, having not done so for years, she was writing a little verse again. A number of people over the years, the Macmurrays included, had tried to convince her to publish her poetry. Marion Angus, she told Neil, was anxious, too, that she should. 'I have many and many a time read your 'Hill Burns', Marion had written to Nan nearly a decade earlier in June 1922:

> It brings back to me a kind of passion, the longing to hear & see & lie among them [the hills]. It does much more, it shows me what miracles can be attained by words. I am carried away by the beauty of the thing which your spirit & the spirit of place between you have conceived. It has something of both & something quite new also—strange—lovely—Nothing so lucid, so precious, yet so restrained could I ever by poor effort attain to! I am lost in confused wonder. You must publish & very soon, that I may not be kept waiting long.[751]

But Nan still did not have sufficient belief in herself as a poet. She poured out her heart to Neil:

> Poetry means too much to me—it seems to me to hold in intensest being the very heart of all experience; and though I have now and then glimpsed something of that burning heart of life—have intimations and hauntings of its beauty and strangeness and awe—always when I try to put these things into words they elude me. The result is slight and small. And then I read something like Hugh McDiarmid's [sic] "You cannot sing until your flight/Leaves you no audience but the light"—and go away humbled and chastened, and shut my lips.[752]

She was beginning to wonder if it was only in a state of 'possession' that she could write poetry: 'and though that might be said to be given and not achieved, yet one must prepare oneself for the possession—it demands discipline of one's whole self, an integrity of one's personality, before "whatsoever powers there be" can possess and use one's force'. She had decided, however, that to be in such a state of possession was physically too taxing. 'I'm too indolent nowadays for such discipline. I shrink too from the subsequent exhaustion. Not being physically very strong, I grudge the way it eats up my vitality.'[753]

Not physically strong? This was a woman who was physically fit enough to be walking the Cairngorms and who, during the past two years had scaled all six summits, some twice over. Nan clearly *was* physically strong. She might have been feeling somewhat fragile after her operation the winter before, but as she admits to Gunn it was cowardice, not the strength-sapping strain caused by these periods of intense creativity, that was really at the root of her writing silence.

It did not matter what others thought of her poetry, it mattered whether Nan thought her writing was good enough. Deep down, she worried that hers was only a mediocre talent and that she was making excuses, laying blaming elsewhere because she could not admit it to herself. 'Isn't it folly', she wrote to Neil, 'to be thus analytic of oneself instead of running to the great business of creation!' To illustrate her point, she used Robert Browning's dramatic monologue 'Andrea del Sarto or The Faultless Painter'. It's an interesting choice because, of course, it contains John Macmurray's mantra: 'but a man's reach should exceed his grasp,/Or what's a heaven for?' Browning's Del Sarto blames his wife for his mediocrity, as Nan went on to explain, 'he put it on his wife, the skunk, that he couldn't be one of the great creative artists, but in his heart he knew well enough that it was all because in himself he was second rate.'[754]

Now it was Nan's turn to need support and encouragement and Neil gave it. But his reply, written on the 15th April, would not have found Nan at home. After posting her letter to Neil, she had taken herself off to Braeview for the Easter holidays, remaining there until the 22nd of April when term re-opened at the Training Centre. Once again the hills revitalised her and despite those protestations of physical frailty to Neil, Nan was re-'possessed'. Between 5th and 20th April 1931, she completed nine poems, eight of which would eventually be published in *In the Cairngorms* in 1934.

Some of these verses Nan sent to Helen Waddell, who responded, 'this stuff is beautiful. I have sometimes wondered to a friend of mine why a countryside like yours and like my own of the Mourne Mountains gets so inadequately into Literature and why it seems easier to write poetry of the English Downs'. Nan's poems wrought in her a sense of the 'wild exaltation, beauty and terror' of the Cairngorms. Helen suggested sending some of her poetry to Constables: 'As you know this is a barren world for poets, but Mr Kyllman is a great lover of poetry, and he has always felt your power of evoking the spirit of the land'.[755] Whether or not Nan took her advice, we do not know, but in the end, *In the Cairngorms* was not published by Constable.

Neil's response greeted Nan on her return from Braemar. Since their first frustratingly brief meeting at the Aberdeen PEN he had been trying to find a time to talk properly with Nan and was due to be in Dundee in the coming weeks, but would only have an hour to spare and that was not nearly long enough to cover everything he had to say about the issues she had raised in her last letter—and not just from a literary perspective. 'I have always a certain second view from the non-literary angle', he explained: 'for I am not really a literary man. I realise this with striking force when I meet many of my friends (eg C M Grieve). I play at it, but I laugh a little too…For I don't know that one ever wants to have an understanding with anything so much as with life.' Here, of course, they were saluting and echoing each other. In her letter back in March 1930, Nan had declared that she was not really a literary person either. Art mattered to them both, but it was life and a grasp of its essential meaning that was at the root of what they were both trying to articulate through it.

Neil also had much to say to her about *The Weatherhouse*:

That book of yours. Good Lord. And your poetry—you make me a little afraid to enter in. Where of course no one can enter

in. Which is not what matters…And when you say that the
result of your poetry is 'slight and small' you make my head
buzz. What I once saw [Lux Perpetua] by way of a sample had
me staggering at a fourth reading. Steady a little, please, and
have a thought for the lowly.[756]

Neil, of course, was by now not so lowly. *Morning Tide* had sold very
well and he was enjoying his new-found fame as a writer. Teasingly,
Nan began her reply on 5th July 1931: 'My dear Best-Seller'. Her letter
was not much more than a note to ask, with her innate courtesy and
the importance of observing social propriety, if they were at home on
Wednesday 29th July as she would be en-route to the Port of Ness
heading for Uig on the western coast of Lewis and if so, would 'Mrs
Gunn allow her to call in the evening?'[757]

'Larachan', Neil and Daisy Gunn's home in Inverness, was often
filled with people. In the early 1930s, Sunday evenings were open house
drop-ins where any number between four and ten people might turn
up. Neil was a great talker and guests would often find themselves still
up at three or four in the morning, a dram to hand. The gently teasing
tone of his correspondence to Nan, was typical. He was, in fact, shy
himself, but adept at drawing out others—as Nan's letters to him reveal.
The relief at being able to 'speak the same language' to someone who
understood and shared her philosophy on life, is palpable. With each
letter, she becomes more forthcoming—most unusual for famously
reticent Nan Shepherd. But then Neil did not consider her 'fey' as she
describes it in the last line of 'Caul', caul" because of her beliefs; to him,
she was clairvoyant. He was thrilled at the prospect of Nan's visit and
asked her to spend as much of the evening with them as possible. Nan
did visit Neil at the end of July. We know this because she refers to it in
her letter of 15th September. But she makes no comment about it.

For an idea of what that encounter would have been like, though,
we have Jessie Kesson's account of her own visit to the Gunns in 1945.
Neil was one of Jessie's literary idols. She would been nervous about
meeting him, but there was a welcoming fire burning in the hearth and
a man who didn't stand on ceremony:

He didn't even sit on ceremony. A tall man, he lengthened
himself out on the floor, leaning his back against an arm chair.
Taking my cue from him I also took to the floor beside him…
We talked through a long afternoon into evening. Replen-
ished and *refuelled* by his wife. Gracious in letting us have space
and privacy to hold our hour and have another.[758]

Six years older than her husband, golden-haired, tall and slim with a wide, warm smile, Daisy did not participate much in these literary meetings, remaining quietly in the background, providing refreshment.

Despite their intellectually flirty correspondence, there is no evidence of any impropriety in Neil's and Nan's relationship over the years. Neil, however, did become emotionally embroiled in a relationship outside his marriage with Margaret MacEwan. Kept secret from even his closest friends the affair began in the summer of 1934, during a period when his marriage was strained. An accident had caused the stillbirth of a much longed for son and, for a time, Daisy withdrew from her husband. Neil's letters to Margaret are very different to those he wrote to Nan (those we have, at any rate). They are guarded and impersonal. Margaret MacEwan's letters to him were destroyed.[759]

'I said you could see these. So see,' Nan wrote to Neil on 15th September 1931 enclosing a sheaf of typed poems. 'Being—as you are now well convinced—a thoroughly lazy one, I send you only such as happen to be already typed…There are about as many more'.[760] She had done nothing further with 'the damnable bits of paper' except to show them to John and Betty Macmurray, who said 'For God's sake get them published!' It is to the Macmurrays that *In the Cairngorms* is dedicated, but as Nan said to Neil: 'Presenting a dedication without making any effort towards publication is rather like buying the pram before the child is conceived, don't you think?'[761]

In the meantime, Nan was holidaying in Uig, in Lewis and had taken with her Neil's short story, 'The Dead Seaman'. She was rapturous about it:

> There aren't minds there but senses. The intellect is put in its place, and the Blessed … are alive in their blood and their muscles and their tingling skin and the whole complex network of their nerves….and just the sense of life that isn't any of these but something beyond.[762]

The sentence ends with her trademark squiggly line. More than an ellipsis, Nan uses it in correspondence at moments either when she is lost for words or when she is retreating into her customary reticence. Here, it is the former. She was often awed by the way Neil Gunn managed to convey the experience she too was striving to capture, and as usual, Nan had struck at the very essence of Neil's story 'the other landscape' integral to his philosophy.

Her poems she had put to one side while she struggled to finish *A Pass in the Grampians*, only to run away from the novel again in September for another 'blessed mountain week'. This time she was headed for Aviemore. 'Perhaps I might even make more poetry, who knows', she remarked to Neil. 'At any rate, I shall see the Cairngorms—and the precipices and the cold, cold snows'.[763]

While Nan was in Aviemore, Gunn was reading her poems, but the letter he wrote to her about them must have been disappointingly brief. 'There's some great stuff', he said, but not all of them, he felt, were flawless. This is true, they are not. Although, he countered, 'they are all exquisitely intent and authentic.' 'The Man Who Journeyed to His Heart's Desire', he thought her most perfect poem. 'The accent is so old and the tone like the line of a long low hill.'[764]

'Union', he admired for its metaphysical quality. He had good things to say, too, about 'Snow', the rhythm-rhyme of the sestet haunting him 'until it becomes almost grievous!'[765] He was keeping them to re-read and comment in more detail. It is apparent from a letter of Nan's that Neil did, at some point, write a more expansive critique. He also suggested she should approach Blake at Faber & Faber to publish her anthology. Unfortunately, this letter of his not amongst those extant in Nan's archive.

Interestingly, Neil made some amendments to 'Caul' which he does not mention in his letter. Neil, like Edwin Muir, wrote in English. It was not that he didn't agree language was important for a nation's identity, but for him, it went beyond language to a nation's cultural tradition, social patterns and, of course, to man's relationship with landscape and the environment. The amendments he made included changing 'wall' in the first line to 'well', and 'waucht' in line six to 'draught', 'wersh' on the next line to 'tasteless' and 'thole' to 'endure'. Basically, he translated into English the dialect he obviously felt would affect an English reader's interpretation—and perhaps diminish Shepherd's audience. Perhaps Gunn thought better of sending her his amendments: the copy Nan sent him remains in his archive and the poem is published exactly as she originally wrote it in *In the Cairngorms* (although a translation of several words appears beneath).

In the first half of 1932, Nan was busy writing verse and trying to work without distractions. Blake had agreed to publish her poems in a Faber & Faber half crown edition and between January and June that year she completed several poems all of which bar one, which remained unfinished, were included in the volume. To let herself go to another kind of work while she was doing that was fatal and while she was not a fan of most novelists' work, for Neil Gunn's she made an exception.

Having bought a copy of his *The Lost Glen* when it was published early in March 1932, for a couple of weeks she had managed to resist the temptation to read the novel which had originally appeared serialised in the *Scots Magazine* in 1928. Detesting serials she had only read the first instalment then, thinking she would wait until the complete novel appeared. It had been a long wait, making it even harder to put the book to one side while she focussed on her poetry. But of course she gave in, sat down and read it from cover to cover and of course, it distracted her from her own writing: 'In the black swirl and air of that first storm—when Ewan's father is drowned—how could I write anymore?'[766] she wailed to Neil in her letter of 26 March 1932.

Neil had endured a mauling in the press for this latest novel. Technically, it was felt to be far less successful than *Morning Tide* and that he had lost his way in it. He was bitter about the reviews. Unlike the critics, Nan understood what Gunn was after in the novel and her effusive and lengthy letter, applied a much needed salve to his wounds. 'It's a much bigger thing than *Morning Tide*', she began, continuing:

> Endlessly amazing is the way you <u>realize</u> the whole. I see, hear, smell, know, every hole and corner and air and angle of your created world…those undulating words and phrases in which you can express so much of what mustn't be expressed else its essential nature must perish. In which you put into words the ultimate wordless darkness in which the spirit sinks and sinks to recreate itself. So few people have put it into words.[767]

What she really admired was that his words not only created the 'mood they seek to embody. They are themselves a spell, potent with movement, rhythm, sound suggestiveness'.[768] To be able to achieve this, Nan felt, was a gift of the highest order. It did not occur to her that she had the same artistry, because at the time she did not feel she had it. *The Living Mountain* was the work about which she was radiant, quite rightly, but that was a few years hence. And in the meantime, the volcano that was *Sunset Song* was about to erupt on the Scottish Scene.

Nan in her 20s.

Chapter Ten

1932-1935

As Hugh MacDiarmid said, Leslie Mitchell's was 'a painfully hurried life'.[769] Born in 1901 in Auchterless, Aberdeenshire, from the age of eight Mitchell lived in Arbuthnott in Kincardineshire, the heart of the Mearns and the land of *Sunset Song*. After four years as a local hack in Aberdeen and Glasgow, followed by eight in the Royal Army Service Corps, in 1925 he married Rebecca (known as 'Ray') Middleton and moved to Welywn Garden City. By 1929, he had turned full-time to writing. Plagued intermittently by gastric trouble which made him feel as though 'rattlesnakes rhumba'd in his stomach',[770] Mitchell wrote feverishly until his death six years later, publishing sixteen books during his short lifetime in categories as wide-ranging as a slave revolt, time travel, biography, politics, exploration and archaeology. But the work for which he is best known is *The Scots Quair* trilogy. Hailed on its appearance in 1932 as perhaps the first really Scottish novel,[771] the first in this trilogy, *Sunset Song* has recently been voted best Scottish novel of all time.[772]

Sunset Song was also the first of Mitchell's Scottish fictional works to appear under his pseudonym, adapted from his mother's maiden name: Lilias Grassic Gibbon. A Scottish pseudonym was deliberate and appropriate—not just to differentiate the work from Mitchell's English novels, or because of its North East setting—but because it was something new and experimental.

The Scottish language issue was one that had divided opinion ever since T S Eliot had suggested there was no Scottish Literature back in 1919. According to Edwin Muir, the Scots language had been in decline for centuries: 'since some time in the sixteenth century Scottish literature has been a literature without a language', he wrote in *Scott and Scotland*.[773] From the early nineteenth century while writers in Europe were producing literature like Baudelaire's *Les Fleurs du Mal*, Eliot's *Middlemarch*, Marx's *Das Kapital*, Scotland appeared to have lost its tongue. It was not until the turn of the twentieth century that the silence was broken, first by Stevenson with *Weir of Hermiston* in 1893, then Douglas Brown's *The House with the Green Shutters* and then by the writers of the 'Renaissance', Nan Shepherd, Neil Gunn, Naomi Mitchison, Eric Linklater, Willa Muir as well as a raft of poets, MacDiarmid included.

The fact was, that with the exception of The Porpoise Press, there was a decided lack of Scottish publishers—meaning new writers had to go to London and pitch their works for an English audience. But this was not the only issue. The problem, according to Mitchell (writing as Lewis Grassic Gibbon) in 'Literary Lights', an essay he wrote in 1933, was that the Scottish writer was forced to write in English and while his prose or verse might be 'impeccably correct...unfortunately it is not English' and to an English reader, sounds somehow foreign. The Scottish writer writing in English, Mitchell decided, was not so much writing as translating himself. Searching for the appropriate word, the Scottish writer 'hears an echo' in a tongue that would bring richness and clarity to his writing. 'That echo is from Braid Scots'.

The trouble was, in most Scots communities, Braid Scots, was not considered genteel. The bourgeois, according to Mitchell, quoted it in inverted commas deeming it inadequate for the 'finer shades of emotion'. As a result, he went on, 'nearly every Scots writer of the past writing in orthodox English has been not only incurably second-rate, but incurably behind the times'.[774]

What Mitchell had identified was a technical problem—how to marry English and Scots so that the work retained a sense of its cultural discreteness. Writing about himself in the third person he then described Grassic Gibbon's technique, which was 'to mould the English language into the rhythms and cadences of Scots spoken speech, and to inject into the English vocabulary such minimum number of words from Braid Scots as that remodelling requires'.[775]

Predicting that it might take another fifty years before a 'Scots Virginia Woolf will astound the Scottish Scene,[or] a Scots James Joyce electrify it' he then damned most contemporary writers:

> with a few exceptions...there is not the remotest reason why the majority of modern Scots writers should be considered Scots at all....The chief Literary Lights which modern Scotland claims to light up the scene of her night are in reality no more than the commendable writers of the interesting English county of Scotshire.[776]

Mitchell goes on to discuss Naomi Mitchison, Gunn, George Blake, Willa Muir, Catherine Carswell, Linklater and John Buchan amongst others before coming to the 'two solitary lights in modern Scots Literature': Hugh MacDiarmid and Lewis Spence. Nowhere in his essay is Nan Shepherd mentioned.

Five years earlier, her own first novel had been praised as one of the best works of Scottish Literature and by the time *Sunset Song* appeared in 1932 Nan Shepherd had published two novels. Both of these works explore the lives of young women in rural communities in the North East, the impact of the First World War on these communities and the choices faced by her female protagonists: both of whom are torn between their longing for education; for wider horizons and their ties to the land from which they come. Martha's journey to intellectual and emotional maturity in *The Quarry Wood* is similar to Chris Guthrie's in *Sunset Song* and her tale is perhaps what Chris Guthrie's might have been if she *had* chosen to go to university.

Shepherd's narrative structure is less showy, less obviously experimental than Grassic Gibbon's but her technique is quietly pioneering. It is a narrative in English, but it is an English which is quite Scottish in its style and makes no apology for using a Doric word when it presents itself. As old Mrs Craigmyle says to Ellen Falconer in *The Weatherhouse*, 'The young man has a good Scots name that won't fit into the metre. You're right. I shouldn't spoil an old name as though I had an English tongue on me—feared to speak two syllables when one will do'.[777] The art of Nan Shepherd's dialogue is that she makes the rhythm, not the words, do the work. She uses only sufficient words to carry the intellectual significance she wants and poses them carefully, so that the sentence or phrase reads as a patter of rhythm in which the reader hears the inflection of the voices. But she manages to begin and end the sentences so that they reflect the nuances of spoken speech and still keep the pace.

Leslie Mitchell and Nan Shepherd never met[778], but he would surely have heard of her and of her novels. At the time, she was as prominent in Scottish literary life as any of the other writers Mitchell discusses. It is odd that Mitchell ignored her work. But he ignored Lorna Moon's *Dark Star which* also anticipates Gibbon's experimental, stream of consciousness style narrative. Moon's work, like Shepherd's, is written in English but has a distinct, North Eastern, idiomatic inflection.

Meanwhile in September 1932 Nan was still trying to finish *A Pass in the Grampians*, which was once again held up while she went on a 'literary tour' of Scotland with Hugh MacDiarmid. She was still writing poetry: 'Images of beauty', 'Ptolemaic System of Love' and 'A Dead Love' were written between October 1932 and February 1933, all of which made it into *In the Cairngorms*. Eventually, she also managed to complete her third and final novel and in the spring of 1933, the same year that *Cloud Howe* (Grassic Gibbon's sequel to *Sunset Song)* was published, Shepherd's *A Pass in the Grampians* appeared in print.

It was largely, well-received. A review in *The New York Times* in September 1933 began:

> Among interpreters of contemporary Scottish life—and recent years have given us several Caledonian novelists of growing distinction—few have attained as complete and individual an art as Nan Shepherd. She excels, as readers of *The Weatherhouse* will remember, in bringing vividly to life rugged and remote and ingrown corners of the earth. Her people, hard-featured and hard-headed Scottish peasants, with their granite frames and life-bitten faces, rude tongues and sparing gestures, seem carved from their own rocky soil. Yet they have warmth and passion at the core, pride and hospitality and a dry, sharp humour.

Like Nan's two previous novels, *A Pass in the Grampians* is set in the 'Nor-east' but this time it is on the Kincardineshire side of the River Dee, in the shadow of Clachnaben. 'Boggiewalls', the grey stone farmhouse home to generations of her fictional Kilgours, she places on the cold side of Cairn O' Mount, near the old military road from Fettercairn in the Mearns[779] to Banchory on Deeside. Now a tarmacked highway, winding through the moorland, heather 'like a dark tide licking its edges,' this Grampian Pass of the book's title was once passage for the reiver[780] and drover and the way Macbeth might have come to cross the River Dee at Potarch, before he was killed at Lumphanan. [781]

Representing a portal to the world lying beyond, the Pass, too, symbolises the passage from girlhood to maturity. As a verb, it not only describes a physical transformation from one state to another but can mean to change, as well as to die. And as the use of the polysemic 'pass' suggests, the novel is all about change, transition and transformation. The text is all movement—backwards and forwards, crossing that symbolic Pass. Even Bella's mother's death is part of this movement— falling from a rick she was thatching in Andrew's stack-yard.

The setting, Nan knew well. The Smith side of her mother's family came from the area and there is much about Boggiewalls, home for generations to the Kilgours, that suggests Dalfouper, just south of the Kincardineshire border where her great grandmother Jean Smith grew up. But for the first time, Nan uses contrast to heighten her portrait of Scottish family life.

On to the grey canvas of Boggiewalls, she splashes the vibrant, brassy Bella. The daughter of one of his servants, after her mother's tragic death, Andrew Kilgour brings up Bella as one of his own. Bella hates the rural life and leaves as soon as she can for London finding fame as a singer, only to return some years later, transformed as 'Dorabel Cassidy'. She then proceeds to shatter the peace, flouting her material success and the pink bungalow all turrets and tiles she is determined to build in the countryside. But it is an ambivalent text: the old order is portrayed alongside the new and neither is given primacy.

In her third novel, Nan returns to the *Bildungsroman* format. Young Jenny Kilgour, grand-daughter of Andrew, is torn between the dour solidity of life on her grandfather's farm and the vulgar, showiness—which to her is exciting and new—of Bella with whom she is infatuated. Jenny is desperate to get beyond the Pass.

While she would resent the label, *A Pass in the Grampians* is the most modernist of Nan's fiction. Like *The Weatherhouse* no one character is given precedence, all are part of the community and all are interrelated—even if they don't realise it. Old and new are contrasted immediately—Durno, driving sheep, encounters Bella in her 'bit car' on the Pass.[782] Andrew Kilgour is against the motor car. Other farmers drive motor cars—'he has even seen a man sit in his car and herd home the cattle he had bought at the Mart',[783] but he insists on mending his cartwheels. Then there is Mary, the epitome of change embodied by the New Woman. Mary has escaped to London, where she is not just a secretary but runs a small typing house. Yet back at Boggiewalls for a holiday, she, too resists change, wanting the place to remain the same for her visits.

At the same time, Nan satirises high modernism, with its experimental art and writing. Mary is confused by a manuscript that had come into her typing house. She 'couldn't make head nor tail of what it meant. The words were all in the wrong places. But the author thanked me for the beautiful typing, so I suppose he meant them like that'.[784] Jenny says of a painting that it is 'the kind of picture that you don't know what it is, all right in Paris and places like that, but rather odd when you know it's the Grassic Burn and the Craig Clach'.[785]

It is the woman who is the harbinger of change, Bella herself, bringing with her the mustard car with its scarlet spokes, her gramophone player and her wireless. But 'the Jezebel'[786] is not staying and the horrid, pink-tiled bungalow will be let to people Bella hopes will make a din, shattering the rural idyll.

In his introduction to Canongate's 1996 edition of *A Pass in the Grampians,* Roderick Watson believes Bella, 'the fat orphan girl who came home to swank', as he describes her, to be one of Nan Shepherd's

'most memorable creations'. She is; as unforgettable as some of her
other creations, like the hairy Bawbie Paterson in *The Weatherhouse*
and the slovenly Emmeline in *The Quarry Wood*. But as Watson recognises, the unapologetically vulgar Bella was a character study ahead of
her time. By the end of the twentieth century there were more of her
ilk appearing in Scottish literature.[787]

In the early 1930s however, not all reviewers thought the character
of Bella Cassidy was successful. But Neil Gunn did. In March 1933 he
wrote to congratulate Nan on 'the Northern Pass through which we
imagine we have to go to make our foray on life':

> all the criticism I've seen dealing with your singer-artist is
> wrong (on the lines that you've succeeded with your natives
> but not with her) because you have realised her not only
> completely but symbolically. In this sense the conception of
> the whole thing is clear & integrated and she is not foreign
> but native & very native.

Neil Gunn, of course, saw immediately what Nan was trying to do as
well the ambivalence in her text. He goes on:

> Indeed you balance her [Bella Cassidy's] reality by giving
> the old man not only austerity but kindliness. Otherwise
> they would have greyed a trifle even before her vulgarity.
> And modern Scotland has the young painter lad. You see
> the problem of the moment: if you have not tightened with
> decision over it.

Neil predicted, once again, that for the undiscerning reader, Nan's
book would seem slight, 'of insufficient wecht'. The average reader
wants 'meat and not vision or poetry' and is not capable of making the
intuitive, imaginative effort required to glean meaning from her text.[788]

Jenny Kilgour's vision of a 'new mode of being' is positioned at the
end of the novel and represented as the wild excitement of Bella and
life in London on the other side of the Pass. But in Jenny's musings,
as well as reflecting the interrelation of man and nature we are now
coming to expect in Nan's writing, there is also a sense of frustration at
the fugitive nature of the very mode of being that has yet to be experienced:[789]

> Her life is rooted deep in earth, its ample rhythms are in the
> movement of her thought…She loves the slow deep satisfac-

tions of the earth, but she has glimpsed now the wild stormy things that stir and pass, once it may be in a lifetime, not subject to the march of the seasons nor the regular recurrences of earth. How shall she gather these, how recognize them when they come, how learn to live not for the anticipated certainty...but for the incredible fugitive approaches of an order whose laws she may not fathom?[790]

Neil's highest praise was for the writing itself: 'This sureness, this spare poise, the naked talk, the drawing to a conclusion'. But he goes on to pinpoint the issue and what makes such a huge difference to Nan's writing in *The Living Mountain*: 'You are surer here than ever before, you are indeed so sure (out of long thought processes) that your detachment at moments may have the air of intricate analysis and even almost of coldness as of an exercise.[791] Nan's detachment was because she had yet to actually experience, what at this stage was still only intellectualised.

Neil clearly thought she had reached a pinnacle of achievement in her writing and had honed her fiction-writing skill, but *A Pass in the Grampians* would be Nan's third and last novel. In March 1933 Neil was awaiting the proofs of an historical novel he had written, *Sun Circle,* which was also published that year. 'No more will it make me a fortune than yours', he suspected, 'and perhaps I don't like history, as my book may show!'[792] But he was optimistic—and it was spring.

That spring of 1933, Nan was in the hills again. This time she was Braemar side and spent the night of 10th April at Thistle Cottage, Maggie Gruer's home in Inverey. Maggie, who was famous for her hospitality to Cairngorm climbers, boasted that she never turned a hiker away from her door.[793] 'Day or night, it was all one to Maggie', Nan was to say of her in *The Living Mountain*. 'No climber was turned away who would sleep on a landing, in a shed, anywhere a human body could be laid. Nor did she scruple to turn a man out of that first deep slumber of the night, the joyous release of an exhausted body, to give his bed to a lady benighted and trudging in at one in the morning'.[794] Many who walked the twenty-one miles from Aviemore through the Lairig Ghru to Inverey spent a night at Thistle Cottage. She charged a shilling a night, or sixpence if you were hard up'. [795]

Two rooms on either side of the front door made up the ground floor. There were a two further rooms upstairs, dormer windows in the sloping roof looking across the road to the woods and a skylight in between. If all the beds were full, including a 'shakedown at the "heid o' the stair" '[796] there was always a bed of straw to be had in the barn at the back. Although Maggie would give up her own bed if needed and sleep in her kitchen chair by the fire, she usually slept in the kitchen in the box-bed in the wall, complete with doors, into which she would climb fully clothed even if male guests were still at her hearthside, drinking a dram and talking a yarn. In the morning she would shout to warn anyone sleeping on the kitchen floor overnight to clear out as she got up to see to the cow in the byre.

On the 10th April, Nan and her friends, Florence Godwin and Nancy Adie, were the only guests.[797] 'When your garments get wetter and fewer, you need only apply to Miss Gruer' reads one of the entries in the *Thistle Cottage Visitors' Book*.[798] If the three had trudged the Lairig Ghru the day before, it would only have been to see the suppressed sparkle in the Pools of Dee. Nan found the narrow defile of the Lairig, the sheer, narrow gash dividing Cairntoul and Braeriach from the Cairn Gorm/Ben MacDhui side, oppressive.[799] Whatever state the hikers were in when they arrived at her door, Maggie would have shown no surprise and just ushered them in to her kitchen, pungent with the smell of hen's meat she was always boiling in a pot on the range. Settling them at her fireside Maggie would then see to the drying of their clothes before pouring a cup of her strong, black brew from her endlessly simmering teapot.

Then, without fail, would come her question 'Weel, ye'll hae an egg?'[800] If not, she would offer a home-made bannock or scone—extra large and hefty as the porridge she kept in a drawer of the kitchen table from where she would slice slabs at breakfast—making one visitors' claim to have set a record by eating six and a half of these 'thick floury delicacies' all the more extraordinary. Once they were fed, Maggie would seat herself at the fireside in her chair[801] and regale her guests with endless tales—usually the one about her letter which was read to the King, or the one about being taken to the door to curtsey to Queen Victoria as she passed.[802] As a baby, Maggie claimed that a draughty wooden cradle with a too-small hood was 'the wey my nose is aye reid'.[803] Whether that was really the case, her nose was claret-coloured and longish and with her iron-grey hair and fierce blue eyes, she had a formidable look about her. Nan described her as witty, acrid when necessary, but living with the glow and gusto that made porridge at Maggie's more than merely food.[804]

Its back to the River Dee, Maggie's home still stands on the road through Inverey. The house looks little different today, so much the same in fact you almost expect to see a Maggie herself standing there, as she is in the photograph of Nan and her two friends taken during their stay. They are all laughing, turned towards Maggie, headscarf tied firmly under her chin, who looks impishly at the camera as if she has just employed the wit for which she was famous.

Well-wrapped against the cold, Nan is elegant, in fur-collared coat and a folded and moulded felt hat that looks like something out of a Picasso painting. The women may have been heading that April morning for the Linn of Dee, half an hour's walk from Maggie Gruer's Thistle Cottage.[805] It is one of Scotland's chilliest places. A favourite haunt of Queen Victoria's, it is a popular beauty spot where the River Dee twists its way through a narrow gorge, carved in the rock by its waters for millennia before tumbling over a precipice into rocky pools below.

The Linn of Dee is hardly a stream, it is more a fierce torrent, but there is something in Nan's poem, 'Singing Burn', to suggest that the sight and sound of it might have been a trigger. There is also the timing: Nan completed the poem on 1st May 1933, three weeks after her stay at Maggie Gruer's. The last but one in her manuscript notebook, it appears first in *In The Cairngorms* and is one of her most lyrical and rhythmically haunting verses. Its first two lines echo in the ear long after first reading:

> 'O burnie with the glass-white shiver,
> Singing over stone,
> So quick, so clear, a hundred year
> Singing one song alone,
> From crystal sources fed forever,
> From cold mountain springs,
> To o'erpersuade the haunted ear
> It new-creates the tune it sings.[806]

The sound of water speaking is something Nan will also bring up in *The Living Mountain*. Standing in the silence on the plateau, she becomes aware that the silence is not complete. 'Water is speaking', she realises, and she goes immediately towards it. For Nan 'all the mysteries' were in the movement of water:

> It slips out of holes in the earth like the ancient snake. I have seen its birth; and the more I gaze at that sure and unremitting surge of water at the very top of the mountain, the more I am baffled. We make it all so easy, any child in school can understand it—water rises in the hills, it flows and finds its own level, and man can't live without it. But I don't understand it. I cannot fathom its power.[807]

Much of the power of the 'Singing Burn' lies in its assault on the senses.

In its hissing sibilance is water's sinister mystery and its rushing, stone-sung sound. A vision which is felt, too, in its clean as crystal water as a 'glass-white shiver'. Without doubt Nan pushed her fingers into the icy water, pitting her own strength against it, shuddering at its cold. The last two lines also return us to the idea of water which Nan explored in 'caul' caul' as the wall': in a mystery of creative energy, it now re-invents, 'new-creates' its tune for our ears. For 'a hundred year' it has sung one song alone. What is suggested by the verse is a need to break with tradition and a call for new forms of writing. As such, the poem springs very much from its context—the Scottish literary revival.

To live all the way through, by living in more than one sense, is to allow body, not mind, to think: 'If I had other senses, there are other things I should know…There must be many exciting properties of matter that we cannot know because we have no way to know them', Nan says in the final chapter of *The Living Mountain*.[808] Already in 'Singing Burn' this sensory, bodily thinking is there. It is Nan Shepherd at her best, this poem. It is right that it comes first in her anthology.

Back in Aberdeen after her hill sojourn, with three novels now in print and her collection of poetry due out the following year, Nan had much to be singing about herself. But just as the Training Centre's summer term was drawing to a close, on 24 June 1933 a review of *A Pass in the Grampians* appeared in *The Free Man*. Headed: 'Scots Novels of the Half-Year', it was written by Leslie Mitchell under his pseudonym, Lewis Grassic Gibbon. 'I suppose other Scots novels have been issued since January, but I haven't read them, and the plan of this book-page is to devote it to books the reviewer has actually read', it began.

Four novels were given Mitchell's critical consideration: James Barke's *The World His Pillow*, Neil Gunn's *Sun Circle,* Christine Orr's *Immortal Memory*, and Nan Shepherd's *A Pass in the Grampians*. Of the four, Mitchell declared, 'one might have been very good, one is good, and two are the dreich yammer of a culture's second childhood'. Barke's work was the one that might have been very good and showed promise. Gunn's was good (although Mitchell found it hard to believe in the antique Scotland he depicted). It was both the women's novels he designated 'dreich yammer'.

Orr's novel about the Edinburgh of the Literary Revival Mitchell deemed 'oh-so-nice and gently satirical, and generally quite damnably dead'. His most damning criticism, however, was reserved for Nan Shepherd's work:

Miss Nan Shepherd writes about farm life in Kincardineshire, a farmer's pretty granddaughter, a prima donna who disturbs the peace, and God alone knows who. I extend my sympathy to the Almighty. This is a Scots religion and Scots people at three removes—gutted, castrated, and genteely vulgarised. [809]

Whether or not Mitchell had read Shepherd's first work, *The Quarry Wood* (which in many ways can be seen as a forerunner to his own first novel *Sunset Song*, not least because it anticipates the 'two Chrisses predicament') is an interesting question. We know he owned a copy of her second, *The Weatherhouse,* but so far can find no trace of *A Pass in the Grampians* in his personal library.[810] In his review Mitchell claims to have read all four of the novels he is reviewing. In the opinion of his biographer, Bill Malcolm, however, the piece is so cursory that he would question how carefully Mitchell had read Nan's third novel, 'if in fact he had read it at all. He had a habit of brusquely dismissing books and trashing writers that he felt weren't worthy of his time'.[811]

Leslie Mitchell (aka Lewis Grassic Gibbon) and his wife Ray.

The last time Helen Cruickshank saw Mitchell, in Edinburgh in late 1934, he was irritable and listless, 'quite without his usual sparkle and verve and he was much thinner'.[812] In the three years leading up to his death in 1935, the 'rattlesnake rhumba' in Mitchell's gut intensified and you can almost feel the dyspepsia permeating the entire piece. It seems rushed, damning and unnecessarily harsh—and not just about Nan Shepherd's writing. There is also an element of competitiveness in it, suggesting Nan had unwittingly trodden on his toes.

Perhaps Mitchell felt that in writing about the Mearns (as Kincardineshire is also known) Nan was encroaching on his own territory. Both *Sunset Song* and *Cloude Howe* are set in Kincardineshire. But not only is *A Pass in the Grampians* setting in a different part of the county,[813] Nan was hardly at 'three removes'.[814] She knew her novel's setting very well—members of her family came from the area. She also still lived in Aberdeenshire. Mitchell, on the other hand, was living in Welwyn Garden City writing about a distant Scotland.[815] Perhaps it was simply her satire of the experimental, stream of consciousness style narrative that struck a nerve—but that, of course, would suppose he had actually read the novel.

Whatever lay behind Mitchell's cursory and damning review, we do not know if Nan actually saw it. It is not among the cuttings her mother kept. But if Nan did read the piece, it would have been hard for her not to have been affected by it. In 1930 she may have confessed to feeling 'positively nasty'[816] towards those critics who she felt over-praised her work, but Mitchell's criticism had gone quite to the other extreme. It must have stung.

In the summer of 1933, shortly after the review appeared, Nan was interviewed for *The Scotsman* by Robert Dunnett.[817] A tea-table was set under an awning in the back garden at Dunvegan and all afternoon they sat, eating Mary's home-made cakes and sipping tea, until the sun left the lupins. They were talking about the Scottish 'Renaissance', modern literature and the problems of technique—all of which were subjects in which Nan Shepherd was extremely interested. It was during this conversation that Nan declared she thought dialect and a typically Scottish arrangement of words were likely to be the two most important features of any national literature Scotland might produce: 'English may be the medium of our national literature, but it will be English as a Scotsman uses it'.

Having said she disapproved of novels which were 'photography', simply reflections of life, Nan then brought up 'a modern Scottish novel which had aroused considerable interest'. 'I liked it', Nan said, 'because I knew the people and the countryside with which it dealt. Very often one had the sense that what one was reading was quite real. And there is a grand sardonic humour about it', she went on, 'the sort of humour which seems quite exclusively Scottish. All the same, I don't think it quite succeeded. The incidents may have been perfectly real, but that is not enough. We want to know not only what happens but what significance it has'.[818]

No names are mentioned. But given the discussion that had been going on before about technique, dialect and an arrangement of words reflecting the rhythms and cadences of Scots speech, it is not too much of a stretch to assume Nan was talking about Lewis Grassic Gibbon's work. Given the timing, she could have been referring to either *Sunset Song* or *Cloud Howe,* both of which had been published by July 1933 and both of which 'had aroused considerable interest.' Many of the critics, in fact, thought the sequel to *Sunset Song* was even better than its predecessor although there were some, particularly in Scotland, whose reviews were not so glowing.[819]

Nan, of course, also knew well the people and the Mearns country-side with which both the novels dealt. But if it *was* Mitchell's work Nan was criticising, she used language far more considered and courteous than his. What she went on to say, however, clarifies not only what she thought this unnamed novel failed to address but also what she strove to reflect in her own writing:

We do not live alone. Society does not exist only for itself. Behind all existence are certain basic laws whose operation is unaffected by human ways. We may be in harmony with these laws, we may rebel against them, or we may simply not under-stand them. In no case can we be indifferent. The artist may think to ignore them, but in so doing he will depict characters existing in circumstances which have no ultimate reality.

By the afternoon's close, young Robert Dunnett, who had recently graduated in English Literature from Edinburgh University, was clearly quite awestruck by 'Miss Shepherd'. It was to writers like her, who were so interested in technique, that Scotland should be looking for the 'Renascent' spirit, he reported. He was clearly looking forward to her next novel. However, interview over, standing at the garden gate, Nan made a confession which startled him: 'I don't like writing really. In fact, I very rarely write. No. I never do short stories and articles and I'm not going to give up teaching. I only write when I feel there's something that simply must be written'. [820]

As we know, Nan was a perfectionist who was unconvinced of her own writing talent. She might well have felt disheartened to the point of giving up by Mitchell's slating of her novel. After all, he was not just any critic, he was a peer who was as much engaged in the Scottish Literary Revival as she. As a fellow author, too, he, more than anyone, would have understood a writer's nagging self-doubt and easily-dented confidence.

His review of *A Pass in the Grampians* appeared in *The Free Man* shortly after it was published and just weeks before *Cloud Howe* appeared in print. And indeed, there is something in the tone of that article and his earlier 'Literary Lights' essay, in which he ignored Nan Shepherd's work completely, to suggest Mitchell's own insecurity. He may well have been keen to avoid inviting comparison between his Scottish novels and hers. He was, after all, writing about a female protagonist in the same part of the country, living in a small community that thrives on gossip and in a Scotland that believes more in the land than in God. 'Only the sky and the seasons endured, slow in their change',[821] Chris reflects early on in *Cloud Howe* and in a *A Pass in the Grampians,* Andrew Kilgour's 'covenant' is with the moor. Shepherd, of course, goes further. Underlying her narrative is an exploration of the metaphysics of landscape—those laws behind existence she was talking about to Robert Dunnett. Moreover, while Mitchell's narrative technique may have been experimentally more ostentatious, it could be seen as a development of what Nan was already quietly pioneering in her own fiction.

Nan's parting comment to Dunnett might well have been a reaction to Mitchell's scathing attack on her third novel, just as it might have been the reason she never produced another one—effectively removing herself from his arena. But it did not stop her writing. In the years that followed she went on to publish exactly what she said she never did—a short story as well as a host of articles. And aside from all her poetry (which does not appear to have been mentioned at all to Dunnett) there was, of course, *The Living Mountain*. Nevertheless, she said little, ever, about her three novels.

★ ★ ★

1934 was a year rich in prose works from Scottish writers, including Neil Gunn's *Butcher's Broom,* but there was little published in the way of poetry. The Moray Press redressed the balance, publishing several books of verse that year, including Nan's, which appeared in the autumn. 'Nancy my dear, they're most lovely—for your first work', congratulated Mure Mackenzie. 'The old ones that I knew already are good enough, heaven knows, but the new ones that I didn't are even better'. Pronouncing them far above her novels, Mure was delighted finally to see them in print, adding, 'I hope they will have the recognition they deserve'.[822]

The autumn term at the Training Centre was a busy one and left Nan little time for her own reading. Wanting to savour it, she had been saving Neil Gunn's *Butcher's Broom* for when she had time enough to give it her full attention rather than read it in snatched half hours. She wrote to tell him how much she had enjoyed it and, although Neil's latest offering had earned him high praise, Nan was un-blinkered: 'I don't think the critics say what to me is the purest fascination of your writing'.

This, for her, was his ability to immerse the reader 'at one and the same time in different planes of being' and was what she aspired to in her own writing. She elaborated:

> I don't think my brain takes in the <u>words</u> but their meaning is moving in my blood before I have properly distinguished them. They're like a pulse of life inside me. Something deeper than conscious intellect recognises their nature. I think you will understand what I mean. But that words should be able to convey this wordless thing—this is what amazes me. Yet they do. Something moving in the blood, yet fashioned into words. O my God! Words aren't meant for that. How by all that is unholy do you do it?[823]

Neil wrote back almost immediately, thrilled by Nan's percipience, delighted that she had seen what the critics had not:

> For if even one other sees them, then they are there, though all the rest of the world be blind…It's odd to have written something that you like and in the same instant to know that you should cut it out 1) if you wish the critics for once to refrain from the word obscure 2) if you want to sell. Whereas the something is not obscure to you at all, but on the contrary, the only clear thing in a waste of pages!

'It's different in poetry', he went on, 'It's no doubt the fashion to expect it there. So you get off with it', he declared before reciprocating with praise for her just-published anthology:

> You have real light: sometimes all light…sunlight, icelight, clear water [ ] *In the Cairngorms* was an ambitious title. You move in it like air and light and running water. What pleasure it gives me to say without politest shadow of reservation what fine poetry this is. It's distilled.[824]

Other reviews were good too and saw the light. 'One might almost say that Miss Shepherd's chief purpose has been to change light into words' said a critic in *The Glasgow Herald* going on to quote extensively from the work.[825] The *Aberdeen Journal* pronounced *In the Cairngorms* 'refreshingly different; at once both individual and universal. The clear light and air of the hills is in these poems; and some have a chiselled beauty as if the poet had taken a boulder and carved it to her mind's will.[826] 'Miss

Shepherd is a mystic, revelatory', went another review in the *Press & Journal*, 'she can discourse upon light as the primal substance rather in the manner of metaphysician than mystic. But generally she expresses it direct, flashing upon startled eyes which see "the unseen at last" '.[827] As Ali Smith said more recently, *In the Cairngorms* 'hymns the combination of nature and intellect'[828] something, too, which was picked up at the time:

> The lyrical strain is, to the reader in the south something new. It has nothing at all in common with the mochy sentimentality of the Kailyard school. In its strength, in its restrained intensity, there is more than a hint of the volcanic fires that were the precursors of the granite of the North East. If the ordered, systemised accuracy of the North East can be effectively combined with the passion of the old fires, we may yet see evolving a type of literature that will stand by itself in its strength and vigour...we have had them in the lyrics of Nan Shepherd.

The *Glasgow Herald* reviewer also noted how Nan's poetry revealed the

changing attitude in Scottish poetry towards 'one of our conventional stage properties, the mountains—once merely the picturesque setting for glorifications of the heather'. *In the Cairngorms* was markedly different, 'one of the signposts on the new road' where mountain, loch and tree are seen not as beauty spots, or parts of a pretty picture, nor as homes of a vanishing clans, but sharply visualised, 'as living spiritual elements, or, at least, inseparably one with the searching spirit of the poet'.[829] It seems Nan had created something new for the 'o'erpersuaded ear' of 'Singing Burn'.[830]

Title page of *In the Cairngorms* first edition.

Still relevant eighty years after it was first published, *In the Cairngorms* was reprinted by Galileo in 2014. '*In the Cairngorms* must rank high as one of the most significant collections of modern Scottish poetry and its author, Nan Shepherd, should really be celebrated as one of [Scotland's] most important poets', wrote Stuart Campbell reviewing the volume of verse for *Northwords Now* in 2014. It took Nan 25 years to complete the poems, he says, which is not strictly accurate. Although Nan was writing poetry prior to university, the poems contained in *In the Cairngorms* were written in a sixteen year period from 1918 to 1934. But he is right, reading her poetry collection gives insight into her non-fiction work. [831]

There is a pattern emerging here, because close reading of Nan Shepherd's fiction, too, gives some insight into her poetry. 'Uncompromising as granite, many of the poems can be as challenging to access as the plateau which inspired them'. 'No poem gives its whole value to the reader without active co-operation of brain and imagination. Each has its own secret, and there is gain for both inward and outward eye when that is found',[832] continued the *Glasgow Herald* reviewer. As a result, once entry is gained, the rewards are even greater.

There was criticism too. 'She can lapse at times into limp lines',[833] said the *Press & Journal* and in 1944, ten years after the volume was published, 'A.M.S.' wrote in *the North East Review* wrote:

> I like Miss Shepherd's verse least when it deals with philosophy and mysticism, when she employs the effect on sunlight on the bare peaks of the Cairngorms to try and prove (not, I think successfully) the existence of another finer world, a world whose essence is pure light, behind and beyond our own. Having no personal knowledge of mystical experiences, I find their description quite unconvincing.[834]

Perhaps the combination of philosophy and mysticism in *The Living Mountain* might not have convinced 'A.M.S.', but in 1944, the project was only in its infancy and more than thirty years would pass before it was actually published.

It was in Loch Avon in July 1934 that for the first time Nan caught a glimpse into Neil Gunn's 'other realm' and provoked her poem 'Loch Avon' which only just made it into *In the Cairngorms*. An eighteen year old Nan had copied into her *Medley Book* Wordsworth's line, 'the breath and finer spirit of all knowledge', along with other nuggets on poetry including Coleridge's 'The best words in the best order' (under which she has written—'equally applicable to prose').[835] It was a distillation of both that was her focus from 1934 onwards, to translate felt experience into words so that it moved in the blood for the reader, just as Neil Gunn's writing did for her. It would take several years.

★ ★ ★

The afternoon of Saturday 23rd February 1935 was bright and cold. An early Spring sun shone on the snow-strewn Grampian hilltops, reddening the fields around Arbuthnott Kirk where it perches on its brae above Bervie Water. Along with many others, Nan was standing in the snowdrop-swathed Kirkyard as Leslie Mitchell's ashes were interred. Just over two weeks earlier, on 7th February, Mitchell had died of peritonitis after an unsuccessful operation on a perforated ulcer. He was thirty-three.

Helen Cruickshank suspected Mitchell was unwell the last time she saw him in Edinburgh, the year before he died. His final letter to her, written in February 1935, revealed her suspicions were correct. He was prostrate, having been in bed with acute gastritis for a fortnight 'on a diet, forbidden cigarettes & loathing humanity'.

'Don't agree about *Grey Granite* it's much the best of the three, as reviewers like Edwin Muir, Howard Spring and Ivor Brown all confirm. Where has your critical faculty gone', he demanded of Helen, 'been reading Aggie whore Mackenzie or summat? Shush!' It was an offensive and unnecessary comment which Helen, presumably, did not share with either Mure or Nan, but it does show Mitchell's disparaging remarks were not reserved for Shepherd's writing alone.

Mitchell ended his letter saying he wished he could come up to see Helen again in Edinburgh that Spring but he was too busy. Or he would be, he said, 'if I ever succeed in escaping my bed & getting on a normal diet again'.[836] But he did not recover and after a simple cremation in Golders Green, Mitchell's ashes were carried up to Scotland.

The kirk, standing on its brae above the winding river Bervie, with its three stained glass windows representing Faith, Hope and Charity satirised in *Sunset Song* 'as the three bit creatures of queans', is just down the road from the school where Dominie, Alexander Gray first spotted Mitchell's talent and encouraged him to write. It was a simple ceremony. Farming folk from all over the Mearns came to pay their respects at the internment.[837] There, too, were Mitchell's parents, his father 'with a face like Saint Andrew of Scotland' and his mother, her lined face working furiously to control her tears.[838] Nan was moved by the spectacle of Mitchell's widow, Ray, 'carrying the casket against her body as though it had been a baby'.[839]

At the graveside, Ray Mitchell spoke a few quiet words: 'A great man is dead. The body is dead but the spirit will remain and will be an inspiration to the people of Scotland now and for many centuries to come'. On his headstone, a simple block of grey granite, his epitaph is taken from the closing passage of *Sunset Song*:

> The kindness of friends
> The warmth of toil
>   The peace of rest.

The night before the service, Helen Cruickshank stayed in a hotel in Inverbervie a few miles east of Arbuthnott on the north-east coast. Clouds of smoke rose from the hillsides where the whin burned, flaming like funeral pyres as the sun set that evening and prompted Helen's poem written in memoriam to Mitchell. Entitled 'Spring in the Mearns', it was published the following year on the anniversary of his death. The last verse reads:

> He who set the flame
> of his native genius
> under the cumbering whin
> of the untilled field
> lit a fire in the Mearns
> that illumines Scotland,
> clearing her sullen soil
> or a richer yield.[840]

Yet Mitchell was not working with untilled soil. The ground had been prepared for *Sunset Song* by other writers of the Scots 'Renaissance', Nan Shepherd and Lorna Moon among them. Whatever Nan thought of Mitchell's slight over her own work, she was clearly not one to bear a grudge and contributed to the Lewis Grassic Gibbon fund established to help Ray Mitchell and her two children after his death. Helen Cruickshank maintained a correspondence with Ray Mitchell for many years afterwards and in a letter written in 1954, Ray asks Helen to convey her love and good wishes to Nan.

In 1960, the Deeside Field Club was planning an expedition for its members to Arbuthnott Church on Saturday 6th August and had asked Nan to give a talk on Grassic Gibbon. She remembered that an unnamed publisher had commissioned another book from Mitchell and that a few days after his death the publisher: 'in the way of all good business, wrote and asked for the return of the advance. Is that correct?' she asked Helen Cruickshank. 'It's the sort of detail that would make members of the Deeside Field, many of whom are very far from literary, realise how stiff was a young man's fight to establish himself and his family through writing.'[841]

Chapter Eleven

1936-1943

1936 was a tumultuous year. It began in constitutional crisis with the death of George V on 20th January and ended with the abdication of his successor Edward VIII in December after his refusal to give up the twice divorced American socialite, Wallis Simpson. Edward lost Scotland's support in September. Instead of opening the new wing of Aberdeen Royal Infirmary, he left the duty to his brother the Duke of York (later King George VI) and wearing goggles which he thought would provide an adequate disguise, he drove his Rolls Royce to Aberdeen railway station to collect Mrs Simpson and whisk her to Balmoral. As Simpson was still married, their love affair was supposed to be a secret. Blinds were fitted to the Rolls as a way of safeguarding her identity. It did not work. 'Down with the American harlot'—Aberdeen's outrage was displayed publicly, daubed on a wall.

'Go now or stay. I have the whole of you' says the speaker in the last line of 'Pardon' completed on 20th April 1931.[842] And five years later, it did seem as though the John Macmurray affair was now firmly behind Nan. All her spare time was absorbed by 'her mountain' and she was distracted, too, by what was going on in Scottish letters. In 'Colours of Deeside', published in 1938, she wrote:

> When I hear strangers call our country grey, I do not, necessarily contradict; for if grey is the universal solvent, melting all colours into itself, looking will resolve them back. Our grey land, our grey skies, hold poised within them a thousand shades of colour.[843]

In 1936, contemporary arts in Scotland seemed grey and lacking in vitality. Concerned that Scotland's cultural gas was ebbing and needed a new outlook a group of people, including Alison Macintyre, Helen Cruickshank and Eric Linklater, decided to do something about it. The Saltire Society was the result.

Like the PEN, the Saltire Society was political and without racial or religious affiliations. Operating in many fields including architecture, publishing, music and the arts generally, its objective was 'to preserve the best in Scottish traditions, encourage new trends and foster the cultural life of Scotland today'.[844] The Society's headquarters was set up in the 17th century town house known as Gladstone's Land. Built by Thomas Gladstone in 1620, with its arcaded front and twin gables it stands, still, in Lawnmarket, Edinburgh. Branches followed all over Scotland, including Aberdeen where, along with Eric Linklater, Nan was an active member and contributor to the booklets printed by the Society.[845]

While the Saltire was busy trying to remedy the dull, grey perception of Scotland's culture, the language debate reached a peak with the publication, in 1936, of Edwin Muir's *Scott and Scotland*.[846] The problem of literature in Scotland, Muir believed, could not be solved by writing a poem in Scots, 'or by looking forward to some hypothetical Scotland in the future'. After the Reformation, English became the Sunday language for serious thought and reflection while Scots was the language of everyday domestic sentiment, not a whole language but only part of one.[847] Scotland continued to produce writers, he went on, but they wrote in a confusion of tongues ranging from orthodox English to the dialects of the various Scottish districts. The only speech they did not continue to use was Scots, as that had disappeared. As a result, from the sixteenth century onwards, Scottish literature was a literature without a language. Scots now lived in a condition of linguistic ambiguity. They 'feel in one language and think in another', Muir said, in his most oft-quoted line from the book.[848]

Basically, in a denial of all that MacDiarmid had achieved through his linguistic experimentation during the 1920s, Muir suggested that the only way forward for Scotland's writers was the use of the English language and English literary traditions. It caused a rift between the two poets that was never resolved.

Having helped found the National Party of Scotland and attacked and pretty much demolished the Scottish literary establishment, by the early 1930s, while still a working journalist, MacDiarmid had come to grief. Penniless, estranged from his first wife and children, he met his second wife Valda, and in 1933 headed for Whalsay in the northeast of the Shetland archipelago. There, however, having overworked and overcommitted himself, he collapsed in 1935 and recuperated in mainland Scotland before returning to Shetland in October of that year.

As well as her work for The Saltire Society, Nan was still much in demand by other associations for lectures and talks. Behind the scenes as well as publicly, she was working to bring to the fore those whose work she believed were misunderstood and whose work was valuable not purely as part of Scotland's literary 'Renaissance' but universally and for the future.

In 1937, Nan gave two talks on MacDiarmid. One was to the Scottish Literature and Song Association, the other was a WEA lecture. Neither audience was highbrow and the Literature and Song Association talk had particularly worried Nan. As their usual fare was either Lady Nairne's songs[849] or a country dancing demonstration, she thought a presentation on MacDiarmid's poetry might fly way over their heads. She was quite certain their mental level would be more Annie S Swan.[850] A first glance at the audience made Nan think she had been right to worry. 'There was one fat, comfortable elderly wife' she said, who 'just needed her shank to complete her'. But this woman took every point Nan made in the most unexpected way. In fact, the whole room did, responding animatedly to the entire lecture. 'You certainly got them',[851] Nan reported back to MacDiarmid afterwards. 'I found myself remembering "Gin I canna win through to the man in the street,/The wife by the hearth—" '.[852]

In both talks, Nan was only trying to make contact between the audience and MacDiarmid, 'to make them feel the dynamic and creative quality of your words'. So she read a great deal of his poetry aloud and she took along a musical friend to the Literature and Song Association, who playing her own accompaniments, sang two of G. F. Scott's settings of his work. 'And they felt and responded all right. No doubt of that'.[853]

Not everyone in the audience was convinced, however. 'Later, there was the usual crop of elderly gentlemen' she admitted, who came up to her and said that while her talk was all very interesting, *they* could not find all that she interpreted in MacDiarmid's work. One even declared he was no poet at all. And because Nan had been trying to make them aware that MacDiarmid was precious to Scotland precisely because he was a poet, 'in the profoundest sense of that maligned word', her retort was cutting. There was the usual cavilling, too, at his using Scots and one kindly soul who felt:

> that Scotland's greatness lay with the folk who did the humble routines duties of life—quite failing to discriminate between the humble routine duty of gathering tatties and the humble routine duty of gathering gossip & reflecting that a country that uses its poets to write the pars on triplets and the presentation to the meenister, is less than generous to its own potentialities.[854]

Post-collapse, part of MacDiarmid's recovery was in the writing of his autobiography, *Lucky Poet,* which he began in 1939 and completed in 1941. Not long after the birth of their son, Michael, then just 'a wee laddie asleep in his basket',[855] Nan popped in on him and Valda. Shortly after Nan's visit, MacDiarmid wrote to her asking for a copy of the talks she said she had given about him in Aberdeen in 1937. 'I can send you no MSS of the two talks I have given in Aberdeen on your work within the last year. I never write lectures. Not even notes for them',[856] Nan replied, although later in the same letter she contradicts herself. Shortly after the WEA Lecture she was asked for an article on MacDiarmid for the *Aberdeen University Review* 'as if in the belief that I'd just hand over the ms. of that'.[857] In 1969, however, when Helen Cruickshank asked if she could quote from this same article of Nan's, she reiterated that 'not a word of it was written, I had then to set to work and write it all down'.[858]

It is more likely that Nan did have some notes for the talks given to WEA, but rather than send those to MacDiarmid in time for inclusion in his autobiography, she wanted to extend and properly consider an article. As she said to MacDiarmid, an article is very different to a talk, which could include the <u>sound</u> of MacDiarmid's work. Its musicality was something vital, she felt, to its interpretation. Nan agreed to write the article but she knew it would take her time to produce and the spring term at the Training Centre was always so busy she had no time to concentrate on anything else. Worried that MacDiarmid would not receive it in time to include it in his autobiography, she promised him a copy anyway.

Written in the early summer of 1938 her essay on 'The Poetry of Hugh MacDiarmid' was meant to be included in the summer edition of the *Aberdeen University Review.* At the last minute 'some Academic Lord' needed space in that issue and Nan was asked whether she might curtail her article or would prefer to postpone it. As her aim was to encourage people to read MacDiarmid, Nan had quoted freely. To cut the words would have defeated her purpose. She was adamant. Refusing to cut the article (which when printed, ran to twelve pages) she agreed instead to its postponement. It appeared, eventually, in the Autumn number of the *Aberdeen University Review* published in November 1938. 'It probably won't express what you think about yourself but at any rate it is the attempt of one reader who loves your lyric to induce others to love it too,'[859] Nan wrote to MacDiarmid in October of that year. In December, as promised, she sent a copy to him in Shetland.

Opinions on MacDiarmid varied in the extreme. 'Guttersnipe genius—Scotland's Public Enemy No 1', or 'the most vital of living

Scotsman,' 'nobody has ever been so Scotch before—he makes even Burns seem like a Cockney by comparison'. MacDiarmid himself admitted that there was an element of truth in all of these descriptions and was unashamed of even those which were the least flattering.[860] He must have been flattered by Nan's article because he quotes extensively from it in *Lucky Poet*.[861]

Reading Nan's study of MacDiarmid's poetry suggests that she wanted more time to consider what she was going to say because she wanted to be searingly honest about it. She opens her essay with a discussion of these polarised opinions:

> Can one be a believer and yet say, as the misbelieving men say, that he writes much pretentious nonsense? Love his work, yet confess his failures? The difficulty arises from the fanatical nature of the responses his work has evoked. Between "the only major poet writing in Europe today" and "The fellow's no poet—the merest charlatan" there seems no plain path for the feet.[862]

Nan was a believer. 'He has qualities which are those of a major poet; I admit frankly to intoxication; I have been drunk for days together on a phrase, a cadence from his work. He can run plain words (*plain* words, the ordinary counters of our speech—not the half-made, rock-hewn inventions of much modern poetry, including his own) into a sequence that is magical in its beauty, that "new-creates" the thing it says',[863] she wrote, reflecting the premise of 'Singing Burn'.[864]

In 1937 Neil Gunn wrote to Nan saying, 'its not the praise or the blame, it's that dull, opaque eye…I'm never worried by my reviews because, I suppose, I know I have had my private fun…Then a seeing eye like yours—and all the original warmth comes flooding on a smile'.[865] Nan now turned her 'seeing eye' to MacDiarmid's work and showed an insight into his poetry and use of language that at the time either exasperated or befuddled many other readers. 'It's not that I canna understand him. I canna even *read* him,'[866] Charles Murray is reported to have said to Helen Cruickshank. Helen was shocked, not only by Murray's comment but also by those who boasted sporadically in the Scottish Press that they were unable to read the Scots language:

> Why this mental blockage? Would we respect a Frenchman who repudiated all desire to know anything about Breton dialect and literature? … Our Scots language is so colourful, graphic, economical, pungent or poignant that I am constantly

surprised it is not oftener used by poets.[867]

It was in this article that Nan also dealt with the antagonism towards MacDiarmid's dictionary-dredging, arguing that new modes of experience needed new words to express them. But, these new words had to be 'right'. 'The over-charged word falsifies—but does the esoteric word communicate?' Here, she reveals her own struggle with trying to find the right words. 'I admit … much failure in communication. I stub my toe against boulders of words that make passage uneasy. Sometimes they yield a meaning to one's labour, sometimes not'. But even if these new words did not yield meaning, Nan believed they were useful to 'sharpen our mood and quicken thought. They must be lived with before they can give us full poetic satisfaction'. Experimentation like MacDiarmid's was healthy, she believed, and would ultimately expand the borders of expression—though which of these 'private words' would actually make it into future language would depend not on his use of them, but on others' dealings with what he has produced.

It was for MacDiarmid's 'swift, illuminating metaphors', however, that Nan reserved her fullest praise:

> For putting aside philology and philosophy, what matters in poetry is neither meaning nor vocabulary, but the fusion of both in utterance that is itself an experience. Such utterance MacDiarmid has, both in English and in Scots, in phrases and in imagery…He is, in fact, a *makar*, creating new life…[868]

She acknowledged that some of MacDiarmid's work came across as propagandist but in order 'create a condition of human society in which men will again hearken to poetry' the poet 'turns political'. To Nan, the poet and the politician were inseparable: 'It might seem comfortable to divide the man up, to say "There goes Grieve the politician, here MacDiarmid the poet. But that would be fatal to the poet. The man is one'. [869] His political creed was hardly relevant. What was relevant, was the vision being his creed. 'That never changes. Always he sees man "filled with lightness and exaltation", living to the full reach of his potentialities'. What followed this statement is a prime example of Nan Shepherd being unafraid to mince her words: 'The actuality is different. Men are obtuse, dull, complacent, vulgar. They love the third-rate… Their reading is "novels and newspapers", their preoccupations, "fitba' and weemen".

MacDiarmid, however, was more than a poet of a particular movement, she went on. Whether you agreed with his ideals or not, his vision was purely accidental to that moment in history and it was valid beyond that moment. For MacDiarmid's political opponents to condemn his poetry *because* they condemn his politics, she said, was 'like refusing a cup of cold water because one dislikes the colour of the cup'.[870] The preoccupation of the younger poets of that era with politics, during the run-up to the Second World War, was not only understandable but inevitable.

★ ★ ★

After weeks of tension, it was almost a relief when, on Sunday 3rd September 1939, war was declared on Germany. The most exposed, geographically, of the Scottish cities, Aberdeen braced itself for bombardment. As scores of men queued to enlist at the recruiting office in the Music Hall, air raid wardens' centres were set up and public buildings, including the Water Works in Cults, were sandbagged. People rushed out to buy blackout materials. Soon, gummed net and sticky paper to protect windows from splintering, black felt, blinds, curtains and blackout paint, even cardboard and drawing pins were in short supply. At night, Aberdeen's streets lay in darkness, only fleetingly illuminated by the lights of a passing tram. But so many of the buildings were of granite that on a clear night, lit by the moon, the silver city gleamed. It was an easy target.

That September, hordes of children from the west of Scotland were evacuated to rural Aberdeenshire. Cults became a Deeside Dormitory, its population swollen with pale-faced, ricketty, young evacuees who arrived at Cults station, labels around their necks, seeking safety from Glasgow. Schoolchildren and students at the Training Centre were drilled in preparation for when the air raid warnings sounded. Gas mask inspection, and practice wearing them, became routine. By November, though, most of the evacuees had returned home. They had come to Cults when there was no need to come, or so it seemed. For the first eight months of the Second World War, nothing happened. Or at least that was how it appeared to the British public who dubbed it the 'Bore War'.[871]

As it turned out, the children returned to Glasgow just in time for the bombing. In January 1940, the Luftwaffe began a series of air raids. The worst, for Aberdeen, was on the 21st April 1943. Twenty-five bombers attacked the city, the last wave sweeping low, machine-gunning the streets filled with civilians running for the shelters. A wall of flame raged at the end of George Street, silhouetting the figures of the ARP and police as they tried to rescue people from the debris as bombs rained down around them. The official casualty list listed ninety-seven dead and over two hundred and thirty injured.

Nan's feelings on war are made clear by a glance at her *Medley Book*. Ezra Pound's lines from *Canto XVIII*, 'War, one war after another. Men start 'em who couldn't put up a good hen-roost' are followed by lines from Tao Te Ching: 'When armies are raised and the issues joined, it is he who does not delight in war who wins'.[872]

The origins of the principal text of Taoism, Tao Te Ching (roughly translated as 'the way of integrity') are uncertain. The general consensus is that it was written around 600 BC by one Lao Tzu, (old master); Nan dates it before 200 BC. Its eighty-one verses are a treatise on how to live in the world with goodness and integrity—still valid—and during the war, for Nan, especially so. She took no delight in war, which to her just further disrupted and divided the world. Any sort of unity now seemed more improbable than ever.

Judging by the translation, Nan's quotation in her *Medley Book* is from Arthur Waley's philological, rather than literary, translation of the text. A member of the Bloomsbury Group, Waley (who deliberately wrote for a more general audience) aimed his book at all intelligent people seeking to understand what was going on in the world around them—'general anthropologists' as he describes them, people bent on finding out how man came to be. *The Way and its Power: A Study of the Tao Te Ching and its Place in Chinese Thought* was published in 1934. His introduction is longer than the annotated text itself, but as Waley pointed out, he saw no way of making the writing intelligible without illustrating how the ideas it embodies came into existence.

The tradition native to China before Buddhism was brought in by the Indian monk Bodhidharma in the sixth century. Taoism was a fertile ground for Zen[873] because of its insistence that Tao can never be properly put into words—its reality can only be apprehended. The first sentence of *Tao Te Ching* claims that 'the Tao that can be spoken of is not the eternal Tao', 'As a thing the way is shadowy, indistinct'. For the Taoist the world is not a collection of separate objects, but a process of energy always in flux. This is 'the way', which manifests in the interaction of complementary opposites, 'yin' and 'yang'—both of which are given equal relevance. The reason Tao is so hard to define is because man is integral to it and as such, cannot stand apart from it and see it objectively. It is this interrelatedness of man with universe that makes the philosophies of Taoism and Zen so alike. Both are concerned with the practical process of learning to live in harmony with the universe—the virtue of non-striving: 'doing it' by 'non-doing'—*being*—which became one of the central tenets of Zen.

To force something, to strain, is futile. The Chinese and Japanese learned to deal with this by turning spontaneous action into an art form—Tai Chi, for example, where a complex series of movements is performed with no sense of exertion, it comes from within. This is the ultimate end of the Taoist or Zen quest—known as 'wu-wei', an action so unforced and natural it loses its ordinariness, deliberation or weighing up. In harmony with the natural, it simply *is*. Now we begin to see how all Nan's reading of eastern philosophies, of Lafcadio Hearn, AE and Tao Te Ching influenced her and was distilled through her own experience into the writing of *The Living Mountain*. 'It is when the body is keyed to its highest potential and controlled to a profound harmony deepening into something that resembles a trance, that I discover most nearly what it is *to be'*, she says and so articulates 'wu-wei' almost at the end of her book.[874]

The Chinese word for landscape literally means 'mountains and water' and the many features of the natural world—rocks, streams, valleys and peaks, rising and falling movements—which were believed to be the material embodiments of yin and yang. Landscape paintings, then, did not simply depict the outer forms of nature, but the energies that infuse the natural world with life. All the patterns of nature, from the highest cliff face to the tiniest stone, the vast ocean to the minute stream, were seen as outward signs of the vital energy that was the basis for all matter. Of all the embodiments of energy, however, the towering, colossal mass of a mountain was the most impressive.

In the first paragraph of *The Living Mountain,* Shepherd illustrates the mountain's yin and yang—'Summer on the high plateau can be delectable as honey; it can also be a roaring scourge. To those who love the place, both are good, since both are part of its essential nature'. And it was to know its essential nature through a process of living that she was seeking.

Exactly when Nan read Waley's translation of the *Tao Te Ching* is hard to determine, but given its placing in her *Medley Book,* it was sometime around the start of the Second World War. With so many men away fighting, the hills were an unpeopled landscape, which suited her. She escaped to them as often as work at the Training Centre would permit, sometimes on her own, sometimes with Grant and Jean Roger. Her other escape was Neil Gunn's fiction.

To take her mind off the 'crump' of falling bombs during the air-raids, in May 1940, she had read Gunn's *Wild Geese Overhead* [875] which had been published the year before. It worked. She could plunge herself into his 'Glasgow Slum' she told him, 'with the sense of having withdrawn from a rank coarse reality to a world seen small and magically clear at the far end of an inverted spyglass'. 'The rank coarseness was good too', she added 'but it doubled my force in dealing with it to take that wizard-journey through the lens'.[876]

She then went on to talk about Neil's *Second Sight*, which had just been published but which was commercially unsuccessful. Yet again, Nan saw what the critics failed to grasp but, more than that, she said, the power of his words themselves dissolved her into a state of *being* that until then, she had only experienced out on the tramp in the hills:

'To apprehend things, walking on a hill, seeing the light change, the mist, the dark, being aware, using the whole of one's body to instruct the spirit—yet, that is a secret life one has and knows that others have. But to be able to share it, in and through words, that's what frightens me. The word shouldn't have such power. It dissolves one's being. I am no longer myself but part of a life beyond myself when I read pages that are so much the expression of myself. You can take processes of being—not that's too formal a word—<u>states</u> is too static, this is something that moves—movements I suppose is best—you can take *movements of being* and translate them out of themselves into words. That seems to me a gift of a very high and sane order. They're like a pulse of life inside me. Something deeper than conscious intellect recognizes their nature. I think you will understand what I mean.'[877]

For Nan, this was a pivotal moment. Her quest was not only '*wu wei*' but, like Neil Gunn, to be able to articulate those *movements of being* so that they were translated out of themselves and into words. Ultimately, of course, she achieved this in *The Living Mountain*. Neil, too, had given her the idea for its subject matter. Back in 1930, he had suggested she replace her wood with a snow-swathed peak: 'You could always stick a peak where a wood should be' he wrote, 'And a snow wreath for a quarry'.[878]

Neil *did* understand what Nan meant in her letter. 'You come uncannily at the heart of the matter', he replied, 'and I feel, well, there's one person anyway. One either sees a thing as you do or one doesn't. That's the sort of conclusion I've come to…without a certain eye many a scene would be unspeakably bleak and boring'. He seems almost embarrassed, though, by her acuity. In an earlier letter of his to Nan, written in 1937, he had talked about 'the sweet embarrassment of understanding'.[879] In his public writing—his novels—Neil felt free to express himself, thinking his innermost thoughts were safe, perhaps, because the critics so often missed the point. In his private writing, Neil was far less expansive and would retreat rather than reveal. It was something Nan also had a tendency to do, drawing a squiggly line in her letters instead of elaborating.

For Neil Gunn, as he wrote in *The Atom of Delight*, 'there is always the inner self that is not going to be touched'.[880] It was the same for Nan. Her version of this appears in Jenny's thoughts in *A Pass in the Grampians*: 'The hard core of herself in Jenny's being remained inaccessible. She was as secretive as frost, stealing on the familiar landscape of herself with a movement no one could detect or influence'.[881]

'When you hesitate before arriving at the word *movements* of being' Neil continued, 'then it is as if you were surprising me in my very lair. Where to put it mildly, I hardly expected to see you—or anyone else.' You can almost feel him blushing with pleasure certainly, but it also seems to have made him a little uncomfortable. Nan hadn't just *seen,* she had stepped right into his lair by which he meant a secret, private place where he sought concealment or seclusion (the English definition of the word rather than the Scots which means a burial place, mud, or mire). He went on:

> You evoke life in its movement of transition, to arrest for an instant the movement and glance of its body and eye, to do something of the same kind to what we call inanimate nature; but somehow it has in it a rare delight…A momentary apprehension of the primordial sense of life, alert, quick-eyed, arrested in a grey rock face…and at the same time a curious half-consciousness of an extra dimension of apprehension, with its momentary thrill. I am not at all sure…that we have not here the beginning of an extra dimension of being. But enough,[882]

And he withdraws once more, changing the subject to his relish of her 'thrawing of his neck' over a cliché in the book: 'Delicious of you. And what a cliché it was. I mean, how few will see it. It was pretty well done'.[883]

Neil's use of the word 'delight' to describe the movement of transition is important. The 'other landscape' he is hinting at, this 'extra dimension of being' he believed man can penetrate in moments of 'satori' (not that he used that word for it) he described as a realm of Delight. Neil's remark, that this can be apprehended through something as apparently as intractable as a 'grey rock face' might also have prompted Nan to use a mountain as both material and metaphor for her book—a way to 'go out' and at the same time to 'go into'.

Going into the mountain was a skill. In Chapter Ten of *The Living Mountain* Nan explains that year by year she grew more familiar with her mountain, its air, light, weather, its burns and tarns, its peaks and dells, its fauna and flora and its 'long blue distances'. 'But if the truth of them is to be told as I have found it I too am involved. I have been the instrument of my own discovering', she admits, 'and to govern the stops of the instrument needs learning too'. She had to train her senses, to look and to listen properly. Her body had to be trained, too, 'to move with the right harmonies'. But of all the skills she taught herself so that she could learn the nature of the mountain, the most compelling was quiescence.

'No-one knows the mountain completely who has not slept on it', she writes. As the mind slips over into sleep, it grows limpid, the body dissolves and 'perception alone remains'. For Nan, those 'moments of quiescent perceptiveness before sleep' were among the most rewarding of her day in the hills. To be 'quiescent', which comes from the Latin 'being still, being quiet', is, of course, '*wu wei*'. It is an unforced and natural state when:

> One neither thinks nor desires, nor remembers, but dwells in pure intimacy with the tangible world…I am emptied of preoccupation, there is nothing between me and the earth and sky…at no other moment am I sunk quite so deep into its life. I have let go my self. The experience is peculiarly precious because it is impossible to coerce…One is tranquil as the stones, rooted far down in their immobility. The soil is no more a part of the earth. If sleep comes at such a moment, its coming is a movement as natural as day. And after—ceasing to be a stone, to be the soil of the earth, opening eyes that have human cognisance behind them upon what one has been so profoundly a part of. That is all. One has been in.[884]

Meanwhile, 1940 passed. Punctuated as it was by bombs and the tragedy of Dunkirk which echoed in the North East as 'ships' of any description were manned from Fraserburgh to Peterhead and headed off down the east coast to France, there was one highlight in the shape of Sheila's wedding. Aged twenty three, she married David Spence Clouston, a vet five years her senior, in Lerwick, Shetland. The wedding was meant to have taken place in Aberdeen, but the exigencies of war relocated it. They married at St Columba's, Sheila in pale blue silk and a straw hat, draped in grey tulle studded with flowers.[885] No doubt Sheila, like all brides, was radiant. Whether or not Nan was able to attend the marriage, we do not know. She would surely not have wanted to miss it. We do know, however, that from then on she went as often as she could to see the 'Shetlanders' as she called them. So did Mary Lawson. Although, as they were unable to leave Jeannie Shepherd on her own until her death in 1950, Mary and Nan were forced to visit separately.

Joy at Sheila's wedding was replaced in April 1941 by sorrow over the death of Charles Murray—and is where this story started. It was from Jessie Kesson that Nan heard the news which had been announced that day on the wireless. Murray was not a fan of the radio. 'Who the hell invented wireless…It screeches on all day till I am deaved,' he exploded in a letter to Alex Keith in 1940.[886]

Having retired from his South African duties in 1924, Charles and Edith Murray returned to Scotland eventually settling, in 1935, at The Lythe, in Banchory, which was nearer than his beloved Alford to old friends like the Shepherds who were only a half hour's bus journey away in Cults. During his last few years, Murray enjoyed a quieter, simpler life. But by the end, he was 'worn awa' as he said in a poem written to commemorate his seventy-sixth birthday. Considered delicate since his schooldays, he was a heavy smoker of both pipe and cigarettes. A severe, persistent cough troubled him. By early April 1941 he was dangerously ill and in the early hours of Saturday 12th April, he died of pneumonia at home, his wife and daughter at his bedside.

The announcement of his death in the Scottish press was picked up and covered in Canada, New Zealand and South African papers. His loss, though, was felt more deeply by his 'ain folk'. His funeral on 15th April 1941 at the West Church of St Nicholas in Aberdeen was, like the man himself, unfussy and modest. Family, close friends and colleagues from his South African years filled the church, but as Nan was on her way to the hills only the day before, it was unlikely that she would have been among the mourners. How fitting though, was the choice of Psalm 121 for the service at St Nicholas: 'I to the hills will lift mine eyes'.[887]

Nan *was*, however, at the opening of the Charles Murray Memorial Gates some fifteen years later on 24 August 1956. She also provided an 'appreciation' of Charles Murray to introduce his last poems, collected in a slim volume which was published in 1969. Her 'appreciation' was reprinted ten years later in a complete edition of his poems, *Hamewith,* published by the Aberdeen University Press. 'Charles Murray was a man one could not miss in a company', she began, 'he had presence: not self-assertive, but dynamic—one felt more alive from being with him.' His verse, Nan described as a poetry of externals, there was nothing introspective, she said, no psychological probing. Murray was wary of intellectual and symbolic poetry, but willing to concede its right to be. 'All his verse', she continued:

> is a record of a way of living already altered and of customs and conventions that have vanished. But it is more than a record, it is an affirmation, of life. These poems have the glow of health on them. Their verve and gusto are the outward and visible sign of an inward assurance that life is livable [sic] and mankind worth knowing. The seed of Charles Murray's power is that he said yes to life'. [888]

Nan wrote another, longer, article for the *Leopard Magazine* and in this and her 'appreciation' she relays the anecdote about the stonemason asking if Murray wanted a job, the same story she included almost verbatim in *The Weatherhouse*. It is a prime example of Murray's humility and a story which, for her, bore repetition because it illustrated an important essence of the man. But there is much in her description of Charles Murray that could be applied to Nan herself.

★ ★ ★

The following year, Nan sent Neil Gunn a short story she had written. It was the first time, as far as we know, that Nan had attempted something in this medium. 'This is really distinguished work', he responded. 'This belongs to what I understand as literature'. He then admonished her: 'Any reference to "inferiority complex" is just tiresome…It's boring— and the slightest bit irritating in face of the true reality. Insight here is profound, essential'. Nan remained unconvinced of her own ability as a writer. She was still striving to express herself in words that lifted the reader into the very experience she was describing so that it exploded from the page 'sticky and rich' as she would say many years later in 1981; so that the words themselves made the experience true. As far as Neil Gunn was concerned she had achieved that. 'All surfaces are seen as surfaces, with the kind of understanding that apprehends completely, without conscious magnanimity. This is distilling, & the purity of the spirit very high'.

He did have some criticism, however. Initially he felt the work was congested, too much was squeezed into the allotted space of the short story medium and her sudden production of whole characters made the story bumpy. Then, not sure whether that was really the problem, he gave the story to his wife to read. Daisy could not quite put her finger on what was actually wrong with it either.

The story was *Descent from the Cross*, which the Scots Magazine printed in February 1943. Neil Gunn is right—the work could easily have been extended to novel length. But Nan was done with novels and experimenting with other genres—after her poetry, the short story was next and then she would try her hand at non-fiction. It was a natural progression. But what she was really trying out, was the distillation Neil Gunn said she had managed.

The story is set in the early 1930s of the post-war depression. Elizabeth, like the female protagonists of Nan's novels, is a member of a small community who is trying to find a way to 'get leave to live'. Nan's trademarks are all there too: her dry wit; her use of the vernacular in dialogue and in the body of the text where it naturally inserts itself; her compassion for her 'tribe' of characters; and her understanding of the pain and joy of everyday living. This time, however, she explores the option of marriage.

Very much the 'New Woman', Elizabeth earns 'a mint' and chooses to marry Tommy Martin, a 'sallow, hag-ridden' man, who had been a prisoner of war.[892] Tongues wag over her choice. What sort of man would live off his wife's earnings? Tommy is to enjoy fame from his book, Elizabeth announces at their wedding. 'Ay, and she believed it too, that was the mischief o't', the narrator comments. But as it turns out 'that she believed in Tommy, and he in her belief in him', begins his slow release from captivity—the trauma of his war years.[893]

The trauma was 'a sort of crucifixion'. Taken prisoner by the Germans, Tommy and five of his engineer comrades, having refused to make munitions for the enemy, were strung up by their wrists in the woods, their toes just off the ground. At the last moment, Tommy is spared and cut down, hence the title *Descent from the Cross*. But at the point when life seemed to have left him, Tommy recounts, 'his brain was never clearer. He seemed to be out of the body…and with superhuman clarity he saw the truth of things… Since that moment of illumination nothing had really mattered but getting it into words.'[894]

In that moment, he tells Elizabeth, he understood something fundamental, 'the basis of a whole philosophy of living…and I think—the thing I saw—could save mankind'. This, he says, is was what he wanted to put into his book, 'if I could work it out'.[895] But the book does not come. Over the first year of marriage only pages of notes appear; nothing coherent. He doesn't work from the beginning, but like Nan herself, works it into shape, fragment, by fragment.

The story reflects Nan's own struggle with writing: the difficulty of finding the right words to translate an experience so that it is felt by the reader. When the book is going well, all is light. Elizabeth and Tommy walk in September fields in 'the sun-saturated atmosphere', 'a day so filled with light that the stubble shone'.[896] Yet only Chapter Five takes form—the rest Tommy grapples with. No matter how hard he toils, how hard he tries to recover the 'sense of seeing deep into truth', he can never quite grasp it again.[897] Tommy's writing of the book is one of the surfaces Neil Gunn means. Beneath that layer is the idea of not forcing, not toiling, the quiescence of '*wu wei*'. Trying to induce satori through meditation also appears in the story: 'Sometimes by fasting, and by discipline of his wandering attention, he strove to induce the moment of vision. The mood came, the sense of seeing deep into truth'.[898]

For Elizabeth, it is while she is listening to Tommy's voice as he explains his philosophy to her, that the moment of vision is induced:

> She didn't know even yet what Tommy's philosophy was. It was vague to her—beautiful and solemn. When he talked of it, new horizons opened before her, but this was less from intellectual apprehension than from the emotion induced by his low vibrating voice and her sense of sharing in a profound experience. At last she was inside.

To be 'inside' something, of course, requires you to have gone 'into' it. In this passage Nan Shepherd manages to illustrate the difference between intellectual apprehension and knowledge gleaned from experience. At the same time she emphasises the struggle to articulate this knowledge through a written text—it is not through Tommy's book that these new horizons open up before Elizabeth, but through his trance-inducing speech.

Tommy's moment of enlightenment mingles Eastern philosophies with Christian and pagan symbols. The 'crucifixion' takes place amongst the birches, pagan symbols of renewal and rebirth:

> life was bursting on every side; and his heart leaped in tumult, he wanted to be part of this force of creation…But what am I to write, he pondered. What have I to write? As though the blaze of sun in the myriad crystals illumined his own inner self, he began to review the contents of his mind; and with the force of a revelation it came to him that he had no philosophy to offer the world, no book to write, nothing to say. And again he felt a sense of release. No more agonising struggle for words; words that had refused him because there was no task to perform…To be nothing, not to matter, to have no importance—how sane it was, and good. He had never really lived till

that morning.[899]

Crystal as metaphor appears regularly in Nan's writing. She uses it to signify clarity. The moment of crystallisation also suggests the energy contained within a crystal. All solid matter is composed of atomic particles arranged in some form of organised crystalline structure, and crystals, too, are believed to contain eons of knowledge and wisdom—the formative life principle. She gives us the interchange, the traffic between Tommy and these myriads of crystal illuminated without but also illuminating within, which leads to his release, his surrender, and in that knowledge that he is 'nothing' he has never felt more alive.

Through Elizabeth, Nan also brings up the matter of the 'well-water'. Tommy's writing, Elizabeth thinks, is not to everyone's tastes. What is selling, she tells him, is war experiences. 'Give the details' she says to him, 'not philosophy. Personal things'.[900] It is an interesting comment, given that *The Living Mountain* is both: philosophy and autobiography.

Descent from the Cross haunted Gunn. He returns to it in several letters. In July 1943 he wrote, 'that last long story has developed a sort of legendary power. These things take their own time. But I am certain you could write a greater story now than ever before.'[901]

Chapter Twelve

1945-1959

N an was thinking about, if not already writing, *The Living Mountain* in August 1943. We do not have her letter to Neil Gunn, but it is clear from his reply that she had outlined the book to him. He was encouraging: 'So forward you go. Having a mountain, too, puts you fair in luck's way'.[902] By 1945 she had completed the 30,000 word manuscript and wrote to Gunn asking if it was the sort of book he would like to read. It was, he answered, and if she cared to send him the script he would read it with delight. In the meantime, he thought 'The Plateau', which was the title she was proposing, sounded 'a trifle square-lined'. 'You're dealing with curves and penetration' he explained. He also felt the book was too short and suggested she increase the word count. Nan must have scoffed at this. 'I know it sounds absurd, it is absurd', he responded. 'However, I'm only telling you what I understand publishers want, with the notion that possibly it's wise when making one's bow, to know about it'. 'It's the sort of book publishers are shy of', he went on. 'A publisher would say to himself: "this is good, but would I even get my money out of it?" You must understand that. It's hellish, but there it is'.[903]

After the war's end on 2nd September 1945, the printing industry was hit not just by paper shortages but by the scarcity of labour. So many skilled men had died and few apprentices had returned to complete their training. Despite the pessimistic tone of his letter, Neil was keen Nan should not feel discouraged: 'As it happens you see, I think you have one of the finest, subtlest minds in Scotland. Your stuff <u>should</u> be appearing. I'm not flattering or talking of greatness or what not. The only value I'm sure of always is quality. It's innate in you'.[904]

Mure Mackenzie did not read the manuscript of *The Living Mountain*, but evidently Nan had told her, too, about the book. 'Knowing you well and the Cairngorms slightly, I am ready to believe it is very good indeed', Mure said in a letter to Nan written the following August of 1946 and offered her some publishing advice. 'It's an awkward length for normal, but just at the moment firms like short books', she observed, contradicting Neil Gunn. '*Country Life* do their books beautifully with very fine photographic illustrations', she went on and suggested Nan could also try Peter Davies and Michael Joseph.[905]

The only person who did read the manuscript of *The Living Mountain* in the late 1940s was Neil Gunn. Nan sent it to him in the autumn of 1945. His response was effusive:

> This is beautifully done. With restraint, the fine precision of the artist or scientist or scholar; with an exactitude that is never pedantic, but always tribute. So love comes through and wisdom. It's not altogether that you deal with essences. Indeed you deal with facts. And you build with proportion, methodically & calmly, for light & a state of being are facts in your world. At one point you talk of other senses there may or might be; and I thought to myself: how many use those they have? And if they have not used them—can they be illumined?[906]

Neil then addressed the practicalities. It was going to be difficult to find a publisher, he warned. Faber was experiencing post-war difficulties and 'were in a terrific jam with printers and binders and stuff'. There was also the size of the book to consider. Nan had clearly taken his advice on the title as Neil now referred to its new one: 'I should like to have this experience of the living mountain on a shelf by me. Friends of the kind are not so many'. On the 30,000 word count, however, Nan refused to budge.

Neil had two suggestions. His friend Alex Salmond might accept it and run it serialised in the *Scots Magazine*. The work would lose nothing by appearing in that form, he thought. His other proposal was to add illustrations or photographs to the book. 'You may not like that idea at first thought. You're wrong. Mountain and loch names that to you evoke magic may not evoke so much to those who never heard them before.' In 1934, Batsford had published George Blake's illustrated *The Heart of Scotland*. Blake's book was about the same length as Nan's. 'Drop them a note', Neil advised, 'saying you have written a book of just over 30,000 words on the Cairngorms, a personal record of the mountains seen in all their phases that might interest hill and country lovers & ask if they might care to see the MS? Make your letter interesting, you water sprite!'[907]

As Nan loathed serials she immediately discounted Neil's first suggestion. Instead she wrote to Batsford at 15 North Audley Street, London W1. The reply, when it came, was courteous but negative: apparently they did not care to see the manuscript. Whether or not they might have accepted *The Living Mountain* for publication if they had actually seen the manuscript we can only speculate. Batsford, now an imprint of Pavilion Books, has not kept Nan's letter.[908] If Nan kept a copy, it probably went the same way as Batsford's polite rejection—into the waste paper basket or, more likely, the fire. The manuscript of *The Living Mountain* went into a drawer in the hall table at Dunvegan and there it stayed for the next thirty years.

After this rebuttal of what Nan considered her finest work, it must have been with some chagrin that she read and reviewed Janet Adam Smith's *Mountain Holidays,* published some months later in 1946 by Dent & Son.[909] Incidentally, Mure Mackenzie had advised Nan against Dent, as they had 'a nasty reputation for sweating their authors'.[910]

'This is a pleasant book', Nan's review opened. Coming from her, this sounds suspiciously like damning with faint praise. 'Pleasant' is not an adjective Nan ever used for works she really admired. It was 'gay', she went on:

> like good talk among friends, salted, sometimes pungent, never stodgy...and towards the end of the book [Adam Smith] sums up admirably a discovery made by everyone who climbs "The pleasure of a whole mountain day is always greater than any of the separate incidents".[911]

Some twelve years younger than Nan, Janet Adam Smith had learnt the craft of mountaineering from her father, George Adam Smith, Principal of Aberdeen University from 1909 to 1935. Her signature appears regularly in Maggie Gruer's *Thistle Cottage Visitors Book* and like Nan in *The Living Mountain,* Adam Smith pays tribute to her idiosyncratic hostess in *Mountain Holidays.* There, the similarities between the two works end. There is some description: 'To walk in a muffled, silent, sightless world, is to feel near to ghosts', Adam Smith writes in her Cairngorm-walking chapter[912] and in her review, Nan picked out a couple of other striking images, among them 'the match stick legs' of the sheep and 'the pungent smell of pine needles, as reviving as a long drink'. But as Adam Smith says in the foreword to the book, it was written purely for pleasure, 'to recall the enjoyment of days on mountains,'[913] and for Nan, the book lacked significance and depth as well as sufficient description.

Although she dismissed the Alps over which Janet Adam Smith 'caracoled', as she put it, preferring her to stick to the hills of home, Nan could not hide her admiration for the girl who could 'walk out of a London office, spend a long night in a train and then walk home through the Cairngorms from Spey to Dee by a different route each time and taking a top or not as the weather allowed. The Scot, one is glad to know, is still a tough.'[914] What Nan really thought of the book, however, is summed up by Malcolm Sutherland. He read *Mountain Holidays* in the late 1940s and having enjoyed it, asked Nan for her opinion of the book. 'She just sniffed' he grinned, 'which said it all'. [915]

In the summer of 1946, the poet, Marion Angus, died. In one of her last letters to Nan she had written: 'I have a feeling that you are at Braemar. I seem to imagine you stepping lightly over the moorland, your golden hair flowing in the wind…For me you are part of the hill country and a kind of emanation of the spirit which lives there'.[916] Marion was right. Nan may have put away the manuscript of *The Living Mountain* but she was not yet done 'drinking that draught' that was the Cairngorms.

It was during that summer of 1946 that Nan first took Malcolm Sutherland's older sister Audrey on her first trip to the hills. 'Audrey returned horrified because Nan had insisted on bathing naked in a tarn', Malcolm recalled. 'It didn't put her off though. The following year she and my brother Joe went up again with Nan'. Malcolm was still a little too young for such a trip. But on their return his brother and sister had been full of their adventure—how they had slept out, during the short summer night, on the plateau behind Ben MacDhui. 'Nan must have watched the weather', Malcolm added. 'You could never really trust it—there could have been a ground frost'.[917]

Malcolm's father was a fruit merchant and Audrey, who had been bound for the family business, instead earned herself a medical degree, followed this with a doctorate and went on to become Medical Officer of Health for Durham. 'Audrey Sutherland did what she wanted to do', according to Ruth Sutherland, but Nan, who was always one to encourage her students at the Training Centre not to conform to society's expectations, may well have had some influence, too. She certainly instilled a love of hill-walking in the three Sutherland children. Many years later, when they returned from their own Cairngorm excursions, Audrey would comment wryly 'Here comes the inquisition' as Nan would appear and insist on hearing all the details. 'Did you see this?' she would ask, endlessly fascinated.

In the run-up to Christmas 1946 any sadness over Marion Angus's death was diminished for Nan by the arrival of a handmade card from Grant and Jean Roger. Announcing the birth of their son Neil, they had enclosed a photograph of him. 'What a live loon!' Nan exclaimed in her reply, adding with her usual acuity: 'How does a man of twelve weeks achieve such an adult sense of humour? Those eyes seem to have looked out on life for a lifetime. What on earth he will be like at twenty-five I can't imagine. You certainly between you produced a person' Nan may not have had a husband and family of her own but she understood the demands they made on a woman's time:

> To run your house, shop, feed and care for your two men, and still have time and strength to make these exquisite Christmas cards—well, it's an achievement though I can understand that now and then you'd like to run away from it all and see a snowy mountain instead of the holes in Grant's socks.[918]

April 1947 found Nan digging in her garden and scrubbing the hen-house. Feeling 'grubby and clean together', she settled down to write to Neil Gunn. *The Drinking Well* had been published the year before. 'About the book:' she begins, 'There's magic in this one'. His first page had transfixed her, so she could hardly turn over to get on with the story. 'I had to live in it,' she explained, 'as I've lived so often in the reality. No-one has caught it in words before, just like this—the way the first light alters things that are familiar, identifies them in a new way in our imagination. It is exquisitely done'. Throughout the book she continued, 'there is a magic of phrase—the kind of magic that obliterates itself, so that the words seem to vanish into the thing they have conjured up'. It was precisely this kind of magic she wanted to manifest from her own writing. But there was no trace of envy in her letter, instead she was delighted by Neil's artistry and quoted line after line back to him. [919]

Nan's delicately perceptive letter restored Neil. Disappointed once again by the reviews of his book he was delighted by Nan's insight as well as by the sentence she used to describe his magic, 'the kind of magic that obliterates itself... I can quote from you too!' he exclaimed 'And how exquisitely you do it! Than that quotation, what more searching could be said on the use of words, of language?'

What Nan had, of course, identified was that Neil's use of words was unselfconscious. Writers whose words called attention to themselves appealed to neither of them. Yet they were living in an era, according to Neil, during which self-consciousness was spreading like a disease: 'The cult of the Ego, the Self—how it is destroying (directly through violence) life itself'. In his latest book, *The Shadow*, 'there is a lassie who has notions of all this', he informed her. However, aside from Nan Shepherd, he wondered how many would actually be able to understand it. 'Geoffrey Faber was fair stumped himself, and fears for my public! But I was adamant'. [920] *The Shadow* came out in February 1948 so as not to jeopardise sales of *The Drinking Well*. The 'lassie' is called Nan.

Discussing his latest book clearly reminded Neil of Nan's latest work. 'You didn't mention any more moves about your hill book?' he observed. Nan had not told him about Batsford's rejection, in fact, for many years, she did not mention *The Living Mountain* at all. Out of sight in its drawer, it appeared, too, to be out of mind.

Both writers were aware that their work was properly appreciated only by the more discerning reader and from his closing remark it seems Neil might have had an inkling of what had happened to the manuscript: 'I can see, Nan, that the world doesn't want the well-water. It doesn't know that it needs it'. It was a comment Nan would remind him of, some thirty years later. In the meantime, it was clear that *The Living Mountain* was ahead of its time. It was not just its length, it was its genre-defiance and its philosophical enquiry. In 1946, the world really wasn't ready for the well water and would not be for some time. However, there is, perhaps, another reason Nan did not pursue publication.

'May you have lovely days and the sun coming', Neil signed off. But winter sat long on the spring of 1947. For days, storms battered Deeside. Sleet still showered from biting winds in early May, ruining the Aberdeen Spring holiday.[921] Eventually, the sun did come and when it did, it shone day after day out of skies so blue Aberdeenshire felt almost Californian.

Now that war was over the Deeside Field Club re-introduced its outings for members. Transport was difficult for those without cars during those post-war years. It took a while for the supply of buses once again to meet the demand and bus companies faced long waits for new vehicles. For Nan, who was a member of the Deeside Field Club, and who never owned a car nor learned to drive so that she was reliant on trains and buses, this might have proved frustrating had it not been irrelevant. She went nowhere that summer. Instead time went astray.

The problem was her thyroid gland. Eventually she underwent an operation to remove nine-tenths of it, but throughout that scorching summer she was forced to lie on a camp bed in the garden, waiting for her pulse to settle and her weight (a mere seven stone) to increase, before the surgeon would touch her. 'I never spent so long at a stretch in absolute quiescence', she wrote, the following February, to Neil. It was an deeply unsettling period for Nan, during which she discovered that the relationship between body and mind was not what she had supposed. She was plagued by anxiety that her essential self had altered—that a stranger was living inside her:

It was an interlude of pure being—later, my doctor said (he isn't an imaginative chiel) that I was "enchanted". But deep down there was a real fear (that only once was able to come to the surface) that this tampering with the odd gland about which in spite of all their knowledge they know so little, might mean an assault on the essential me. And when I was beginning to recover, to go about again and try to live with my new self. I had two bouts of panic... All I knew was that I had lost my poise—my inner serenity—the balance that is the precarious all that separates us from non-being and could not retrieve it. And (while one is living through these things they seem eternal) I had to face the question whether my former poise had not been a matter of the spirit at all but merely the result of a generous supply of thyroid—an accident of matter. To find I couldn't believe in mind anymore—in something that was independent of the flesh and its mysteries—shook me very badly.[922]

It was most unlike Nan to be so forthcoming, even to Neil Gunn. It bored her, she said, to talk about herself, 'it doesn't seem important enough to justify the trouble.' Such an outpouring, then, shows just how much the experience had shaken her. In 1954 she sympathised with a friend who had 'badly lost her self-confidence as a consequence of losing her superabundant thyroid essence. It's such a low miserable business, finding one's balance again after an endocrine disturbance.'[923] Ultimately, Nan did regain her balance but it took nine months and was quite possibly why, in the meantime, she did nothing more with *The Living Mountain;* it was, after all, about *being.*

During this period, in February 1948, lying in bed undisturbed, she read Neil's *The Shadow* straight through. 'Time and again in your book I find that you had already set down things that I discovered'. The novel had fascinated her. But she suspected Neil of nefarious work. 'By giving this girl who loved air and water and light, and who couldn't find all of human nature in a formula, by giving her my name, did you wish on me the things that have been happening to me the last year?' she joked.

The conflict for Neil's 'Nan' is a fight, really, between the integrity of love and the integrity of life:

I can understand how disrupting it would be to know you loved someone who could not see things that you knew as integral to both life and love. And the loveliness of the non-human world, of sky and earth and water, is not enough to heal that wound. To be quite satisfied with these exquisite and healing things is to refuse life.[924]

Nan could have been talking about herself. Her philosophies on life and those of John Macmurray had, after all, diverged. Although her comment is ostensibly about 'Nan' in *The Shadow* who is in love with Ranald, a man who shuts out life, Nan knew that while the natural world has its compensations and healing properties, to be fully *living,* one needs to be fully *in* life.

The Shadow was Neil Gunn's antidote to the darkness and negativity in much of the literature around at the time and while it considers the causes and effects of war, it cannot really be described as a 'war' novel. 'Nan', a young Scotswoman is recovering from a nervous breakdown on a croft in the Highlands with her widowed Aunt Phemie. Her breakdown is caused partly by the horror of living through London's Blitz but mostly by the spiritual bankruptcy of her Marxist lover, Ranald. At first 'Nan' seems to be making progress, but suffers a relapse after hearing of the brutal murder of a neighbouring crofter and the unsolicited attentions of an artist, Adam, whose ideas about nature are very different to hers. 'Nan's' eventual recovery is due to her optimistic, educated and practical Aunt Phemie and the bond between the two women which deepens as the story progresses.

The novel's ambiguous ending did not quite satisfy Nan Shepherd. It felt unfinished to her and she found herself wanting to know what happened to Ranald when he returned to London and how he lived with himself as a consequence of his rather violent actions. Typically, she had pinpointed the weakness of Neil's novel. The character of Ranald feels unreal. As he is viewed for the most part from the outside, it is hard for a reader to identify with him or to see quite why 'Nan' loves him.

It took Neil nearly a month to reply to Nan Shepherd's letter and when he did, on 23 March 1948, he seemed almost embarrassed by her uncharacteristic and lengthy revelation about her illness and mental state, dismissing it in a couple of lines: 'That was a terrific time you had. I had heard nothing about it. You make it very vivid. I hope you are fine now and taking the sun in'. He was also quick to assure Nan that the eponymous heroine of *The Shadow* was not based on her: 'No, I didn't call the girl Nan because of you; at least I don't know why I called her the only name I could call her, because she herself knew it was like a cry'. [925]

Yet there is *so* much of Nan Shepherd in 'Nan' of *The Shadow*. In three parts, each related to 'Nan's' mental condition, the second and third parts of the novel are structured as a straightforward narrative. Part One, however, is a monologue in the form of letters, written but not necessarily sent, from 'Nan' to Ranald. 'Nan' even writes like Nan Shepherd. The prose is complex. Contemplations of nature are interspersed with philosophical musings and self-analysis, literary allusion and sometimes simple, apparently innocent, expression. 'Nan' of *The Shadow* even uses dashes in the same way as Nan Shepherd, whose letters are scattered with them in her haste to get her thoughts down on paper or to skip over what she would rather leave unsaid.

Neil Gunn was as perceptive as Nan Shepherd. He would have gleaned much about her over the years not just from her letters but from reading of her works, too. A passage early on in *The Shadow* is reminiscent of Nan's own description of plunging into a mountain pool, its water so cold she feels stricken, annihilated, before life pours back in *The Living Mountain*.[926]

> —I plunged and gasped and it's a wonder you didn't hear me. Such shuddering ecstasy! Then in a moment—the water was warm. It was all about me and soft and warm...Not having wherewith to dry myself, I did a little dance on the old rock, and then I sat on it.[927]

There is also an account of 'Nan' having fallen asleep 'when I lost consciousness, when either I fell asleep or thinned away on sun and wind' which is redolent, too, of Nan Shepherd's feeling of dissolving as she slips into sleep out on the mountain.[928]

The woods of Nan Shepherd's novels creep into the epistolary narrative too: 'A gorge, wooded with birches...I love birches', 'I came near the first of the birches...I like trees, particularly small birches, because they bring back my childhood'. It is in the birch wood that 'Nan' has an encounter with the stranger, Adam. 'In the wood there is a clearing, an open space'.[929]

There are also stylistic parallels. Nan often opens her writing with a simple sentence: 'The other day I was very angry with you.', or, 'I hope you'll arrange that visit to Aberdeen'. 'Nan' starts letters similarly: 'I have discovered the world!', or, 'A terrible thing has happened'. The text, which mixes these with longer and more complex sentences seems also to echo the way Nan and Neil write to each other, as if they were in conversation.

It is likely that even if it was sub-conscious, Neil's 'Nan' was inspired by his interaction and correspondence with Nan Shepherd and by her writing. But as Nan was to say after his death, she and Gunn recognised each other; in many ways they were twin spirits. Neil Gunn's biographers, Hart & Pick, concluded that:

> if Gunn was self-conscious about the book, it is not surprising,

because not only is it deeply personal, but his feelings are Nan's. He was quite clear both emotionally and intellectually that our salvation must come through women—from intuitive perception and not from the analytic intellect.

He refused to accept a 'new' role for women, however. [930]

Perhaps Neil did not call 'Nan' after Nan Shepherd, but 'the cry' he talks about in his letter, is the same cry, he acknowledged, that is in some of Nan's poetry: 'Your little poems about the earth had that cry in them. Even the cold spring water on the hillside. The spirit cry out of the peewit body'.

'Ranald will be of no use to her, I'm afraid', was Neil's response to Nan's comment about the book's ending:

Kronos will devour his children. That's the way the world is shaping. The world, ordered by men, will destroy what Nan stands for…Totalitarian or Marxist man, in action, will have no feeling of guilt. And the individual doesn't matter much, and his emotional reactions not at all.

'Don't grow despondent' he counselled, 'not while the sun shines and one can still give the silent cry'. He was keen to hear from her again. [931]

If Neil did hear from Nan between March 1948 and January 1949, there is no letter extant in the archives. It is quite possible she did not write again in between. In October 1948, Nan's mother Jeannie was taken ill. For ten days, the doctors thought she would not pull through and although she did, for a long time afterwards she needed continuous care. On top of that, one of Sheila's children was down from Shetland recuperating at Dunvegan after an operation. Throughout all this, Nan had to keep up the appearance of a 'calm judicial appraisal of literature in the presence of students', as she put it, [932] at the Training Centre. Life, with its very real and domestic responsibilities, claimed her full attention and she could not slip away, as she so often did, into that 'other world' which she so often inhabited.

Instead, her portal was Neil's next novel, *The Silver Bough,* which was published in October 1948. Nan bought the book as soon as it appeared in print but was forced to set it aside until January when she could read it as she liked to, in one sitting. Interestingly, the character of Anna, 'beautiful, with a beauty that inhabited her' standing 'against the moonlit world with an extraordinary authenticity', Nan picks out to use as an example of Neil's use of language. 'You use words so that they stop being words—are thinned out until they become just life, still retaining the shape of the worlds that moulded it into meaning'. 'I can't begin to criticise this book', she went on, 'because I've been in. Words like crock of gold aren't sesame to me but sesame grows all over these walls. It's sesame for me when you say 'moving slowly as if shepherding invisible things into the house for the night'.[933]

Neil's response, 'I can't promise you that I'll go on writing books for the pleasure of hearing from you', suggests he had not heard from Nan during that ten month period. We can only speculate whether this was because Nan was simply busy, or whether it was because she was disappointed by his apparent dismissal of her breakdown post thyroid operation. She said no more about it in her letter of January 1949. Neil was happy, though, to hear her mother had recovered.

But Jeannie Shepherd's recovery was temporary. Eighteen months later, she died at home in Dunvegan, shortly after midnight on the 18th March 1950. She was eighty-five, not a bad 'innings' for someone who was apparently too ill to leave the house for over fifty years. According to the certificate, her death was caused by Arterio Sclerosis[934] and Cerebral Thrombosis. No other contributory, underlying or longterm, illness is cited. Whatever was the matter with Jeannie Shepherd remains opaque.

At the age of only fifty seven Nan had lost brother, father and mother. She was the last Shepherd remaining at Dunvegan which, as Mary Lawson stayed on as housekeeper, was now a household of two. The relationship between Nan and her mother, without any testimony, is hard to gauge. But given that since birth, Nan's life had been bounded by her invalid mother, it would have been natural for her to feel a sudden sense of freedom. And Nan still had a lot of living left to do.

★ ★ ★

In October 1950, a few months after her mother's death, Nan wrote four poems inspired by a visit to the north-west coast of Scotland. All four continue the topos of *The Living Mountain,* crystallised in verse. Although 'Achiltibuie' was shown to Sheila Hamilton when she interviewed Nan in 1976, like the manuscript of *The Living Mountain,* these verses, too, remained hidden from public view. Handwritten on loose sheets tucked inside her poetry notebook, none of these poems has been published.[935] Those nine months of imbalance were now firmly behind her; it seems she had regained her poise:

'Achiltibuie'

Here on this edge of Europe I stand on the edge of being.
Floating on light isle after isle takes wing.
Burning blue are the peaks, rock that is older than thought,
And the sea burns blue—or is it the air between?—
They merge, they take one another upon them.
I have fallen through time and found the enchanted world.
Where all is beginning.
The obstinate rocks
Are a fire of blue, a pulse of power, a beat
In energy, the sea dissolves
And I too melt, am timeless, a pulse of light.

(4th October 1950)

To use Nan's own description, there is magic in this poem; 'the kind that obliterates itself so that the words vanish into the thing they have conjured'.[936] It is one of her best. The surfaces Neil Gunn admired in Nan's short story, *Descent from the Cross,* are made explicit here: 'They merge, they take one another upon them'.

The poem itself works on several levels to draw the reader into the experience. The dashes are used for pause, so that the reader is halted, just as the speaker is, as they try to distinguish what is being seen. The rhythm, particularly of the last few lines, cleverly emulates the lapping of waves on the shore. Even the poem's line lengths suggest the series waves follow: a longer seven, followed by a shorter five. Sea, air, rocks—all is blurred, dissolved as the speaker also becomes one with the landscape. Here is the 'movement of being'. The following day, it seems the weather changed.

'Next Morning'

This morning the rocks are adamant—we knew they were—
Monsters, planting their feet against the gale.
The bright sea is itself, and could be no other,
Sharp and hard, cavorting and lashing its tail.

A world in the active mood, knowing the grammar of now,
The present tense, a fierce exultation of act,
No meanings that cannot be shouted, no faith but is based
On the tough, the mendacious intractable splendour of fact.

(5th Oct 1950)

All the weather's fury is depicted in this poem. Nature's unleashing of its power is as glorious as it is terrifying—the rocks and sea personified as monsters and serpent. Unlike 'Achiltibuie', where the surfaces are softened and blurred, here they are definite. In the second stanza, the play on language rules: 'grammar', 'active' and 'present tense' are all used to evoke being in the moment. 'Mendacious' and 'intractable': scientific fact would have you believe otherwise, but in the face of all this furious weather, the speaker asks, how could science and fact be anything other than lies? The double negative, 'no meanings that cannot be shouted', lends weight to this refusal to acknowledge any other interpretation of 'truth'.

'On a still morning'

I hear the silence now.
Alive within its heart
Are the sounds that can not be heard
That the ear may not dispart?

As white light gathers all –
The rose and the amethyst,
The ice-green and the copper gleam,
The peacock blue and the mist –

So if I bend my ear
To silence, I grow aware
The stir of sounds I have almost heard
That are not quite there.

(6th Oct 1950)

Standing in the silence on the plateau, 'I become aware that the silence is not complete', Nan Shepherd wrote in *The Living Mountain*.[937] While 'On a still morning', with its 'stir of sounds…not quite there', plays again with this idea it is surely more about the glimpse of knowledge that comes through all the senses, prismatic within the 'white light' of crystal. To accept the silence, when the voices in one's head cease, is to bend your ear to the 'movements of being', the poem appears to suggest.

There is something of John Cage's 4'33" here. A composition of varying lengths of time, it does not rely on sounds themselves to create structure, it simply *is*, with or without any noise that might have been made during its performance. Silence was an endless source of inspiration for Cage in the 1950s—one of his most prolific periods. Out of it, the music welled into being in a way that sounds remarkably similar to Neil Gunn's 'being told' where to go in his writing and to Nan Shepherd's feeling 'possessed'.

The last of the four poems written in 1950 is:

'Rhu Coigach'

A headland on the Atlantic

Thrusting at me the gaunt rocks cry:
This is the end, there is nothing further to know,
Here is the last foothold, the whelming wave is beyond
There is no more for the mind to undergo.

But the rocks lie: there is negation to undergo
To know oneself blank, blind, worthless, rejected, done,
A stranger in the outwash of a bitter sea.
This too must be apprehended, its savour won.

(Oct 1950)

Looking out at the headland, which appears at first to indicate an end, in the second verse the narrator of Rhu Coigach sees it is not so—there is more to be apprehended. This is echoed in *The Living Mountain*; knowledge is not total, but infinite, the journey is always on-going. And while we must be cautious about identifying the narrator of this poem with Nan Shepherd, knowing the context in which it was written, which was shortly after her mother died, it is hard to ignore the parallels. With her mother's death came an ending. Nan's life so far had been full: of love, loss of love, loss, and grief. Surely, the speaker of this poem asks, there is no more for the mind to have to endure. But as the second stanza concludes, whatever life throws next—in this case negation—those feelings of worthlessness, of nothingness, however overwhelming, must be savoured too. And there *was* grief and loss still to come.

In 1955 Mure Mackenzie died suddenly in Edinburgh. Nan wrote a portrait of her friend and comrade which was published that spring in the *Aberdeen University Review*. In it she listed Mure's considerable achievements which were all the more extraordinary given that as well as being almost totally deaf, without her glasses, Mure was as good as blind. But as Nan said, 'her mind was muscular, her judgment mature and she had the habit of hard work and fire in her bones. The recognition, however, took time'. [938]

The following year Nan retired from the staff of the Training Centre. Almost immediately Sir Thomas Taylor, then Principal of the University of Aberdeen, asked if she would take on the editorship of the *Aberdeen University Review.* Those years spent as an undergraduate as editor of the *Alma Mater,* now stood Nan in good stead. Printed from the 1950s to the 1960s by Aberdeen University Press[939] under the management of Harold Watt—for a subscription of sixteen shillings— the bi-annual *Review* was distributed free to all members of the university's alumnus association.[940] From 1956, all editorial communications were addressed to Nan at Dunvegan.

Working from home must have been an enormous change to Nan's routine after forty years of commuting during term-time to the Training Centre in Aberdeen, but the *Review* kept her busy. As well as the proof-reading and 'make-up', books for review flowed in to Dunvegan. The editorship also helped keep Nan abreast of 'literary doings'. She enjoyed the work. It was 'fun', she reported to Neil Gunn 'and enlightened me about many things in and around the University that I wouldn't have believed otherwise'.[941]

'Apparently, like yourself, I am now retired', Neil announced to Nan in 1957. His latest work, *The Atom of Delight* had been ignored by critics and 'the lave' and effectively put 'a full-stop to book-making', he told her.[942] The meaning of *Atom* was pretty much missed by all. The book was based on events in Neil's childhood but it was more philosophical meditation than autobiography—little can be gleaned from it about the man himself. Like Nan, Neil was more comfortable fictionalising autobiography in his novels. Genre-defying as *Atom* was and therefore not easily categorised which, as Neil had anticipated, offended 'the literary pure of heart', he had clearly enjoyed writing the book—an entire chapter of which he devoted to *Zen in the Art of Archery.*

From the 1950s onwards Neil was reading works on Eastern philosophy, among them Suzuki's essays, Alan Watts's *The Way of Zen* and Paul Reps's *Zen Flesh Zen Bones.* At some point Nan must have mentioned to Neil her own reading on the subject, either in letters no longer extant or during one of their meetings, because in this letter of his written in 1957, Neil reminds her how much 'ideas' meant to her in her formative years. Whereas, for him, they were not so valuable:

> From the beginning systems of philosophy or psychology were troublesome to me for two reasons: because my mind could not accept premises and so got bored, and because they did not necessarily stem from their author's experiences. So

I thought I would write something that did, and even use the earliest experiences to show they persisted and interpreted the later ones. Which took me into some weird fields, I admit. [943]

He still felt it had been worth it, however, just as he still hoped for at least one decent review.

Nan had struggled with Neil's *Other Landscape* which had appeared in 1954. It was not one of his better books, she thought, and said so:

I have to admit that its surrender to me was only partial. I understood the 'other landscape' yes. Yet the fable of the tale seemed to me to be struggling to express either something that wasn't in it, or else something I can't understand. I can get through to the other landscape, but I can't get through by the particular door you open here. [944]

But Nan understood exactly what Neil was attempting in *Atom* and quoted tracts of his work to demonstrate it in her letter to him. 'How much I do delight in your quotations', Gunn replied, 'for they show you were there with me' and once again, he remarked on their twinned minds: 'it is a rare country to have someone with the recognising mind in and even alongside. So you just watch your step'. [945] She did: the disappointing reaction to *Atom* just proved that her own genre-blurring, philosophical meditation was best left tucked in its drawer.

She was still writing, however. In 1959 she published 'Wild Geese in Callater' in *The Deeside Field*. She had written articles for the magazine before, including the 'Colours of Deeside' in 1938. That piece appears to be a kind of pre-writing for *The Living Mountain* and 'Wild Geese' takes an episode recounted in the book and expands on it.

A gamekeeper she does not name (but who was most likely Sandy Mackenzie, the 'mighty gamekeeper on the Rothiemurchus side' of the Cairngorms) once told Nan that on the night of every fifteenth of October, hundreds of migrating geese descend upon Loch Einach, [946] 'filling its hollow with the rushing of their wings'. There, they pause on their journey from the north-west, he said, and urged her to go. Nan had never gone to Loch Einach on the fifteenth of October and had no idea if the date was correct, but she was, of course, entranced by the idea that this was some kind of 'ancient earth-magic, the creatures obeying the turning of the earth in its orbit'. It was not unusual to see flocks of geese flying towards the south at that time of year. Nan had once spent an entire October day that was punctuated by their 'harsh, alien cry' in Glen Einach, but she never saw Sandy's birds.

In 'Wild Geese', she describes the flight of those she *has* seen on a blustering October day in Glen Callater. Although there is a discrepancy between the two versions in the number of geese, it is the same episode she recounts in *The Living Mountain*. Rather than retrieve her manuscript from its hiding place she apparently reconstructed the incident from memory. Having clambered up to the watershed only to be 'buffeted and mishandled' by the gale raging from the south, Nan soon dropped down once more to the shelter of the valley-head. It was then that she saw the geese, flying quite low, on the other side of the water. 'They made a handsome phalanx, some eighty strong, in perfect formation, steady and straight, with a sharp clean arrow-head'.

Passing the point where Nan was standing, the geese reached the watershed—and the wind. As she watched:

> ...the point of the arrow was blunted, the leading bird swerved to the right, the next two or three bunched together, then a new bird struck out as the leader and the line went on: but only for a moment—the new leader also swerved, the birds bunched, another individual took over the leadership and the line again went on, straight and true. But again the leader swerved and the birds bunched for a moment till yet another flew ahead and the formation righted itself. The birds, however, had had enough. When the fourth leader swung right about each bird wheeled along with her—or was it him? a youngster learning the game? Without disorder, so swiftly that one had hardly seen it happen, they were again in clean sharp formation, back down the valley they had just come up.[947]

Then, so swiftly that Nan could hardly believe she had seen it happen, the geese were once again flying in a 'clean, sharp formation' back down the valley from which they had just come. 'On the far side of the water a diaphanous cloud had gathered and the birds flew into it. I strained my eyes to watch them, but they grew fainter and fainter, now a silverpoint, at last a wraith, a memory of shape—I could not have sworn that I was still seeing them', Nan said. She had no idea where they went, nor at which loch or tarn they eventually landed, nor even how long they were diverted from their course. What stayed with her, however, was the ease and purpose in their deflected flight. 'The birds faded out into the cloud like an embodiment of mystery; they came and they were gone'.[948]

As the same episode was related in *The Living Mountain* it most likely occurred between 1928 and 1943, in which case Nan can be forgiven for the inaccuracy and embellishment of the number of geese (which in her hill book number twenty-seven). The description is more concise and arguably more compelling in *The Living Mountain*: 'they flew into a cinder-grey cloud, in an undulating line like the movement of a fish under water'[949] but either way, it was a memory she had retained ever since.

The sight of geese in flight never failed to move her. Hearing their honk overhead would be enough to set her searching the sky for a glimpse. One wintry morning, not long before she wrote 'Wild Geese', a skein passed so close over her head as she stood at the door of Dunvegan, that she could count the individual birds. 'There were ninety-six of them, one edge of the plough-share more than twice the length of the other'.[950] These living encounters, moments of bird or animal life that crossed moments of Nan's,[951] were a vital reconnection, reinforcing her sense of interrelatedness with the universe. This was not something that could be learned from books. In those encounters, as she says in 'Wild Geese' all the 'primeval forces are there, made for a moment visible'.[952]

Chapter Thirteen

1960-1970

960 opened with an ending. Grierson was dead. Nan wrote an obituary of her beloved Professor for the *Review* which was published that Spring.[953] A few months before his death, she had made the journey from Aberdeen to Cambridge to visit him. Aged ninety, the legend that was Professor Grierson was still sprightly despite a body progressively crippled by arthritis. In a photograph of him taken then, he is standing, supported by a walking stick in each hand, a little stooped around the shoulders perhaps, but dapper, a crisp, white handkerchief in the breast pocket of his suit. In another, later close-up of Grierson, although by now almost bald and his face furrowed further, his eyes, behind his familiar round rimmed spectacles, remain alert.

By Nan's visit, Grierson's arthritis had confined him to a downstairs room in the nursing home. His mind, too, had grown fragile and intermittently lost its moorings: 'the bush without the burning', she described him in his obituary. The bright, burning bush was a trope Nan had explored in a poem written in February 1933 and included in *In the Cairngorms*. She refers to it because it was the image of Grierson as she remembered him from his Aberdeen days, as all bright light, the man himself at once consumed, eclipsed and irradiated by the fire of his own intelligence. The bush, too, is resonant of the tree of knowledge and it was Grierson's mind, his intellectual passion, that hooked Nan:

> In that pure ecstasy of light
> The bush is burning bright.
> Its substance is consumed away
> And only form doth stay,
> Form as of boughs, but boughs of fire,
> That flicker and aspire.[954]

But during her visit, Grierson, Nan said, could be recalled readily enough, 'if one had the right magic'. Clearly she did: the word 'Aberdeen' was all the anchor she needed to bring Grierson back. Eager and animated, his voice strong and resonant, his corrugated face creased further with laughter as he talked of his days in Aberdeen.[955] As he acknowledged in his autobiography, the last two or three years of his work at Aberdeen University, which coincided with Nan's time there as an undergraduate, were the happiest period of his life.[956] Then, a matter of months after Grierson's death, Nan saw for the last time another man who had made an impact on her and who she also immortalised in her writing.

In 1960, the Deeside Field Club celebrated its fortieth anniversary with the presentation of a fifty-one inch stone pillar bearing a landscape indicator which was installed high above Braemar, on Morrone. Around the indicator's circular top, from its central compass radiates a key to the location of a wide sweep of Cairngorm peaks, the meanings of their names, their heights above sea level and their distances from the indicator, as well as the club's coat of arms and lines by the poet George Stephen. Under an ominous sky as many as two hundred of the club's town and gown members—doctors, lawyers, teachers and Deeside estate owners—tramped up the hillside through the Birkwoods to a lower slope of Morrone to watch the unveiling.

As they stood among the heather and juniper waiting for the ceremony to begin, drenching rain came suddenly and—just as suddenly—stopped. Then, not to be outdone, precisely at the moment Major Gordon unveiled the indicator, the elements put on their own show and a rainbow arced its way over the Quhoich valley.[957] Not that Nan would have cared. She disliked rainbows. Their smug regularity annoyed her. The less obvious, more rarely discerned, was more beautiful and valuable to Nan Shepherd. The only 'rainbow colouring' she cared for was the one found 'in spray', or 'on broken edges of cloud', or best of all, 'in the broch around the moon'.[958]

1960 was the year Nan last set eyes on Jimmy MacGregor. He was already a stricken man. 'The swiftness had gone. Speech and movement were slow and difficult', she said later. That autumn, she was staying at Braeview once again with the MacGregors and was sitting with them at their fireside, when their niece burst in. A long line of stags was passing on the face of Morrone, she told them. Leaving the old man by the fire, Nan and Amelia MacGregor charged up the hill to stand at the top gate and watch:

> The stags stood out against the sky, then disappeared into a dip. We were about to turn away when they appeared again, taking the next flank of the hill with a perfection of grace. We stayed on, watching. Then I was aware that James MacGregor

too was with us. He had made his slow painful way up to see
again a sight seen a thousand times and still desirable.[959]

It was a good last memory of this man of whom Nan had grown so
fond. He died a few days after Christmas and is buried in the cemetery
you pass on the road on the way into Braemar. From there you can see
Morrone rearing its head and just make out the brick-red roof of the
recently restored croft above Braeview, the house 'up-by', which was
home to Jimmy's forebears, the Downies.

But 1960 was not all gloom; there was good news too. The
Shetlanders were soon to be Shetlanders no more. Their house was on
the market; Sheila had found a house in Banchory they wanted to buy.
Nan was cheered by the thought of having her 'adopted' family closer
to home and reported the news, excitedly, to Helen Cruickshank.[960] In
June, she managed to fit in a visit to Loch Toridon before the Clous-
tons came to stay and 'time fizzled up'. From then on she was kept
busy with a special edition of the *Review*. It was to be the highlight of
Nan's years as editor of the magazine.

That year, the University was celebrating the Centenary of the
fusion of Aberdeen's two colleges, King's and Marischal. Nan's idea for
this centenary issue was inspired. Collecting and collating a survey of
the staff, from Principals to Sacrists and Servitors of Aberdeen University over the hundred year period, using contemporary stories and
reminiscences as well as drawing from old class records and early issues
of the *Review* and *Alma Mater,* she produced a magazine that was not
only riveting to read, but which became a valuable historical document.
So successful was her Centenary Review, it was published, in toto, in
1963 as Part Four of *The Fusion of 1860: A Record of the Centenary
Celebrations and a History of the University of Aberdeen 1860-1960.*

In April 1961 Cuthbert Graham started a weekly poetry corner
in the Saturday magazine of the *Aberdeen Press & Journal*. The idea was
to publish new verse by living writers in the North East of Scotland,
but so that this new work should be seen in the context of a long
and distinctive cultural tradition, Graham included many well-known
poems from the past. These, he hoped, 'the young people of the region
would feel to be somehow part of their background'.[961] The *North
East Muse*, as Graham's poetry corner was called, became compulsive reading. His choice of works had readers like the poet Flora
Garry, reaching for her scissors on a Saturday morning to add another
clipping to her growing pile.

Gin I canna win through to the man in the street,
The wife by the hearth,
A' the cleverness on earth'll no mak' up
For the damnable earth[962]

So runs MacDiarmid's oft-quoted quatrain. Yet to 'win through', to be 'spoken in the factories and fields' and 'in the streets o' the toon'[963], a poet has to be made accessible. This is exactly what Graham did. Down from the dusty shelves of libraries and bookshops came the words of forgotten poets of the North East, to be pushed through letterboxes and on to Aberdeenshire breakfast tables on Saturday mornings.[964] Not only did Graham's 'corner' make poetry more accessible, he provided a valuable platform for those poets whose work he printed. For some, it was the first time their verses had seen the light of day. But it was useful, too, to others, like Nan Shepherd who may have been better-established, but whose work by 1961, was slipping into obscurity.

What was also so important about the *North East Muse,* as Flora Garry pointed out, was that it reminded Aberdonians of their origins. 'The North East produces a special breed of folk, whether we live in Auchnagatt, Birmingham or Kalamazoo. We're a distinct racial group, bound together by ways of work and thought, by traditions, by a speech that refuses to die,'[965] she said. And as Graham's *Muse* proved, week in, week out, the vernacular was still very much alive. Many of the younger poets were writing in Doric. In 1970, Cuthbert Graham was heartened to see the vernacular verse written by the *North East Muse's* youngest ever contributor, who was aged twelve. 'Certainly', he remarked, 'the idea that the use of the Doric is inimical to intellectual force or subtlety ought by now to be killed stone dead'.[966]

So popular was the *North East Muse* that in 1977 an anthology was printed. Nan's 'Loch Avon' and 'A Girl in Love' were included, neither of which were in Doric, but then only three of her *In the Cairngorms* verses *were* in the vernacular. Nan, though, was tiring of the debate. 'One can talk and talk and get nowhere' she said in a letter to Helen Cruickshank.[967] She was still one of MacDiarmid's staunchest advocates and took the trouble to write, telling him how pleased she was so many of the Aberdeen undergraduates students gave their allegiance to him in a university debate in November 1960,[968] but the following year, for Nan, was a silent one.

In August 1961, after her pulse had been 'playing some silly tricks for a while', she was referred to a specialist who whisked her off to Foresterhill Hospital. There, she was subjected to so many different tests that, as she joked to Helen, she thought the doctor 'must now know everything about me except why I am.' [969] After a cardiograph, blood tests, a radio-iodine test in case her thyroid had gone toxic again (luckily it hadn't) a chest and throat x-ray and finally, a Barium meal, Nan was sent home to Dunvegan to rest.

There she waited anxiously to hear whether or not she would have to forgo her usual week at the Edinburgh Festival. A regular festival-goer since its inception in 1947, Nan had been looking forward to that year's programme—the Joseph Epstein memorial exhibition in particular—and having booked her week of events as far back as March she was keen not to miss it. In the end, she was allowed to go, on doctor's orders to 'live with the utmost rectitude'[970] and not to attempt to see any of her friends. So while she forfeited her usual 'pow-wow' over the latest 'doings' of the 'literary elite' with Helen, at least she did not miss out on the sight of Epstein's muscular, winged 'St Michael' suspended via scaffolding over Waverley Market.[971]

Post-festival and back in Cults, Nan was still under strict instructions to take things easy but with the University Press breathing down her neck over the Autumn issue of the *Review,* September and October 1961 were busy. Reaching the point where it was taking her a week to do what normally she would have run through in an evening, she was forced to out-source the work on the galley proofs of that edition.

That winter, Nan went into hibernation, venturing out to nothing but Saltire meetings (only because by then she was Chairman, otherwise she would have cut them) and the occasional Chamber concert. By Easter 1962 she still had little energy. She tired quickly and was unable to do anything strenuous. 'But what the hell', she wrote to Helen Cruickshank, 'I'm nearly seventy and can surely go down the hill as gaily as I climbed it'. Claiming to have enjoyed her 'silent year', she remarked, 'it's wonderful how little one really needs the dash of the world'.[972]

In early June 1962 she rallied sufficiently to take a holiday with Jean and Grant Roger in Kintail, at the head of Loch Duich. It was new territory for her and while she could no longer climb the heights, there was still plenty for her to see and explore. She and Mary were then kept busy entertaining Sheila's youngest boys, Magnus and John, who came to stay at Dunvegan for the last fortnight in June. A photograph taken then shows a pale and skinny but still smiling Nan. Holding on to a tree for support, she is standing in the river with boys who are fishing with makeshift tackle: string for lines and sticks for rods.

September brought endless rain and walloping winds. The garden at Dunvegan was a jungle. Nan worked in it when it stopped raining—it rained again and she would go back to find a new crop of weeds in possession of it. And like those dry-spells between showers, Nan's good-health was short-lived.

The following Easter of 1963 she 'nearly went over the edge' as she described it. On Good Friday, a couple of days after what would turn out to be her last public appearance at the Saltire conference, Nan collapsed. Snatched up by ambulance, she was rushed into hospital for an emergency operation where surgeons, as she put it to Neil Gunn, 'hawked out a bit of her insides'. Quite what this 'bit' was, we do not know (it could not have been her appendix as this had already been 'hawked out' during her late thirties) and Nan does not elaborate in her letters to Neil Gunn and Helen Cruickshank on the subject. But then, in those days, it was not 'done' to discuss this sort of thing in detail. To Helen, Nan made light of her ordeal, masking her disappointment over a trip to Rome planned, originally, for the following week: 'It was pretty sensible to do my collapse before I went away instead of in some odd corner of the Italian landscape. It might quite literally have been See Naples and die!'[973]

Die, she did not. But it was a slow climb back to normal life. Lassitude leaks through the lines of her letter to Helen in July 1963. 'Lying on my garden chair in a blaze of evening sun which has followed a day of gloom and rain and my writing pad has gone done except for one sheet which to my consternation turns out to contain the beginning of a letter I had never finished...', she wrote. Unable to summon the energy to fetch another pad from the house, she carried on her letter to Helen on the one to 'Mary' that she had begun, crossing out the two lines and the address and continuing on the 'dishonoured page'.[974]

Although Nan made it to the Edinburgh Festival that year and even managed a ten-day holiday in Rothiemurchus, she was still 'badly fagged', she said. 'I don't want to use my wits at all but just potter doing the lighter garden jobs. And on Monday I have to go to Echt twelve miles away to talk to the Women's Guild, alackaday and still alackaday partake of tea beforehand at the Manse. How can one make hostesses understand that taking a hospitable meal is purgatory'.[975]

September of 1963 found Nan, as usual, in the thick of proofreading and make-up for the Autumn *Review*. Much as she had enjoyed her seven years as editor and learnt a great deal about things in and around the University she would never have believed in otherwise,[976] she was beginning to find a lot of drudgery in the work, which she could no longer now take in her stride. She thought she would relinquish editorship of the magazine, once the Autumn issue was out. 'It's become too much for my ageing body!' she explained to Jessie Kesson.[977]

Nan Shepherd was now seventy years old. After the 1963 Autumn issue of the *Review* was published, she did give up its editorship. To that last edition, celebrating the Jubilee of the University Review (1913-1963) she contributed an article of her own. 'Aberdonian Salt stings best in the Aberdonian Tongue' she says, her pride palpable in the piece. Graduate after graduate shows here how well he remembers the true taste of that speech', she goes on and then lists those whose works had been printed in the *Review*. Among those contributions, she mentions Flora Garry's 'Tib Tocher's Dochter', 'with its inimitable evocation of the vanished life led by Professor's Ladies in the far-off days when the speaker was a student of King's and the later, soberer days when she was merely a professor's wife'.[978]

Nan, too, had been a student of King's in those far-off days when female undergraduates were still relatively novel. In 1964, seventy two years after women were first admitted to the University of Aberdeen, the first female professor was appointed. That same year, Nan Shepherd joined the ranks of the scarlet gowns. Recognising the contribution she had made to education, as well as her years as editor of the Review, the University of Aberdeen conferred on Nan Shepherd the honorary degree of LL.D.[979]

Congratulations poured in. Will Christie penned 'Nunc est Bibendum'[980] honouring Nan's achievement, a poem which obviously tickled her as it escaped her 'pitching out' session and made it into her archive:

> My Nannie's awa, my Nannie's awa,
> She's nae langer Nan, but a DOCTOR sae braw[981]
> Is the news that cam' dirlin' throu' fluckkers o' snaw.
> Her goun will be scarlet, blue-braidit at that,
> Wi' a black velvet bonnet instead o' a hat—
> She'll wear LL.D wi' an unco[982] éclat
> Fu' crouse may we craw[983]![984]

Neil Gunn wrote to Nan on the 19th July, the day he learned of the news:

> I was delighted to see your name among the learned Doctors in today's *Scotsman*. Some considerable time ago I remember having a talk with the late Professor Rex Night[985] and strongly backing his notion that you should be so honoured. We are at last in the same class![986]

It had been a while since Neil had been in touch and during that time Daisy had died. Nan, of course, had written as soon as she heard. 'I got your letter of understanding when my wife died, & put it aside from many, & then having answered it involuntarily in my mind I thought I had written it and am still uncertain', he explained. Neil was not well. An operation two and half years earlier had left him tired and he was still undergoing tests. 'However, I can still float out into things', he wrote, adding, 'in this, we have always gone the same way, & it's a way with silent companionship in it. So if I didn't really write to you, still I did'.[987]

'No, you didn't writer earlier but that was no matter. It wasn't needed,' Nan replied by return, pleased to hear from him, nonetheless. 'How good of you to welcome the new girl to the class of Canon and Civic Law! I still think it quite fantastic to be there although it hasn't made any difference to me that I've been able to fathom'.[988]

Whether it made any difference to her or not, Dr Anna Shepherd was always quick to point out that her LL.D was conferred. 'What did you do your PhD in?' Cameron Donaldson, a close friend and neighbour in the 1970s, asked Nan one day when they were out walking together. She stopped and turned to him: 'I didn't *do* a PhD. Mine was an honorary degree'. 'That was me put in my place', Cameron laughed. 'Oh, she could be very direct, Miss Shepherd. And that was fine'.[989]

Excitement over the degree aside, although Nan was well again, her doctors were still insisting she limit her activities. This was frustrating her. 'I still want to do a lot of living', she railed in a letter to Neil Gunn that summer of 1964, her usually neat, regular handwriting spiky with indignation, the words running into one another. She was, however, enjoying having her thoughts to herself once more:

I can again just <u>be</u>. A cessation of doing in which one begins to know being. Frightening sometimes. One rushes off to do things in order to escape from it. As though human nature were fit for such a miracle as contemplation! There's one thing about a body that doesn't function aught: it gives you leisure from too much activity, and at the same time pulls you back by its demands from too deep an immersion in Being.[990]

Typically, of course, Nan could not stand to be inactive for long and although she had given up work on the *Review*, she was finding ways to escape too much contemplation.

In December 1962, the poet John C Milne died suddenly. He and Nan were close. They had known one another for years. A contemporary of hers at Aberdeen University, Milne was later also a colleague at the Training Centre where he was Master of Method. As well as being Godmother to his daughter, Nan also became a member of his memorial committee. In addition to Milne's Doric verse collected in 'The Orra Loon', which had been published in 1946, he left behind enough work for another volume of poetry, none of which had been revised for the press.

Nan took on the task of arranging, discarding and undertaking all the minutiae of being an editor and in 1963 Milne's *Collected Poems* was published by the Aberdeen University Press. She did a good job. If Nan had grown tired of the Doric debate, she had not tired of promoting work in the Aberdeenshire dialect. The book ran through three editions, recouping the subscription monies raised by the memorial committee to fund its printing and making enough on top to give Milne's widow a sum of money too.

As a member of the Charles Murray Memorial Committee, Nan was invited to talk at the Centenary Celebrations held at Murray Park in Alford on 26th September 1964. There is no hint of fatigue in her voice. All her years of experience of public speaking are revealed in this one existing recording. Pausing for dramatic effect, unhurried, each word crystal clear and carrying across the assembled crowd, her voice is still strong and vibrant, her wit as dry and sharp as ever.

★ ★ ★

Over twenty years had passed since Nan and Jessie Kesson had 'tired the sun with talking' that day on the train, and although the two women had corresponded fairly frequently since then, in May 1962 it had been some months since Nan had heard from her. Aside from listening to one of Jessie's plays broadcast on the radio or being told about one of her television appearances—which, as she did not own a set, she missed—Nan felt out of touch. She wrote, anxious for news.

Jessie had been having a difficult time. With never a day's illness before in his life according to Jessie, Johnnie Kesson suffered two heart attacks in as many years. 1960 to 1962 was an anxious period, during which Jessie became the sole breadwinner as well as Johnnie's carer. Somehow, in between her various jobs (which included working at Woolworths as well as posing as a Life Model) and nursing Johnnie, she had managed to complete another novel. She replied to Nan's letter enclosing a copy of the manuscript of *Glitter of Mica*.

Nan was delighted to hear about the new book:

It's good to know that a sound and lovely thing can make its way in a world so given over to perverted values. And *Glitter of Mica* is a good title. I was quoting that line "glitter of mica at windy corners"—not long ago in a speech at a Glasgow/Aberdeen University luncheon.[991]

Nan praised the novel in her review: 'Mrs Kesson's art is blessedly clean and taut. She is pitiless to her words, casting out the weaklings, the redundant, the merely decorative'. But she was critical too: 'She is equally pitiless to her characters. One feels a dimension missing—perhaps the dimension of loving-kindness'.[992]

Glitter of Mica was not a great success. Reviews of the book were mixed and sales soon slowed. Understandably, Jessie was defensive about the work she had hoped to turn into a film script and disappointed when she was told it was not adaptation material. Having claimed earlier in her article 'Nan Shepherd: In Recollection' printed in *The Aberdeen University Review* in 1990 that she always accepted Nan's opinion of her work, Jessie then goes into a somewhat lengthy defence of the novel:

> She didn't approve of *Glitter of Mica*. She thought that much of its dialogue was 'coarse'. Since she was neither a prig nor narrow-minded I knew that she genuinely felt that to be so. I didn't accept that. Nor was I offended. I think I understood the reason for her opinion. *She* herself also knew country workers well, their way of life, their Doric tongue. *She* would have been at ease in their company. But to refer again to Wifies and Ladies, *they* might not have been quite so much at ease in *her* company. Recognising her as a Lady and educated, out of respect for that, they would not have been so forthcoming in their language. She might never have heard them use the strong words we used automatically in our daily lives. Words never intended to be blasphemous, but used simply as emphasis—God Almichty, Good God, By God, and God Be Here. Equally, in a sexual context, our words were down to earth and uninhibited, '*clean* dirt'. An accurate description.[993]

Of course this is entirely possible. But Jessie seems to be forgetting that Nan Shepherd had lived for many years with Mary Lawson. Mary with her 'tongue that could clip clouts' was certainly forthcoming in the language she used around Nan. It was from Mary that Nan learnt some of her 'saltiest' phrases and slotted them into her own works.

Perhaps because she felt Jessie had enough to worry about with

Johnnie's ill-health, Nan made no mention of her own spate of serious illnesses. She kept writing, asking after Johnnie, how Jessie's work was going and if she had managed to place any.[994] As well as her constant literary encouragement, it was those other little touches of Nan's, too, that Jessie was to remember:

> Never a letter reached me in London but came with a token flower from that garden. She had imaginative kindness, not simply confined to the giving of seasonal gifts but rather to gifts in season. A lambswool scarf would arrive, "to keep your neck warm now that cauldrife Winter is here".[995]

The years from 1964 onwards were quiet ones. Other than keeping up with her correspondence and making the occasional public appearance, from 1964 Nan still seemed not to need the dash of the world—which was just as well. In February 1966 Cults station closed to passenger traffic, leaving Nan completely reliant on the bus service running to and from Cults into town. She was still to be seen out on the tramp though and often went from Dunvegan across to the other side of the Dee, via the Shakkin' Brigie, as far as Blairs College and back.

On one of these walks, time turned back. A visit to Lupin Island, which lay on this route just off the south bank of the Dee halfway between Ardoe and the Shakkin' Brig, had been a rite of early summer during Nan's childhood. In the years following the October 1920 spate which had stripped the islet of its flowers, the river breached the parapet between the bridge and the south road, washing up an enormous bank of stone on to the north side. The main current poured on to the south pier instead of between the piers and the bridge became unsafe to use. A bulldozer shifted the washed up shingle, leaving it piled in an island so that the current broke on it forcing it once again between the bridge piers. In 1963 the islet was still bare shingle. The following year it flushed with green and in May 1965, out walking, Nan was startled to find the island once again ablaze with lupins. She *had* thought these were somehow her old lupins, restored to life, seeds, roots, miraculously resurrected. Of course Grant Roger put her right. This was a fresh colony of plants, the empty shingle lying just out of the river's reach—the perfect place for a fresh crop of seeds carried downstream to germinate.[996]

Nevertheless, the sight provoked Nan into picking up her pen again. In the Autumn of 1965 she wrote a short piece called 'The Lupin Island' which was published the following year in *The Deeside Field* magazine. At the time, the future of the Shakkin' Brig was uncertain. It still is.[997] But as Nan said in her article, at least the efforts to save it had restored the lupins.

The sight of the lupins may have reinvigorated her, but towards the end of the 1960s Nan's health was still precarious. 1968 was a quiet year. Spring came in late March. Weeks of sunshine produced masses of flowers and then suddenly winter barked back, with snow on the ground and blustering winds. Nan was destabilised by a series of 'silly little accidents', as she called them. None of them were serious, she said, although they had resulted in a broken nose and a glorious black eye, 'but one coming just when the one before was concluding its effects resulted in a summer when I never felt really free!'[998] She missed the Edinburgh Festival that year. In mid-December, when darkness descended so early that on some days it never seemed light at all, she wrote to fellow Scot and writer Edith Robertson.

The two women had known one another since 1931 when Nan, who at the time was immersed in her own verse-writing, had come across Robertson's work and written to compliment her, particularly on her lyrics. 'They have a rhythm so quiet and yet so powerful—like the movement of a brimmed river',[999] she said, illustrating her own talent for imagery. The two writers shared an interest in the culture and language of the North East and during Nan's years as editor of the *Review* she had done her best to print Robertson's work in the magazine. Hampered by restrictions on space caused by soaring printing costs in 1961, however, Nan had been forced to turn down one of her lengthier poems. She was delighted, then, in 1968, when two collections of Edith Robertson's work appeared in print.[1000] 'I hope you have had some real satisfaction from your published volumes', Nan began a letter to her in December 1968. What followed, however, reveals Nan's own state of mind:

> Is the creative urge still working? I think you are a wonderful creature not to lose your spiritual and mental élan. I feel so flattened in my old age! Living at a low tempo and achieving nothing—except the production of a few flowers in my garden and a few visits to people older than myself.[1001]

Nan's body was letting her down. Her roaming restricted, her hill walking days long behind her, she felt spiritually, mentally and creatively stifled too.

★ ★ ★

After much exploratory drilling in the hostile waters of the North Sea, in December 1969 commercial quantities of oil were discovered at the Montrose Field, about 135 miles east of Aberdeen.[1002] The oil boom began, swelling the economy of Aberdeen as well as its population. Leafy Cults, perched on the banks of the Dee, with its recently built secondary school,[1003] its nucleus of convenient shops and its proximity to the city as well as to the curve of beach four miles east at Aberdeen, was bound to be a sought-after area. Property developers swooped. 'Aberdeen grows taller and taller and Cults is no longer a village', Nan wrote disconsolately to Edith Robertson. 'The houses stretch up and up the hill as far as my childhood's playground, the Quarry Wood'.[1004]

Saddened by the changes wrought on Cults, Nan was relieved that most of the building was going on behind Dunvegan, 'at least they can't build up my view in front, where the ground goes down too steeply to the river. So I still rejoice in space and distance and the sky'.[1005]

Development has continued since Nan's death in 1981. There has been some building below the old Deeside Railway Line; however, it is the trees lining it which have grown taller and taller and now obscure some of her view of space and sky. But Nan was not to know this then and, in any case, she soon had a more pressing preoccupation.

Chapter Fourteen

1971-1978

1 971 was an odd sort of year. It began with the postal strike lasting from January to March and, in the meantime, Britain went decimal. As soon as the strike was over, Nan had pictured herself rushing to resume contact with all those friends with whom she hadn't been in touch by phone. 'But the disinclination to write grows on me', she confided to Helen Cruickshank, when she finally put pen to paper that April.

Aside from the Lewis Grassic Gibbon Exhibition in the Aberdeen Art Gallery, which was timed to coincide with the first airing of *Sunset Song* on television, 'nothing much happens up here', she said. Hundreds had poured into the gallery for the exhibition. Nan, however, was no more impressed by it than she was by the television adaptation of his book, which seemed to her, 'not much above the "Both nicht" standard'.[1006] Then, shortly after Nan and Mary spent an idyllic three days with Sheila in Kermore 'up the Noran Water',[1007] something did happen.

Towards the end of April 1971, Mary, who was by then eighty-seven, was involved in a road accident which left her seriously injured. Knocked down by a car, her leg was so badly broken she spent five months recovering in hospital. Nan visited her every day. After a few weeks, when Mary's big toe went black and sores on her feet refused to heal, it looked as though an infection had set in. Nan grew anxious. Drugs to increase Mary's circulation seemed, at first, to be working and her skin began to look more human and less like 'a grey wrinkled animal's hide',[1008] as Nan described it. An x-ray revealed that despite the bone in Mary's leg having been splintered, it seemed to be healing. But Nan's relief was short-lived. The gangrene she thought they had avoided had taken hold and Mary's leg was amputated.

Given her ordeal, in the photograph of Mary being presented with her Red Cross Medal in hospital, she looks surprisingly well. Always a slight woman, she looks even slighter, although she is still impeccably neat in her quilted bed-jacket. Holding her certificate in her hand, propped against crisp pillows, her bespectacled face is turned to the camera. Judging by the gleam of amusement in her eyes and the awkwardness of the four people clustered around her bedside—as though they are uncertain laughter is appropriate in the circumstances— it looks as though she might well have been 'clipping clouts' with her tongue. It had been a while since Mary Lawson had been seen around Cults in her Red Cross uniform, but how very gratifying it must have been for her to have been rewarded for her efforts over the years.

Mary was redoubtable. Despatched from hospital towards the end of summer, she arrived back at Dunvegan with an artificial leg which she set about learning to use 'with verve and gusto', according to Nan, although she still needed a lot of attention and care. Obviously Dunvegan's stairs were now too much for Mary, so the dining room was turned into a bedroom for her. Her bed, which was positioned on the wall adjoining the wood-panelled hall, had a pulley system installed above it so that she could hoist herself up. On more than one occasion their neighbour, Cameron Donaldson, was summoned to Dunvegan because Mary had fallen and could not get up. 'I haven't had a man lift me like this in a hundred years', Mary would scream in her broad Scots accent, amid snorts of laughter all round.[1009]

Mary's accident reversed the two women's roles. At the age of seventy-eight, Nan now became full-time nurse and companion as well as housekeeper. A visitor to Dunvegan during this period remarked that 'the mistress appeared to be Mary Lawson, the servant, Dr Nan Shepherd'.[1010] Jessie Kesson said that Mary Lawson was 'much, much more than a retainer, but Nan paid the price'.[1011] However, according to Cameron Donaldson, there was never any question that Nan would not look after Mary. 'She looked after me for years, so…', Nan shrugged. Nor was there any feeling that Mary was a usurper. As far as Nan was concerned, Dunvegan was Mary's home.[1012]

Always averse to domesticity (and in any case, she was elderly herself by then) Nan enlisted help with the running of the household. A local woman came in to 'do' for her and then there was Peggy MacPherson. 'Not all there', 'man mad' and always 'plastered in heavy make-up', Peggy lived up the Quarry Road at number 19 and although she would come down to Dunvegan to help, she wasn't allowed into the house because apparently she wasn't to be trusted. 'No, no, we can't have Peggy doing that', Mary said—she was 'too rough', but she would do the windows and any exterior work needed.

'On one occasion there was a painter on a ladder outside the house,' Cameron Donaldson remembered. 'Peggy 'was up the ladder after him and Miss Shepherd called to Peggy "get off, leave the man alone!" ' [1013]

Peggy MacPherson could talk and talk. Once started it was difficult to stop her and many in Cults simply found her too much. Not Nan, who left money in her will to Peggy—a revelation which came as no surprise to Malcolm Sutherland. According to him, 'Nan liked a lot of lame ducks'.[1014] It was more than this though. As much as she was conscious of community, Nan was also fascinated by people, their quirks and qualities. Her novels are populated with such individuals whose character, however small their role in the drama, she draws deftly and swiftly, often in only a couple of lines. Annie Craigmyle in *The Weatherhouse,* is just one example: 'There was no false sentiment about Miss Annie: nothing flimsy. She was hard-knit, like a home-made worsted stocking, substantial, honest and durable.'[1015]

While Mary lived, Nan's ear was regularly tuned to the Doric.[1016] Visitors to Dunvegan remember sitting talking in the little parlour off the kitchen. Every so often Mary would butt in with some pithy comment and Nan would roll her eyes and tut. But there was no animosity. Before Mary's accident, she and Nan were visiting Malcolm and Ruth Sutherland. Just as they were about to leave, Mary stood up and starting plumping the cushions. 'You mustn't do that in other people's houses!' Nan said, laughing. Mary 'didn't give a hoot' and just carried on. No offence was taken.[1017] They were foils for one another.

Mary survived a further five years after her accident before dying of heart disease and pneumonia aged ninety-two on 21st April 1976. How strange the old house must have seemed without her. For some seventy years—most of Nan's life—Mary had been a constant presence. Fittingly, she was buried from Dunvegan, leaving Nan (who was by then eighty-three) living there alone.

Although Mary's time was not always spent in bed, those five years of nursing her must have taken their toll. Yet despite describing herself, laughingly, as 'a geriatric'[1018] to Helen Bain who visited during this period, Nan was still remarkably agile. She was 'swark', says Cameron Donaldson, out 'on the tramp' most days along the old railway line and although it was beginning to be beyond her, Nan carried on working in her garden. She was still entertaining at Dunvegan too.

For all her warmth and hospitality, however, Nan was still undomesticated. The house had no central heating and after Mary died Nan rarely lit a fire. 'She didn't bother with things like that', according to Cameron Donaldson. If he and his young sons were invited over, he would tell the boys to keep their coats on.

Nan in the garden at Dunvegan.

Nan would make sure her store of children's toys was fetched from behind the red, woollen-curtained alcove in the sitting room and laid out ready for the boys to play with, but the tea, by the time she poured it into china cups, would be stone cold.

Dunvegan is a chilly house in winter, and despite new windows and the installation of central heating, its current owners say it remains so. Apparently, Nan didn't notice the cold. She would spend her evenings reading in front of an electric fire, a Shetland blanket draped over her knees. At night, whatever the weather, she slept with her bedroom window open to the elements. But then, a battering by the elements, be it rain, wind, sleet or snow, made Nan Shepherd feel more vital, more keenly alive. That 'elemental feel' is a constant refrain, running from her first to her last work: 'Washed by the rain she felt strong and large, like a wind that tosses the Atlantic or a tide at flood—'.[1019]

In the summer, if she wasn't outside, according to Helen Low, another neighbour in the 1970s, Nan was almost always to be found pottering among her plants in her garden room, the sun porch of Barbara Balmer's painting. Barbara provided the kind of intellectually robust friendship Nan needed more than ever during this period. In the 1970s her circle of literary comrades was dramatically diminishing: Neil Gunn, Helen Cruickshank and John Macmurray all died before the decade was out.

Correspondence between Neil and Nan had dwindled during the late 1960s, but in September 1971 she wrote to him. The National Library, planning an exhibition to honour the writer on his eightieth birthday, had asked if she would lend some of Neil's letters. Digging them out and reading them again she said:

> I can see that I kept them from sheer exhilaration over the stupendous things you used to say about my work, conceited little brat that I was. But there is also in some of them some interesting light shed on your own work in progress. Am I allowed to lend these?[1020]

'It was wonderful seeing your handwriting again', Neil's reply began. 'I have often thought about you, & still think that some of your poems about 'finding yourself' in remote places are about 'the greatest', if I may use a joyous colloquialism'.[1021] Neil had been ill. A severe bout of trigeminal facial neuralgia had left him exhausted. After spending some time in hospital, it was decided not to operate and so he was back home again, he said, but weaker than ever. As for the National Library: 'give 'em what they want', he told Nan. 'I've striven against publicity, but it's no use'.[1022]

Nan wrote one last time in November 1971. Old codgers aren't we? But still with an eye to the dew and the morning'. She was sympathetic over his facial neuralgia, which is, as she said, 'a nasty, spiteful sort of pain':

> Peace to your tormented nerve-endings—Pain is somehow worse when it attacks close to the brain. I suppose a big toe could be equally painful, and disturb the mind as much, and yet it doesn't diminish one in the same way as a pain in the head—I wish one could do something to help you bear yours.[1023]

Neil deteriorated over the following year and after spells in and out of hospital, he died on 15th January 1973. At his funeral, held in the cemetery high above Dingwall near Braefarm House, the mourners were all good friends, but whether they included Nan Shepherd, is not known. It seems likely that she would have attended, if she were able. But with Mary needing so much of her time and care during that period, it just might not have been possible.

Undoubtedly Nan grieved the loss of her old friend, but it was not long until she lost another. At the beginning of the long, hot summer of 1976, only two months after Mary's death, came John Macmurray's end. He had never fully recovered from cancer surgery and towards the end of 1974 his health really began to deteriorate. He died in his bed at home surrounded by his family. A talented, remarkable man who 'did not measure easily' during his lifetime, read his obituary in *The Times*.[1024] At his funeral service and cremation held at Morton Hall Crematorium in Edinburgh on 25th June, as is traditional with Quaker services, there was no music. Betty minded about that. She insisted music was played at her own funeral in 1982.[1025] Her remains were laid alongside John's ashes in the small cemetery adjoining the Friends' Meeting House at Jordans.

The Macmurrays had moved from Jordans to Edinburgh in the early summer of 1969 and bought 8, Mansionhouse Road which they shared with Betty's nephew Duncan Campbell, his wife Jocelyn and their four children. Finally, John was able to enjoy something of the community living he had dreamed of. Although he and Betty lived in a separate section of the house, the two families ate together, the Campbell children popped into see the Macmurray's on a daily basis and the garden was very much a joint enterprise.

Nan often dropped in on the Campbell/Macmurray household when she was in Edinburgh. But with John gone, one side of their triangle went too. Betty and Nan certainly stayed in touch and met once more at least. Jocelyn Campbell drove Betty up to Aberdeenshire visiting some of her old haunts on the way and dropping in for tea at Dunvegan. But it was a fleeting visit, Jocelyn said, and what the two old friends talked about, she did not recall.[1026] It's not unreasonable to suppose that John came up in conversation. After nearly sixty years of marriage, John's death hit Betty hard. And Nan had loved him too.

In March 1972, relieved to hear that Helen Cruickshank, who had also been in hospital, was still frail but now back at home, Nan wrote to her old friend. Her letter is a mixture of comments on nature, gardening and literary affairs—those common interests which bound the two women. Enclosing a pair of silk stockings so that Helen might not feel 'laid up', she added, 'don't think I'm being extravagant,—they were a gift from someone who certainly quite correctly observed that I have big feet, but didn't allow for their skinniness. I couldn't possibly fill these out, so please wear them for me'. Knowing how much Helen loved her garden at Dinnieduff, to encourage her, Nan described the quiet optimism of spring appearing in her own:

> Are you able to go into your garden? Mine is alive, with small buds half through the earth that are to be glory of the snow and scilla and dog tooth violets in a few days' time. One piece of forsythia, one gentian—a thousand snowdrops—golden crocuses protected from the beaks of my bird population by black pepper—but the purple ones, for the first time in my experience, torn to shreds. Sheer spite, I fear.[1027]

'A report came this morning that Aberdeen is to have a PEN luncheon in June. It's the first I've heard of it', Nan continued. 'The notice says that the north-east members are arranging the luncheon and I am wondering who the north-east members are!'[1028] The Aberdeen PEN may have gone quiet, but Nan was still unflagging in her efforts to promote the work of newer writers as well as those whose work she was concerned was disappearing from the Scottish literary scene. In 1972, the Aberdeen branch of the Saltire Society asked Nan to give a talk on North East poetry in the last quarter of the century. Helen Cruickshank's *Collected Poems* had been published the year before, in 1971, and Nan wanted to include some of her work:

> Cuthbert Graham says, yes, distinctly you are part of the North East. May I use you? Read one or so of your poems? I don't know just what pattern there will be in my tapestry but it will have J C Milne, Flora Garry and George Bruce in it, and some younger men like Ken Morrice[1029] (probably quite unknown to you!).[1030]

'Be well, my dear', Nan ends. It is the last letter, dated 9th March 1972, that we have of their extant correspondence in the archives.

Helen's final years were beset by illness. A stroke in 1973 left her reliant on a zimmer-frame and despite her determination to live independently—which she did for some years—her last few months were spent in a nursing home. Even here, apparently, she entertained an endless stream of guests and managed to maintain her staggering, global correspondence with those 'from aa' the airts'. And she was still writing poetry until the very end, leaving unfinished a poem about a woman who cannot stop for death because she has too much to do. Helen died in March 1975 without seeing the publication of her memoir, *Octobiography* which appeared the following year. In its penultimate chapter she was optimistic about Scotland's literary outlook, which 'in poetry and fiction writing seems most promising'. The future of Scottish women poets, however, she did not care to predict.[1031]

In 1969, when Helen was writing her memoirs, she asked to borrow from Nan's essay on Hugh MacDiarmid. In return, she offered to help with an article Nan was putting together on the poet Marion Angus. Helen sent her a bumper bundle of the poet's letters, which, as Marion's handwriting is often almost illegible, were 'sometimes snorters to get through'[1032] and many were undated. But in Nan's reply to Helen written in February 1969 she sounds more upbeat. Clearly she was thriving on the challenge presented by the letters and by copyright issues arising from the Marion Angus article. She was enjoying writing again. February was 'a month of wild snow storms followed by a sudden slushy sloppy thaw,' but the sap was rising, as she was wont to say to her Shetlanders.[1033] 'There are snowdrops galore and hundreds of aconites and a few primroses and hepaticas. So spring will come'.[1034]

The Marion Angus article was not the first one Nan had written about the poet. In 1947, a year after Marion's death, *The Scotsman* had published Nan's tribute to her. This second piece was prompted by a conversation with Marion's cousin, Tyrone Guthrie, who had asked Nan if Angus's work was still read and if she thought it would last. 'Deeside place-names, burns and hills, sing their way into her lyrics on page after page, and when people quote Deeside they always seem to leave her out', Nan complained to Helen Cruickshank.[1035] The article was Nan's way of rectifying this. 'Poet of Deeside', as it was called, appeared in the jubilee edition of *The Deeside Field* magazine in 1970 and is as sensitive and perceptive as her piece for *The Scotsman*. Marion's letters, Nan lodged with the Aberdeen University library, hopeful, as she said to Helen, that:

> if anyone in the future should wish to write a thesis on Marion Angus[1036] or even include her in a thesis, there would be matter here for such work...Some day I suppose someone will put you in a thesis...odd to think that a few hundred years hence Marion Angus and you may be dug out of oblivion together.[1037]

But what of Nan Shepherd? She makes no mention of her own contribution to literature. Helen Cruickshank, Marion Angus and Mure Mackenzie, whose letters to her Nan also deposited with Aberdeen University, were not the only ones, surely, she hoped would be dug out of oblivion. As Hugh Walpole had predicted in June 1928, along with several other writers' works Nan Shepherd's novels had been buried almost as soon as they were born: 'Of *The Quarry Wood* I have seen only one review. For three of these novels I asked at three of our leading London bookshops; there was not a copy to be had nor had any of three booksellers whom I questioned heard of them'. This would not have astonished him if they were negligible works, but in his opinion *The Quarry Wood,* for one, was not: '*The Quarry Wood* has some poetic descriptions of nature in it which are a real addition to English literature; it is honest, courageous and unsentimental'.

'Now you may say,' Walpole continued, 'good work always comes to the top;' meaning that, even if these women writers had not won full recognition with their first books, they only had to persevere and success would come. But in 1928 that was no longer true, he said. These women will perhaps write three or four novels but 'the reviews will remain few, the advertisements fewer, the sales fewer yet; they will receive perhaps recognition from a small inner group who are passionately interested in literature'.[1038] How eerily prophetic his pronouncement turned out to be. By the late 1960s Shepherd's three novels and poetry anthology were all out of print. Like Marion Angus, Mure Mackenzie and many others, Nan Shepherd, too, seemed to have disappeared from the literary landscape and been forgotten.[1039]

Towards the end of 1976, Nan tripped and fell against her armchair, hurting her shoulder. Carted off to hospital, an oxygen mask was held over her face while the doctor re-set her shoulder. 'We wouldn't do this for a younger person' she heard the nurse say, 'but with an auld craitur like this…'. It seems extraordinarily rude to say this in Nan's hearing. Clearly the nurse assumed that because Nan was elderly, she must be deaf too. But this insensitivity met with Nan's usual wry humour: 'I have a real chip on my shoulder now', she chuckled to Sheila Hamilton, the journalist who came to interview her at Dunvegan in the winter of 1976.

Hamilton had turned up that day determined to find answers to her questions, only to be left, like so many journalists before her, frustrated by Nan's reticence. 'Over 40 years ago, Nan Shepherd was acclaimed as a writer of genius', Hamilton's article begins, continuing:

> "That's what you call a passing reputation," shrugs Miss Shepherd, a twinkle in her eye. You get the impression that it doesn't really matter that much to her. Although she is a

well known and highly respected figure in literary circles Miss Shepherd (83) might be termed the forgotten authoress of Cults.

In a letter to Nan written in 1959, the poet Rachel Annand Taylor had asked 'Why, I wonder, did you give up literature so early?'[1040] In 1976, Hamilton posed the question again answering it, initially, with a quotation gleaned from Dunnett's 1933 feature on Nan: 'She once confessed that she didn't really like writing and only wrote when she felt there was something which simply had to be written'.[1041] Dunnett's article was among the press cuttings kept by Jeannie Shepherd which Nan, rather reluctantly, brought out during the interview saying that she hadn't seen some of them. Waving them around laughing, Nan seemed surprised: 'I had some extremely good reviews', Hamilton reported her saying, 'reading out snippets as if they were about some other person's work, not her own'. 'Such accolades', Hamilton remarked, 'and yet since the thirties, Miss Shepherd has published no major works'. But during that interview, when she asked Nan the question again, directly, Nan apparently admitted, 'it just didn't come to me anymore'. Having been stonewalled, even if gently and wryly, Hamilton then comes to her own conclusion: 'Writer of genius gave up' ran the headline of her article printed on 15th December 1976 in the *Aberdeen Evening Express.*[1042]

How that headline must have pricked. Nan Shepherd may not have published any major works since the 1930s, but she had not given up writing. In addition to the articles printed during the intervening years in the *Scots Magazine, The Scotsman, The Deeside Field* and the *Aberdeen University Review,* there was her short story, *Descent from the Cross,* the four unpublished poems written in the 1950s and, of course, there was *The Living Mountain.*

Hamilton's probing, however, resulted in more than Nan usually gave away—even to some of her closest friends. As well as the press cuttings, she was even persuaded to fetch copies of her books, kept on the little bookcase in her bedroom. Nowhere, however, in Hamilton's article is there any reference to *The Living Mountain.*

Yet even before that interview, *The Living Mountain* had been on Nan's mind. In her last letter to Neil Gunn, written in 1971, she said, 'Do you remember once saying the world wasn't ready for the well-water? They didn't know they needed it?'[1043] Neil's own philosophical meditation, *The Atom of Delight* had been misunderstood and pretty much ignored by critics in 1957. By the 1970s, however, the West was much more receptive to Eastern thought and, as Neil rather delightedly reported in a letter to Nan, to finding 'other means of inducing "transcendental state".

'I have done a fair amount of reading on the "revelations" that follow on a dose of a certain drug (Aldous Huxley was quite interesting about this experience)', he said. But Neil felt this was a 'false samadhi': 'the more you experience of the genuine light or enlightenment the more profoundly it irradiates even the flesh; whereas the more drugs the more diseased the flesh (& mind) becomes'.[1044]

Such moments of enlightenment, for Nan, in the early 1970s were fewer than they used to be. 'Does one lose the power, or the sensitivity?'[1045] she asked Neil. His response was to suggest that if she had cultivated the habit of enjoying the light, 'the light will be there in the dark moments', adding that if she felt the light was diminishing she had only reread one of her old poems, '& sit still in the middle of it'.[1046] By 1971, Neil's writing was achieving the recognition it deserved. 'Two professors (one American, one Japanese)', he reported, 'pursue me, for they really believe that I have written important works.' Nan was pleased: 'How glad I am that the world feels that it wants you. You are so good for the people who think they can explain everything'.[1047]

Whether it was because she thought the world was now ready for the 'well water'; or because she wanted to re-read the work in which, she felt, 'the light' was best articulated and 'sit still in the middle of it' (as Neil had suggested); or whether it was a reaction to Sheila Hamilton's jibe that she had given up, we cannot be certain. It may have been a combination of all these things. What we do know is what Nan did next, which was to open the drawer in her hall table and take out the manuscript of *The Living Mountain*.

★ ★ ★

'I confess it was with some considerable delight that I re-read the manuscript of *The Living Mountain*. I'm glad you like it', Nan replied to Helen Bain after the book was finally published in 1977. In her foreword, Nan says that on reading it again, she realised that the tale of her traffic with a mountain was as valid in 1977 as it was over thirty years ago when she put away the manuscript. 'Thirty years in the life of a mountain is nothing—the flicker of an eyelid', she says. But during that time, the world had caught up with her.

'Nature writing' as a genre did not exist in the 1940s when Nan was writing *The Living Mountain*. By the 1970s, though, cheap flights to far-flung destinations meant that writing about remote places was very much in vogue. In 1977, Bruce Chatwin burst onto the literary scene with his first book, *In Patagonia*, documenting his quest to the farthest reaches of the region. *A Time of Gifts*, the first of Patrick Leigh

Fermor's trilogy charting his walk in 1933, aged eighteen, from the Hook of Holland to Constantinople, was also published that year, as was John McPhee's book about Alaska, *Coming into the Country*. All were very different in style and all were by men. The following year, Peter Matthiessen's *The Snow Leopard* appeared.

Out of the four, it was Matthiessen's work Nan most admired. She even copied out a long passage from it into her *Medley Book*—her last entry, in fact. She chose an extract where the writer, crawling on hands and knees on a precarious mountain ledge, pauses for breath and is awed by the trance-like state of the 'B'on-pos' who pass him: 'On they come, staring straight ahead as steadily and certainly as ants, yet seeming to glide with an easy, ethereal lightness, as if some sort of inner concentration was lifting them just off the surface of the ground.'[1048]

It's not surprising Matthiessen's account of his odyssey to Nepal's Crystal Mountain appealed to Nan. Like *the Living Mountain* his work is part spiritual quest, part exploration of an exterior wilderness and is threaded, too, with Tao and Zen.[1049] *The Snow Leopard* is also a metaphor: it did not matter to Matthiessen, as he came to understand, that he never caught sight of a snow leopard. The snow leopard was not the point— any more than the peaks were the point for Nan Shepherd. It was all about the journey.

Although Neil Gunn was the only person who ever read the manuscript of *The Living Mountain* in the 1940s, since then, others had seen it. 'She certainly showed it to my mother', said Erlend Clouston, 'who encouraged her to re-present it to a publisher'.[1050] But the person who really persevered with Nan, pestering her to get the book into print and who must also have read the manuscript, was Harold Watt.

Managing director of Aberdeen University Press from 1946 to 1992, Harold lived just the other side of the old Deeside Railway line in Cults. As well as being almost a neighbour, Harold knew Nan well from her days as editor of the *Review,* which was printed by the AUP. 'Harold actually told me', said Cameron Donaldson, 'that he was always on at her to publish *The Living Mountain*'.[1051]

Until January 1978 when the company was purchased by Robert Maxwell's Pergamon Press, the AUP was a printer not a publisher. Nan herself explained the difference to Helen Cruickshank in 1971 when Helen was looking for a publisher for *Octobiography:*

The U Pr [Aberdeen University Press] are printers and not publishers. They do not undertake advertising and distribution, both of which must be met by the author. They do beautiful work, good paper, good print, pleasant volumes—but they're cursed dear, very expensive indeed'. [1052]

Nan had managed to finance John C Milne's anthology because of the many subscriptions given as a memorial after his death and as the book ran through three editions it eventually paid for itself, making enough of a profit on top for the Memorial Fund to give a sum of money to his widow. Similarly, the little Charles Murray volume, *The Last Poems,* published for the Memorial Trust by the AUP in 1969, was reprinted in 1970 and eventually just paid for itself.[1053]

First edition of *The Living Mountain*, 1977.

Harold's Watt's pestering, however, paid off. In October 1977 *The Living Mountain* was printed by the AUP in a relatively short run of 3,000 copies. Nan took the advice Neil Gunn had given her back in 1945. He felt that the book's 30,000 word length needed illustrations of some kind, or photographs, to complete it.

As he predicted, Nan didn't like the idea then but by 1977 she had apparently come round to his way of thinking. Ian Munro's[1054] black and white illustrations accompanied the text which included a map on the opening page alongside her foreword, written in August 1977.

As its author, Nan told Helen Cruickshank, she was responsible for advertising and distribution. This would explain the dearth of reviews and the fact that she was so generous with the number of copies she signed and gave away to her friends. Erlend Clouston remembers his mother, Sheila, grumbling about the way the National Trust for Scotland was displaying Nan's work as well as boxes and boxes of the books lying around the house. Cameron Donaldson has one of these originals. Signed by Nan, it says, simply 'To Joan and Cameron in friendship'. 'It's a family heirloom', he says, 'It's an amazing book'.

Cuthbert Graham was just as rapturous in his review for the *Press & Journal* which appeared the day *The Living Mountain* was published, the 27th of October, 1977.[1055] 'The magic of the Cairngorms told unforgettably', his piece is titled and opens: 'Dr Nan Shepherd, Aberdeen's Grand Old Lady of Letters has given to the world a little masterpiece'. Long before *The Guardian* described it, in 2011, as 'the finest book ever written on nature and landscape in Britain',[1056] Graham saw its value:

> She calls it 'The Living Mountain' in the singular, because she sees the entire Cairngorm plateau as one—a wonderful wilderness, in which is it possible for man, not merely to resuscitate his jaded spirits but to come to a new understanding of himself and the nature of reality. She is not the only Scottish writer who has recognised in the Cairngorm plateau a touchstone of Being with a capital B. Other poets like the late John C Milne and artists like Thomas Train have done that, but she has worked out the implications more fully and, in more exquisite prose, than anyone has done before her.

As Graham recognised, hill walkers, climbers and skiers would all love the book, but it was not aimed at them alone, 'It is for everybody who has ever puzzled over the mystery of life'. Nor, as he said, does *The Living Mountain* profess to be any kind of reference book: 'It offers no technicalities or scientific 'gen' as such. But it brings into focus much deep and detailed knowledge of the mountains in every mood, in all weathers, at every season of the year'. He was sure it was the kind of deluxe paperback that should make a Christmas bestseller.

Ken Morrice was given the book for Christmas and wrote to congratulate Nan, enclosing 'The High Mountain', a poem he dedicated to her and which, he said, was inspired by *The Living Mountain*. 'Your book is (as they say) really something', he declared. 'Rarely can such acute observation be matched by a gift for poetic expression. "Gentle" it is not: powerful, muscular, vivid, experimental…The experience of reading it stays with me'.[1057] Not everyone, however, was so keen on *The Living Mountain*.

Cairngorms guru Adam Watson, is not a fan and in 2016 published a detailed critique of the work in which he says: 'Always I have found her book fanciful, contrived and fundamentally anthropocentric. I read it once, and it meant little to me'. Having re-read it when preparing for his review his opinion remained unchanged.[1058] Helen Bain's father-in-law also 'thought it a load of tripe'; nor did it go down well with her son, a keen climber. But as Helen observes, 'None of these men got it'.[1059] As well as a philosophical enquiry into the nature of being, *The Living Mountain* is littered with minutely detailed observation of the hills and their flora and fauna, but deliberately avoids documenting the kind of scientific data, the 'gen' as Cuthbert Graham put it, for which these male readers were, perhaps, looking. They did not, as Graham clearly did, see what Nan Shepherd was trying to do.

Aside from Graham's review, there was little other publicity. She may have been an ardent promoter and encourager of others' works but Nan Shepherd was never one for self-recommendation. Many people were unaware she had even written another book until *The Living Mountain* first appeared in print that autumn of 1977. Jean Roger, who, along with her husband Grant, was often with Nan in the hills during the Second World War when the book was actually being written, confessed, 'I didn't know about it until after it was published'.[1060]

So quiet was its initial launch that even Erlend Clouston, who at the time was a journalist for *The Guardian,* wasn't aware the book had been published until a copy landed on his desk in 1983. The literary editor sent him a bundle of books to review and to his amazement, among them was Nan's, 'which I'm not sure I knew had even been published', he admits. 'It was a great sense of a circle being completed to be able to provide what I think was the first national review of the book'.[1061] 'A stunning and loving analysis of the lure of high and lonely places', Erlend describes it, ending: 'It is likely to make a famous memorial for a private and perceptive author who died two years ago.' And so it has.

Robert Maxwell was keen that AUP should become a publisher rather than a printer of academic books.[1062] In 1979 Colin MacLean was taken on to grow this side of the business and did so, publishing several works which have since become classics (including *The Living Mountain* which he reprinted in an identical format in 1984). That same year, Canongate Classics reprinted all Nan Shepherd's works, collected under the title *The Grampian Quartet,* with incisive introductions to each provided by Roderick Watson.

Watson had first come across Nan Shepherd when he was writing about Hugh MacDiarmid and had been impressed by the insight she had shown in her 1938 essay on his verse. He had no idea then, that Nan herself had written novels and poetry, let alone a work of non-fiction. 'They have been most unfairly forgotten', he says of her novels which, in his opinion, 'deserve a key place in that line which runs from *The House with the Green Shutters* to *A Scots Quair* and beyond'.[1063]

It is Robert Macfarlane who is largely responsible for the recent resurgence of interest in Nan Shepherd. 'I knew the Cairngorms long before I knew *The Living Mountain*' he says, 'I first read it in 2003, and was changed. I had thought I knew the Cairngorms well, but Shepherd showed me my complacency. Her writing taught me to *see* these familiar hills, rather than just to look at them'. [1064] As well as reviewing her work in the press, Macfarlane devoted pages of his own books to Nan Shepherd,[1065] with the result that in 2008 Canongate published *The Living Mountain* individually and then reprinted it in 2011.[1066] All Nan's works were available once more—except, that is, for her poetry anthology. Copies of *In the Cairngorms* were rarer than hen's teeth until Galileo's reprint of 2014.

But all this was in the future. 'Writer of Genius gives up', wrote Sheila Hamilton in December 1976. Ten months later Nan Shepherd produced her masterpiece. Imagine her wry smile. 'People were stunned', said Malcolm Sutherland. 'Some knew of her novels but as Nan never mentioned them, neither did they. Then when *The Living Mountain* came out, well…'.[1067] In 1977 Nan's light was shining bright.

Chapter Fifteen

1979-1981

Nan Shepherd's last years were not so joyous.[1068] By 1979 she was growing less mobile and now very seldom ventured into town. Endings were on her mind: 'I must tell you of a lovely death that has just taken place,' she wrote to Jessie Kesson in November:

> I had a cousin, ninety years old, a little lively Jenny Wren of a woman, with her tail always cocked. The other week she was being collected by friends to go to a whist evening. She said, "Just wait till I blow out my lamp". She blew it out—and her own life at the same moment. What a lovely way to go.[1069]

Nan Shepherd's light was not so swiftly or neatly extinguished. It began to fade towards the end of that year.

Now aged eighty-six, her pulse was up to its old tricks. 'They've told me my heart is "just a leaky old thing" ', she wrote to Jessie in early December, 'my pulse rate has gone down to 40 and is slower than two tortoises. So they are giving me a pacemaker into my heart. It's not a big operation, a week or ten days in hospital, and they say it's being done successfully on people a good deal older than me'.[1070] The corollary of this, however, was that Nan would be leaving Dunvegan in the Spring. The old house with its steep brae up to the gate and its large garden, were more than she could cope with.

For as long as she could remember, Nan had lived at Dunvegan. All her life (as she was so fond of saying to interviewers) she had slept in the same, narrow bedroom with its wide views of the Dee valley and she may have hoped that, like her father, mother and Mary before her, she would be buried from the house. But it was not to be. When, over forty years earlier, Nan wrote *Descent from the Cross* she could not have predicted that someday she would have to leave her home. Yet her description of Tommy, discharged from hospital and dependent on the care of his mother in law, suggests she had imagined the wrench. For a long time, Tommy lay 'looking at the line of hill from his bedroom window. Leaving that before he was compelled would hurt'.[1071]

Leaving Dunvegan now that she was compelled, defeated in old age by the old house and garden, would hurt Nan too. Typically, though, she hid her pain, joking instead to Jessie Kesson: 'It'll be odd for me to have a new address, for I've never lived anywhere but here. But if people <u>will</u> take on more than the allotted share of life, they shouldn't take on more than the allotted share of space!'[1072]

The move, to what Nan called her 'snail shell residence', the old kennel-man's cottage behind 'Oakleigh', Sheila Clouston's home in Auchattie, Banchory, was planned for the end of April 1980. Much smaller than Dunvegan, Oakleigh Cottage would contain Nan herself, but there was not nearly enough room for all her belongings and certainly not for her vast collection of books. And so, the operation at Christmas to fit the pacemaker having been successful, post-recovery, Nan spent the spring of 1980 clearing out her possessions. Neighbours and friends who dropped in to Dunvegan to see her were asked to help themselves to whatever they liked from her bookshelves. As it turned out, though, the move to her 'snail shell' never took place.

On Sunday 20th April 1980, Mike Radford's adaptation of Jessie Kesson's semi-autobiographical novel, *The White Bird Passes,* aired for the first time on television. Following the film, was a short documentary featuring Jessie herself talking animatedly about the ups and downs of her life and, appreciatively, of 'the Lady in the Train's' part in it all. Although she was not a fan of television (it was only after Mary's accident in 1971 that she had rather begrudgingly been persuaded to purchase one) Nan was really looking forward to watching the film. In March 1980, as the date drew nearer for the showing, she had written encouragingly to a very nervous Jessie: 'I suspect you feel twinges of apprehension— something that can't be helped. Especially with something so personal as this is bound to be…Love to you, my dear, and a stout heart for the day'.[1073]

White Bird was a triumph. Ecstatically reviewed, it won the Scottish TV Drama award and turned Jessie almost overnight into a celebrity. She was inundated with fan mail. Letters poured in 'from a' the airts',[1074] but nothing came from the one person whose critical opinion really mattered to her. As she said later, Jessie was convinced that only serious illness would have prevented Nan from writing to her; she was right.

In preparing for her 'flittin'[1075] from Dunvegan, Nan had overdone things. On Monday 21st April 1980, the day after Jessie's film was shown on television, she collapsed at home and lay unconscious for several hours. By chance, Bunty Mackie, a nurse whose parents kept the family bookshop and newsagents in Cults and who had been a good neighbour to Nan in her last years, chauffeuring her around and keeping a friendly eye on her, happened to pop in to Dunvegan that Monday afternoon and found her. Given oxygen and rushed by ambulance to Aberdeen's Royal Infirmary at Foresterhill, Nan eventually came round. But she was confused and disorientated and it was several days before she was fully cognisant.

For a week she was convinced she was waking in a different bed to the one in which she had fallen asleep, believing that:

> at night the whole ward moved out to a wood in Drumoak and came back and I with it in the morning, and that I walked into the ward and said, I've brought it all back safe. For they couldn't leave the wood out because of the vandals, and I had said, I'll keep the vandals away (the conceit of me!). I can see the wood—I played in it as a child.[1076]

Possibly caused by medication or a lack of oxygen to the brain, Nan's hallucinations might also have been the result of her anxiety over leaving Dunvegan. After all, she had collapsed at home and regained consciousness to find herself somewhere completely different. Either way, as she lay in her hospital bed she decided she should say no to moving to Sheila's cottage, 'for I'd be very little use if Sheila was ill. Indeed I was, I realised, to be very little use at all'.[1077]

After two and a half weeks in hospital, however, Nan made an almost complete recovery and was feeling so much better she forgot her intention to say no to the cottage. Despatched for two weeks' convalescence at the Glen O'Dee Hospital in Banchory, during which preparations for her move were completed, on 30th May Nan was all packed and ready to be collected when the Ward Sister came to see her. She brought bad news. Sheila, who had already suffered one heart attack a few weeks before Nan's own collapse, had suffered another much worse one. Her doctors said they must give up the idea of living together.

The hospital was very good about it all and Nan was told she could stay on till a place was found for her. Nonetheless, it was a worrying time for her. Concerned about Sheila and uncertain about where she would end up, as Dunvegan was already leased to tenants, it was a huge relief when, just over a week later, a room fell vacant at a residential care home in Torphins. 'I had luck's own grin over me', Nan wrote, her relief palpable in the long-awaited letter she wrote to Jessie Kesson on 29th June 1980. 'By all that is wonderful, it couldn't be better', she continued. 'Annesley House is a country house now adapted for six elderly and afflicted women (which is what I am now). We have a room apiece…and can put anything we like of our own into the room & stay in it as long as we wish'.[1078] The largest of the residents' rooms, Nan's faced south and from its window she had a view 'up country' to Clachnaben.[1079]

A dusky pink, slate-turreted, Victorian building, when Nan was a resident there in the early 1980s, Annesley House was still surrounded by parkland. Houses cluster closer to it now but, standing on the pink–gravelled path bordering its immaculate lawn and looking south, there are still long views to the rock topped Clachnaben.

It is ironic that Nan's view was of that particular hill, described in *A Pass in the Grampians* as, 'the great crag that looked so friendly and familiar from the farms, like the hunched back of an old labourer, but from one angle on the moor, grew sinister, like a hooked claw'.[1080] The novel is set in the shadow of Clachnaben and the 'Pass', the high road once from south to north which runs a few miles south-east of Annesley House.[1081] In the text, Nan replicates the climb she took so many times herself: 'up and still up to the Pass, while the great crag changed shaped behind them and new peaks came into view; and then the summit and the leagues of undiscovered country that were lying there below him, blue and incredible as talk of death'.[1082] But in 1981, Nan's climbing days were long behind her and talk of death not so incredible in a 'waiting room' like Annesley House.

A Pass in the Grampians ends with Jenny Kilgour, on the brink of womanhood, deciding she 'must get beyond the Pass. Beyond it, her granduncles, her father and her aunt, went each in turn'.[1083] Many of her own relatives had journeyed beyond the Pass. Nan Shepherd never did; she remained in Aberdeenshire all her days. For Jenny, the Pass is 'the symbol of her going'.[1084] Its meaning, at this point in her life, would not have been lost on Nan.

What she thought about an afterlife is articulated in a letter to Jessie Kesson:

> I understand your sense of a gulf opening at your feet when you think of 'after'. I too have no belief in a life after death—at least I keep an open mind over it acknowledging that the lovely philosophies I once held, and can still see to be so desirable, may indeed be true. I can grasp that there may be a realm of life, an order of living, as imperceptible to me just now as fragrance to a man who has no sense of smell. But my reason does not accept it. And yet—I suppose that is just itself a density.[1085]

In the meantime, from her room with a view at Annesley House, Nan could look on Clachnaben. But it was not just looking she was doing. Jean Roger said of Nan: 'You felt she was part of the mountain, she absorbed its spirit'.[1086] And even as an old woman, Nan Shepherd was still able to 'live all the way through',[1087] as she puts it in *The Living Mountain*. To be able to walk out of her body and into her mountain, for her was *all,* and it sustained her. Jessie Kesson recognised this. 'I'm glad you look on Clochnaben [sic] "Your" hills', she wrote in a letter to Nan on 18th July 1980. 'I know you do more than look. 'You "Know" the "feel" of it beneath your feet, the sting of its rain on your face— you breathe the hill smells. I know this because I, too, can <u>merge</u> my being into beloved places. Not quite the same thing, but a blessing despite'.[1088]

Not quite the same thing as her large garden at Dunvegan either, but still a blessing, was the window box on the ledge outside her room. This Nan planted up and watched carefully for the sap-rising signs of spring—always her favourite time of year. As for any other entertainment, aside from reading, there was little offered at Annesley House except for the TV set in the residents' sitting room which, she said, 'speaks well but is abominable to look at'.[1089] All the residents met for meals in a dining room with a large oval table round which they all sat, their portions of food deposited in front of them. Mealtimes might have been more entertaining than the despised television but as three out of the six women were deaf there were 'six knives and forks busy in a sad silence'.[1090]

Although her handwriting was deteriorating, Nan's wit was very much alive in her letters from this period; her interest in her fellow human beings undiminished. It was their uniqueness, their individual quirks which fascinated her and she was still able to paint tragi-comic cameos of her fellow residents, who were a good set of women, she said, with interesting pasts:

> One is in her ninetieth year and play-acts. I think she's practising death bed scenes. She refused for a while to eat, sometimes staying in her room and calling down that she didn't want any lunch, sometimes persuaded to sit at table, she ostentatiously rose and walked to the side table and deposited her full plate there & then sat in high majesty and self-approval till we had all eaten. Funny and pathetic.[1091]

While she was content at Annesley House, Nan was never fully acquiescent at being in a 'Home'. 'It came on me so suddenly', she admitted to Jessie. 'It was a fortnight after I came here that I really <u>felt</u> it. Before that

I just accepted dumbly. Somehow I never thought I'd be homeless! And they told me that a pacemaker enabled old people to stay in their homes instead of taking up places in homes'.[1092]

'The size of a matchbox', Nan gleefully told friends George and Fiona Heraghty who visited her at Annesley House in the summer of 1980, pulling open the collar her blouse to show them the scar left by surgery to install her pacemaker just below her clavicle.[1093] The device, which was supposed to have granted her a more independent lifestyle and hadn't, then let her down again. In August 1980, discovering that a wire had slipped, her doctors informed Nan she would have to go back into hospital for a further operation. She tried to remain optimistic, but her letters began to lose their sparkle. 'The sun shines and the fields change colour and the roadsides have a new crop of wildings and all is well,' she wrote to Jessie Kesson.[1094] But all was not well. The second operation fixed the problem with her pacemaker, but not long afterwards Nan's legs failed her.

She had gone out for a short walk in the grounds of Annesley House and slipped on a patch of ice. Her legs gave way beneath her and, having fallen, she could not lift herself up again. Like most care homes, to help with the smooth running of the place, mealtimes at Annesley House were strictly observed. This, of course, heaps unnecessary anxiety in the residents and, while Nan lay incapacitated on the frozen ground the insult to injury was compounded, by worry that she would be late for lunch. 'The indignity to self', as Jessie said in one of her last letters to Nan, 'is worse than the actual pain and discomfort, which can in some measure be alleviated, it's that other thing that hurts'.[1095]

In early 1981, Nan was still writing letters, but it was a slow process. Let down by her legs which had carried her so easily for so many years in the hills, her memory was now beginning to go too. 'Forgetting is one of the things age accustoms you to', she wrote to Barbara Balmer, 'we never lose things here, but we mislay them constantly'.[1096]

She was caught out occasionally, too, by moments of confusion. In late January, she was lying in bed, half awake, a number of things jostling in her mind, when she opened her eyes to see the word 'MAGGIE-KNOCKATER', large and plain, emblazoned in an arc in a room which was otherwise dark and silent. The name of a hamlet near Craigellachie, Nan knew of Maggieknockater but had never been to the place, nor did she know anyone who lived there. Perplexed, she mentioned it to her fellow residents. A prophetic vision, they suggested. But what it was prophesying Nan had no idea and continued to ponder.

'Thinking things out', though, was something Nan Shepherd had always done and was still doing. Perhaps aware that time might be running out for her, she was focussed on the subject. 'Oh dear. I do get muddled over this business of time', she confessed to Jessie Kesson. 'It's one of the most puzzling things one can think about. That we so often measure it by the motions of sun and other heavenly bodies is, I think, one of the obstacles—intensity of experience has nothing to do with solar measurements'.[1097]

By January 1981 she had puzzled it out. In *The Living Mountain,* she describes the water at Loch A'an being so clear that 'gazing into its depths one loses all sense of time, like the monk in the old story who listened to the blackbird'.[1098] She then quotes Burns:

> Water of A'n, ye rin sae clear,
> Twad beguile a man of a hundred year'.[1099]

To explain her workings out to Barbara Balmer, Nan used the same analogy:

> Time. I always knew that time didn't matter, but it took old age to show me that time is a mode of experiencing. The old story about the monk who listened to a blackbird for an hour and then found it had been a hundred years (and the Reformation had taken place) is just an example of what we all know—that we can gaze at a lovely scene for what seems a minute or two but is really an hour. Or conversely that if we are in a situation of extreme suspense, a minute can seem a year…but if one is to write about that, to convey its inwardness, how is it to be done? How get [sic] an experience into words so that the words make the experience true?

she went on:

> A gifted creative writer, uses words that transform what he is saying—quite simple words they may be, but they carry his whole theme on to a level where the reader can share the experience. It's as though you are standing <u>experiencing</u> and suddenly the work is there, bursting out of its own ripeness… the life has exploded, sticky and rich and smelling oh so good. And that's the word (or it may be a whole phrase) that makes the ordinary word magical…and gives the reader a new experience.[1100]

To be able to use words to convey something wordless was a gift Nan Shepherd was always quick to spot and praise in others. She believed Neil Gunn had it. When she wrote applauding *Butcher's Broom,* to illustrate his talent, Nan quoted his description of Mairi: 'Indeed in her steady unthinking darkness, she might have walked out of a mountain and might walk into it again, leaving no sign'.[1101] But then, her letter was written in December 1934, a few months after her experience at Loch Avon, so she understood exactly what Neil meant: a merging of being so absolute, mountain and man are one. Of course, it would never have occurred to Nan Shepherd to suggest that her own writing achieved exactly this kind of transformation and illumination for her reader. She remained reticent about herself and her talent to the very end.

The end, when it came, was at 8.30 pm on Friday 27th February 1981. Just two weeks after her eighty-eighth birthday, Nan Shepherd died of pneumonia[1102] at Woodend Hospital, Aberdeen, three and a half miles from the house in which she had lived nearly all her life. Pneumonia, often called the 'old man's friend', is common amongst elderly patients who remain lying in the same position for long periods of time. As Nan became more and more immobile, fluid normally dispersed by activity built up in her lungs. It would have been a drowning sort of death—but, treated in hospital, at least it was a pain-free and dignified dissolution of being.

In *Descent from the Cross,* written when Nan was still young and vital, she gives us, through Tommy's eyes, a perspective on death:

> Elizabeth wanted to give him all the richness of life into his remaining hours. She didn't yet understand…that all the richness of life could be felt in merely being. His passivity was not vacant. It was full with the miracle, eternally renewed of being. He could never get enough of the single wonder of life.[1103]

Towards the end, Nan may have been sitting or lying for long periods but for someone who had lived her life with such fervour, it is hard to imagine that her passivity was any more vacant than Tommy's. She knew, too, that all the richness of life could be felt in merely being. Death, to Nan Shepherd, was simply the dissolution of being and 'to face death alone in the darkness of the night, slowly to inure oneself to contemplate dissolution, that could be borne'.[1104] 'We knew she was ready to go', Sheila Clouston said afterwards, it made her passing more acceptable'.[1105]

The *Aberdeen Press & Journal* printed an announcement of Nan's death on 2nd March 1981, respectfully inviting all friends to her funeral two days later at 2pm in Cults East Church. It was a simple service, not hugely attended. One friend who was not present, much to her distress, was Jessie Kesson.

Jessie had been giving a reading of *The White Bird Passes* to the English Faculty at St Andrew's University when a man in the audience asked: 'Who was the Lady in the Train?' Jessie told him. 'Nan Shepherd is dead. She died this morning', he said. Somehow, Jessie managed to go on with the reading. 'I did it for Nan Shepherd, as she would have wanted me to do, and the last thing I could do for her'. But Jessie was so upset by the news, she stayed overnight in St Andrews. The following morning she rang the *Press & Journal* to find out about the funeral only to discover it had taken place that day—and with her so close. 'I would have gone a lot further than Aberdeen to say good-bye' she wrote in a letter to Sheila Clouston'.[1106]

Sheila had done her best to notify as many people as possible of Nan's death, 'mostly elderly ones who had been her contemporaries' she explained in her reply to Jessie. 'I did make a small attempt to write to you, but I was so sure that you would hear through literary channels'.[1107] Sheila met Jessie only once during Nan's lifetime, but had heard about her often. 'Nan had such faith in you and a true fondness' she said, writing later to Jessie to congratulate her on being awarded a doctorate by the University of Dundee: 'How pleased and proud our dear Nan Shepherd would have been! I wish she had known of this honour.'[1108] In 1990, when the shock of Nan's death had diminished somewhat, Jessie was able to write about her for the *Aberdeen University Review*. She remembered that some twenty years earlier, she had told Nan about the loss of a close friend. 'Think of this', was Nan's response, 'She was graced by you'. 'The gist of this article could also be contained in *one* line', Jessie wrote, '*I* was graced by Nan Shepherd'.[1109]

'You're like a lovely day in the hills',[1110] was the last line of Neil Gunn's final letter to Nan. 'It was a lovely compliment' she said, and an 'all sufficient goodbye'.[1111] As romantic and fitting as the idea might be that Nan's ashes were scattered in her beloved Cairngorms, according to Kathleen Jamie the practice is altering the chemical balance of the soil, 'fertilising it with phosphorous and calcium to the detriment of rare alpine plants'.[1112] Nan Shepherd would not have approved. Like Mairi in Gunn's *Butcher's Broom* she would no doubt have preferred to walk into the mountain again, leaving no sign. Instead, she lies buried with her father and mother in the family lair at Springbank Cemetery on the outskirts of Aberdeen, just two miles from Dunvegan.

An unassuming, rough-hewn, granite tombstone lists the names, dates and ages at their deaths of John, Frank (buried at Bloemfontein), Jane and Anna (Nan) Shepherd. There are no other words, no memorialising inscriptions or verses of remembrance. There are larger, more elaborate monuments including one for William Kelly and his wife Mary in the row of graves among which the Shepherds' sits. Trees overhang the cemetery, the grass is neatly mowed. It seems somehow too orderly, too neat and domestic a resting place for Nan Shepherd. But it is peaceful; a good place to be. And there are more ends than the grave.

A Note on the Text

Nan Shepherd's punctuation, grammar and spelling have been followed in quotations from her commonplace books, manuscript notebooks, articles and letters. Scottish place-names vary in spelling; I have tended to use Nan Shepherd's.

All references to Nan Shepherd's fiction are to Canongate's 1996 collection of her works contained in *The Grampian Quartet*. References to *TLM* are to Canongate's 2011 edition and to *ITC* are to Galileo's 2014 edition.

Abbreviations

ABDN:	University of Aberdeen Spec Coll	JK:	Jessie Kesson
AE:	George William Russell	JM:	John Macmurray
AHS:	Aberdeen High School	LGG:	Lewis Grassic Gibbon
AHSM:	*Aberdeen High School Magazine.*	*LM*:	*Leopard Magazine*
		MB:	*Medley Book*
AJ:	*Aberdeen Press & Journal*	NSA:	Nan Shepherd Archive
AM:	*Alma Mater*	NLS:	National Library of Scotland
AMM:	Agnes Mure Mackenzie	NS:	Nan Shepherd
APIG:	*A Pass in the Grampians*	NR:	Neil Roger
AUR:	*Aberdeen University Review*	NMG:	Neil Gunn
		PMN:	*Poetry Manuscript Notebook*
AUP:	Aberdeen University Press	RAT:	Rachel Annand Taylor
		SB:	*Sheila Book*
BB:	Barbara Balmer	SC:	Sheila Clouston
BM:	Betty Macmurray	*SM*:	*Scots Magazine*
CM:	Charles Murray	*SO*:	*Scots Observer*
DB:	Deirdre Burton	TC:	Aberdeen Training Centre
DEB:	*Deirdre Book*	*TDF*:	*The Deeside Field*
DFC:	Deeside Field Club	*TLM*:	*The Living Mountain*
DFTC:	*Descent from the Cross*	*TQW*:	*The Quarry Wood*
EC:	Erlend Clouston	*TS*:	*The Scotsman*
GL:	*Gleanings*	*TW*:	*The Weatherhouse*
HC:	Helen Cruickshank	UOE:	University of Edinburgh
HJCG:	Herbert Grierson		
HM:	Hugh MacDiarmid		
ITC:	*In the Cairngorms*		

Select Bibliography

Manuscript Sources

NSA is held at the NLS. Also at NLS are the literary papers of AMM, CM, JK, LGG and NMG. The papers of JM and BM can be found in The John Macmurray Collection at UOE which also holds NS's letters to HC and HM.

ABDN holds NS's letters to AMM, MA, Edith Robertson, and from RAT as well as the records of the AHS, DFC, TC, the papers of Cuthbert Graham, HJCG, William Kelly, CG the *Thistle Cottage Visitors' Books* and the *Shelter Stone Visitor Books.* Testimonies of Mary Esslemont, Stella Henriques, Flora Garry and Winifred Black can be accessed from the Oral History Archives, ABDN. Mary Esslemont's notes for her address to Former Pupils of AHS association can be found in AHS archive at also at ABDN.

In private hands are Betty Macmurray's unpublished memoirs, NS's letters to Barbara Balmer, to Jean Roger and from Francis Bonnyman Kelly to Jeannie Kelly and the Smith/Tough family tree.

Works by Nan Shepherd

The Quarry Wood, (1928) Canongate, 1996.
The Weatherhouse, (1930) Canongate, 1996.
A Pass in the Grampians, (1933) Canongate, 1996.
The Living Mountain, (1977) Canongate, 2011.
In the Cairngorms, (1934) Galileo, 2014.
Descent from the Cross, SM, 1943.

'Faerie Land Forlorn', *AM,* 1914.
'On Noises in the Night', *Saturday Westminster Gazette,* 1915.
'Smuts', *Saturday Westminster Gazette,* 1916.
'Pixies and Or'nary Peoples', *AHSM,* c. 1919.
'Things I shall never know', *The Gala Rag,* 1934.
'Town and Gown: The Pageant of Aberdeen University', *TSM,* 1934.
'The Poetry of Hugh MacDiarmid', *AUR,* 1938.
'The Colours of Deeside', *TDF,* 1938.
'Women in the University: Fifty Years', *AUR,* 1942.
'Mountain Holidays by Janet Adam Smith: Review', *NLS,* 1946.
'Marion Angus', *SM,* 1947.
'Agnes Mure Mackenzie: A Portrait', *AUR,* 1955.
'The Charles Murray Memorial Trust', *AUR,* 1958.
'The White Bird Passes by Jessie Kesson: Review', *AUR,* 1958.

'Wild Geese in Glen Callater', *TDF,* 1959.
'Sir Herbert Grierson', *AUR,* 1960.
'James MacGregor and the Downies of Braemar', *TDF,* 1962.
'Aberdonian Salt', AUR, 1963.
'Glitter of Mica by Jessie Kesson: Review', *AUR,* 1963.
'The Lupin Island', *TDF,* 1966.
'Charles Murray, An Appreciation', '*Charles Murray: The Last Poems',* AUP,
    1969, (reprinted in *Hamewith: The Complete Poems of Charles Murray,*
    AUP, 1979).
'Marion Angus as a poet of Deeside', *TDF,* 1970.
'Charles Murray: The Poet of "Hamewith"', *LM,* 1978.
'Schools and Schoolmistresses', n.p., n.d., NSA.
'The Old Wives', n.p., n.d., NSA.

Articles and Reviews

'Miss Anna Shepherd, M.A.', *AM,* Supplement, 12 Dec 1917.
'Miss Anna Shepherd', 'Women Citizens', n.p. n.d., NLS.
'Aberdeen Flower Show', *AJ,* 24 Aug 1906.
'Address by Former Pupil, Now an Authoress', *AJ,* 27 Jun 1930.
'A Woman on Burns (A Novelists's Verdict)' NSA, n.p. c. 1934.
'Best sellers went to this party', n.p., n.d., NSA.
'Chairman's Report on AHS', *AJ,* 29 Jun 1906.
'Clash of Generations in Modern Novel', *AJ,* 25 Mar 1931.
'Cultural Hope of Scotland', *AJ,* 5 Feb 1934.
'Cynthia', 'Scottish Women Writers', *The Scotsman,* 14 Nov 1931.
'Death of a Deeside Farmer: Mr James Tough,' in *AJ,* 8 Oct 1890.
Dunnett, R. F, 'Nan Shepherd: One of the Scottish "moderns" ', *The Scotsman,*
    c. Jul/Aug 1933, pp.341-342.
Donald, Louise, 'Nan Shepherd', *LM,* Oct 1977, pp. 20-22.
'Fluent Speaker' in 'Social News of the North', *AJ,* 14 oct 1935.
Forrest, Vivienne, 'In Search of Nan Shepherd', *LM,* 1986, pp. 17-19.
Grassic Gibbon, Lewis, 'Scots Novels of the Half Year', *Free Man,* 24 Jun 1933.
Hamilton, Sheila. 'Writer of Genius gave up', *Aberdeen Evening Express,*
    15 Dec 1976.
Jubilee Celebrations of the High School', *AJ,* 1 Mar 1924.
Kesson, Jessie, 'Nan Shepherd: In Recollection', *AUR,* 1990, pp. 187-191.
Kyle, Elizabeth, 'Modern Women Authors', *Scots Observer,* June 1931.
Macfarlane, Robert, 'I walk therefore I am', *The Guardian,* 30 Aug 2008, p.21.
Macfarlane, Robert, 'Introduction' to *TLM,* Canongate, 2011.
McBain, John, 'Obituary' in *AJ* 19 Jan 1925.
'Modern Scottish Drama', *AJ,* 20 Dec 1939.

'Review of *TQW*', *Illustrated London News,* 16 Jun 1928.

'Review of *TW*', *Illustrated London News,* 22 Mar 1933.

'Review of *TW*', *The Scotsman,* 24 Feb 1930.

'Review of *APIG*', *The Scotsman,* 9 Feb 1933.

'Summer Graduation at Aberdeen', *AJ,* 12 Jul 1915.

Taylor, Coley, *Dutton's Weekly Book News,* 1928.

'Town Council Scholarships', *AJ,* 5 Aug 1907.

Walpole, Hugh, 'New Writers and Their Work', *T.P's Weekly,* 30 Jun 1928.

Watson, Adam, 'Seton Gordon compared with some recent writers on the Cairngorms', *Essays on Lone trips, mountain-craft and other hill topics,* Paragon, 2016, pp. 12-18.

Welfare of Youth prizewinners', *AJ,* 25 May 1907, 30 May 1908, 8 Jun 1909.

Other works cited:

AE, *The Candle of Vision,* Macmillan, 1918.

Adam, Ruth, *A Women's Place 1910-1975,* Chatto & Windus, 1975.

Adam Smith, Janet, *Mountain Holidays,* Dent & Son, 1946.

'Address by Former Pupil, now Authoress', *AJ,* 26 Jun 1930.

Alison, James (ed.) *Poetry of Northeast Scotland,* Heinemann, 1976.

Allan, John R, *North East Lowlands of Scotland,* Yeadon's, 2009.

Allbut, Henry Arthur, *The Wife's Handbook,* W J Ramsey, 1886.

Anderson, R.D., *Education and Opportunity in Victorian Scotland: Schools and Universities,* Oxford University Press, 1983.

Anderson, R.D., *The Student Community at Aberdeen 1860-1939,* AUP, 1988.

Anderson, R.D., *Education and the Scottish People, 1750-1918,* Clarendon Press, 1995.

Bishop of Winchester and Committee, *The Army and Religion: An Enquiry and its Bearing upon the Religious Life of the Nation,* Association Press, 1919.

Brown, Hamish, *Seton Gordon's Scotland: An Anthology,* Whittles, 2005.

Brown, Ian & Riach, Alan, *The Edinburgh Companion to Twentieth Century Scottish Literature,* 2009.

Browning, R., 'Andrea del Sarto' in *Men and Women,* Chapman & Hall, 1855.

Blaikie, Andrew, *Infant Survival Chances, Unmarried Motherhood and Domestic Arrangements in Rural Scotland 1845-1945,* Local Population Studies, 1998.

Carter, Gillian, 'Boundaries and Transgression in Nan Shepherd's *The Quarry Wood* in Anderson, Carol & Christianson, Aileen, (eds.) *Scottish Women's Fiction,* Tuckwell Press, 2000, pp.47-58.

Craig, Cairns, *The Modern Scottish Novel: Narrative and the National Imagination,* Edinburgh University Press, 1999.

Carswell, Catherine, 'Proust's Women' in *Marcel Proust: An English Tribute,* Turtle Point Press, 2016, pp. 66-77.

Carter, Jenny, *The Biographical Dictionary of Scottish Women*, Edinburgh University Press, 2006.

Craig, Cairns, (ed.) *Vita Mea: The Autobiography of Sir Herbert J.C. Grierson*, AUP, 2014.

Costello, John, *John Macmurray: A biography*. Floris Books, 2002.

Clarke, Mary, *A Short Life of Ninety Years*, Caledonian Press, 1973.

Crawford, Robert, *Scotland's Books: The Penguin History of Scottish Literature*, Penguin, 2007.

Cruickshank, Helen, *Octobiography*, Standard Press, 1976.

Cunningham, Shirley, *A Store of Memories*, Waverley Press, 1991.

De Purucker, G., '*Questions We All Ask': Lectures on Theosophy*, California, 1930.

Diski, Jenny, *Skating to Antarctica*, Virago, 2005.

Duff, David (ed.) *Queen Victoria's Highland Journals*, Hamlyn, 1997.

Dymock, Emma & Palmer McCulloch, Margery (eds.) *Scottish & International Modernisms: Relationships and Reconfigurations*, Association for Scottish Literary Studies, 2011.

Eliot, T. S., 'Was there a Scottish Literature?', *Athenaeum*, 1 Aug 1919, pp. 680-681.

Fraser, W. Hamish, & Lee, Clive H, (eds.) *Aberdeen: 1800-2000 A New History*, Tuckwell Press, 2000.

Gibbon, Lewis Grassic, 'Literary Lights' in *The Speak of the Mearns*, Polygon, 1982, pp.128-139.

Gibbon, Lewis Grassic, *Cloud Howe*, Millward Press, 2011.

Glasgow Women's Studies Group, *Uncharted Lives: Extracts from Scottish Women's Experiences, 1850-1982*. Pressgang, 1983.

Graham, Cuthbert, *Portrait of Aberdeen and Deeside*, Robert Hale, 1972.

Graham, Cuthbert, *Historical Walk-About of Aberdeen*, Aberdeen Corporation Publication, 1975.

Graham, Cuthbert (ed.), *North East Muse Anthology*, 1977, Aberdeen Journals Ltd.

Graham, Cuthbert, *The Press and Journal North East Muse Anthology*, Aberdeen Journals, 1977.

Gramich, Katie, 'Caught in the Triple Net? Welsh, Scottish, and Irish Women Writers in Joannou, Maroula, *The History of British Women's Writing 1920-1945*, Palgrave Macmillan, 2015, pp. 217-232.

Grieve, Christopher, *Contemporary Scottish Studies:* First Series. Leonard Parsons, 1926.

Groome, Francis (ed.), *Ordnance Gazetteer of Scotland 1882-4*, T. C. Jack, 1901.

Gunn, Neil, *The Atom of Delight*, Polygon, 1986.

Gunn, Neil, *The Silver Bough*, Whittles, 2003.

Gunn, Neil, *The Shadow*, Whittles, 2006.

Hart, Francis Russell, & Pick, J.B., *Neil M Gunn: A Highland Life*,

John Murray, 1981.

Hearn, Lafcadio, *Gleanings in Buddha Fields,* Kegan, Trench, Trubner & Co, 1897.

Hodgkiss, Winifred. *Two Lives,* Yorkshire Art Circus, 1983.

Holden, Katherine, *The Shadow of Marriage: Singleness in England 1914-1960,* Manchester University Press, 2007.

Howard, Roy, *Cults Past and Present,* Centre for Scottish Studies, 1988.

Jallan, Pat, *Women, Marriage and Politics,* 1860-1940

Jamie, Kathleen, 'A Lone Enraptured Male: The Wild Places by Robert Macfarlane, *London Review of Books,* Vol. 30 No. 5 · 6 March 2008, pp. 25-27.

Jamieson, John, *Dictionary of the Scottish Language,* William Nimmo, 1867.

Kain, Richard, & O'Brien, James, *George Russell (AE),* Bucknell University Press, 1976.

Knox, William, *Lives of Scottish Women: Women and Scottish Society, 1800-1980,* Edinburgh University Press, 2006.

Kynoch, Douglas, *Scottish [Doric]-English / English / English-Scottish [Doric] Concise Dictionary,* Scottish Cultural Press, 1996.

Lawrence, David Herbert. *Pansies* (1929) in *The Complete Poems of D H Lawrence,* Wordsworth, 1994.

Le Blond, Elizabeth, *True Tales of Mountain Adventure For Non-Climbers Young & Old,* E P Dutton, 1903.

Lumsden, Alison, 'Journey into Being': Nan Shepherd's *The Weatherhouse'* in Anderson, Carol & Christianson, Aileen, (eds.) *Scottish Women's Fiction,* Tuckwell Press, 2000, pp. 59-71.

MacDiarmid, Hugh, *The Company I've Kept,* University of California Press, 1967.

MacDiarmid, Hugh, 'Neil Gunn and the Scottish renaissance' in Scott, Alexander & Gifford, Douglas, *Neil M Gunn: The Man and the Writer,* Blackwood, 1973.

MacDiarmid, Hugh, *The Letters of Hugh MacDiarmid,* Hamish Hamilton, 1984.

MacDiarmid, Hugh, *Lucky Poet: A Self -Study in Literature and Ideas,* Carcanet, 1994.

Macfarlane, Robert, *Landmarks,* Hamish Hamilton, 2015.

Macmurray, Elizabeth Hyde, *Out of the Earth,* Peter Davis, 1935.

Macmurray, Elizabeth Hyde, *Now and Then: Memoirs of Elizabeth Hyde Macmurray: 1891-1982,* unpublished, private hands.

Macmurray, John, *Journals 1908-1913,* unpublished, Macmurray archive, University of Edinburgh.

Macmurray, John, *Freedom in the Modern World,* Faber & Faber, 1935.

Macmurray, J. 'Search for Reality in Religion' *The Swarthmore Lecture,* 1965, published as *Search for Reality in Religion,* Quaker Home Service.

Malcolm, William, *A Blasphemer & Reformer: A study of James Leslie Mitchell / Lewis Grassic Gibbon,* AUP, 1984.

Matthiessen, Peter, *The Snow Leopard,* Vintage, 2010.

McClure, J. Derrick, *Doric: The Dialect of North East Scotland,* John Benjamin, 2002.

McMilland, Dorothy and Byrne, Michel (eds.) *Modern Scottish Women Poets,* Canongate, 2003.

Moore, Lindy, *Bajanellas and Semillanas, Aberdeen University and the Education of Women* 1860-1920. AUP, 1991.

Morrison, Toni, *Sula,* Knopf, 1973.

Muir, Edwin, *An Autobiography,* Canongate, 2010.

Muir, Edwin, *Scott an Scotland: The predicament of the Scottish Writer,* Polygon, 1982.

Muir, Willa, *Belonging,* Hogarth Press, 1968.

Murray, Charles, *Hamewith: The Complete Poems of Charles Murray,* AUP, 1979.

Murray, Isobel, *Jessie Kesson: Writing her Life,* Canongate, 2000.

Murray, W.H., *Mountaineering in Scotland, Undiscovered Scotland,* Diadem, 1979.

Neate, W. R., *Mountaineering and its Literature,* The Mountaineers, 1978.

Palmer McCulloch, Margery, *Scottish Modernism and its Contexts 1918-1959: Literature, National Identity and Cultural Exchange,* Edinburgh University Press, 2009.

Palmer McCulloch, Margery (ed.) *Modernism and Nationalism: Literature and Society in Scotland 1918-1939,* The Association for Scottish Literary Studies, No 33, 2004.

Pick, J.B., (ed.) *Neil M Gunn: Selected Letters,* Polygon, 1987.

Prospectus, AHS, 1915-1916, Aberdeen School Board Offices.

Riach, Alan and Grieve, Michael, (eds.) *Hugh MacDiarmid: Selected Poetry,* New Directions, 1992.

Robbie, William, *Aberdeen: Its Traditions and History,* Wyllie & Son, 1893.

Ryan, C. *What is Theosophy? A general view for Enquirers.* Theosophical University Press, 1930.

Simpson, Douglas, *A tribute offered by the University of Aberdeen to the memory of William Kelly, LL.D, A.R.S.A',* AUP, 1949.

Smith, Ali, 'Shepherd, Anna (1893-1981)', *Oxford Dictionary of National Biography,* Oxford University Press, 2004.

Stanley, Liz, *The auto /biographical I,* Manchester University Press, 1992.

Stephenson, Tom, *Forbidden Land: The Struggle for Access to Mountain and Moorland,* Manchester University Press, 1989.

Steven, H. *Rising to the Challenge: 100 Years of the Ladies' Scottish Climbing Club.* (2010) Scottish Mountaineering Trust.

Student Handbook, 1912, 1913, 1914, 1915, ABDN.

Suzuki, Daisetsu Teitaro *An Introduction to Zen Buddhism,* 1934. (A series of articles originally written for *New East* magazine and published in Japan, 1914-18).

Tagore, Rabindranath. *The Gardener,* Pendle Hill Classics, 1915.

The Army and Religion: An Enquiry and its Bearing on the Religious Life of the Nation, Macmillan, 1919.

Thomson, May, 'Maggie Gruer' *TDF,* AUP, 1981, p. 956.

Thoreau, Henry, *Walden,* Vol 2*, Houghton, Mifflin & Co,* 1882.

Tzu, Lao, *Tao Te Ching: Translated with notes by Arthur Waley,* Wordsworth, 1997.

Watson, Adam, *The Cairngorms,* Scottish Mountaineering Trust, 1992.

Watson, Roderick, '…to get leave to live. "Patterns of Identity, Freedom and Defeat in the Fiction of Nan Shepherd, in Schwend, Joachim and Drescher, Horst W, (eds.) *Studies in Scottish Fiction: Twentieth Century,* Peter Lang, 1990, pp.207-218.

Watson, Roderick, 'To know Being': Substance and Spirit in the Work of Nan Shepherd', in Gifford, Douglas and McMillan, Dorothy (eds.) *A History of Scottish Women's Writing,* Edinburgh University Press, 1997, pp. 416-427.

Webster, Jack, *Grains of Truth,* Black and White, 2013.

Wilson, James Maurice, *Three Addresses to Girls at School,* 1890.

Notes

1	*TLM,* p.108.
2	NS to BB, 15 Jan 1981.
3	NS to NMG, 28 Sep 1971.
4	Diski, 2005, p.220.
5	Stanley, 1992, p. 67.
6	Carswell, 2016, pp. 66-77.
7	AMM to NS, 1925.
8	AMM to NS, 12 Jul 1927.
9	*TLM,* p.1.
10	*TLM,* p.108.
11	NS to NMG, 14 May 1940.
12	*TLM,* p.14.

13 In her account of their first meeting in 'Nan Shepherd: In Recollection,' (*AUR,* 1990, p. 187) JK misquotes the line from CM's 'Hamewith' as 'The road that's never weary'.

14 Doric, the classical dialect of ancient Greece spoken in Doria and used for poems of songs and rural life, is a term used to describe a distinctive sub-set of Scots. In 1792 the dialect used by Allan Ramsey in his pastoral play *The Gentle Shepherd* (1791) was christened 'Scotland's Doric' by Banffshire-born academic Rev. Alexander Geddes. 'Doric' was adopted then as a name for Scots in general. Towards the end of the 19th century when a school of writing headed by William Alexander developed in Scotland, particularly in the North East, publishing articles and stories in the local dialect on subjects of local interest, Doric began to be established as the medium for literary and polemic prose and poetry. Although the term fell into disuse during the 20th century, 'Doric' has been revived in the North East, its use preferred to 'Scots' as a means to illustrate the very distinct features of its regional dialect (McClure, 2002, pp.1-48). NS uses the term in *APIG:* [David Kilgour] fell readily into the Doric, however, when he heard the shibboleth, using it pithily and with good humour'. (APIG, p. 15) (See also note 1016.)

15 JK, *AUR,* 1990, p. 188.

16 *ibid.*

17 NS, '*The White Bird Passes: Review*', *AUR,* 1958.

18 'Bennachie' in *Hamewith: The Complete Poems of Charles Murray,* AUP, 1979, quoted by NS, 26 Sep 1964, transcribed from a recording.

19 JK, *AUR,* 1990, p. 188.

20 *ibid.*

21   NS to JK, 22 Dec 1979.
22   NS to JK, Jan 1981.
23   NS, *The White Bird Passes: Review, AUR,* 1958.
24   JK, *AUR,* 1990 p. 189.
25   *APIG,* p. 30.
26   *LM,* 1945.
27   JK, *AUR,* 1990, p.189.
28   *TQW,* p. 116.
29   JK, *AUR,* 1990, p.190.
30   Taylor, 1928.
31   Walpole, 30 Jun 1928.
32   'Cynthia', 14 Nov 1931.
33   Helen Bain, 2016.
34   *AM,* 12 Dec 1917.
35   Quoted in Forrest, 1986, p. 18.
36   JR, 2014.
37   *TQW,* p. 56.
38   DB, 2017.
39   *TQW,* p. 208.
40   Roderick Watson has identified this and elaborates in Watson, 1990, pp.207-209.
41   *TQW,* p.4
42   *TQW,* p. 210.
43   *APIG,* p. 111.
44   Jocelyn Campbell, 2015.
45   DB, 2017.
46   Cameron Donaldson, 2016.
47   JK, *AUR,* 1990, p.189.
48   *The Guardian,* 2008.
49   JK, *AUR,* 1990, p. 190.
50   *TLM,* p. 11.
51   Meteorological Office, July 1934.
52   *TLM,* p. 15.
53   *TLM,* p. 12.
54   No-one has been able to give me a definitive answer as to whether or not NS could swim.
55   In Indian and Tibetan Buddhist traditions this is known as 'Nirvana'. For consistency I have used Zen terms.
56   Thoreau, 1882, p.318.
57   Suzuki, 1934.
58   NS to NMG, 14 May 1940.
59   *TLM,* p. xliii.

60   *TLM*, p. 108.

61   *ITC*, p. 2. Translation: Loch Avon, Loch Avon, how deep you lie/ Tell none your depth and none shall I/Bright though your deepmost pit may be/You'll haunt me till the day I die/Bright, and bright and bright as air/You'll haunt me now for evermore.

62   Dunnett, 1933, p. 341.

63   *TLM,* p. 108.

64   *TLM,* p. 1.

65   Suzuki, 1934.

66   Watts, 1957.

67   Hearn became a Japanese citizen in 1894.

68   Hearn, 1897.

69   Buddhist Scripture.

70   *GL.*

71   *ibid.*

72   Suzuki, 1934.

73   NS to NMG, 28 Sep 1971.

74   *ibid.*

75   *TLM*, p.106.

76   *TLM,* p.108.

77   Bodhidharma (also known as Daruma in Japan) was an Indian Buddhist monk commonly considered the founder of Chan Buddhism in China (later known as Zen in Japan).

78   Suzuki, 1934.

79   George Mackie, 2016.

80   NS to F. R. Hart & J.B. Pick, 1978, quoted in Hart & Pick, 1981, p. 84.

81   NS to NMG, 14 May 1940.

82   *APIG*, p. 20.

83   *TLM*, pp. 106–107.

84   NS to NMG, 4 Apr 1947.

85   *TW,* p. 43. The average croft is around five hectares (12 acres), although they can range in size from half a hectare to over 50.

86   Census, 1851.

87   According to their marriage certificate, John Shepherd Jr wed Ann Barron in Echt's Free Church on 11th February 1849.

88   Until 1975, Strachan (pronounced 'Strawn') was a parish in Kincardineshire.

89   Haugh: a low-lying meadow by the side of a river.

90   Canmore Collection, Scotland.

91   *TW*, p.44.

92   The book is not among those left in Nan's literary estate, but might have been one of those given away to friends, or sold, when she was

93   *TW,* p.57.

94   *AJ,* 8 Oct 1890.

95   Census, 1861. Another daughter, Christina, born in 1853, had died
        in 1860.

96   *AJ,* 8 Oct 1890.

97   Smith/Tough family tree compiled by Jeannie Shepherd in the
        1930s, private hands.

98   Francis Bonnyman Kelly was not her only suitor. Alongside his
        keepsake is another: signed on the reverse 'with the kind love of your
        sincere friend, C I Lethesson'.

99   Francis Bonnyman Kelly to Jeannie Kelly, Mar 1861.

100   *TW,* p. 22.

101   The leopards have also been attributed to Sidney Boyes, the sculptor
        who designed the bronze panels on Union Bridge, but as Kelly
        used a similar leopard on his design for the Aberdeen Savings Bank
        in Union Terrace and sketches of the finials are in the Kelly archive at
        Aberdeen University it seems likely the 'cats' were Kelly's, not Boyes's
        creation.

102   Aberdeen City Council is considering replacing the
        'outmoded cats' although many want to save them and an
        auction of cat sculptures was held in 2016 for the purpose.

103   Simpson, 1949.

104   *TW,* pp. 43-45.

105   *TW,* p. 52.

106   *TQW,* p.1.

107   Forrest, 1986, p.17.

108   Scots: sloping.

109   *TQW,* p. 2, p. 187.

110   'Contraception' was a word not used until after WW1,
        and although invented and publicised in the very respectable *Wife's
        Handbook* in 1886 (published a year after John and Jeannie
        married) which included a note about 'Malthusian Appliances', it
        was not readily available. Other han the unreliable practice of *coitus
        interruptus*, the decrease in birth numbers is attributed to separate
        bedrooms, abstinence, prolonged breast-feeding and possibly, an
        increase in the number of abortions.

111   NS, *TDF*, 1938, p.10.

112   Duff, 1997, p.7.

113   Not, as has been suggested in previous accounts of Nan Shepherd's
        life, in Peterculter. The confusion has arisen because historically
        Cults has been located within several different units. For much of its

history Cults, together with its neighbouring Pitfodels, was placed under the parish of Banchory-Devenick—most of which lies south of the river Dee. In 1890 the Cults portion of Banchory-Devenick contained Pitfodels, Cults, part of Murtle and part of Countesswells. In 1891, a boundary change occurred transferring Cults to the parish of Peterculter. Today all these areas are included in the City District of Aberdeen.

114   Howard, 1988, p. 64.
115   *TW,* p. 5.
116   Jean Roger, 2015.
117   Malcolm Sutherland, 2016.
118   Head of Speech of Drama, Elizabeth Henry was a contemporary of NS's at Aberdeen Training Centre. She died in 1986. Quoted in Forrest, 1986, p. 17.
119   Beard, George, M.D., 'Neurasthenia or Nervous Exhaustion', *The Boston Medical & Surgical Journal,* 29 Apr 1869, p.217.
120   Myalgic Encephalomyelitis.
121   Marris Murray to NS, 30 Sep 1979.
122   NS, *LM,* 1978, p. 17.
123   *SB.*
124   *The Auld Doctor and other poems and songs in Scots,* 1920., *The Lum Hat Wantin the Croon and other poems,* 1935, *Poems and prose,* 1983.
125   Howard, 1988, p. 160.
126   *SB.*
127   *ibid.*
128   Malcolm Sutherland, 2016.
129   Dunnett, 1933, p. 342.
130   *TW,* p. 7.
131   NS to BB, 15 Jan 1981.
132   *DFTC,* 1943, p. 345.
133   *TLM,* p. 28.
134   *TLM,* p.103.
135   *TLM,* p.53.
136   *TLM,* p. 58.
137   NS, *TDF,* 1966, p. 43.
138   Muir, 2010, p. 15.
139   *TW,* p. 45.
140   CM to Bella Walker, 24 May 1925.
141   *SB.*
142   *ibid.*
143   *ibid.*
144   *DEB.*

145   Fiona Heraghty, 2016.

146   *TQW*, p. 208.

147   *TQW*, p. 4.

148   NS, *AHSM*, c. 1919.

149   NS to NMG, 14 Mar 1930.

150   She is referring to George Bernard Shaw's 1923 play, *Saint Joan*.
       The hens' laying again, at the end of Scene 1, is interpreted
       as a sign from God of Joan's divine inspiration.

151   NS to NMG, 14 Mar 1930.

152   NS to NMG, 14 Mar 1930.

153   *TW*, p. 45. Whether or not Frank was red-headed, like his sister, can
       only be guessed at from extant photographs in sepia or black and
       white, but certainly his hair is a lighter shade than both his parents'
       and appears closer in hue to Nan's.

154   CM to NS, n.d. (Given the content of his letter, which refers to
       Frank being alive, it must be pre-1917.)

155   At 59 Carlton Place.

156   The felled conifers have since been replaced with larch trees. You
       can still walk right up to the top and on to Countesswell's Wood.

157   One of three cairns mentioned in Groome's Ordnance *Gazeteer*,
       1884.

158   Cist: ancient coffin, or burial chamber.

159   *TQW*, p. 2.

160   *TQW*, p. 4.

161   Quoted in Houston, R.A., *Scottish Identity: Literacy and Society in
       Scotland and Northern England 1600-1800*, Cambridge University
       Press,
       2002, p.6.

162   Anderson, 1983. pp.2-10.

163   By 1883 the school leaving age had risen to fourteen.

164   The old endowed school building and its neighbouring school
       house remained until the late 1960s when they were demolished to
       make way for the building of Rorie Hall. Apartment blocks and
       the scout hut now stand where they once did, off School Road.

165   The Scottish academic year begins in the third week of August.

166   Peterculter School Board log, Aberdeen City Council.

167   Dec 1881-Mar 1882.

168   On her death certificate, the cause of death was given as
       'Hemiplegia—duration 17 days'. It was an experience NS drew
       on in *The Quarry Wood*.
       Aunt Josephine's death from cancer is protracted. The doctor
       came and went, a death certificate in his pocket, just in case, '
       marvelling when the epic would end. He carried it for five days,

because Josephine Leggatt, seventy-nine years of age, and griev
ously afflicted with cancer, would not die'. There are moments of
comic pathos as relatives gather at the bedside watching and
waiting for the inevitable. 'What are ye sittin' there glowerin'
at me for like a puckle craws a' in a raw?' Aunt Josephine
demands of her sisters. (*TQW,* pp.205-6*)*.

169   Mary, the youngest of Ann's children, had died aged fifteen
in 1882, her husband in 1892 and then in 1895, Robert, her
oldest son died in mysterious circumstances in a hotel room in
Aberdeen. Robert had followed his father into farming. In 1882
he married Jane Greig, a farmer's daughter from Durris in
Kincardine and moved with her to farm land in Old Machar (
then a parish in south-west Aberdeenshire which included
much of Aberdeen). At 7.30 am on the morning of 4th May 1895
Robert Shepherd was found dead in bed at the Royal Hotel,
Bath Street in Aberdeen. The cause of death on the certificate
signed by John Shepherd is given as 'Supposed Poisoning
—Sudden.' He was forty-six years old.

170   In NS to NMG, Nov 1971, she says Mary had been with the family
for over sixty years, which agrees with the Census information.
The 1901 Census lists Isabella Gordon, aged 19, as the family's live-
in domestic servant while Mary Lawson is recorded as living in
as a domestic servant with the Ferres family in South Kirktown.
Mary Lawson's name is not listed at Dunvegan until the 1911
Census.

171   DB, 2015.

172   *TQW*, p. 10.

173   *SB.*

174   JK. *AUR,* 1990, p.189.

175   Blaikie, 1998, p.40.

176   Survey of parishes conducted by Paddock cited in Blaikie, 1998, p.40.

177   Nelly Dick may not have been a relative either. There was a 'Nellie'
who was maid at Dunvegan in 1920 and it is possible Mary kept in
touch with her and visited (DB, 2015).

178   DB, 2015.

179   The 1891 Census lists: Elizabeth Jane Reid, Domestic Servant aged
11; Mary Jane Wilson, scholar, aged 11, Robert Sharp aged 10,
scholar; William Esson, aged 9, scholar; Mary Lawson, aged 7,
scholar; James Rainie, aged 4 and William Forbes aged 1.
The 1901 Census records only Robert Sharp, general labourer
on the roads and William Forbes, scholar aged 11 both 'grandsons'
still living with Mrs McGhie.

180   *TQW*, p. 15

181   There were charitable children's homes set up during the Victorian
        era—Barnardo's, National Children's Homes and Waifs and Strays
        Society. Barnardo, however, did not set up his first home for boys
        until 1870, following this some years later with a girls' shelter.
        Barnardo's homes were also established in Scotland and ran until
        the 1970s —although there were none in Aberdeenshire.
        It was not until 1948 Children's Act that local councils took respon
        sibility for their provision in Britain.

182   *TW*, p. 49.

183   Forrest, 1986, p. 17.

184   NS commented on the effect of the use of English rather than
        Scottish at rural primary schools in an article published in *AHSM*
        entitled 'Schools and Schoolmistresses': 'The mother tongue for the
        bairns there is Gaelic. They come to school innocent of English. The
        teacher, a Gaelic speaker herself, must harden her heart and pretend
        not to understand the answers to her English questions that come so
        readily in the Island speech'. n.d., NSA.

185   EC, 2015.

186   'Cynthia', 1931.

187   Doric: kind.

188   Cameron Donaldson, 2016.

189   Quoted in Forrest, 1986, p.17.

190   NS to JK, 18 Sep 1963.

191   Forrest, 1986, p. 17.

192   *SB*.

193   Cults was in the parish of Banchory-Devenick until 1891 when
        the boundary was changed and the village was absorbed into the
        parish of Peterculter.

194   The church hall remains to this day behind the newer, Cults West
        Church, built in 1916.

195   Evangelist revival movements had been rippling through Scotland
        since the eighteenth century and by the 1830s had gathered
        momentum, eventually causing the 1843 schism in the Church
        of Scotland known as the Disruption. Patronage was the main issue.
        Ministers of the established Church of Scotland were chosen by
        patrons—landlords and the crown. After ten years of wrangling,
        the evangelicals succeeded in securing a majority in the
        General Assembly, getting through a Veto Act, allowing a congrega
        tion to reject a patron's choice of minister.
        This was challenged by a number of patrons and ministers and when
        legal appeals to Westminster and the House of Lords failed to

resolve the conflict, the Evangelicals staged their 'walk out'.

196   John Shepherd's parents, John Shepherd and Ann Barron married in Echt's Free Church 1849 only a few years after the Disruption. Andrew, John Shepherd's brother was a Free Church minister in Chryston, Glasgow living in the United Free Church Manse (see note 197). According to their marriage certificate (dated 6 Mar 1861) Jeannie Shepherd's parents were established Church of Scotland. By the time Jeannie married John Shepherd, as their marriage certificate confirms, Jeannie, like her husband, was Free Church.

197   In 1900 the Free Church united with the United Presbyterian Church of Scotland becoming The United Free Church of Scotland. Eventually, in 1929, the United Free Church was reunited with the established Church of Scotland so that the The Kirk on the Brae became known as Cults East Church. Almost completely obliterated by fire on 19 January 1941 (not, as it was believed at the time by enemy fire but as the result of a faulty boiler vent) only the spire and stair tower remain of the original church.

198   Paterson & Scott, *The History of Cults East Church 1843-2005* quoted in 'Cults East Story', Cults Parish Church website.

199   *TW,* p. 184.

200   According to the *AJ,* on 15 Jun 1907, NS won Mr Maitland's prize in the Junior Section on New Testament and Catechism with 356 marks.. On 30 May 1908 NS was 4th prize winner for the shorter catechism and on 8 Jun 1909 she was awarded 3rd place in the Middle Section with 338 marks.

201   *AJ, 8* Jun 1908.

202   *TQW*, p. 20.

203   *APIG*, p. 88.

204   *ibid.*

205   Macmurray, *Now and Then,* p. 4.

206   Macmurray, E. H., 1935, p.7.

207   Wilson, 1890, p. 10.

208   *AHSM*, 1926.

209   Another notable alumni was the poet Rachel Annand Taylor who was one of the first women students at the University of Aberdeen from 1894 to 1897 and who taught at the High School afterwards for a time which earned her a yellow plaque on Harlaw Academy's wall. Nan would not have been among her pupils as by the time she joined the school as a pupil, Annand Taylor had married and moved to London (via Dundee). We know the two women were acquainted, however, from an extant letter at ABDN.

210   'A brief history of Aberdeen High School for Girls', Harlaw
       Academy website.
211   *AJ,* 19 Jan 1925.
212   Robbie, 1893, p. 422.
213   Quoted in Esslemont, 1967. Dorothy Kidd went on to become
       headmistress of Aberdeen's Albyn School.
214   Robbie, 1893, p.422.
215   Esslemont, 1967.
216   After her husband James's death in 1833, which left her a substantial
       fortune, Mary Emslie (1780-1868) purchased two acres at Albyn
       Place and built the Aberdeen Female Orphan Asylum to train girls
       for domestic service which opened in 1840 with around 50 girls.
       In 1891, Miss Emslie's institution closed and was sold to the Aberdeen
       School Board. It re-opened as the new High School for Girls, two
       years later. (Robbie, 1893, p. 407.)
217   *Prospectus* 1915-1916.
218   *Prospectus* 1915-1916
219   *AJ,* 29 June 1906.
220   American feminist activist Susan B. Anthony declared in 1896 that
       the bicycle 'has done more to emancipate women than anything
       else in the world.' In *A Wheel Within A Wheel: How I Learned to
       Ride the Bicycle,* published in 1895, temperance reformer and
       suffragist Frances Willard asserted, 'I began to feel that myself plus
       the bicycle equaled myself plus the world.'
221   *TQW,* p. 22.
222   Schoolhill was named originally for the Grammar, the oldest school
       in Aberdeen (also said to be one of the oldest in Britain) which was
       founded there in about 1257, moving to Carden Place in 1863.
223   Webster, 2013, ch.9, p.1.
224   The 'Auld Hoose' was built on the site of the old
       Dominican (Black) Friars building and although fee-paying from
       1881, RGC still enjoyed considerable support from benefactors.
225   Quoted in Fraser & Lee, p.10.
226   Pupils like Nan, who lived some distance away, were permitted
       to stay in school for a two course lunch at a cost of 2/6 a week.
227   Esslemont, 1967.
228   *AJ ,* 29 Jun 1906.
229   *ibid.*
230   *AJ,* 19 Jan 1925.
231   Lucy Ward was Head Elf at AHS from 1894.
232   In 1902, along with various of the town's 'gowns', (its academics
       and university staff) Ward attended a meeting at Aberdeen's

Palace Hotel for the purpose of considering 'the enlargement of the sphere of women's usefulness'. (*The Nursing Record and Hospital World,* 5 April 1902).

233   Lucy Ward quoted in *AJ,* 24th June, 1929.

234   Margaret Iverach, science teacher at AHS, quoted in *AJ,* 24th June, 1929.

235   NS to NMG 14 Mar 1930.

236   *TQW,* pp. 26-28.

237   Clarke, 1973, pp.13-14. Despite her disappointment with much of the school's teaching, Mary Clarke fulfilled the school's aim for its pupils, going on to become headmistress of Manchester High School.

238   *TQW,* pp. 18-20.

239   *Prospectus,* 1915-1916.

240   Macmurray, E.H., 1935, p. 90.

241   *AJ,* 12 Aug 1906.

242   By the 1930s, the uniform had changed to blue tunics on school days and white ones on prize days. White hats and school ribbons were worn when 'out of school' on science expeditions.

243   *AJ,* 27 June 1930.

244   *AJ,* 1 Mar 1924.

245   Unfortunately the school keeps records of former pupils for seven years only and records do not go back as far as 1912, nor are there any School Magazines prior to 1926 kept in the school archives.

246   Town Council Scholarships awarded to Anna Shepherd and Laura McLeod. £12 each tenable for 3 years, successful competitors entering the fourth class at High School for Girls, *AJ,* 5 Aug 1907.

247   Macmurray, E.H., 1935, p. 89.

248   For continuity she is referred to as Betty throughout.

249   Macmurray, E.H., *Now and Then,* p. 18.

250   Betty says she had a love/hate relationship with the sea (Macmurray, E.H., *Now and Then,* p. 16) however she also says she 'loved to dip her bare feet' into the River Dee (Macmurray, E.H., *Now and Then,* p.15).

251   *TQW,* p. 79.

252   *TQW,* p.110, p. 42.

253   *TQW* p. 107.

254   Macmurray, E.H., *Now and Then,* p.20.

255   Macmurray, E.H., 1935, p. 91.

256   Macmurray, E.H., 1935, p. 89.

257   Also for the Gordon Mission, in Natal, Africa.

258   On a salary of £80 a year, a joint of meat at Christmas and a ration of coal, meal and vegetables.

259   Macmurray, E. H., 1935, p.7.

260   Macmurray, *Now and Then,* p. 19.

261   NS, *AUR,* 1942, p. 174.

262   'These things were not done under bushels', Nan continues: 'A generation of impact on public opinion lay behind the 1892 Ordinance enabling several Scottish Universities to admit women to degrees. 'The press and the law courts paraded them. Society had them through hand. Scotland had been in the fray too.'(NS, *AUR,* 1942.) The fight for medical educations raged in Edinburgh more furiously than elsewhere but since 1870, Edinburgh had been running a women's class for literature. St. Andrews instituted for women an LL.A equivalent to an Arts degree and Glasgow founded St Margaret College. From 1892 it was up to each Court of each Scottish university to decide whether *able* meant *willing* to admit women. Aberdeen admitted them at once to degrees in all Faculties.

263   NS, *AUR,* 1942, p.171.

264   James IV died in Battle of Flodden in 1513.

265   William Elphinstone, statesman and Chancellor of Scotland, obtained the Foundation Bull of the University of Aberdeen (originally the College of St Mary) issued by the Borgia Pope (Alexander IV) dated 10 February 1494 during James IV's reign.

266   Quoted in Graham, 1975, p. 33.

267   First Class Honours was awarded to a woman for the first time in 1899.

268   NS, *AUR,* 1942.

269   Moore, 1991, p.48.

270   Her name does not appear in any of the 1911 newspaper lists either for bursary awards or Carnegie Grants.

271   George Campbell had been unwell for some time before his wife, who believed more 'in the efficacy of her own writings to ease pain' (Macmurray, *Now and Then,* p.21) than medicine, called in a doctor. The prognosis was gloomy. After an unsuccessful operation George was given a year to live. He did exactly that. Almost a year to the day, on the 7th May 1910. It must have been a slow and agonising death. By the end he was simply too tired to fight the cancer. The cause of his death according to the certificate was 'Carcinoma of the Rectum' and 'Exhaustion'.

272   After George Campbell's death Mr Davidson, the Laird, promised Mrs Campbell an allowance of £50 a year. According to Betty, Davidson only paid it for six months, stopping it when he heard that Duncan Campbell had been seen walking in Aberdeen with

a silver-knobbed stick and was outraged at the extravagance. (See Macmurray, E.H., *Now and Then,* pp. 7 & 21.)

273   Macmurray, E., H, *Now and Then,* p. 21.

274   Macmurray, E.H., *Now and Then,* pp. 21-22.

275   Macmurray, J., *Journals,* 12 Aug 1911.

276   For insight into John Macmurray's philosophical stance I have drawn on Costello's scholarly: *John Macmurray: A biography,* as well as from some of John Macmurray's own work, including *Freedom in the Modern World,* 1935.

277   The John Macmurray Fellowship is doing its best to redress the balance.

278   Quoted in 'Scottish Diary', *Times Educational Supplement,* 25 Jun 1976, p. 3.

279   County of Dumfries since 1928.

280   Macmurray, J, 1935, p.174.

281   Macmurray, E. H., *Now and Then,* p. 1.

282   Macmurray, E.H., *Now and Then,* p.19.

283   Macmurray, J, *Journals,* 26 Dec 1908.

284   Frank was at RGC from 1904-1908.

285   Macmurray, E.H. *Now and Then,* p. 19.

286   Jocelyn Campbell, 2015.

287   Macmurray, E. H., *Out of the Earth* p. 108.

288   Macmurray, E. H., *Now and Then,* p.19.

289   Macmurray E.H., *Now and Then,* p. 20.

290   Macmurray, E.H., *Now and Then,* p. 21.

291   Macmurray, J., *Journals,* 31 Jan 1911.

292   Macmurray, J., *Journals,* 20 Jul 1911.

293   Macmurray, J., *Journals,* 29 Oct 1911.

294   Macmurray, E.H., *Now and Then,* p. 21.

295   Macmurray, J. *Journals,* 4 Feb 1912.

296   Macmurray, J, *Journals,* 18 Jul 1911.

297   Luke Cromar in *TQW* and Gilbert Munro in *APIG.*

298   *TQW,* p. 42.

299   Jocelyn Campbell, 2015.

300   *TQW,* p. 48.

301   Macmurray, E.H., *Now and Then,* p.22.

302   *ibid.*

303   *TQW,* p. 55. Duncan and Betty's financial situation during those years is also detailed in Macmurray, E. H., 1935, pp. 133-135.

304   *TQW,* p. 48

305   Macmurray, E. H., 1935, p. 133.

306   *TQW,* p. 108.

307   TQW, p. 49

308   Macmurray, J. 1935, pp.156-157.

309   EC, 2014.

310   AMM to NS, 12 Jul 1927.

311   NS, *PMN.*

312   NS to BB, 15 Jan 1981.

313   AMM to NS, c. 1932.

314   *TQW*, p. 154.

315   *TQW*, p. 153.

316   Until 1860 Aberdeen University has had the curious distinction
       of being two universities, their eventual fusion forced by circum
       stance when the old buildings of Marischal College (founded in
       1593) were demolished. Rebuilt to Archibald Simpson's design,
       when the new College opened in 1844 it was said to be
       the second largest granite building in the world and considered a
       masterpiece of granite carving. In *TQW*, Marischal is described in
       less than flattering terms as 'a sort of rival grocer's shop across
       the street from King's' but this has more to do with the art
       students, who were based mostly at King's College and were loyal
       to its cloistered, more rarefied atmosphere. (NS, 'Town and Gown',
       AUR, Autumn 1958).

317   Quoted in Graham, 1975, p.34

318   Allan, 2009, p. 243.

319   *TQW*, p. 51.

320   Semilina, Tertiana and Magistrella were the other female
       adaptations of the male names.

321   In 1900, Perthshire-born Myra Mackenzie became Aberdeen's first
       female graduate in medicine. She went on to have a successful and
       prominent medical career and was appointed Resident Physician
       and Surgeon at the Aberdeen Royal Hospital for Sick Children
       and later as School Medical Inspector for the County of
       Staffordshire.

322   Stella Henriques, ABDN.

323   There was a reason for this. Many of the male students were
       heading for careers in either the church or legal, medical and
       scientific professions. Aside from teaching, there were few employ
       ment opportunities open to women then. Education was offered
       as a university subject from 1901 and those intending to become
       teachers were permitted to attend the university arts curriculum
       without being connected to a teacher training centre.
       Other women, who were attached to a training centre, were also
       allowed to attend the university and take a couple of specialist

subjects, usually English, a modern language and Education.
The number of women in the university was also increased by the
presence of non-matriculating student teachers who attended
classes taught by non-professorial staff. As a matriculated student,
NS was not among their number.

324   *Student Handbook,* 1912, 1913, 1914 & 1915.

325   Although many a poor male student, ashamed to appear in his
        'Sunday best', was also deterred 'by the lack of that conventional
        mark of polite society—a dress suit', (Anderson, 1988, p. 6).

326   *AJ,* 1912-1915.

327   Testament to their friendship is that Dankester even presented Nan
        Shepherd with a book which, judging by the date, 11 Nov 1916,
        was on his retirement.

328   *TQW,* p. 51.

329   *TQW,* p. 53.

330   Mary Esslemont, ABDN.

331   *TQW,* p. 62.

332   Aberdeen's new English class was different to the three
        other Scottish universities'. The Act of 1858 which had united
        King's and Marischal colleges under the umbrella of one University,
        had laid down an Arts curriculum of seven compulsory subjects.
        The seventh subject was to be English Literature. As Aberdeen had
        a strong history of nature studies, the university pleaded for Natural
        History to be the seventh subject offered. The plea was granted and
        Literature was given a place as part of the course in Logic and
        Rhetoric offered by the brilliant and beloved Professor Minto who
        died before his one hundred lectures were completed.
        (Craig, 2014, pp. 70-71.)

333   *TQW,* pp 51-52.

334   NS, *AUR,* 1960.

335   *ibid.*

336   *ibid.*

337   Flora Garry, ABDN.

338   NS to HM, 22 Oct 1938.

339   NS, *AUR,* 1960.

340   Rather than specialise, NS took the three year Ordinary
        degree rather than the MA introduced in 1889.

341   *Alma Mater* was the students' magazine at Aberdeen University.
        Founded in 1883, it was noted amongst contemporary
        student magazines for the high proportion of good verse contributed
        to it by its readers. Replaced in 1934 by the *Gaudie,* it was
        subsequently revived in an altered form and continued to be

published until 1965.

342   *AM,* 1917.

343   *ibid.*

344   *TW,* p. 85

345   *TW,* pp. 171-2

346   *TW,* pp. 53-4.

347   The Mitchell Hall, designed specifically for graduation ceremonies, was part of the extension of Marischal funded by Charles Mitchell, a wealthy Newcastle shipbuilder who died just before it opened in 1895.
(Anderson, 1988, p.70.)

348   *AJ,* 12 Jul 1915.

349   *ibid.*

350   In July 1914 the number of graduates and students matriculating was 1059. Twelve months later there were only 832. While the number of women students graduating remained the same, the number of men doing so was reduced by over 230. Since 1914, the number of students and graduates who were wounded or who had given their lives for the cause had been dramatically increased through the heavy fighting in which the 4th Gordons had been engaged throughout the spring and summer in Flanders, particularly by the action in June between Ypres and Hooge. Members of the University Company of the regiment had distinguished themselves, but the number of casualties was great. The following year at the Somme, even heavier losses were sustained. (*AJ,* 12 Jul 1915).

351   *AJ,* 12 Jul 1915.

352   Aberdeen University's motto is *Initium sapientiae timor Domini* which can be translated from the Latin to mean '*The beginning of wisdom is fear of the Lord*'. A quotation from the Old Testament, Psalm 111, verse 10, it also appears in the Book of Proverbs (9:10). The motto adorns the archway beside New King's on the High Street at the King's College campus. It also appears on college certificates.

353   *TQW,* p. 93.

354   Of the 4,539 students who graduated between 1901 and 1925, 67.8% of women and 27% of men went into education.
11 % of women and 42% of men went into medicine.
(Watt, Roll of Graduates, ABDN.)

355   The *Encyclopaedia of Religion and Ethics* was originally published by T&T Clark in Edinburgh, and Charles Scribner in the United States. The volumes were issued in increments, vol.1 in 1908;

vol. 2,3,4 in 1910; then 1912, 1914, 1915, 1916, 1917, 1918, 1922, and the Index in 1926 as vol. 13. After Hastings's death in 1922, John Selbie and Louis Gray took over its editorship and completion.

356   NS thought the job was ideal for Agnes Mure Mackenzie, whose post as Junior Assistant in the English Department (which was for a statutory three years) had come to an end by 1917 and whose prospects were looking bleak. Nan found lodgings for Mure on Lower Deeside, near Dunvegan, so that her friend could take the job at Hastings' *Encyclopaedia,* where she was employed until 1920 until post-war difficulties led to Hastings' publishers withdrawing much of their financial support and she was forced to find alternative employment. Mure moved to London to work as Lecturer in English Literature at London's Birkbeck College. (NS, 'Portrait of AMM', *AUR,* 1955.)

357   In 1905, teacher training provision in Scotland had been reorganised and responsibility for it taken over from the church by the government. The two teacher training colleges in Aberdeen, run by the Church of Scotland and the Free Church were established in the early 1870s in response to the 1872 Education Act which called for the formal training of teachers. By 1905 they were struggling to keep up with the demand for places and could no longer cope with the more complex courses required in more specialist subjects by student-teachers. Duly disbanded, in their stead the secular, Aberdeen Provincial Training Centre was created in 1907.
The Training Centre changed its name in 1959 to Aberdeen College of Education and then again in 1987 to the Northern College of Education following its merger with Dundee College of Education. In 2001, the College merged with the University of Aberdeen to become the Faculty (now School) of Education. A new site at Hilton Campus was created in the 1960s. (TC archive, ABDN.)

358   Now part of The Robert Gordon University.

359   Opened in Charlotte Street in 1828, the Practising school was handed over to the Free Church Education Committee and moved to John Street in 1904. In 1909 it became the Aberdeen Demonstration School and was under the direction of Alexander Bremner. The school closed when the Training Centre moved to the Hilton campus in the 1960s.

360   Flora Garry, ABDN.

361   Grace Law, 2017.

362   *TQW,* p. 107.

363   Mary Gall, 2017.

364   'Women Citizens', n.p.,n.d. NSA.

365   'Best sellers went to this party',n.p., n.d. NSA.

366   NS, Charles Murray:Programme of Centenary Celebrations, 26 Sep 1964, transcribed from a recording.

367   *AJ*, 14 Oct 1935.

368   Forrest, 1986, p. 18.

369   JK, *AUR*, 1990, p. 190.

370   Malcolm Sutherland, 2016.

371   'Women Citizens', n.p. n.d.,NSA.

372   Mary Gall, 2017.

373   NS to HM, 9 Jan 1938.

374   Mary Gall, 2017.

375   *ibid*.

376   *ibid*.

377   Forrest, *LM*, 1986, p.18.

378   Mary Gall, 2017.

379   Grace Law, 2017.

380   *TQW*, p. 69.

381   When Tillotson refused to publish Hardy's *Tess of the D'Urbervilles* because of its graphic content in 1891, Hardy produced a bowdler ised version, without the seduction, violation or baptism scenes, which was serialised in *Graphic.*

382   Malcolm Sutherland, 2016.

383   *AJ*, 19 Apr 1922.

384   According to the TC, ABDN, for the academic year September 1918 to August 1919 the highest paid male member of staff was Alec Bremner who was earning £42 per month and the highest paid female member of staff was May Young on £24 per month. The remaining staff members were on salaries of £12 per month. There is no mention of NS, but then she was not a full-time member of staff until the start of the academic year in September 1919. I was unable to find later staff salary records in the archives. But given that the average working class wage was at that time around 20 shillings a week, her salary was not an inconsider able amount. As a part-time member of staff, NS would have been paid much less. According to her, in 1914, for essay correction and tutorial work, Mure Mackenzie was paid a meagre £30 a year. (NS, *AUR*, 1955, p. 134.)

385   'Women Citizens', n.p.n.d., NSA.

386   NS to NMG, 14 March 1930.

387   Forrest, *LM*, 1986 p. 18.

388   'I never write lectures. Not even notes for them'. NS to HM,
       9 Jan 1938. See also notes 833–834.

389   Mary Gall, 2017.

390   Donald, 1977, p. 2

391   For nine of those twelve miles there was not a house to be seen.
       But it was not just the isolation these ex-pupils often had to endure.
       Teaching practice in city schools was not, NS thought, decent
       preparation for the life of a teacher in these rural posts. See NS,
       'Schools and Schoolmistresses', n.d., NSA.

392   Mary Gall, 2017.

393   Scottish Leaving Certificates.

394   FSJ to NS, c. 1915.

395   *TW*, p. 45.

396   George Thomson had a son, George Watt Thomson born 15 Oct
       1880, from his first marriage to Isabella Watt. She died in 1880.

397   The Thomson's two sons went early into the retail trade. Aged
       fourteen Stephen was a grocer. His older brother William, in 1901,
       was a draper living in Ferryhill, Aberdeen, suggesting that the family
       moved to be closer to him.

398   Isabella Thomson, the oldest of the six daughters, was born in 1885
       and died in 1900 aged 15. She is buried with her father in
       Longside. Of the other Thomson girls, we know that Harriet
       Thomson married Arthur Edward McRae Smith in 1920.
       They had one daughter. Charlotte Thomson never married. In 1963
       her address was Bogroy Hotel, Kirkhill, Inverness-shire. Jennie
       Thomson died in 1979.

399   Sources for this section: Imperial War Museum, 2016, and 'The Life
       of a Woman Worker', The Royal Arsenal, Woolwich, 2016.

400   *Civil Engineer's Listing.*

401   The novelist Edith Nesbit leased Well Hall House from 1899 to
       1911. Demolished in 1930, it is said to have provided Nesbit
       with inspiration for some of her writing, where it appears as 'The
       Red House'.

402   Archibald Cameron Corbett Society, 2016.

403   Now a golf course.

404   Now Eltham station.

405   On his marriage certificate Frank Shepherd is recorded as 'Mechan
       ical Engineer, Shop Manager, Royal Arsenal Woolwich'.

406   HC Deb, 'Written Answers, Commons', Hansard, 8 Nov 1916,
       Vol 87.

407   Afrikaans: 'fountain of flowers'.

408   *TW*, p.45.

409   Mary Gall, 2017.

410   *TW*, p. 63.

411   Also in the picture is Euphemia Cruden (suggesting that by then she and Jeannie had patched up their differences over the lace knickers), her daughter Hilda Sutherland and her son Joe Sutherland.

412   To date, I have been unable to trace either the name or cause of death of Frank and Alice's daughter (although there was an outbreak of Scarlet Fever around the time she died). SC has written on the back of the photograph without naming the little girl or her mother who is described as 'Nan's sister-in-law'.

413   Alice's mother, Isabella Thomson, died in 1916 before her daughter's marriage. After her mother's death Alice moved from 'Briars' to 'Cloves', on the south side of the Deeside Railway Line but where she was living in the period between her return from South Africa and her daughter's death is not known. The Saxon's passenger list cites Wales as Alice Shepherd's ultimate destination.

414   On their marriage certificate Alice's address is the same as her husband's: 'Bank House, Torphins' and her occupation is given as 'Housekeeper (Widow)'.

415   Latin: Perpetual Light.

416   In the mss of the poem, NS has used the archaic 'alway', *PMN*.

417   Grierson believed 'it is only in the fragments of Sappho, the lyrics of Catullus, and the songs of Burns…that one will find the sheer joy of loving and being loved expressed in the same direct and simple language as in some of Donne's songs', (Grierson, *Donne's Poetical Works,* 1912, pp.xlii-xliii.) As a student of Grierson's, this may account for the number of extracts from Sappho and Catullus in *GL* and *MB* and for her allusions to them in her own works.

418   *GL*.

419   *TLM*, p.93.

420   AE is an abbreviation of 'Aeon' meaning life, a vital force, being.

421   Yeats, W.B., 'Nobel speech', 15 Nov 1923.

422   MacDiarmid, 1984, p. 751.

423   An excerpt from Yeats's one-act morality play *The Hourglass* (1903).

424   *The Theosophical Path*, Jan. 1930, pp. 3-4.

425   In Sanskrit *sat* or *tat*.

426   Ryan, 1930.

427   de Purucker, G., 1930.

428   Quoted in Kain and O'Brien, 1976, p. 78.

429   Macfarlane, 'Introduction' *TLM*, p. xix.

430   NS, *TDF,* 1938, p. 10.

431   *TLM*, p. 2.
432   To AE, nature was magic—beyond the scope of religion—and to
       access this magic required a retreat from the basic tenets of Irish
       Catholicism and its strict system of penitence and forgiveness of
       sins. It was Christianity, theosophists believed, that had disconnected
       people from nature and embroiled it instead in politics. The principles
       of theosophy, as 'universal truth', 'divine nature, visible and invis
       ible' permeate all AE's poetry but are probably best-explained in *The
       Candle of Vision* (1918) a memoir of his visions not yet published
       when NS first came across his poetry. Here, he relays his encounters
       with what he calls 'super-nature' in his visionary moments, his dream
       -states where the natural world seems to transform itself, and his
       journey into self. If NS read the book when it came out, there
       is no evidence to support it in *Gleanings*. But the thinking in AE's
       memoir and in NS's own spiritual autobiography, *The Living
       Mountain,* is somewhat analogous.
433   AE, 1918, p.54.
434   Dana is the patroness of AE's thought and work. The mother of gods,
       the first spiritual form of matter: beauty, Dana can 'enchant the trees
       and rocks and fill the dumb brown earth with mystery'. She appears
       in 'The Place of Rest' as the Mighty Mother who 'smites through
       pain'. In 'Desire', the narrator searches, in an 'eternal toil' for 'the high,
       austere and lonely way' turning 'to Thee, invisible, unrumoured still:
       White for Thy whiteness all desires burn'.
       'Frolic' parallels children dancing on a beach with stars shouting, sun
       chasing the moon, 'The game was the same as the children's/They
       danced to the self-same tune'. In 'Immortality, the reader is urged to
       'pass like smoke or live within the spirit's fire...as smoke we vanish/
       though the fire may burn'. In 'Epigram' we have the 'infinite'
       murmuring its ancient story' wakening, 'primeval fires'.
435   Meteorological Office, Feb 1918.
436   *PMN.*
437   'In from the great processional of space,/From the tramp of stars'
       appears in a poem written the following year, 'Fires', *ITC*, p. 4.
438   *PMN.*
439   *TW,* p. 56.
440   *APIG*, p. 74.
441   *PMN.*
442   *TQW,* p. 129.
443   *TQW*, p. 102.
444   Macmurray, E. H., *Now and Then*, p.25.
445   Assigned to the 40th Field Ambulance Unit he was dispatched to

Salisbury Plain where he remained at the Tidworth training camp
until August 1915.

446   Betty graduated third class from Aberdeen University in 1915.
(*AJ,* Jul 1915.)

447   Macmurray's parents were by then living in Crouch End as John's
sisters, Ella and Lilias, were working for the civil service in London.

448   England and Wales civil registration index 1916-2005.

449   In her memoirs, Betty says Mary Beedie was a 'companion'
to her mother (Macmurray, E.H., *Now and Then,* p.21). According to
the 1901 census Beedie was a domestic servant at Home Farm,
Inchmarlo.

450   Meteorological Office, Jan 1917.

451   Macmurray, E. H., *Now and Then,* p. 1.

452   Macmurray, E. H., 1935. p. 145.

453   *TQW,* p. 85.

454   Macmurray, J. 1965.

455   The book is a remarkable collection of soldiers' personal responses
to the effect war was having on their religious faith. It seems most
likely that the section on 'Trench Fatalism' in the book can be
attributed to John Macmurray although he is not identified by name,
but as an officer of a Scottish regiment. (*The Army and Religion,*
1919, pp. 168-169.)

456   *TW,* pp.54-55.

457   *TW,* p.56.

458   *TW,* p. 171.

459   Macmurray, J. 1965.

460   *ibid.*

461   Aside from the timing of the extracts in *Gleanings,* 'Fourteen
Years' is repeated with reference to the duration of Mary Kilgour's
love for Gilbert Munro, with whom she used to 'philosophize'.
Once again, Nan Shepherd's fiction explains oblique references
in her poetry.
(*APIG* p.52.)

462   Hamilton, 1976.

463   Smith, 2004.

464   Macmurray E H, *Now and Then,* p. 47.

465   JM to BM, 1923.

466   Quotation attributed to Dorothy Parker.

467   *APIG,* p. 51.

468   *TQW,* p. 76.

469   *ITC,* p. 44.

470   *ITC,* p 43.

471   AMM to NS, Jan 1923.

472   *TQW, p.* 86.

473   *TQW, p.* 108.

474   *TQW,* p. 115.

475   Macmurray, E H, *Out of the Earth,* 1935, p.223.

476   *ITC,* p. 47.

477   *TQW,* p. 126.

478   Browning, 1855. Andrea Del Sarto was a sixteenth century
Italian artist working with Michelangelo and Raphael in Rome.

479   Macmurray, E.H., *Now and Then,* p. 21.

480   Macmurray, E. H., 1935, p. 155.

481   She was acquainted with Browning's 'Andrea del Sarto',
however, as she refers to it in NS to NMG, 2 Apr 1931, when
discussing her own poetry writing. (See note 654.)

482   *TQW,* p. 88.

483   A Hindhu, Tagore's religion was of the relationship of man with
nature and with God, a relationship whose goal was oneness with
God (Bramah)—oneness meaning absorption into God and
therefore loss of identity. What NS seems most taken with,
however, is his collection of 'the lyrics of love and life'
in *The Gardener* translated by Tagore from their original Bengali in
1915 and dedicated to W B Yeats.

484   In her *Medley Book,* NS erroneously gives the date Tagore won the
Nobel prize as 1914.

485   Patrons of the society included Professors Grierson, Japp,
Anderson and George Adam Smith.

486   *MB.*

487   *TQW,* p. 122.

488   *TQW,* p. 123.

489   Quoted in NS, AMM: 'A Portrait', *AUR,* 1955.

490   *Without Conditions* 1923. *The Quiet Lady* 1926. *The women in
Shakespeare's plays* 1924 Two more novels followed, a play, and
two works of literary criticism: *The Process of Literature* and
The Playgoer's Handbook to the English Renaissance Drama—
during the 1920s. Then, *An Historical Survey of Scottish Literature
to 1714,* 1933, a biography: *Robert Bruce, King of Scots* 1934 and
two historical novels for younger readers on Bruce: *I was at
Bannockburn* (1939) and *Apprentice Majesty* (1950). *Robert Bruce,
King of Scots* was included retrospectively into her six-volume
history of Scotland as volume two. The other volumes were *The
Foundations of Scotland* (1938), *The Rise of the Stewarts* (1935),
The Scotland of Queen Mary and the religious wars 1513–1638 (1936),

The Passing of the Stewarts (1937), and Scotland in modern times 1720–
1939 (1941). In 1940 she produced The Kingdom of Scotland: a short
History and a school textbook history, A History of Britain and Europe
for Scottish Schools in 1949. She also published a four-volume series,
Scottish Pageant (1946–1950), a series of translated extracts from
primary sources for a mass audience.

491   NS, 'AMM: A Portrait', *AUR,* 1955.

492   *ibid.*

493   *ibid.*

494   HJC Grierson to AMM, 14 Jan 1914.

495   Suffragism was replaced with quiet lobbying leading eventually to
the 1918 Representation of the People Act which gave votes to
women over thirty who met the property criteria (40% of the
total population, then, of women in the UK) and extended the vote
to all men over twenty-one. It was the 1928 Equal Franchise Act
that extended the vote to women over twenty-one.

496   NS, *AUR*, 1955.

497   Oliver quoted in NS, 'AMM: A Portrait', *AUR*, 1955.

498   Hodgkiss, 1983, p. 39.

499   Clachnaben is one of Aberdeenshire's most distinctive hills,
standing at 589 metres it is visible from many points on Lower
Deeside. It is also the Grampian of NS's *A Pass in the Grampians.*

500   AMM to NS, 1921.

501   AMM to NS 12 Jul 1927.

502   AMM to NS, Dec 1920.

503   *ibid.*

504   Even before the war there hadn't been enough men to go round.
From the 1870s women outnumbered men in census figures, caused
by the numbers of men emigrating to the Colonies and the deaths,
in infancy, of more males than females. The war just amplified an
on-oing issue.

505   Nan could hardly have missed the critical cartoons or the newspaper
articles on the 'surplus women'. *DFTC,* written when she was fifty
years old, shows her very clearly conversant with the 'phenomenon'.
Elizabeth, 'began to be aware she was shut out from something, but
there was no sesame for that door. She stayed out and went on
working. She worked like a puppy at a sandbank...Shoulders
squared she marched on life with such zest that she had nearly
forgotten the door without the sesame'. (*DFTC*, p. 345.)

506   Hodgkiss, 1983, p. 44.

507   *DTFC,* p.345.

508   Macmurray, E. H., *Now and Then,* p. 26

509   Macmurray, E. H., unpublished journals, 1922.

510   *TQW,* p.146.

511   CM to George Walker, 8 Aug 1922.

512   CM to Edith Murray, 15 Jul 1920.

513   'When I was his guest in Capetown and Pretoria, he was keen to
        know what was happening to poetry 'at home' and was even then
        a reader, I remember, of Edith Sitwell' (NS, 'The Charles Murray
        Memorial Trust', *AUR,* 1958).

514   Afrikaans: verandah.

515   NS, 'Introduction' to *Hamewith,* 1979, p. ix.

516   *ibid.*

517   *APIG,* p. 15.

518   Macmurray, E.H., *Now and Then,* p. 27.

519   Lourenco Marques in Delagoa Bay (now Maputo Bay in
        Mozambique) grew from a settlement of a few flat-topped hovels
        on a sand-spit in the 1870s to a flourishing town of about
        twenty thousand inhabitants by the 1920s and was fast becoming
        the place to go.

520   NS is made conspicuous by her absence from Betty's memoirs.
        She is referred to once, as a friend during Betty's university years
        (Macmurray, E. H., *Now and Then,* p.22). We know Nan stayed
        with the Macmurrays though because in Charles Murray's letter
        to George Walker dated 8 August 1922, that when Nan left
        them, she was going on to stay with friends in Johannesburg.
        Betty makes no mention of Nan accompanying them to Delagoa
        in her memoirs, or in her 1922 journal (although she has pasted in a
        20 centavo note from the trip). That Nan did go—is evident
        from references to Delagoa in *TQW (* p. 147).

521   Macmurray, E. H., *Now and Then,* p. 29.

522   *TQW,* p. 147.

523   *TW,* p. 161.

524   'See page 201' Betty adds after this, referring John to a passage
        where Maribel discusses a Cubist sketch of hers with David
        —a sketch Agnes cannot fathom.

525   Lawrence, D H. (1929) 1994, p. 625.

526   In Max Plowman to John Middleton Murray, 13 Jun 1932,
        Plowman claims John Macmurray once confessed this to him
        (*Bridge into the Future: Letters of Max Plowman,* London: Andrew
        Dakers, 1944, p. 424).

527   Macmurray, E. H., 1935, p. 191.

528   Macmurray, E. H., *Now and Then,* p. 46.

529   Macmurray, E. H., unpublished journals, 1922.

530   Macmurray, E. H., 1935, p. 184.
531   *ITC, XV.*
532   *ITM*, p.45.
533   *ITC*, p. 27.
534   Macmurray, E.H., 1935, p. 215.
535   Macmurray, E. H., 1935, p. 227.
536   Macmurray, E. H., 1935, p. 226.
537   *TQW,* p. 117.
538   *TQW* was published in 1928, the same year D H Lawrence's *Lady Chatterley's Lover* was published in Italy (and in Paris the following year). Lawrence's work was banned in Britain until 1960, which gives some indication of the prudishness of the reading public.
539   Inspired by the landscape around Gavin Maxwell's house at Sandaig Kathleen Raine's phrase from *The Marriage of Psyche* (1952), was borrowed by him for the title of his best-known book, *Ring of Bright Water* (1960).
540   Macmurray, E. H., 1935, pp. 212-3.
541   *ITC,* p. 49.
542   *TW,* p. 112.
543   *TW,* pp. 77-8.
544   *GL.*
545   Enclosed with NS to NMG, 15 Sep 1931.
546   *ITM*, p. 51.
547   *ITM*, p. 39.
548   NS to JK, 12 Aug 1979.
549   Quoted in Dunnett, 1933, p. 342.
550   Quoted in Kyle, 1931.
551   Hamilton, 1976.
552   *TQW*, p. 184.
553   Morrison, 1973, p. 92.
554   *TQW*, p. 210.
555   Cunningham, 1991, p. 28.
556   AMM to NS, circa 1923.
557   The etymology of 'Maggie' is more straightforward: 'child of light'.
558   *TQW*, p. 64.
559   *TQW*, p. 125.
560   *ITC*, p. 48.
561   Macmurray, E. H., 1935, p. 223.
562   *TQW*, p. 177.
563   Macmurray, E.H., *Now and Then,* p. 45.
564   St Francis referred to his body as 'Brother Ass'.

565 AMM to NS, 1925.

566 *ibid.*

567 *ibid.*

568 *TQW,* pp. 124-125.

569 AMM to NS, 1925.

570 AMM to NS, 1925.

571 Kail: a type of brassica, or cabbage. The critical term 'Kailyard'
    is thought to have come from an old Scots song used by Ian
    Maclaren: 'There grows a bonnie briar bush in our Kailyard, And
    white are the blossoms on't in our Kailyard' in his preface to
    Beside the Bonnie Brier Bush (1894).

572 *TW,* p. 75.

573 Quoted in Kyle, 1931.

574 Kyle, 1931.

575 A 'Celtic renascence' in Literature and Art had been proposed as far
    back as 1895 by Patrick Geddes. It was the way forward, he said,
    for 'the revival and development of the old Continental sympathies of
    Scotland (a line MacDiarmid was later quick to adopt). In 1921,
    journalist and poet William Jeffrey asked 'Is this a Scottish poetry
    renaissance?' in his review of the first series *Northern Numbers* first
    produced by Grieve in 1920.

576 1922 was the year T S Eliot's *The Wasteland* first appeared in Dial
    Magazine, James Joyce's Ulysses was published in Paris and in
    London, D H Lawrence produced *Aaron's Rod* which was followed
    by Virginia Woolf's first experimental novel *Jacob's Room.*

577 NS, *AUR,* 1938, p. 57.

578 It was not that Grieve drank a lot of whisky, it was just that,
    according to Willa Muir, it did not take much to intoxicate him.
    (Muir, 1968, p. 116.)

579 *The Chapbook,* Aug 1922.

580 Eliot, 1919.

581 For the sections on the Scottish 'Renaissance' I have relied
    heavily on Palmer McCulloch, M., 2009.

582 *The Chapbook,* Oct 1922.

583 David Murison to NS, 10 Jan 1952. Other antagonists coined
    the term 'Plastic Scots' for it to suggest something artificial and a poor
    'phoney'. Synthetic Scots' was a term first used by Denis Seurat about
    MacDiarmid's language in *Sangschaw* and *Penny Wheep.* See also
    Cruickshank, p. 77.

584 David Murison to NS, 10 Jan 1952.

585 Grieve in *Dunfermline Press,* Sept 1922 reprinted in Palmer
    McCulloch, 2004, p. 24.

586 NS, *AUR,* 1938, p. 55.

587   In May 1923 Grieve, who was struggling with the format
        of *The Chapbook* published a new weekly magazine, *The Scottish
        Nation*.
        Despite its title and in this first edition, the call for the freeing of
        Scotland from English influence, the magazine's agenda was not
        explicitly political. There were articles on music, new fiction,
        contemporary art, religion and ethics as well as articles on Gaelic
        language, education, employment and politics. International art and
        affairs was a regular feature through which Grieve introduced the
        work of European writers, discussions of Russian poetry and essays
        by Muir on D H Lawrence, for example. *The Scottish Nation* was
        modelled on Orage's *The New Age* which never made a profit and
        without financial backing, the magazine proved eventually
        unsustainable. Scotland in the twenties was not a land full of wealthy
        patrons who would sponsor such enterprises and as time went on,
        despite the fact that most of its contributors were doing so freely,
        Grieve himself under various pseudonyms was actually writing
        most of the pieces. By December 1923, both *The Chapbook* and *The
        Scottish Nation* ceased to appear. A monthly magazine, *The North-
        ern Review* was published by Grieve the following year but as this,
        too, had no outside funding, it ran for only four issues.

588   Penny wheep: the weakest kind of small beer sold at a penny
        a bottle. (Jamieson, 1867, Vol 1, p. 713.)

589   Quoted in Dunnett, 1933, p. 341.

590   LGG, 1982, p. 129.

591   The reader was Desmond Hughes (see AMM to NS, 1927).

592   AMM to NS, 1927.

593   Constable and Company was founded by Archibald Constable, a
        bookseller from Edinburgh, Scotland, in 1795. After his death in
        1827, the company suffered financial difficulties until his grandson,
        (also Archibald) reinvigorated it in 1890, opening a London office.
        On his retirement in 1893 he handed over the company to his
        nephew H. Arthur Doubleday. Doubleday added Otto Kyllmann
        and William M. Meredith as partners in 1895, with Michael Sadleir
        joining the company in 1912. In 1999, Constable and Company
        merged with Robinson Publishing to become Constable and
        Robinson.

594   AMM to NS, 1926.

595   AMM to NS, 1926. In fact, Kyllman, who was born in Manchester,
        was of German rather than English descent. Both his parents had
        emigrated from Germany to England in around 1860 with their
        respective families. Otto Kyllman's father, Eduard Kyllman
        was born in Nordhhein-Westfalen in 1838 and his mother, Matilda

Borchardt, in Preussen, in 1844.

596   JK, 1990, p. 190.

597   *ibid*.

598   AMM to NS, c. 1923.

599   AMM to NS, 19 May 1926.

600   *Glasgow Herald,* 1928.

601   W.S.M., n.p. 1928.

602   *Buffalo Times,* Aug 1928.

603   Taylor, 1928.

604   Quoted in Taylor, 1928.

605   n.p. n.d. NSA.

606   W.S.M., n.p., 1928.

607   *ibid*.

608   Walpole, 30 Jun 1928.

609   Evelyn was the only daughter to marry. Widowed not long after, she returned home to live with her sisters. Andrew and Jane Shepherd's only son, Andrew Barron Shepherd died aged four of croup in 1891.

610   Helen Bain, 2016

611   Jean Roger, 2014.

612   AMM to NS, 12 Jul 1927.

613   NS to AMM, 9 July 1928.

614   *ibid*.

615   Young Lindsay Lorimer finds herself living in a female community among generations of Craigmyle and Lorimer women and to some extent can be seen as on a journey to 'become' her adult self before marriage to Garry Forbes. The novel goes further than *TQW,* asking questions about identity that go beyond female emancipation.

616   Quoted in Dunnett, 1933, p. 341.

617   Kyle, 1931.

618   *TW,* p.5.

619   *TW*, p. 199.

620   *TLM,* p. 101.

621   *TW*, p.9.

622   *TW,* p.164.

623   *TW,* p. 118.

624   *SO,* 1930.

625   *TS,* 24 Feb 1930.

626   *Illustrated London News*, 22 Mar 1933.

627   Helen Bain, 2016. Undeterred, she found copies in the library and read them anyway.

628   NS to NMG, 14 Mar 1930.

629   NMG to NS, 10 Mar 1930.

630   NS to NMG, 14 Mar 1930.

631   Later the 'Scottish National Party'. NMG joined the National
       Party of Scotland a year after it was formed in 1929. He was
       also a member of the Committee on Post-War Hospitals in 1941
       and the Commission of Inquiry into Crofting Conditions in 1951.

632   Quoted in MacDiarmid, 1973.

633   Grieve, 1926.

634   NMG, 'Hugh MacDiarmid', 1962, Box 8, NLS.

635   Quoted in Murray, 2000, p. 175.

636   Quoted in Hart & Pick, 1981, p. 84.

637   She first wrote to him via *The Porpoise Press* which had published
       his collection of short stories earlier in 1929.

638   NS to NMG, 19 Aug 1929.

639   The *Scots Magazine* first appeared in 1924, its aim to provide
       'a high class literary periodical devoted entirely to Scotland and
       things Scottish'. From 1927, under the editorship of James Bell
       Salmond, the magazine was injected with fresh energy. Salmond
       printed various of the 'Renaissance' writers' work, NS's included
       among them were her poem 'Lux Perpetua' in 1929 and her short
       story *Descent from the Cross* in 1943).

640   NMG to Hodder & Stoughton, 19 May 1929.

641   James Bell Salmond took over editorship of *The Scots Magazine* in
       1927.

642   NMG to NS, 26 Aug 1929.

643   *SM,* Nov 1938.

644   NMG to NS 26 Aug 1929.

645   NS to Francis Hart & J B Pick 1978, quoted in Hart & Pick,
       1981, p. 84.

646   NMG to NS, 26 Aug 1929.

647   NMG to NS, 10 Mar 1930.

648   NS to NMG 14 Mar 1930.

649   By 1931 there were several in China and South America.

650   Galsworthy asked his friend Herbert Grierson, by then Professor of
       English Literature and Rhetoric at the University of Edinburgh, to
       consider founding a PEN centre for Scotland. Grierson passed on
       the task to Grieve.

651   Cruickshank, p. 68.

652   PEN representatives: in Inverness, NMG; in Glasgow, William
       Jeffrey, George Blake and Marion Lochead; in Dundee, J B Salmond.
       Edinburgh's PEN was presided over by Lady Margaret Sackville and
       J. Liddell Geddie, Professor Grierson, Charles Grave and Lewis
       Spence were also members. (Cruickshank, p. 75.)

653   AMM to NS, 1932.

654   Cruickshank, p. 59.

655   Cruickshank, p.76.

656   In 1920, Helen Cruickshank heard that a C M Grieve (then only
        a name to her) was inviting contributions to *Northern Numbers* and
        she sent him some of her verses. They began to correspond
        and in 1924 she met Grieve for the first time. (Cruickshank, p. 58.)

657   'After the story of Elijah and the pious widow who always
        placed her small "chamber in the wall" at the Prophet's disposal'
        (Cruickshank, p. 75).

658   The meeting was held to honour Ronald Campbell Macfie
        (1867–1931) a poet who by then had been rather forgotten. HC
        makes no mention of whether she appreciated his poetry and I can
        find no reference to him in NS's extant papers.

659   NS, *TDF,* 1970, p. 9.

660   NS, *SM,* 1947, p. 37.

661   Cruickshank, p. 76.

662   Quoted in 'Will Braid Scots Die Out? Timorous Use of Old Speech:
        Miss Marion Angus's Forecast', *AJ,* 9 Dec 1930, p. 6.

663   Many thought Marion Angus's poetry sprang from frustration—
        unhappy love, love betrayed, lover unrequited, love sated,
        is a recurring theme in her poetry. (NS, *SM,* 1947, pp. 37-44.)

664   Cruickshank Collection, 5 Dec 1930, University of Stirling.

665   Cruickshank, p. 59.

666   Cruickshank, p. 60

667   Doric: wasn't bashful.

668   This one was a party given to celebrate Christopher Grieve's return
        from Liverpool in 1931.

669   Scots poet Nannie K Wells (1875-1963) was a colourful personality
        who collaborated with MacDiarmid on an unpublished biography
        of Alexander Stewart (the Wolf of Badenoch). An avid supporter
        of the Scottish Literary Renaissance, Wells, who worked for the
        foreign office during the first World War, was a Scottish Nationalist
        and Secretary Deputy of the Scottish Nationalist Party from the
        late 1920s to early 30s. She wrote regularly for the *Scots Mag-
        azine and The Free Man* (the latter founded in 1932 by Robin Black,
        who although sympathetic to the nationalist cause claimed no
        affiliation to any particular party).

670   NS to HC, 9 Sep 1962.

671   Edwin Muir's first book, *We Moderns* was published under the
        pseudonym Edward Moore in 1918.

672   *First Poems,* 1925 and *Chorus of the Newly Dead,* 1926.

673 Muir, 1968, p. 114.

674 Muir, 1968, p. 115.

675 *ibid*.

676 Muir, 1982, p.2.

677 Grieve, 'Scotsmen Make a God of Robert Burns' *Radio Times*, 17 Jan 1930, p. 137.

678 One of MacDiarmid's most overlooked works *To Circumjack Cencrastus* was published in 1930, four years after what is generally considered his modernist masterpiece, *A Drunk Man Looks at the Thistle*. Yet as well as being pivotal in the poet's development it actually contains some extraordinarily fine writing. . It is typical of NS to have seen and appreciated this.

679 Carswell, 'The "Giant Ploughman" Can Withstand His Critics', *Radio Times*, Feb 1930.

680 NS to NMG, 14 Mar 1930.

681 'A Woman on Burns' n.p. c. 1934, NSA.

682 *TQW*, p.102.

683 After leaving South Africa in November 1922, the Macmurrays moved to Oxford.

684 'A Woman on Burns' n.p., c. 1934, NSA.

685 From 'Morgan' in Thomas, E., *Cloud Castle & Other Papers*, Duckworth, 1922.

686 Proverb of Asaro of Papua New Guinea: Knowledge is only a rumour until it lives in the muscle.

687 'Cairngorms', as the range is now called on maps and in guidebooks, is a nickname taken from Cairn Gorm, the best-known hill in the massif. These hills are actually Am Monadh Ruadh (the red hill-range) but as Nan Shepherd uses the moniker 'Cairngorms', so have I.

688 *TLM*, p.106.

689 Quoted in Le Blond, 1903, p. ix.

690 There is some dissent over the height of this record-setting ascent which is recorded as being anything between 22,735 and 23,263 feet. According to the American Alpine Club, in 1906 the summit of Pinnacle Peak in the Nun Kun was estimated to be 23,264 feet. The third highest summit of the Nun Kun massif, according to the Jammu and Kashmir Tourist Board it measures 6,930 metres (22,736.22 feet).

691 914.4 metres.

692 Quoted in Steven, p.10.

693 *Shelter Stone Visitor Books*, ABDN.

694 *TLM*, p.1.

695   The reason for this is because the Cairngorms stand exposed to winds from north around to the south-east, which are the main snow-bearing winds in Scotland and is why coastal Aberdeenshire experiences more snow and frost than Skye. As the hills lie in the centre of Scotland, their climate, too, tends to be more continental so that the weather there is warmer in summer and colder in winter than in the surrounding coastal areas. (Watson, p. 29.)

696   The Automatic Weather Station on the summit of Cairn Gorm holds the record for the highest recorded windspeed in the UK. 176 mph was observed at 11:48 on the 3rd Jan 1993. The lowest ever recorded temperature in the UK, according to the Met Office, was −27.2C in Braemar, Aberdeenshire, in 1895 and 1982 and in Altnaharra, Sutherland, in 1995.

697   Cairngorms National Park Authority, 2017.

698   *TLM*, pp.18-19.

699   *TLM*, p. 107.

700   *TLM*, p.2.

701   *TLM*, p. 6.

702   Making it the highest loch of this size in Britain (Watson, p. 76).

703   *TLM*, p. 17.

704   *TLM*, p. 16.

705   *TLM*, p. 7.

706   *TLM*, p. 7.

707   NS, *TDF*, 1962.

708   *ibid.*

709   *TLM*, p. 85.

710   Deas: a wooden bench which, turned over and rested on its arms became a table and if the seat was raised up could be used as a bed.

711   NS, *TDF*, 1962.

712   A chimney, or a chimney canopy of any type, according to the *Dictionary of the Scots language,* the lum at Downie's Cottage is a wooden structure that hings (hangs) on the wall over the cooking fire. It was a style of chimney commonplace in old traditional cottages. Because of its large volume it tended to gather and direct the smoke, rather than draw it, as a narrow masonry chimney is designed to do, but despite this, was clearly a fire hazard.

713   John Duff, 2016.

714   *TW*, p. 10.

715   NS, *TDF*, 1962.

716   *TLM*, p.58.

717   Jean Roger, 2014.

718   Neil Roger, 2015.

719   It may not have been a honeymoon snap. There is another, unidentified woman in the group, bespectacled in a tightly belted mac who is standing next to Mrs MacGregor.

720   NS, *TDF*, 1962.

721   NS to HM 11 Oct 1938.

722   NS, *TDF,* 1962.

723   NS, *TDF,* 1962.

724   *TLM*, p. 89.

725   *TLM*, pp. 85–89.

726   *ITM*, p.4.

727   *TLM*, p. 107.

728   NS, *TDF,* 1962.

729   NS to NMG, 14 Mar 1930.

730   NS to NMG, 17 May 1940.

731   NS to NMG, 14 Mar 1930.

732   *ibid.*

733   NS, *SM,* 1947, p.40.

734   NS, *DFTC*, p. 354.

735   *ITM,* p. 50.

736   *ITM,* p 38.

737   *ITM*, p. 50.

738   *TW*, p. 52.

739   Siepmann, in 'Foreword' to Macmurray, J, 1935, p. 8.

740   The brainchild of Charles Siepmann, Head of the Talks Department and Secretary to the Central Council for Adult Education, the broadcasts were part of the BBC's thrust towards Adult Education which was developing swiftly in the late 1920s to early 30s. In April 1929, it was decided to extend the series on 'Mind and Body' to include 'philosophical problems'. Macmurray's talks made broadcast history and 'Today and Tomorrow: A Philosophy of Freedom', the pamphlet John wrote to introduce them, was a best-seller. Letters poured in from all over the country —from all social classes. By 1930, John was in great demand as a speaker but aside from a few academic articles he had published nothing else. This was deliberate. Wanting to let his ideas mature, John had vowed not to publish anything until he was forty. On 16th February 1930 he had turned thirty-nine and his twelve BBC talks became his first book, *Freedom in the Modern World*, published by Faber & Faber in 1933.

741   NMG to NS, 25 May 1930.

742   *TLM*, p. 23.

743   NS to NMG, 2 Apr 1931.

744   *The Modern Scot* took over Grieve's more avant-garde role in the
        early 1930s. It was owned and edited by an American, James H Whyte,
        who was a supporter of the political and cultural aims of the 'Scottish
        Renaissance'. Unlike Grieve, Whyte had money and could pay
        contributors well and continuing where Grieve left off, maintained
        European connections and encouraged new writing in all three
        of Scotland's indigenous languages. At the outbreak of war in 1939,
        Whyte, a bi-sexual who scandalised the St Andrew's community
        where he lived by openly cohabiting with his partner, fell victim
        to the spy mania sweeping Britain and returned to America.
        (See Palmer McCulloch, 2009, pp.22-24). Back in 1931,
        though, Neil Gunn still had high hopes that Whyte, whom he
        described as intelligent, would develop his critical skills.

745   NMG to NS, 29 Mar 1931.

746   NMG to NS, 29 Mar 1931.

747   AMM to NS, 1930.

748   Helen Waddell to NS, 12 May 1931. The Irish poet, translator
        and playwright Helen Waddell, who was a friend of members of the
        Bloomsbury set like Yeats and Woolf and who enjoyed a personal and
        professional relationship with Sassoon, was also published by Constable.
        She never married, but for many years enjoyed a very close relation
        ship with with Otto Kyllman.

749   NS to NMG, 2 Apr 1931.

750   *TW*, pp. 9-10.

751   MA to NS, June 1922.

752   NS to NMG, 2 April 1931.

753   *ibid.*

754   Browning, 1855. Although Browning does not feature in *GL or
        MB* NS was obviously well-acquainted with the work and perhaps,
        too, with John Macmurray's mantra—it would seem otherwise
        to be quite a coincidence. (See also notes 478 and 418.)

755   Helen Waddell to NS, 12 May 1931.

756   NMG to NS, 15 Apr 1931.

757   NS to NMG, 5 Jul 1931.

758   Quoted in Murray, 2000, p. 174.

759   According to Hart & Pick, by 1936, Daisy and Neil were reconciled.
        Despite the Gunn's move from Inverness and MacEwan's move to
        London in 1938, making it more difficult for the two to meet, the
        relationship continued, if somewhat intermittently until the 1960s.
        MacEwan never married. To do so would have meant the end of her
        relationship with Neil and she was not prepared to jeopardise it.
        (Hart & Pick, pp. 129-131.)

760 NS sent: 'Blackbird in Snow', 'The Apple Tree', 'Achiltibuie', 'Winter Branches', 'Illicit Love', 'A Girl in Love', 'Love Eternal', 'La Vita Nuova', 'Union', 'The Man Who Journeyed to His Heart's Desire', ' The Hill Burns', 'In Separation', 'Snow', 'Caul', caul' as the wall' and which is not among those attached to Nan's letter in his archive. I can find no trace of this poem, it does not appear in *PMN*, neither does 'Union'. 'Achiltibuie' is not in *PMN*, but among the loose poems which are dated 1950.

761 NS to NMG, 15 Sep 1931.

762 *ibid.*

763 *ibid.*

764 NMG to NS, 1931.

765 *ibid.*

766 NS to NMG, 26 Mar 1932.

767 *ibid.*

768 *ibid.*

769 MacDiarmid, 1967, p. 223.

770 LGG to Dorothy Tweed, 18 Jan 1932.

771 George Malcolm Thomson to HC, 21 Aug 1932.

772 Public Poll conducted by BBC Scotland published 17 October 2016.

773 Muir, 1982. p.6.

774 LGG, 1982, p. 130.

775 LGG, 1982. p. 139.

776 LGG, 1982. p. 139.

777 *TW*, p.81.

778 William Malcolm, Mitchell's biographer talked to Nan Shepherd after Ray Mitchell's funeral in 1978 and thinks she said then that she and Mitchell never met (email, 2015). I can find no evidence to suggest otherwise.

779 Also known as Kincardineshire.

780 Reiver: border raider.

781 This is referred to in the text. 'Macbeth came that way,' Jenny Kilgour says to her grandfather. 'They killed him at Lumphanan …he must have crossed the river at Potarch' (*APIG, p.* 27).

782 *APIG*, p. 2.

783 *APIG*, p. 24.

784 *APIG* p. 30.

785 *APIG*, pp.29-30.

786 *APIG*, p. 53.

787 Watson in 'Introduction' to *APIG*, pp.ix-x.

788   NMG to NS 24 Mar, 1933.

789   APIG, p. 115.

790   *APIG*, p. 115.

791   NMG to NS 24 Mar, 1933.

792   ibid.

793   Stephenson, 1989, p.128.

794   *TLM*, p. 85.

795   In the 1920s there was a move to prevent cottagers at Inverey
         taking in boarders. This would have been a calamity for Maggie
         who relied on the income, keeping her earnings in a ewer.
         A letter to the press was dispatched on her behalf and read out
         in the House of Commons. 'When the King heard it' Maggie
         used to say, 'He fairly danced, and said, Maggie could have all the
         visitors she wanted and Balmoral has to be open two days in the
         week. I held my heid fu' high,' she said, determined as ever.
         (Thomson, 'Maggie Gruer' *TDF,* 1981, p. 956.) Janet Adam
         Smith also recalls Maggie telling the story of the attempt to prevent
         Inverey tenants taking in visitors, From then on, it was 'How are you
         to-day Miss Gruer?—and a car sent up for me at the election to vote
         for the Tories. I take the car, but...' she grinned as she recounted
         how her chief antagonist now treated her. (Adam Smith, *1946,* p. 26.)

796   Thomson, 1981, p. 956.

797   *Thistle Cottage Visitors' Book*, 10 April 1933.

798   *Thistle Cottage Visitors' Book*, May 14-17th 1929.

799   'I can conceive of no good reason for trudging through the
         oppressive Lairig Ghru except to see them [the Pools of Dee]
         TLM, pp.23-4.

800   Thomson,1981, p. 956.

801   Maggie Gruer's chair was so famous it was presented to the Cairn-
         gorm Club after her death.

802   Adam Smith, 1946, p. 26.

803   Thomson, 1981, p. 956.

804   *TLM*, p.85.

805   It is also possible they had come from the Linn of Dee the day before
         and stopped at Maggie Gruer's for the night before heading home
         the following morning when the photograph was taken.

806   *ITC*, p.1.

807   *TLM*, p. 27.

808   *TLM*, p. 105.

809   LGG, 24 Jun 1933.

810   There are no references to *TQW* in Mitchell's book reviews, essays or
         correspondence. His copy of *TW,* is held in his personal library at

Edinburgh University Library Special Collections (Spec Coll3630). William Malcolm, 2017.

811   William Malcolm, 2015.

812   Cruickshank, p. 90.

813   'Kinraddie' of *Sunset Song,* closely resembles Arbuthnott. The fictitious Segget is described in the opening lines of *Cloud Howe* as being 'under the Mounth, on the southern side in the Mearns Howe, Fordoun lies near and Drumlithie nearer' (LGG, 2011, p.2). Shepherd's *APIG* is set in the shadow of Clachnaben, nineteen miles from Arbuthnott and nearly sixteen miles away from Drumlithie via the old military road.

814   LGG, 24 Jun 1933.

815   The Mitchells moved to Welywn Garden City in 1931. When he was writing *Sunset Song,* Mitchell apparently used the *Geography of Kincardine* published by Collins in 1875 as well as a map of the area to refresh his memory. (Munro, 1966, p. 71).

816   NS to NMG, 14 Mar 1930.

817   Later a war correspondent, broadcaster and publicity officer for the BBC, after graduating from Edinburgh University in 1932, Robert Forrest Dunnett was editorial assistant at *The Scotsman.*

818   Quoted in Dunnett, 1933, p. 342.

819   See reviews in *AJ*, 3 August 1933 , *Glasgow Herald* 3 Aug 1933 and *The Scotsman* , 27 July 1933.

820   Quoted in Dunnett, 1933, p. 342.

821   LGG, 2011, p. 17.

822   AMM to NS, 25 Oct 1934.

823   NS to NMG, 7 Dec 1934.

824   NMG to NS, 16 Dec 1934.

825   *Glasgow Herald,* 14 Nov 1934.

826   *AJ,* 31 Oct 1934.

827   *AJ,* Nov 1934

828   Smith, 2004.

829   *Glasgow Herald,* 14 Nov 1934.

830   *TLM,* p.1.

831   Campbell, 2014.

832   Glasgow Herald, 14 Nov 1934.

833   *AJ,* n.d. NSA.

834   *LM,* Oct 1944, p.5.

835   *MB.*

836   LGG to HC, c. Jan 1935

837   'Mr J L Mitchell's Funeral at Arbuthnott', *AJ,* 25 Feb 1935.

838   Cruickshank, p.90.

839   NS to HC, 11 May 1960.

840   Cruickshank, p.92.

841   *ibid.*

842   *ITC,* p. 51.

843   NS, *TDF,* 1938, p.8.

844   Cruickshank, p. 98.

845   The Saltire Society still exists, its headquarters now in Fountain Street, Edinburgh. Eric Linklater's son Magnus has been President since 2011.

846   Before Leslie Mitchell's death, he and Christopher Grieve had planned a series of small books about Scotland to be called *The Voice of Scotland* which Routledge was willing to publish. The intention of the series, originally, was that each writer should choose a figure or subject and enquire what he/she or it had done for Scotland. Writers included NMG, Eric Linklater, Compton Mackenzie, William Power and the Muirs. Edwin Muir, realising as he began to write on Scott, that 'a much more promising subject for inquiry would be what Scotland had done for him, led him to consider the question of the writer in Scotland generally 'a position which is both unhappy and unique. That in turn raised the whole question of Scottish Literature and language as the vehicle for that literature (Muir, 1982, p.1).

847   Linguistically, Muir said, Scottish Literature could be divided into 'Early Scots, Middle Scots, and Anything at All'. The first two periods showed a certain homogeneity of language and because of that, a certain style. The third, which began with Knox and the acceptance of the English translation of the bible, signalled the 'disintegration of the language of Scots literature and the disappearance of a distinctive Scottish style (Muir, 1982, p.6).

848   Muir, 1982, p.8.

849   Carolina Oliphant later Lady Nairne (1766-1845) collected Scottish folktunes and modified or wrote her own words to them. They were published for many years under the pseudonym Mrs Bogan of Bogan.

850   Swan, a Scottish romantic fiction writer, whose work was dubbed Kailyard for its parochialism and sentimentality, was also editor of *Woman at Home* and author of penny weeklies like the *Annie Swan Annual.*

851   NS to H McD 9 Jan 1938.

852   *ibid.*

853   *ibid.*

854   NS to HM, 9 Jan 1938.

855   *ibid.*

856   NS to HM, 9 Jan 1938.

857   *ibid.*
858   NS to HC 24 Nov 1969.
859   NS to HM, 11 Oct 1938.
860   MacDiarmid, 1994, pp.91-2.
861   See MacDiarmid, 1994, pp-90-1.
862   NS, *AUR,* 1938, p.49.
863   *ibid.*
864   *ITC,* p.1.
865   NMG to NS, 5 Jun 1937.
866   Cruickshank, p. 77.
867   *ibid.*
868   NS, *AUR,* 1938, p. 56.
869   NS, *AUR,* 1938, p. 51.
870   NS, *AUR,* 1938, p. 52.
871   Now known as Chamberlain's 'phoney war', at the time, it was referred to as the 'Bore' or 'funny' war while the Germans referred to it as 'Sitzkreig'(sitting war). Little in the way of actual fighting on land happened during this period, although there was some action at sea and in the air.
872   *MB.*
873   Ch'an to the Chinese.
874   *TLM,* p. 106.
875   *Wild Geese Overhead* was originally a short story called 'Whisky' which Gunn developed into a novel exploring the Glasgow slums. Gunn had been wrestling with the charge of escapism levelled at his novels and in writing this novel in a setting in which he, personally, would not feel at home, wanted to prove that he could deal with slums and deprivation as well as any other writer.
876   NS to NMG, 14 May 1940.
877   NS to NMG, 14 May 1940.
878   NMG to NS, 25 May 1930.
879   NMG to NS, 5 Jun 1937.
880   Gunn, 1956, p.85.
881   *APIG,* p. 109.
882   NMG to NS, 17 May 1940.
883   In her letter of 14th May 1940, Nan criticised his English characters in *Second Sight* and his use of cliché: 'and on suitable evenings provided some exquisite light effects'—'You, who can write like an emanation of the moor, to write in clichés like that!' NS to NMG 14 May 1940.
884   *TLM,* pp. 90-2.
885   EC, 2015.

886   CM to Alex Keith, n.d. circa 1940.
887   Charles Murray's ashes, however, were not strewn on 'his' Bennachie,
but   beneath a polished, granite stone in Alford West Kirkyard.
888   *ibid.*
889   NS to BB, 15 Jan 1981.
890   NMG to NS, 8 Nov 1942.
891   *ibid.*
892   *DFTC*, p. 345.
893   *DTFC*, p. 347.
894   *DTFC*, p. 347-8.
895   *DTFC*, p. 348.
896   *DFTC*, p. 349.
897   *DFTC*, pp. 349-50.
898   *DTFC*, p. 350.
899   *DTFC*, pp.351-2.
900   *DTFC*, p. 355.
901   NMG to NS, 26 Jul 1943.
902   NMG to NS, 23 Aug c. 1945.
903   *ibid.*
904   *ibid.*
905   AMM to NS 16 Aug 1946.
906   NMG to NS, 30 Oct 1945.
907   *ibid.*
908   Batsford is now an imprint of Pavilion Books based in Gower St, WC1.
         Having moved several times since 1945 they have nothing in the archives
         pre-1970s let alone from 1945 and had no comment to make on why
         TLM was refused. Conversation with Pavilion Books 29 Jul 2016.
909   Interestingly, NS owned a copy of *The Mountain Way*, anthology of
         prose and verse collected by RLG Irving which was also published by
         Dent & Sons and which she bought in 1939, a year after its publication.
         Dent also published Janet Adam Smith's *Mountain Holidays*, but it seems
         NS took AMM's advice.
910   AMM to NS, 16 Aug 1946.
911   NS, 'Mountain Holidays', Review, n.p. 1946.
912   Adam Smith, p. 20.
913   Adam Smith, p. v.
914   NS, 'Mountain Holidays' Review, n.p. 1946.
915   Malcolm Sutherland, 2016.
916   MA to NS, 8 Jul (n.d.)
917   *ibid.*
918   NS to Jean Roger, 28 Dec 1946.
919   NS to NMG, 4 Apr 1947.

920   *ibid.*
921   3rd to 5th May in 1947.
922   NS to NMG, 24-29 Feb 1948.
923   NS to HC, 21 Nov 1954.
924   NS to NMG, 24-29 Feb 1948.
925   NMG to NS, 23 Mar 1948.
926   *TLM,* p.104.
927   Gunn, pp 13-14.
928   *TLM,* p. 90.
929   Gunn, 2006, p. 9.
930   Hart & Pick, 1981, pp.208-9.
931   NMG to NS, 23 Mar 1948.
932   NS to NMG, 28 Jan 1949.
933   NS to NMG, 28 Jan 1949.
934   Hardening of the arteries, it is associated more commonly with men over the age of fifty.
935   Except for 'Achiltibuie' which appears in Roderick Watson's introduction to Canongate's quartet of Nan Shepherd's work published in 1996.
936   NS to NMG, 4 Apri 1947.
937   *TLM,* p. 22.
938   NS, 'AMM: A Portrait', *AUR,* p. 138.
939   The Aberdeen University Press was taken over by Robert Maxwell and the Pergamon Press Group in 1978.
940   Membership of the Aberdeen University Alumnus Association was open to all graduates, teaching and administrative staff and the university court.
941   NS to NMG 19 July 1964.
942   NMG to NS, 27 Jan 1957.
943   NMG to NS, 27 Jan 1957.
944   NS to NMG, 9 Jul 1954.
945   NMG to NS, 27 Jan 1957.
946   Nan Shepherd's spelling as it appears in 'Wild Geese in Callater'. It is often also written 'Einich' and Eanaich'.
947   NS, *TDF,* 1959, p. 10.
948   NS, *TDF,* 1959, p.10.
949   *TLM,* p. 68.
950   NS, *TDF,* 1959, p. 9.
951   *TLM,* p. 67.
952   NS, *TDF,* 1959, p.9.
953   NS, *AUR,* 1960.
954   *ITC,* p. 11.

955 NS, *AUR*,1960.
956 Cairns, 2014, p. 134.
957 *DFC* leaflet on the Morrone indicator.
958 NS, *TDF*, 1938, p.10.
959 NS, *TDF,* 1962
960 NS to HC, 25 May 1960.
961 Graham, 1977, p.8.
962 MacDiarmid, from 'Second Hymn to Lenin', in Riach and Grieve, 1992, p. 134.
963 *ibid*.
964 Garry in Graham, 1977, p.4.
965 Garry, 'Foreword' to Graham, 1977, p. 3.
966 *ibid*.
967 NS to HC, 23 Apr 1962.
968 NS to CMG, 24 Nov 1960.
969 NS to HC, 11 May 1960.
970 *ibid*.
971 NS to HC, 18 Aug 1961.
972 NS to HC, 23 Apr 1962.
973 NS to HC, 18 Jul 1963.
974 NS to HC 18 Jul 1963.
975 NS to HC 29 Sep c.1963.
976 NS to NMG, 19 Jul 1963.
977 NS to JK, 18 Sep 1963.
978 NS, *AUR*, 1963 p102..
979 Doctor of Laws.
980 Latin: Now we must drink
981 Doric: fine, fine-clothed.
982 Doric: extraordinary.
983 Doric: how bold may we boast/crow.
984 Christie, 'Nunc est Bibendum' NSA.
985 Eminent psychologist Rex Knight who died in March 1963 was a colleague of Nan Shepherd's at the Training Centre and previously lecturer at Aberdeen University.
986 NMG to NS, 11 Jul 1964.
987 NMG to NS, 11 Jul 1964.
988 NS to NMG, 17 Jul 1964.
989 Cameron Donaldson, 2016.
990 NS to NMG, 19 Jul 1964.
991 NS to JK, 15 Sep 1962.
992 NS, 'Glitter of Mica' Review, *AUR,* 1963.
993 JK, *AUR,* 1990, pp. 189-90.

994 NS to JK, 19 Dec 1964.

995 JK, *AUR,* 1990, p. 191. In her letter to Jessie, Nan was quoting the first line of Charles Murray's poem, 'Winter', 'Noo that cauldrife Winter is here' (Murray, 1979, p.28).

996 NS, *TDF,* 1966, p.43.

997 Derelict now, as recently as 2007 plans were made to restore it, but funding has still to be secured.

998 NS to HC, Dec 1968.

999 NS to Edith Robertson, 17 Jan 1931.

1000 Edith Robertson's *Collected Ballads and Poems in the Scots Tongue* and *Translations into the Scots Tongue of Poems by Gerard Manley Hopkins* were both printed in 1968 by *AUP.*

1001 NS to Edith Robertson, 19 Dec 1968.

1002 It was not the first North Sea find. Earlier in December 1969 the Ekofisk Field was discovered in Norwegian waters. It was not until 1975 that the first oil was pumped ashore in North East Scotland.

1003 Cults Academy, built in 1967. A newer building on the school's playing field replaced the original 1960s school in 2009.

1004 NS to Edith Robertson, 19 Dec 1968.

1005 NS to Edith Robertson, 19 Dec 1968.

1006 NS to HC, 17 Apr 1971.

1007 *Up the Noran Water* is the title of Helen Cruickshank's first collection of poetry published in 1934, as NS acknowledges in her letter to Helen dated 17 April 1971 by enclosing the phrase in inverted commas.

1008 NS to HC, 6 Jun 1971.

1009 Cameron Donaldson, 2016.

1010 Forrest, 1986, p. 19.

1011 Quoted in Forrest, 1986, p. 17.

1012 Cameron Donaldson, 2016.

1013 *ibid.*

1014 Malcolm Sutherland, 2016

1015 *TW*, p. 3.

1016 According to Adam Watson Nan Shepherd 'did not use the absurd term Doric or The Doric in her books, and likewise in her conversation'. She does, however, use 'the Doric' in *APIG*, p. 15.

1017 Malcolm Sutherland, 2016.

1018 Helen Bain, 2016.

1019 *TQW*, pp. 102-3.

1020 NS to NMG, 28 Sep 1971.

1021 NMG to NS, 24 Mar 1970.

1022 NMG to NS dated 1970 but is more likely to have been 1971.

1023   NS to NMG 28 Sep 1971.

1024   *The Times,* 23 Jun 1976, p. 17

1025   Betty Macmurray died on 19th May 1982.

1026   Jocelyn Campbell, 2016. May Anderson may also have come up in
        conversation. When Betty had last seen her, post-lobotomy, May was
        unrecognisable, bloated and coarse. Betty could not bring herself
        to visit May again and we do not know if NS kept in touch.

1027   NS to HC, 9 Mar 1972.

1028   *ibid.*

1029   Ken Morrice (1924—2002) was a prolific poet writing in both
        English and Scots whose work is still included in anthologies. Leaving
        the navy in 1949 to pursue a career in psychiatry, his poetry was widely
        published in Scottish literary periodicals as well as in several collections
        of his own. (*Scottish Poetry Library.*)

1030   NS to HC, 9 Mar 1972.

1031   HC, 1976, pp.168-170.

1032   NS to HC, 26 Jan 1969. HC's letter to NS is not extant, but
        from NS's reply it appears this was how HS described Marian Angus's
        letters.

1033   DB, 2017.

1034   NS to HC, 4 Feb 1969.

1035   *ibid.*

1036   In 2006 Aimee Chalmers published a thesis on Marion Angus:
        The Singin' Lass, Polygon, 2006, which includes selected writing and
        an overview of her life and work.

1037   NS to HC 26 Jan 1969.

1038   Walpole,30 Jun 1928.

1039   It was not just Scottish women writers who were affected by this
        treatment. In 1971, Ray Mitchell (LGG's widow) living in Welwyn
        Garden City remarked to Helen Cruickshank about the lack of
        marketing there was in England of Scottish books:'It's Scottish and the
        English won't even try to read it' Ray Mitchell to HC 31 Mar 1971.

1040   RAT to NS, 30 Aug 1959.

1041   Dunnett, 1933, p. 342.

1042   This may have been the sub-editor's heading rather than Sheila
        Hamilton's.

1043   NS to NMG, 13 Nov 1971.

1044   NMG to NS, 24 Mar 1972.

1045   NS to NMG, 13 Nov 1971.

1046   NMG to NS, 24 Mar 1972.

1047   NS to NMG, 13 Nov 1971.

1048   Matthiessen, 2010, p.142.

1049   In the late 1970s Matthiessen was a novice Buddhist. His wife (whose death he was still grieving when he was writing *The Snow Leopard*) had introduced him to Zen Buddhism.

1050   EC, 2015.

1051   Cameron Donaldson, 2016.

1052   NS to HC 6 Jun 1971.

1053   *ibid.*.

1054   Ian Munro and his wife Mary were friends of NS from the 1960s. See NS to HC, 26 Jan 1969.

1055   *AJ,* 27 Oct 1977.

1056   Quoted 2011 Canongate edition.

1057   Ken Morrice to NS, 26 Dec 1977.

1058   Adam Watson, 2016, p.15.

1059   Helen Bain, 2016.

1060   Jean Roger, 2014.

1061   EC 2015

1062   Unfortunately, its ties to the Maxwell Group brought about the AUP's demise. Put into administration in 1992 it was wound up eventually in 1996.

1063   Watson, Introduction to *TQW,* 1996., p. ix.

1064   Macfarlane, 2015, p. 65.

1065   *The Old Ways,* 2012, *Landmarks* 2015. Macfarlane also retraced NS' steps in the Cairngorms for a BBC 2 programme, 'Secret Knowledge' aired 2 Dec 2014.

1066   Over 50,000 copies have been sold.

1067   Malcolm Sutherland, 2015.

1068   SC to JK 14 Apr 1984.

1069   NS to JK, 29 Nov 1979. There is no first cousin I can trace who died between August (the date of her previous letter to Jessie Kesson) and November 1979 aged ninety. Of her first cousins who had died by 1979, none that age. The oldest was Evelyn Shepherd who died in Cults aged 86 in 1972. It may have been a second cousin.

1070   NS to JK, 22 Dec 1979.

1071   NS, *DTFC,* p. 364.

1072   NS to JK, 22 Dec 1979.

1073   NS to JK, 13 Mar 1980.

1074   JK to SC May 1980.

1075   *ibid.*

1076   NS to BB, 2 Feb 1981.

1077   NS to JK, 29 Jun 1980.

1078   NS to JK, 29 Jun 1980.

1079   Also known as Clochnaben, which is how it is spelt in *APIG*.
1080   *APIG*, p. 81.
1081   *APIG*, p. 27. The old military road, said to be the way
        Macbeth came.
1082   *APIG*, p. 24.
1083   *APIG, p.* 111.
1084   *APIG*, p. 112.
1085   NS to JK, 15 Sep 1962.
1086   Jean Roger, 2014.
1087   *TLM, p.* 105.
1088   JK to NS, 18 Jul 1980.
1089   NS to JK, 29 Jun 1980.
1090   *ibid.*
1091   *ibid.*
1092   *ibid.*
1093   Fiona Heraghty 2016.
1094   NS to JK 28 Aug 1980
1095   *ibid.*
1096   NS to BB, 15 Jan 1981.
1097   NS to JK, 28 Aug 1980.
1098   *TLM*, p. 3.
1099   Burns, Robert, 'Tam O'Shanter' quoted in *TLM*, p. 3.
1100   NS to BB, 15 Jan 1981.
1101   *ibid.*
1102   Cause of death recorded on certificate as 'Hypostatic
        Bronchopneumonia'.
1103   *DTFC*, p. 367.
1104   *DTFC*, p. 365.
1105   SC to JK 14 Apr 1984.
1106   JK to SC, April 1984.
1107   SC to JK, 14 Apr, 1984.
1108   SC to JK, 16 Feb 1984.
1109   JK, *AUR,* 1990, p. 191.
1110   NMG to NS, 1970.
1111   Quoted in Hart & Pick, 1981, p. 84.
1112   Jamie, 2008, p. 25.

INDEX